THE
HOLY MAN
OF TOURS

The Life of Leo Dupont

M. L'Abbé Janvier

THE
HOLY MAN
OF TOURS

— OR —

The Life of Léon Papin-Dupont

Who Died at Tours in the Odor of Sanctity, March 18, 1876.

Translated from the French of

FR. PIERRE DÉSIRÉ JANVIER

A Priest of the Holy Face

First published with the Approbation of the Archbishop of Tours, in French as *Vie de M. Dupont*, 1879.

Ⓒ Free of copyright. With the Evangelists and Saints throughout history, you are *encouraged* to copy and freely share this material for the glory of God and the salvation of souls!

Paperback ISBN: 978-1-945275-31-9
Hardback ISBN: 978-1-945275-32-6

CONTENTS

AUTHOR'S PREFACE
  To the Abridged "Life of Mr. Dupont." 1

CHAPTER I
  Birth of Léon Papin-Dupont — His Youth — His Marriage. 5

CHAPTER II
  His Arrival at Tours — His Attitude as a Fervent Christian. 23

CHAPTER III
  His Correspondence With Grace — His First Efforts in the Work of Reparation. 33

CHAPTER IV
  His Works of Charity — His Conversations. . . . 47

CHAPTER V
  His Vocation — His Relations With Sister Saint-Pierre — La Salette. 57

CHAPTER VI
  His Daughter. 75

CHAPTER VII
  Mr. Le Pailleur and the Little Sisters of the Poor. 93

CHAPTER VIII
  Various Works of Charity. 107

CHAPTER IX
  The Nocturnal Adoration. 121

CHAPTER X
  THE WORK OF ST. MARTIN. 147

CHAPTER XI
  SATAN AND THE MEDAL OF ST. BENEDICT. 173

CHAPTER XII
  THE HOLY SCRIPTURES. 191

CHAPTER XIII
  COMMENCEMENT OF THE DEVOTION TO THE HOLY FACE. 199

CHAPTER XIV
  SECOND PERIOD OF THE DEVOTION TO THE HOLY FACE — CERTIFICATES. 223

CHAPTER XV
  HIS CORRESPONDENCE. 241

CHAPTER XVI
  DEATH OF HIS MOTHER, HIS AFFECTION FOR HIS RELATIVES AND FRIENDS. 259

CHAPTER XVII
  THIRD PERIOD OF DEVOTION TO THE HOLY FACE. . . . 277

CHAPTER XVIII
  LOURDES. 293

CHAPTER XIX
  HIS LOVE OF THE CHURCH. 307

CHAPTER XX
  HIS FAITH, HIS HUMILITY. 319

CHAPTER XXI
  HIS HOPE — HIS LOVE OF GOD — HIS MORTIFICATION. 341

CHAPTER XXII
  HIS DEVOTION TO THE SACRED HEART, THE BLESSED VIRGIN, THE SAINTS, THE ANGELS, AND THE SOULS IN PURGATORY. 355

CHAPTER XXIII
   Fourth Period of the Holy Face.......... 375

CHAPTER XXIV
   Prussian Occupation — the Commune — Pontmain...................... 385

CHAPTER XXV
   Isolation and Suffering — Last Period of Devotion to the Holy Face............ 395

CHAPTER XXVI
   His Last Illness — His Death............ 407

CHAPTER XXVII
   The Oratory of the Holy Face — Conclusion... 431

VRAIE IMAGE
DE LA
SAINTE FACE DE N. S. JÉSUS-CHRIST
conservée et vénérée très-religieusement à Rome, en la Basilique de Saint-Pierre au Vatican.

AUTHOR'S PREFACE

To the Abridged "Life of Mr. Dupont."

IN PUBLISHING, under a new form, the "Life of Mr. Dupont," we are guided by the advice of judicious and estimable persons; at the same time, we correspond to the expressed desire of many friends.

This second edition does not materially differ from the first. It has the advantage of being more within the reach of the community at large, and it will, consequently, do greater honor to the memory of Mr. Dupont, and will render his name more popular. We have retained the characteristics by which he was so well known. The admirers of our holy friend will find him portrayed with his noble and calm physiognomy, the heroic perfection of his virtues, the charming traits of his character, his exuberant piety, even his personal peculiarities. He is always the man of God, the "just" living the "life of faith" and prayer. But he is particularly and above all, the man of reparation, the adorer of the Holy Face. This controlling feature is presented entire, and with the prominence it deserves. The work of reparation, such as the social wounds of our age demand, and such as Mr. Dupont inaugurated in his parlor, is exhibited in its origin, development, and early results, with its expressive emblem, and the efficacious means our Lord Himself deigns to offer: adoration of the Holy Face. From the example of this worthy servant of Christ and the Church, we hope the reader may be induced to follow the providential impulse which is, at the present time, so strongly urging generous souls to works of reparation, and which seems to be the pledge of the Divine mercy, the harbinger of a brighter future.

We dedicate this volume to the friends of Mr. Dupont and to all the servants of the Holy Face. By their aid and under their auspices, may it be circulated, read, and attain the end for which it was written—the glory of God and the salvation of souls! It is particularly addressed to persons living in the world, members of the Christian family, and to the youth of our schools. To both we offer a Saint as a model, and we may justly say:

He is one of you. Behold him! He is clothed as you; he breathes the same air; he lives in the midst of the world like yourselves. He respected and honored the barrier which separates you from the priesthood and the religious state; but he never passed it. He was a student, a husband, and father; he fulfilled, to the last, the common duties of the family and friendship. If, in order to serve God and the poor, he expends his money, his time, his faculties, his whole life with prodigality and love, he does so, not in consequence of a previous promise, nor by being obliged thereto by a particular vow. The only vow which bound him to Jesus Christ and the Church, was that which binds you, the sacred vow of baptism. His character of Christian was sufficient for him; in it he finds his strength, his consolation, and joy. Read and consider… Do more; study and imitate.

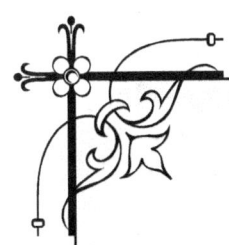

Chapter I

Birth of Léon Papin-Dupont — His Youth — His Marriage.

Léon Papin-Dupont, the devout servant of the Holy Face and of St. Martin, was born January 27, 1797, in Martinique, where his father, Nicolas Léon Papin-Dupont, the descendant of a noble family of Brittany, had sought a refuge from the revolutionary excesses committed in his native island, Gaudeloupe, by the agents of the Convention. He had married a noble and wealthy Creole of Martinique, Mademoiselle Marie Louise Gaigneron de Marolles, who, in a few years, was left a widow with two children, Léon the elder, and Theobald, younger than his brother by four years. Léon was baptized at Lamentin in the Church of St. Lawrence, his sponsors being his grandfather, Jean Baptiste Papin-Dupont, and his maternal aunt, Marie Rose des Verges de Maupertuis.

His childhood passed under the guardianship of his mother, an amiable and accomplished woman, gifted, according to her contemporaries, with many attractive qualities as well as solid virtues, who early instilled into her son a veneration for the great truths of faith, and a love for the service of God.

A trifling incident of his boyhood evinces the frankness of his character and the candor of his soul. He attended a school in the town with other children of his age. It happened one day that the pupils, taking advantage of the absence of the master, amused themselves instead of attending to the duty assigned them. Hearing the uproar, the teacher returned promptly to the room, but apprised of his approach, the boys had quietly resumed their places and had, apparently, been engaged in study. The master inquired into the cause of the disorder, and demanded who were the ringleaders. To judge by their account of themselves, they had behaved with perfect propriety. Only one, the little Léon, acknowledged that he had been playing instead of studying. As he was ingenuously accusing himself, the bell rang for recreation: "Oh! my little friend," said the teacher to him in a grave manner, "you do not deserve to remain in the company of these good children, you can go play," and sending him to recreation, he severely reproved the others, and obliged them to continue their studies. When relating this circumstance in his old age in his usual pleasant manner, the servant of God was accustomed to laud, in the highest degree, sincerity and frankness, which, he said, had always proved advantageous to him.

When his age required a more extensive course of study than that pursued at the village school, his mother placed him in an institution in the United States. The political events which were agitating France, forced upon Madame Dupont this painful separation. It was at the period when France, and indeed all Europe were in arms in consequence of the great wars of the empire. The English, revenging the brilliant victories of Napoleon on the Continent, had defeated the French in the colonies. In 1809, they obtained, a second time, possession of Martinique, and held it until 1815. For two years Léon remained at boarding school in the United States; thence he went to France, and continued his education at the college of Pontlevoy. He had the happiness of making his first Communion at the age of twelve. Although we are ignorant of the particular circumstances attending this solemn act, we know that Mr. Dupont always regarded this grace as the greatest he had received during his life, and he would often say that his soul had been then inundated with a heavenly joy.

In this sacrament, as from its source, he derived that ardent and tender devotion for the holy Eucharist which so eminently characterized him, and which enabled him, whilst yet a boy, deprived of his father, separated from his mother, surrounded by dangers and temptations, to preserve his innocence and keep the faith.

Providence, however, raised up for him a second father, in the person of his maternal uncle, Count Gaigneron de Marolles, who invited him annually to pass the vacation at his castle of Chissay, on the borders of Touraine. There, in the society of his two cousins, the young Marolles, his brother Theobald who had likewise been sent to Pontlevoy, his cousin Mademoiselle de Beauchamp, and Mademoiselle d'Audiffredi, a young Creole of Martinique, a pupil of Madam de Lignac, at Tours, Léon not only enjoyed the happiness of a home circle, but also profited by the example of a pious family. The ties of friendship he thus contracted were strong, disinterested and lasting. Of a sympathetic and cheerful disposition, he won the affection of all who were associated with him. "He was," say those who composed the young company assembled during the summer months at the castle of Chissay, "an amiable, attractive child. Sprightly, active, eager to contribute to the pleasure of others, he was the life and soul of the innocent games and amusements of our age, was ready to take his part in any sport, never tired of dancing, driving or riding, whilst he displayed at the same time a strength of resolution, an energy of will, a tenacity of purpose which was unyielding, and which often astonished us." The following incident strikingly illustrates this characteristic.

One day at Chissay, Léon had climbed on the large outer gate which gave admittance to the grounds of the castle.

His cousin, Alfred de Marolles, had mounted on the other side of the gate upon which he was swinging violently. Léon had placed his thumb exactly in the spot where it would be caught, should the gate shut. Alfred continued his sport, but said several times to his cousin: "Take away your thumb, Léon, or I shall crush it." Léon replied: "Well, crush it, if you choose, I will not move it." A moment afterwards the gate closed upon the thumb of the obstinate and self-willed Léon, who received so terrible a wound, that the thumb was completely crushed, and that part of his hand was disfigured for life. In this resolute and decided character, we discover the material upon which grace will act, to build the edifice of the most solid and heroic virtues.

In 1815, his studies had terminated. A peace had just been definitely concluded upon the continent, and according to the stipulation, the English were to depart from Martinique. The young Dupont was thus enabled to return to his mother, who, having been left a widow at the age of twenty-two with large possessions to manage, had been united in a second marriage to Mr. d'Arnaud, an extensive landholder at Lamentin, and a member of the Colonial Council. As the schools of the island offered no advantages for a finished education, Madame d'Arnaud did not retain her children with her for any length of time, but sent them to the mother-country in order to prepare them to enter an honorable career in life. Léon, being destined for the magistracy, went to Paris to pursue his studies. He occupied with his brother, Theobald, a furnished apartment in the house of an excellent Christian woman, Madame Contour. Besides the public lectures which he attended, he followed a course of reading under the direction of a private tutor; his family appropriated to him an annual allowance of ten thousand francs.

We find him immediately upon his arrival at the capital received into the brilliant aristocratic society of that period, for which his birth, fortune and elegant manners eminently qualified him. He was frequently in company with the celebrated Laurentie, with Dr. Pignier, a fervent Christian and with many other young men distinguished by their talents and virtues. He was, however, more intimately associated with a former college companion, who had become a priest, and who already commenced to enjoy the reputation which, later, cast so bright a lustre around his name. We speak of the Abbé Frayssinous. By his superior intellect and eminent virtues, this friend of his childhood exercised over the young Creole, a strong and salutary influence, and Léon Dupont owes in a great measure, to this illustrious friendship, the resolution we shall soon see him make, to devote himself to a life of fervent piety and good works.

And, in truth, a residence in Paris was not without its dangers for a young Creole, twenty-one years of age, at a distance from his family, handsome, rich, noble hearted, and with time at his disposal. Léon was profuse in his expenditure, and consumed entirely the large income furnished him. Without disregarding the essential requirements of a Christian life, he yielded to the attractions of fashion and the frivolities of the world. Like other young men in high society, he had his vehicles and handsome horses; he frequented the salons of the nobility, drove his equipage in the Bois de Boulogne, loved dancing, attended balls, where his reputation, fine appearance, and elegant manners, won for him the notice of many mothers, who desired to secure him as a member of their family. His reputation was unsullied, and we have reason to believe that his heart always remained pure. Whilst his life was worldly, it never ceased to be Christian. His intercourse with persons of every rank was marked by such good breeding, that his friends had given him the sobriquet of the "Marquis of Politeness." Later in life, laughing at this surname, he related how upon one occasion he had brought disgrace upon it by his manner of acting. It was in Martinique, shortly after his return from Paris. One day at Lamentin, a visitor indulged in strong invectives against the martyr king, Louis XVI, for whom this noble family professed the deepest veneration. The "Marquis of Politeness" lost his temper, and rising, he said to the visitor: "Sir, here is your hat!" and he dismissed him without further ceremony. His good mother, Madame d'Arnaud, was present at this scene, and she often rallied her son upon his want of courtesy.

But at Paris, his delicate and pure conscience could not long remain at rest amid frivolous and worldly amusements. God spoke to his heart, and made him feel that this useless life, without purpose, was not such as he should lead. How bitterly in future years he deplored the time he had thus wasted! In his letters and conversations, he never alluded to this period without expressing his deep regret. His humility even exaggerated its consequences; he speaks of himself as living amid the mire of the world. "I required a powerful grace," he says, "and suddenly, the light shone upon me and. made me realize the importance of leading a Christian life and attending to the great affair of salvation. I was obliged to break certain habits, whilst at the same time my heart clung more closely to the friends whom I had first met." This he called the period of his conversion. He himself tells us the circumstance which was the exterior cause of the graces he afterwards received.

He was in want of a servant to attend to his horse and carriage. The porter of the hotel where he was lodging, offered his services to procure him a jockey who would suit him in every respect. The offer was accepted, the porter met on the street one of those little Savoyards who were then so numerous in Paris, obtaining a support as chimney sweeps. He called in the boy, interrogated him, and being satisfied that he would perform properly the duties required of him, he cleaned, dressed him in a suitable manner, and instructed him so well, that he soon became a skilful jockey with a pleasing address. But, lo! after commencing satisfactorily the performance of his new duties, the ex-chimney sweep one day was not at his post at the proper time. Mr. Dupont inquired where he had been, and what had caused the delay. He learned from his jockey that a fervent Christian named Bordier, in company with several other young men, was interested in the little Savoyards of Paris, that he assembled them on certain days in the basement chapel of the Foreign Missions, instructed them in the Faith, and prepared these poor children for their first Communion. His new jockey, who was only twelve years old, was of the number, and his presence at one of these assemblies had been the cause of his delay. Curious to ascertain the truth of the statement thus made him, the young Dupont went in person at the hour appointed to the place of meeting, and there he found a respectable man, surrounded by a crowd of children, who were listening to his instructions with the greatest attention, and who seemed to love him as a father.

Touched by the scene and filled with admiration for Mr. Bordier, he wished to see him in his own home. During his visit, the young student gave an account, in the sprightly manner so natural to him, of a party of pleasure he had accompanied a few days previous to the Bois de Boulogne, but lamented that it had been interrupted by a violent storm, in consequence of which, he had returned home exhausted by fatigue and drenched with rain. Mr. Bordier ingenuously acknowledged that he had not noticed the storm; and observing that his visitor appeared surprised, he mentioned that, at the hour alluded to, he was in Church assisting at Vespers. "But," exclaimed the young Dupont, "it was not a Sunday!" "No," replied Mr. Bordier, "but it was a feast of the Blessed Virgin;" and he named some minor feast which had been celebrated during the week. These simple words made a deep impression upon the young man; he withdrew in confusion, and was mortified upon reflecting that, although professing to be a Christian, he was so ignorant and so unworthy of the name.

Thenceforth he was the intimate friend of Mr. Bordier, and requested to be his associate in his work of charity towards the little Savoyards. From this resolution resulted the change in his manner of life. The work itself always remained dear to him. As soon as he fixed his residence at Tours, he continued there what he commenced in Paris. He assembled on certain days the little chimney sweeps of the city in the chapel of the Carmelites, taught them the catechism, heard them recite their prayers, and prepared them for their first Communion. Wherever he might be, if he met a Savoyard in the street, he never failed to give him alms. I never see one," he would say, "without emotion."

His intimacy with Mr. Bordier made the young Dupont acquainted with another more important work. We speak of the congregation of the Blessed Virgin which, at that time, was highly esteemed for the immense good it was accomplishing in Paris. Established after the revolution by Father Delpuits, an old Father of the Society of Jesus, the association numbered among its members the flower of the young men of the city, those who reflected honor on their illustrious names by their virtues and talents.

The young Dupont, then about twenty years of age, had no sooner heard of the congregation than he requested to be admitted. Being received, he obeyed the rules and performed the exercises of charity without human respect, carefully and with the fervor and simplicity which belonged to his character. The following incident will illustrate this.

Once when on a journey, he passed a Sunday at Nantes, and entering a church early in the morning, he requested one of the pastors of the parish to hear his Confession, as he wished to Communicate. The priest, seeing before him a handsome young man evidently belonging to the fashionable world of Paris, doubts his sincerity and hesitates to hear him; so unusual it was for a young man in high life to brave human respect and publicly demand holy

Communion on an ordinary Sunday. Mr. Dupont, divining his suspicions from his embarrassed manner, informed him frankly that he belonged to the congregation of Mary, and was accustomed to approach the Sacraments every week. The pastor equally surprised and pleased received him cordially.

Léon was most generous and kind hearted in relieving the wants of poor families. A Catholic bookseller of Paris relates the following circumstance: "In 1821, I was present at the meeting of the creditors of a poor stationer, the father of a family, who was bankrupt, and obliged to suspend payment for want of fifteen hundred francs. Mr. Dupont entered the store to make some purchases. He was so struck by the sadness depicted on the countenances of the gentlemen assembled, that he asked the cause. On receiving the reply, he pointed to the street and said: 'Take my horse and tilbury, sell them and pay the debt.' This spontaneous act of charity made such an impression upon the creditors of the poor merchant, that they did not push him for immediate payment, and by degrees, he was enabled to recover himself and continue business. I should not be surprised," observes the narrator, "if the sanctity of Mr. Dupont dated from that period."

Grace, in reality, gradually transformed his life and character and led him on to perfection. The excellent Madame Contour, who was brought in daily contact with him, and to whom he often confided his little troubles and difficulties, always spoke of him in the highest terms. She said of him that even when he yielded to his natural vivacity, he so quickly regained his self-control, his repentance was so frank and sincere, that he won more esteem by his act of virtue than he lost by the fault.

One day, as he was about to leave the house, Léon missed a note of a thousand francs which he had intended to change. He eagerly looks for it; he is pressed for time, as friends expect him. Besides the anxiety and precipitation of the search, he is troubled by the fear of failing in politeness to those who are awaiting him. All these feelings are expressed in his gestures, the tones of his voice and his exclamations of annoyance. He becomes impatient, and then suspicious. He had sent for Madame Contour who aided him in his search. At last in a passion he pointed to his servant and said: "There is the culprit: he only has been here." The servant turned deadly pale, but did not speak. Madame Contour replied: "Calm yourself, Mr. Léon; I will examine into this affair. You are obliged to meet friends. I will advance the money you require today; leave me your keys, I will make a thorough examination." Satisfied for the moment, Léon thanked her and went to fulfil his engagement, but still suspicious of his servant. After his departure, his landlady opened every drawer of his writing desk, and searched them without success. At last, the idea occurred to her to remove the drawers, when to her great joy she found the note pressed against the back of the desk where it had been caught by the drawer. The poor servant had followed his master and, of course, was ignorant of the fortunate discovery. Madame Contour met her young guest on his return and handed him the bank note. She had scarcely time to explain to him where she had found it, when without a moment's hesitation, Léon cast himself on his knees before his servant, begged his pardon with tears, and in his generosity, never omitted an opportunity which offered to repair the injury he had done him by his unjust suspicions.

Towards the close of his residence in Paris, a circumstance procured him, as he says, "the honor of making the acquaintance of Madame Barat, the venerable foundress of the Religious of the Sacred Heart." We give the account in his own words; we shall discover in it more and more his extreme modesty, and the kind of good works which occupied him at that time.

"A lady," he says, "addressed me one day in the parlor of a mutual friend, and gave a rather imperative direction. 'Go see the Superioress of the convent in Varenne street'—it was the old Biron hotel bought by Madame Barat, in 1820—' and try to obtain from her a deduction on the board of the Misses de X—. The family is pecuniarily embarrassed, and the friends cannot appear personally in the matter. A disinterested stranger can more delicately make the agreement.' Although perplexed at being selected for such a mission, I discharged it as simply and with as little awkwardness as possible. Madame Barat received me cordially, explained the reasons which influenced her decision to refuse the deduction requested, notwithstanding her personal interest in the family. My confidence increased as she continued to speak; we came to terms; she made a slight abatement in the charge, and I paid the remainder of the portion which the family de X— were unable to meet. In order to avoid wounding their feelings, they were not informed of our arrangements which remained a secret between Madame Barat and myself."

Thus already the zeal and virtue of the young Dupont designated him as one to whom the most delicate missions could be safely entrusted, and his reserve and generosity proved him worthy of the confidence reposed in him. During his whole life, he continued the virtuous friendships and the intimacies he then contracted. He visited afterwards and kept up a correspondence with Madame Barat, as well as with other ladies of the Sacred Heart. Mr. Bordier went several times to see him at Tours, and, at last, bequeathed him his whole fortune. Dr. Pignier, the Abbé Lacroix, and many others, remained his faithful and devoted friends.

The above account contains all that is reliable and interesting concerning his life whilst a student at Paris. We subjoin a little incident, giving it in his own words. It illustrates strikingly his prominent characteristics, frankness of character and candor of soul.

"Whilst I was studying law," he says, "I received instructions from a private tutor, and I exempted myself, of my own will, from attending the public lectures. The time for my examination was drawing near, when I would be required to present certificates attesting my presence at the lectures. What could I do? I determined to visit the Professor at his own home, and make a personal application to him. I did not know his residence, but having made inquiries I went to the designated street and number, and asked the porter if the Professor had returned. 'He has this moment passed you,' he answered, 'and has gone to his room. Follow him.' I introduced myself to the Professor, with whom I was not acquainted, whom I had never even seen before, and made known to him the object of my visit, which was to obtain the certificates necessary to admit me to my examination. He politely requested me to be seated, and interrogated me immediately as to my assiduity in in attending his lectures. Then I acknowledged frankly and without disguise, that I had never been present at any of the lectures, that this was the first time I had even had the honor of seeing him, which I must plead as my excuse for the impoliteness of which I had just been guilty in not saluting him when he passed me in the hall. This simple admission on my part, seemed to make a great impression upon him; for, instead of reproaching me as I deserved, he exclaimed quickly: 'Ah! here is one, at least, who admits his absence. You are the first I have found with sufficient sincerity and frankness to state his case truthfully. All the other students, under similar circumstances, persist in denying their fault. According to their own account, they are models of exactitude, and never absent themselves from a single lecture. If I remark to any among them: 'I noticed you were not present on such a day;' they invariably reply: 'You are mistaken, sir, I was certainly there; you did not notice me.' 'Would you believe,' he continued with increasing animation, 'that recently a student whom I was reproaching for non-attendance at the lectures, had the audacity to tell me that if I had not seen him, it was because he was hidden from me by the intervening pillar. Now there is no pillar in the hall.' After speaking for some time in the same strain, he said: 'My young friend, come two or three times. Since you tell me that you have pursued a course of study under a private teacher, I believe you, and I have confidence in your acquirements. I will put some questions to you to satisfy myself as to the extent of your information, and I will sign the requisite certificates.' This, in reality, he did for me."

His law studies were not unprofitable to him. He received an appointment in the royal court of Martinique, whither he returned and joined his mother, being then twenty-four years of age. The profession of law, in which he now held an honorable position, was agreeable to him, but he felt another attraction; even before his departure from Paris, his thoughts turned towards the ecclesiastical state, and he expressed his desire to enter the Seminary of Saint Sulpice; his friends, his family, Madame d'Arnaud, all opposed his design. Such were his dispositions on his return to his native island. He there continued the kind of life he had led in Paris, devoting himself to works of piety and charity; whilst at the same time, he allowed himself the amusements of young men of his age, and took his part in the social pleasures of the family. He was skilled in all athletic exercises, loved the chase and long rides on horseback; his company was eagerly sought at balls and parties; but his reputation remained untarnished; he was always regarded as a virtuous young man, manifesting on all occasions and sometimes in a striking manner, a sovereign horror for vice, and for all that had even the appearance of vice.

One day he gave vent to his strong feeling on this point with a colonial vivacity excusable considering the motive which actuated him, and his position as councillor of the court. He was assisting at High Mass on a Sunday in the parish church of Lamentin. A mulatto girl, decked in the finery so pleasing to feminine coquetry, was turning her head from side to side, trying to attract the attention of those around her. "As we were standing during the Preface," says Mr. Dupont, "I became so indignant on seeing the airs of the woman, that from my pew, the door of which separated me from her, I leaned over and gave her a box on the ear which quieted her immediately." In this summary punishment, inflicted by the young councillor, we have evidence both of the strength of his faith and the purity of his heart.

His zeal was equally apparent in the practice of works of mercy and of charity; and in all these works, he regarded primarily their moral and religious aspect. Soon after his return to Martinique, he adopted a little girl, his godzealdaughter, and during his whole life watched over her with paternal solicitude and tenderness. Learning that this child, the daughter of a French officer, had lost her father, and that the family had selected for her godfather a gentleman, very rich, but not desirable in a religious point of view, he offered to present her at the baptismal font with the intention of taking upon himself her future support and of sending her to be educated at the Sacred Heart by the Religious of Madame Barat. When she had attained her seventh year, he sent her to France on board of the *Elizabeth*, which was freighted with sugar. She still lives and remembers how Mr. Dupont took her to Lamentin to pass several days before embarking, sending to her at table the little birds he had killed, and finally accompanying her to Saint-Pierre, ascending the ladder of the ship before the child, who held on to the spurs of her godfather. After a passage of fifty-two days, she was placed at the Sacred Heart of B——, and the pious councillor never ceased to guide her by his letters and advice, and to aid her in every manner.

His brother, Theobald, soon joined him in Martinique, but he shortly afterwards was attacked by a fever, which carried him off in three days. This sudden and unexpected death, whilst it was a terrible blow to Madame d'Arnaud, influenced the future career of her elder son. Léon, when at Paris, had felt his heart moved by a vague desire to embrace the ecclesiastical state. We are told that he would then gladly have renounced civil preferment to enter the Seminary. In Martinique his mind was possessed by the same idea, and he confided to his mother his hopes and aspirations. Madame d'Arnaud, a woman of strong feeling and still young, was disquieted by his designs and expressed great opposition. By the advice of his friend, the Abbé Landas, a worthy priest, Léon relinquished the project, and one day asked and obtained his mother's consent to demand in marriage Miss d'Audiffredi.

Miss d'Audiffredi was in the twenty-fourth year of her age. Mr. Dupont had been acquainted with her for a long time. Like himself, she had been educated in France. Whilst he was pursuing his studies at the College of Pontlevoy, the young girl was in Tours, at the boarding-school of the Ursulines, directed by the Reverend Mother de Lignac. Under such guidance, Caroline had grown up in piety and in the exercise of every virtue. Being at a distance from her home and country, she was accustomed to pass her vacations at the castle of Chissay, with Mr. de Marolles, an acquaintance and friend of her father, where Léon Dupont also went during the holydays. Her education being completed, she had returned to Martinique about the same time as the young student. She is represented to us by those who were acquainted with her as a woman of great virtue and amiable disposition, but of a frail constitution. The nuptial Mass was celebrated with great solemnity the 9th of May, 1827, in the Church of Our Lady at Trois-Ilets, a small town where the family d'Audiffredi resided.

Not long afterwards, Mr. Dupont established himself at Saint-Pierre, in order to be nearer the court, where his duties as a municipal officer frequently called him. He purchased in this village a fine property called "l'hôtel des

Follets;" he jokingly named it "la maison Follette." The gardens are adorned with several ponds of water; one was particularly beautiful, and in this, accompanied by his brother, he had often, when a boy, amused himself in swimming; he was an expert swimmer, and delighted in exercising his strength in feats of agility.

The hôtel des Follets is still standing. When he left Martinique, it was purchased by the city authorities of Saint-Pierre, who established in it a seminary, directed by the Fathers of the Holy Ghost. It is a vast and important estate, rising as an amphitheatre along the declivity of the hill, offering by its fine position a view of incomparable beauty. The house faces the sea, on the heights of the parish of "Strength," at the extremity of the street of "Good Children," and it is reached by a path known under the name of "Ascent to Heaven;" names significative to Mr. Dupont, who often made them the theme of his mystical commentaries, or the subject of a laughing remark.

There the councillor of the royal court of Saint Pierre, with his amiable and virtuous wife, fixed his residence. Alas! they were not destined to live long together. This charming abode was to become suddenly the scene of a great joy and a great sorrow. God often presents in the state of marriage a bitter sacrifice to be accepted, whilst bestowing, at the same time, benedictions and holy joys. Mr. Dupont experienced at Saint-Pierre, as at Paris, an attraction to a life of piety and a degree inconsistent with the wordly pleasures and family joys towards which his natural tastes inclined him, and which his position in society required of him. God, in order to fix his wavering will, was about to strike a heavy blow. Like Abraham, the father of the true believers, He will call upon this pious layman to leave his home and native land, and He will show him another land where, not by the priestly office, but by the apostleship of prayer and charity, he is destined to be the tutor of orphans, the support of the poor, the salvation of sinners, the model of the Christians of his time. This vocation has appeared to us uncertain, and thwarted by man: contact with suffering and the light derived from trials, will unfold it clearly before him.

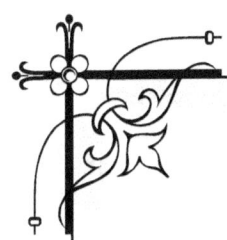

Chapter II

His Arrival at Tours — His Attitude as a Fervent Christian.

Mr. Dupont had been married five years when God gave him a daughter. She was born October 4, 1832, and was named Mary Caroline Henrietta. The name of Henrietta has a history connected with it. Mr. Dupont had commissioned a friend in Paris to purchase for him a little carriage. It so happened that the furniture of the palace of Charles X. was being sold, and among other articles was the carriage which had been used by the little Duke of Bordeaux, Henry V. His friend obtained possession of it and forwarded it to Martinique; the father, delighted by the circumstance, desired the name of Henrietta to be given to the new-born babe for whom it had been procured.

Henrietta was baptized immediately after her birth, but the solemn ceremonies were deferred eight months. A magnificent festival celebrated the event at the hôtel des Follets. "Suddenly," relates a relative of Mr. Dupont, "it was noticed that the young mother had disappeared. For a long time she was sought in vain. At last, Léon found her by herself weeping. To the inquiries as to the cause of her sorrow, she said she would not raise her child, that she herself would die. Was it a presentiment? However that may be, she died a short time afterwards. Although she was known to be in delicate health, she was not considered ill. She asked, however, for a priest, requesting him to administer to her the last sacraments. As the priest refused, observing to her that she was not ill, she insisted, saying: 'You will not have time to return? It happened as she said. It was another priest, near at hand, who was summoned hastily to administer the last rites of the Church. She expired August 1, 1833, eight months after the birth of her daughter. Léon loved his wife devotedly, and this sudden blow affected him deeply; his grief was such as to bring on an illness which caused his friends great anxiety."

When he had rallied a little, he was advised to visit the continent. As the frail health of his daughter was a source of continual anxiety, he determined to leave Martinique and seek in France a climate more suitable to himself and his daughter. He obtained a leave of absence from the court, but finally sent in his resignation of the office of councillor. Mr. Dupont enjoyed at that time the large fortune left him by his father; his mother's income was also considerable; he was thus enabled to live in a handsome and independent manner. Towards the end of May, 1834, he sailed from Martinique and landed in Bordeaux with his mother, Madame d'Arnaud, who had been a widow nearly five years, his daughter, Henrietta, two years and a half old, Alfred, his negro boy, and Adele, a mulatto girl, a cousin of Alfred. From Bordeaux he went to Nantes to visit his uncle, Mr. de Beauchamp, who entertained him hospitably in the city and also at his country-seat, Gringuenières, situated on the borders of Maine and Anjou. He left there his mother and daughter for several months, whilst he was making arrangements to establish himself at Tours, which he had selected for his residence.

Many circumstances combined to induce him to give the preference to that city: the mild climate which appeared to him particularly suited to his daughter's delicate constitution; the reputation of the illustrious and good Doctor

Bretonneau, whom he had known from his childhood, and under whose care he desired to place Henrietta; the proximity of the castle of Chissay, where he had passed so many happy days in his childhood, and whither the kindness of his old uncle, the Count de Marolles attracted him, and finally and more than all the rest, the expressed wish of his deceased wife. Madame Léon Dupont, as we know, had been educated at Tours with the Ursulines, by Madame de Lignac; she preserved so filial and loving remembrance of the instructions and counsels of her venerated mistress, that feeling her death approaching, and considering the future of her infant daughter, she begged her husband not to confide the education of the child to any other than the Superioress of the Ursulines of Tours. Léon promised to comply with her wishes, and this was the principal motive which brought him to the city of St. Martin. Providence had also His designs over him which were to unfold themselves later.

After having had charge of the mother, Madame de Lignac saw the daughter entrusted to her care. Mr. Dupont selected a house in the cathedral parish, where he was a near neighbor of Dr. Bretonneau, and not far from the convent of the Ursulines. He occupied that dwelling about two years, when he was forced to move in consequence of the extension of Buffon street, which passed exactly through the ground occupied by his residence. It was at that time he became a tenant, at first, and then proprietor of the house in the street Saint Etienne, which was destined to be sanctified and rendered illustrious by his presence, and which he was to occupy to the end of his life.

Hardly was he settled, when he resumed the good works of piety and charity which had engrossed his attention in Martinique. At the same time, the old idea of a vocation to the priesthood presented itself to his mind. He asked himself if the moment had not arrived to realize it, to abandon the world, to leave the care of his daughter to his mother, and to enter Holy Orders. Being intimately acquainted with Madame de Lignac, and reposing entire confidence in her spiritual discernment and judgment, he opened his heart freely to her, and described his uncertainty with regard to his vocation to the ecclesiastical state.

"He consulted me," she says, "requesting me to point out a confessor. I mentioned Mr. Jolif du Colombier, then pastor of the cathedral. He was delighted with him, and until deprived of him by death, consulted him as his spiritual director, and often thanked me for the introduction to him."

Madame de Lignac adds: "Mr. du Colombier spoke to me of Mr. Dupont's desire, and we agreed entirely in our opinion. We thought he would do more good and exercise a more extensive influence by remaining in the world. He yielded his judgment to our united advice."

From that time he devoted all his energies to lead a fervent, Christian life, openly professing his faith by his words and his example. The course he pursued created considerable sensation in the city. At this period, not long after the revolution of 1830, human respect exercised a sovereign empire over men of every class. Very few ventured to fulfil publicly their religious duties. They attended church by stealth, and concealed certain acts of exterior piety from the eyes of others. Therefore, it was an extraordinary circumstance to see a layman like Mr. Dupont, of polished manners, agreeable in social intercourse, of high family and enjoying a large fortune, willing to appear pious and devout, following the priest as he carried Viaticum to the dying, serving Mass when the occasion required it, joining in the processions of the Blessed Sacrament on Corpus Christi, or bearing a flambeau in his hand at the meetings of the Confraternities of the Sacred Heart or of the Blessed Virgin. To the silent influence of example in the cause of religion, he added fervor in his conversations, speaking unhesitatingly of God and religion in any company whatever, and doing it with a charming grace, a deep conviction, an uprightness and wisdom, which challenged the approval even of those who taxed him with exaggeration. Sometimes the sight of certain public scandals excited his zeal and led him to the commission of acts of vigor to which the good people of Tours were unaccustomed. As he was passing along the street one day, his eye fell upon an immodest picture exposed at the door of a shop. He stopped, thrust his foot through the canvas, and paid the price demanded by the owner, upon condition that he would never again display publicly any similar paintings.

The conduct of Mr. Dupont was a powerful protest against the cowardly concessions of certain men, who, in reality, loved and reverenced religion, but who had not the moral courage to practice and honor it before the world. Everything about him claimed respect. Imagine the former royal councillor of the Antilles, with his tall, upright figure, his high, broad forehead, his noble bearing, his calm, serene countenance, his toilette free from extravagence, but always exquisitely and irreproachably neat, assisting at the public office of the parish, exhibiting in his exterior, with as much dignity as modesty, the sentiments of strong faith and ardent love for God by which he was animated. What admiration he won from all who came in contact with him! I was a young seminarian at that time. Never shall I forget the impression made upon me when I saw him serving Mass in some one of the cathedral chapels, or holding the cords of the canopy during processions of the Blessed Sacrament. So much modesty, piety and angelic fervor in a simple layman, a man of high birth, was an unexpected phenomenon at that period: it was a revelation to me of what the faithful of the Church must have been in the time of the Apostles.

Mr. Dupont was soon chosen administrator of the cathedral property. No one was better suited to bear the title. He resided in the parish; the pastor was his confessor; he was assiduous in his attendance at the Church Office, and like the Christians of former times, was often present even on week days. He had acquired the habit of reciting daily the entire Office, such as is said by priests, and he subjected himself to an exact observance of the hours allotted for the different portions. A young curate of the city went, on one occasion, to make his Confession to the Canon Pasquier, and met Mr. Dupont, who had visited him for the same purpose. The pious layman proposed to him to say the Office together whilst they were waiting for their confessor. The ecclesiastic, who was not acquainted with Mr. Dupont, was astonished on hearing such a suggestion made by a man evidently of high position in the world.

These holy practices did not interfere with his social relations. Mr. Dupont frequently mingled with persons of his own rank, received and returned the visits of his friends, with whom his intercourse was of the most cordial kind. His conversation was sprightly, animated by pleasant anecdotes and witty repartees. He was what we may call a great talker, but, at the same time, a most agreeable conversationalist. Later in life, he gave a more spiritual and mystical turn to his remarks; but his intercourse was then chiefly with persons of dignity, or souls blessed with choice graces. Even his acquaintances of rank in the world, although sometimes considering his piety unseasonable, and his fervor exaggerated, could not withhold their admiration or refuse the respect due to his virtue.

The frequentation of the sacraments having become a habit in his youth, contracted by the obligation imposed on him as a member of the Congregation of the Blessed Virgin, he continued to be faithful to his duties in Martinique. When settled at Tours, he took advantage of his freedom from official charges to approach the holy table more frequently. Nearly every day he Communicated, either at the cathedral or in the chapel of some Religious community, according as circumstances or devotion dictated. So desirable did the happiness of communicating appear to Mr. Dupont, that he was surprised to find his pious practice a subject of comment. The very sight of the altar filled him with emotion, and drew from him ardent expressions indicative of the vivacity of his faith. One day, a priest of the cathedral noticed him standing alone, as if absorbed in contemplation, at a short distance from one of the side chapels, where the Bread of Life had been distributed to the faithful at the early Mass. Seeing him approach, Mr. Dupont stopped him, and pointing to the Communion cloth spread over the railing, said in a low tone with an accent of faith and admiration; "How good is God! Behold! The table is set! The feast is prepared, the Master awaits His guests... All are invited... No one is excluded or refused. Yes, God is good! Where can we find the great ones of the earth who keep a table always ready for those who present themselves? Why do not all come?"

What he thus said privately in the ear of a friend, he did not hesitate to repeat openly as circumstances suggested the thought. He urged to frequent Communion those over whom he possessed any influence. His piety in regard to the Holy Eucharist was solid and enlightened. Besides studying books of controversy, he read the best ascetic authors. Gifted with an upright mind and sound sense, he was not influenced by sentiment in matters of doctrine or principle, nor controlled by his imagination.

We have proof of this in a small book which he published in 1839 under the following name: "Faith Strengthened and Piety Reanimated in the Mystery of the Eucharist." The work is divided into two parts. In the first, he enumerates the proofs generally adduced by theologians in support of the dogma of the real presence: the words of scripture, the testimony of the Fathers, tradition, and the Greek and Latin liturgies. These proofs are presented with force, clearness and precision; it is a learned and concise polemic work, in which the quotations are given verbatim. The second part, which is moral and mystic, contains a series of meditations on the Eucharist, selected from those of Father Avancini and from the "Eucharistic Month" of Father Lezcari.

Unpretending in form, simple and natural in style, this work gives us a fair idea of the friendly discussions and the controversial disquisitions in which Mr. Dupont willingly engaged with Protestants, or unbelievers. The magisterial style of the former councillor of the royal court of Saint-Pierre, was not without a salutary effect. At the time when he published it, there still remained a taint of Jansenism in our midst. Men, professing to be Christians, lived more like Protestants than Catholics, and whether through indifference, human respect or obstinacy, habitually abstained from holy Communion. Mr. Dupont, by his pen, his conversation and example, exerted himself strenuously to counteract this fatal habit. To his eyes, faith in the real presence was the germ of every virtue, the fertile root on which all private devotions should depend. It was the rule he adopted for himself. If then the life of this fervent Christian, appears to us springing up under the eye of God and before man as a noble, vigorous tree, adorned with flowers and fruit, let us remember that the sap, which vivifies it, is devotion to the Blessed Eucharist.

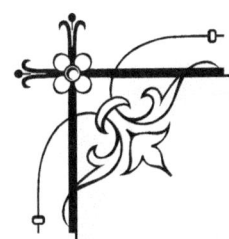

Chapter III

His Correspondence With Grace — His First Efforts in the Work of Reparation.

At Tours, Mr. Dupont found himself intimately associated with two noble families, with whom he was united both by the ties of relationship and friendship—the family of Beauchamp and of Marolles. Availing herself of their vicinity to Tours, Madame d'Arnaud was accustomed every year to pass a few months with her grand-daughter, Henrietta, at Gringuenières, the country seat of the Beauchamp. Mr. Dupont generally accompanied them there, but did not remain long at the castle. He usually devoted that time to solitary excursions, or to pilgrimages to neighboring shrines.

Those who knew him well, represent him as an indefatigable walker and an intrepid huntsman. To walk for leagues through woods and over rough paths, seemed to him a mere trifle. "One night," says a relative, "he returned thoroughly drenched from some excursion, during which he had been obliged to cross a wide and deep stream in order to reach a pathway on the opposite side. Being occupied all day by the cares of a numerous family, I was frequently obliged to write or work at night. Léon noticed the light in my room and called me. I welcomed him cordially, and made a good fire to dry his clothing. But how can I tell you all that he ate! He was dying of hunger! It gives me great pleasure, I said to him, to see you with so good an appetite, and to complete your repast, I will bring you some of the best pears from the fruitery. My aunt, Madame d'Arnaud, was asleep; in the morning I amused her and the family by relating what had passed the previous evening."

Gringuenières was distant only four leagues from the Abbey of Solesmes and from the chapel of Notre Dame du Chêne. Dom Guéranger had been a fellow-student of Mr. de Marolles; and thus his cousin, Mr. Dupont, had every opportunity and facility of visiting, in his cloister, the illustrious restorer of the Benedictine order in France. From this period dates the close friendship which united the Abbot of Solesmes and the holy man of Tours, and which time and circumstances only rendered stronger. Mr. Dupont went frequently very early in the morning to Notre Dame du Chêne. He always returned on foot and fasting, arriving in time for the family breakfast.

In Touraine, he was also near Chissay, whither he was attracted by associations of his childhood, and the warm affection testified by his uncle, Mr. de Marolles. When visiting there, he indulged in his old taste for riding on horseback and hunting; but he reproached himself for gratifying these inclinations; such a life appeared to him idle and useless for the soul. "I do nothing for God," he would say; and the attraction to a penitential and perfect life became daily more and more marked. It was at Chissay that grace finally triumphed over this privileged soul.

In 1837, he went there with his mother and daughter; three days after his arrival at the castle, he was illumined by a supernatural light which made a deep impression upon him, and of which he has himself revealed the principal circumstances. On the 22d of July, the Feast of St. Magdalen, after Communion his eye rested on a picture of St. Theresa, and suddenly his soul was enlightened, and he comprehended the necessity of resolutely embracing Christian mortification. The grace was so marked that every year, wherever he might be, he celebrated in the secrecy and joy of his heart the anniversary of that day of benediction. Not long afterwards, when reading the life of the seraphic Teresa, he met with the following passage: *"I declare that I commenced to comprehend the things pertaining to salvation, only after I determined to disregard the demands of the body."* He considered this an additional grace, as it furnished him with greater light for his guidance, and he ever viewed this memorable event as his starting point in the path of perfection. It may be that he then had a presentiment of the future, and of those ties which were to unite him so closely to Carmel—an intuition of the great work of reparation to which, in the designs of God, he was to be called.

Circumstances had, sometime previously, brought him in communication with the virgins of Carmel. Mr. Dupont had been a resident of Tours for several months, when, desiring to visit the chapels of the city, he entered that of the Carmelites. It was the chapel of the old monastery in Banchereau street, where the community then lived. His attention was attracted to the picture above the grand altar representing the mystery of the Annunciation. Besides the artistic value of the painting, which was ancient and belonged to the Italian school, Mr. Dupont observed that the attitude of the various personages differed entirely from that usually ascribed to them. In this, the Blessed Virgin is seated, and regards with modest dignity the heavenly ambassador, who, bending respectfully, seems to acknowledge in her the Mother of God and the Queen of angels. The pious visitor, having finished his prayers in the chapel where his soul was stirred by an unwonted emotion, asked at the parlor for the prioress, at that time, Mother Mary of the Incarnation. He imparted to her his impressions of the altar piece, and learned that it was prized as one of the most precious treasures of the community, on account of the miracle of which it had been the object. During the revolution of 1793, after the spoliation of the convent, this picture, through the secret designs of Providence, had alone remained hung against the wall of the church which had been converted into a storehouse. An offer was made to the proprietor by some individuals, who wished to purchase it for the purpose of arranging it as a theatre. The owner was about to conclude the sale, when one of his clerks with as little religion as himself, entering to attend to some business affairs, noticed that the picture was wet, although it was placed forty feet above the floor, and not the slightest moisture appeared on the wall. He examined it attentively, and, at last, mounting a ladder he discovers with terror that tears are flowing in two streams from the eyes of the Blessed Virgin, that they run to the bottom of her dress, the blue color of which is spotted by the water. Whether this circumstance was the cause, or some other motive, the sale was not effected, and the dress, without having been touched, resumed its original freshness. Impressed by these details, Mr. Dupont, from that moment, was particularly devout to that chapel, and entertained a strong affection for the community.

As the monastery is under the invocation of the Incarnation, he conceived for this adorable mystery an especial devotion, as well as for the Archangel Gabriel, who was its ambassador. When the daughters of St. Teresa transferred their residence to the house they now occupy, in the street of the Ursulines, the precious picture was removed and placed in the new chapel, where it may still be seen above the high altar. Mr. Dupont continued to venerate it, and several times wished to have it photographed, but was forced to abandon the design, because there was not sufficient light thrown upon it. In his last illness, he declared that he beheld it with the eyes of his soul, and he requested to have his bed turned, so that he might see the rose window, saying it was a consolation to him. A few days before his death, fixing his eyes upon it, he said to his servant, Adele: "How Carmel shines! It is brilliant with rubies and emeralds!" The Carmelite nuns remarked with admiration that his death took place on a Saturday, the day consecrated to the Virgin Mother of God, and on the 18th of March, feast of the Archangel Gabriel, whom he had so much honored.

Several other holy friendships held a large place at this time in the life of Mr. Dupont. There lived at Tours a worthy canon of the metropolitan church, regarded as a wise director, a man of good works, M. l'Abbé Pasquier, the founder of the present orphan asylum. Both clergy and laity considered him a saint. The Archbishop, Monseigneur de Montblanc, had selected him for his confessor, consulted him on all occasions, and desired to receive the last sacraments at his hands. Mr. Dupont became acquainted with him, and as the bad health and constant occupations of Mr. Jolif du Colombier often prevented him from attending to his penitent, Mr. Dupont finally placed himself entirely under the spiritual direction of Mr. Pasquier. He saw him nearly every day. In the evening he recited Matins and Lauds with him and M. l'Abbé Verdier, a young deacon, who had been sent to aid him in the charge of his orphan asylum.

Through this canon he made the acquaintance of another holy priest, M. l'Abbé Botrel, who still lives, and with whom Mr. Dupont remained on intimate terms till his death. These three holy men conversed upon God and united in prayer. When Mr. Pasquier, in 1836, established his orphans outside the city in the old convent of St. Francis of Paula, near Plessis-lez-Tours, Mr. Botrel accompanied him there. Notwithstanding the distance, Mr. Dupont rarely failed to visit these two friends daily. The tomb of the thaumaturgus of Calabria, near which they took their solitary walks and where they entertained themselves with pious conversation, the antique walls built by the Minims, the vast enclosure in which formerly arose so celebrated a church, everything in this memorable place, suggested to the fervent layman projects of works of reparation, and all he saw aroused his zeal to restore the memory of the patrons of the country.

It was on that spot and during a conversation with these two men of God, that Mr. Dupont broached the subject of the reconstruction of St. Martin. When he first fixed his residence at Tours, he was astonished and grieved to find the name of the great Bishop, to whom his native isle was dedicated, totally effaced from the hearts of his fellow citizens. He sought, in vain, in the centre of the city for the exact spot where rested the remains of the thaumaturgus of Gaul, in order to pray there; no trace marked the sacred place; the very remembrance of it was lost. There was even a fatal mistake existing in this respect. It was erroneously supposed, from judgments based upon plans published at a certain period, that the glorious sepulchre lay under the public street, and as it was considered an impossibility to induce the authorities either to condemn the street or to turn it in another direction, the hope of restoring the tomb to the veneration of the faithful was abandoned.

One day, Mr. Dupont turned his steps towards the supposed location, venerating in his heart the memory of the holy Pontiff. As he had but recently arrived in the city, he interrogated the inhabitants of the neighborhood, and a good old woman, a vender of vegetables, explained to him, in her way, that the tomb of St. Martin was not in the street as was generally said and believed; that the engineer, who had been employed to locate a street over the ruins of the ancient church, intended, it is true, to draw the line so that it would pass above the site of the tomb, but that "during the operation, St. Martin had caused his instrument to deviate to the right," she said, "in such a manner that the engineer had failed to carry out his design." Mr. Dupont paid but little attention at the time to the remark of the good woman. He concluded that the true location of the sepulchre, venerated by the whole world for so many centuries, was no longer known.

At least, although ignorant of the exact spot, he would offer the homage of his prayers near it, and from that day he often stopped at the corner of St. Martin and Descartes streets, when passing through the city to satisfy his devotion. Whoever might be his companions, whatever the weather, he never failed to take off his hat, and recite in a low voice that verse of the Psalmist which he applied to the tomb and basilica of St. Martin. *"Benigne fac, Domine, in bona voluntate tua Sion, ut ædificentur muri Jerusalem."* "Deal favorably, O Lord, in Thy good will with Sion, that the walls of Jerusalem may be built up." It had not, at that time, occurred to any one at Tours to build up the walls of the antique and celebrated edifice; those who had formerly conceived the idea had abandoned it as chimerical and impracticable. Mr. Dupont, alone, did not doubt that the project would, at some future day, be carried into effect. He made it the object of his unceasing petitions to Almighty God, regarding the rebuilding of the basilica and the restoration of pilgrimages to the shrine, such as they had formerly been, as two things not only possible, but indispensable for the salvation of France and the regeneration of society. Possessed by this thought, he was accustomed to set out, generally alone, but sometimes accompanied by one or two friends, about nightfall, and he made through the silent streets, what he called his "way of the cross," which consisted in reciting, as they walked along, the *Miserere* and other prayers, kneeling and praying on the ruins of churches or chapels which had been destroyed or profaned. He numbered fourteen of these; the basilica of St. Martin held the first place in his affections; after this came St. Julien, St. Clement, the Cordeliers, the Minims, the Jacobins, &c. Each of the above was a station where he would stop and offer to God on his knees the most fervent acts of reparation.

The ruined churches and desecrated sanctuaries of Tours were not the only ones which were visited by this fervent Christian in a spirit of reparation. A secret attraction led him to all the shrines consecrated by the piety of our ancestors to our Blessed Lady and the saints. If he felt any preference, it was for the poorest and the most dilapidated.

The devotion of pilgrimages seemed innate in him. It was the principal motive which led him to undertake his distant excursions and frequent journeys. Even when business affairs or the exigences of propriety caused him to go upon a journey, he never failed to take advantage of it to visit, as a pilgrim, the celebrated places and even the least frequented sanctuaries, which were either directly on his route or not far removed from it. From this attraction arose his idea of composing a book unique of its kind.

In 1840, he accompanied to Havre a relative who was about to embark for the colonies. His friend, desiring to make his Confession before leaving France, applied to the parish priest, and during the day made him a visit of courtesy in company with Mr. Dupont. This simple circumstance was the commencement of a long and close friendship between the priest of Havre and the pious layman. Whenever business affairs called him to Havre, he received hospitality from his friend, the curate of Notre Dame. In the frequent pious conversations they had together, and which Mr. Dupont rendered so interesting by the lively expression of his faith and by his great zeal to procure the glory of God, they discussed the means of serving the Church and contributing to the good of souls.

Mr. Dupont, who, among all the practices of devotion, esteemed the most highly those which did homage to the Blessed Virgin, thought immediately of the pilgrimages which were formerly so common, and which were still made in various places. Thence he conceived the idea of a book, in which different pilgrimages should be proposed to the piety of the faithful under the form of "Visits to Mary for Every Day in the Year."

The environs of Havre offered a specimen of those antique sanctuaries towards which his soul was so strongly attracted: it was the little chapel of Our Lady of Gournai, at that time totally neglected. Situated in a fertile and charming valley, it had been, before the revolution, a place of pilgrimage for all the parishes of the country in its vicinity. Mr. Dupont went thither with his friend, the priest, and through devotion carried away with him, as a memento, some of the water from a fountain which flowed beside the chapel.

In like manner, he made a pilgrimage to Our Lady of Grace, another renowned sanctuary of Normandy, on the road from Havre to Harfleur. "He prayed there," says his companion, "with his usual fervor, and received from the chaplain, as a souvenir of the holy spot, a small fragment which had been broken from the statue."

These two pilgrimages accomplished with such dispositions in company with a pious and learned priest, the conversations which ensued, the supernatural impression made upon him personally, all confirmed Mr. Dupont in the project he had conceived. His idea was to describe, and visit in imagination as many shrines as there are days in the year. France alone, without speaking of other Catholic countries, presented a sufficient number of such places consecrated to the honor of Mary; but it was necessary for him to know them well. To obtain the requisite information, he must open communication with some learned ecclesiastic, or with a competent and obliging layman of each diocess. This was no easy task; but whilst the author foresaw all the difficulties, he did not lose courage. Being on terms of friendship with persons who resided near these shrines, and who could enter into his views, he did not hesitate to make use of them to obtain the notes he needed for his work. He undertook several journeys for that purpose, collected documents, and made inquiries in every direction; he wrote to Germany and even to America, neglecting no means of arriving at the truth.

He was thus enabled to furnish the reader with a lecture and a visit, not for every day in the year as he desired, but for every other day and even for every day during the month of May. Each pilgrimage is the subject of a "historical notice," which, giving a description of the place, enables the reader to visit it in imagination. The greater part of the historical notices were accompanied by an engraving representing the sanctuary, which was the object of the pilgrimage. The work appeared in 1842, with the approbation of Monseigneur de Montblanc, Archbishop of Tours.

Notwithstanding some imperfection in the arrangement of the book, it proved very valuable by contributing to render the ancient devotion of pilgrimages more practical and popular, and the servant of Mary had the happiness of seeing his simple publication aid the magnificent development which this devotion has acquired in our days. The work was intended by the author to be a kind of manual for the use of pilgrims. He commences it by summing up, under the form of preliminary counsels, the dispositions with which pilgrimages should be made, if we desire them to be spiritually profitable.

For him a pilgrimage was a solemn act of religion. As far as possible, he performed it on foot and fasting; he never omitted receiving Holy Communion. He was alone the first time he made the pilgrimage to Candes, the place rendered memorable by the death of St. Martin. The traveller at that time did not meet the same facilities and the rapid transportation we now enjoy. Mr. Dupont arrived at Candes only at eleven o'clock, and the curate of the parish had finished his Mass some time previous. However, addressing the venerable pastor, who was in the church, Mr. Dupont asked the favor of communicating, saying that he had assisted at the Holy Sacrifice early in the morning. The curate of Candes, to whom he was a perfect stranger, unaccustomed to see men of rank ask for Communion under similar circumstances, distrusted him and dryly refused. The pilgrim, without a word, resigned himself to the loss of Communion and quietly knelt upon the bare ground, interiorly rejoiced at being despised. God soon recompensed him. The good curate, perceiving that he was dealing with a simple, fervent Christian, offered to render the service he had just refused.

He had the habit of speaking indirectly of himself as "the pilgrim." He used the name familiarly, and it was commonly applied to him by his friends. He answered as readily to the appellation as to his own name. The "dear pilgrim" took pleasure in making a personal application of the expressions so frequent in the Scriptures, in which man is called a "traveller," a "stranger" here below. A stranger to all except God and the things of God, passing through the world without being attached to anything on earth, he was truly "the pilgrim." None had more perfectly the spirit; none put it more seriously into practice; he went from one sanctuary to another, praying, meditating, or conversing piously with the friends who were induced, by his example or solicitation, to accompany him. His enthusiasm won a cheerful acceptance of these invitations. He was, on a pilgrimage as elsewhere, say those who knew him, the most amiable and obliging of travelling companions. Without any effort to put himself forward, and without affectation, he was attentive even to the personal comforts of each individual, thoughtful and ingenious in providing for every want, profiting by his great experience in these kinds of excursions for the benefit of the party, delicate in his attentions and courteous to all, enlivening the conversation and relieving the tedium of a long journey by interesting and sprightly anecdotes; in a word, as a perfect gentleman, putting every one at his ease. The friendships he contracted on these occasions were unalterable and lasted as long as life.

There were in Touraine shrines forgotten and abandoned. Mr. Dupont preferred to visit such as these, and strove to restore them to the veneration of the faithful. He never failed to leave an abundant alms at every shrine. He foresaw, twenty years in advance, the immense good that pilgrimages were destined to do in France, and he proposed them as a most efficacious means of arousing the faith of the people; willingly would he have traversed France from shrine to shrine, openly bearing the pilgrim's traditional staff.

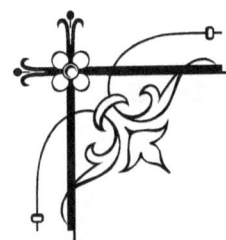

Chapter IV

His Works of Charity — His Conversations.

THE SERVANT of God, next to assiduous visits to the churches in which our Lord dwells, and to the sanctuaries where the saints are honored, had nothing more at heart than visiting the suffering poor. The conference of St. Vincent de Paul had just been established at Tours, and Mr. Dupont immediately requested to be admitted as a member.

He became, from the first, associated with the honorable and virtuous men of the city, and soon acquired a marked influence over them. The modesty of his demeanor won the sympathy of his fellow members, quite as much as the fame of his virtues and the example of his piety. To those who knew him well, who caught a glimpse of the celestial light which illumined his soul, and who knew in what magnificent charities he expended his income, and often a portion of his principal, it was a strange and edifying sight to behold him come every week to the conference, asking a small alms of a few pounds of bread, which he scrupulously offered in the name of all to some poor family. He gave an account of his visit, and with exquisite delicacy, replied to all the questions put to him. He rarely volunteered to speak; and if he wished to make a suggestion, he first consulted the President or some member of the Board. He put himself forward as little as possible.

He particularly delighted in these reunions, because he met there such society as he preferred—Christians reputed pious and fervent, or whom he strove to render such. Without any assumption on his part, he formed in the midst of the conferences of St. Vincent de Paul, a phalanx of devout men of which he was the head, and who were unconsciously influenced by the enthusiasm of his lively faith and ardent piety. When he was about to establish the nocturnal Adoration, these members of the conferences formed the principal nucleus of adorers.

As to the poor, he visited them much more frequently than the other members, and gave far more abundant alms than was allotted to each; and yet, at the weekly meeting, the treasurer could affirm that Mr. Dupont was present, simply by looking in his purse. How he loved the poor! With what interest he watched the result of an illness! A former President writes: "I had mentioned to him a family whom I was visiting. It was that of a tiler named Talon. The unfortunate man, having fallen from a roof, had been terribly mangled. His life was a long martyrdom; but he had become very pious and perfectly resigned. Mr. Dupont went to see him from time to time, encouraged and consoled him. One morning we met at the cathedral, and he said to me with a countenance radiant with joy: 'Talon is dead! I kissed his heart before the chill of death had frozen it.' The sight of a Christian death delighted him."

Visiting the poor, and pious conversations with his fellow members, attracted Mr. Dupont to the conferences of St. Vincent de Paul. But the official part of the meetings, the formal assemblies, reports and settling of accounts were distasteful to him. He willingly left this to others, and would never consent to accept any office. He chose rather the practice of good works.

CHAPTER IV

The conference of Tours had under its direction, at that time, says one of the presidents, a number of different kinds of works, such as the superintendence of apprentices, instruction of soldiers and classes of adults. Mr. Dupont comprehended their importance and was deeply interested in them. For a long time he devoted a portion of his evenings to the class of adults, which was assembled three times a week. One hundred and fifty workmen of various trades and ages received lessons in reading, writing, grammar and arithmetic. Mr. Dupont never absented himself; from seven to nine o'clock he was at his post, ready to receive all who presented themselves, but choosing for his own pupils the most ignorant, those who did not even know their letters. When, through his exertions, they had commenced to spell, he advanced them to the class of another member, by whom they were taught to read.

He never seemed so pleased as when seated on a bench, surrounded by these poor people in their working clothes, covered with dust and impregnated with the bad odors exhaled from their work and their miserable huts. He never manifested the slightest repugnance, but radiant with joy, he would frequently stop some member of the conference as he passed, and claim his admiration for the knowledge and progress of some poor man, who had, by hard labor, succeeded in spelling a word of two or three syllables. On such occasions, it was necessary to congratulate the master, to compliment and encourage the pupil. "He is improving, he is improving," Mr. Dupont would say, "he will succeed." Among others, there was a sort of colossus, a laboring man, quite young and very dull, who was an assiduous scholar of Mr. Dupont. During four consecutive years, Mr. Dupont devoted several hours three times a week to the task of cultivating this untutored mind. Although the perseverance of the young colossus, in his efforts to learn to read, was not crowned with success, it obtained for him something far more precious. He was as ignorant of his religion as of his letters, and if he did not learn his lessons, he learned the way to the Church; he attended Mass regularly, said his prayers and approached the sacraments. Mr. Dupont was right in saying: "He improves, he will succeed."

His zeal was not less in the care of the soldiers than it had been for the class of adults. With them, however, his efforts were not restricted to instructions; his attention must be given also to their amusements and games. Mr. Dupont made no difficulty in taking his part in them. By his unfailing kindness, and charming simplicity in speaking of God and His wonderful works, he excited the interest of the soldiers, and his friends say that on many occasions they were not only surprised, but touched by the manner in which they listened to his pious remarks, which awoke in them the sentiments of their youthful days, and remembrances of their childhood. The man of God gave no regular discourse, nor any address which had the appearance of a discourse; the soldiers were neither formally assembled, nor seated to hear him; but a group of men would collect around him in the garden or in the recreation hall, would come and go as they liked, asking him questions, and receiving his answers with unfeigned delight.

Mr. Dupont excelled in, what we may call, this family intercourse; in such circumstances his heart expanded, was at ease, and poured itself out naturally. He had the gift of familiar conversation. His diction was easy, clear, elegant, picturesque, in good taste, and without pretension or affectation; he entirely lost sight of himself, never sought to impose his opinions, even when he clung to them energetically through conviction; but both through a motive of prudence, and an humble distrust of self, he avoided discussions or contentions, unless in cases where there was question of moral right or wrong, or of a dogma of faith; for then he did not hesitate to enter into a discussion, but always in a calm, cordial manner, never wounding any one, although, at times, he was sharp and ironical when speaking of anti-Catholic prejudices and false doctrine. His clear and solid argumentation recalled the former magistrate of the Antilles; he had reasons peculiar to himself, ingenious and just repartees, which left his adversary without reply. His honesty of purpose, his candor, his delicacy of feeling, as well as the sincerity of his opinions, were so evident, that his opponents would yield the controversy through courtesy.

The learned and celebrated Dr. Bretonneau, himself an untiring and charming conversationalist, for a long time a neighbor, and always a friend of Mr. Dupont, would endure in religious matters, his reproaches, his piquant observations, his urgent solicitations, until at last, in self-defence, he would rush from the room and take refuge in the garden.

When Béranger, the well known lyric poet, established himself at Tours towards the end of his life, and fixed his residence not far from Saint-Etienne street, Mr. Dupont, in his pious proselytism, interested himself deeply in the soul of his new neighbor. He undertook to convert him. His conversation seemed to please the Parisian poet; he only persuaded him, however, to read St. Paul's Epistles.

Mr. Dupont was inexhaustible in his stock of religious news, pious anecdotes, and accounts of miracles. He possessed the talent of relating them in an agreeable manner, entering, sometimes into details, which were always ingenious and edifying, even when they were long and minute; he threw into them a glow of imagination and a biblical poesy, which brought vividly before the mind the persons or things he was describing; and he represented to the life, by his voice and gesture, what he was narrating.

He did much good by his conversations in families and small companies, where he was always cordially welcomed. He took pleasure in visiting at houses where he could speak freely of God; he did this with an "ineffable" charm, to use an expression which was familiar to him. But if he happened to meet company who gave another turn to the conversation, he quietly withdrew.

His friends often contended for his society. "One evening," says one of them, "as we were leaving the conference of St. Vincent de Paul, I invited him to pass the remainder of the evening with me. Mr. de Noricourt was equally desirous of having him at his house. We agreed to toss up for him. We were on the side walk of the Rue Royale. Mr. Dupont laughed heartily, and amiably accompanied home the friend who won him."

At his own house, he received all who called upon him, and continued the conversation as long as they chose, provided they spoke of God, or things appertaining to God. "To speak of God, or to keep silence," was already the motto he had adopted. He did not refuse even serious controversies with Protestants or Freethinkers. On these occasions, he appeared, not only as an agreeable conversationalist, but a skilful polemic and a true Christian apologist. We give an example.

A wealthy and erudite Englishman, named William Palmer, was passing some time at Tours, and although a Protestant, often visited Mr. Dupont. They had long, amicable discussions together, particularly on the real presence in the Eucharist. This was Mr. Dupont's favorite subject; and he returned to it the more willingly with his learned opponent, because he maintained that all true Anglicans admitted the real presence. "You are the only Englishman," said Mr. Dupont, "whom I have heard express such an opinion. For instance, Mrs. Bruce, with whom I corresponded for a long time, did not believe in it." Mr. Palmer insisted that the lady had been misunderstood, and he asserted positively that no member of the Anglican Church could know his Catechism and deny the real presence. What was his astonishment, when Mr. Dupont arose and handed him an Anglican work entitled Crossman's Catechism, in which a doctrine directly contrary to the real presence is positively taught. Now this Catechism, which was a sort of theological commentary of the Anglican doctrines drawn up by Dr. Crossman, had been published with the approbation of the "Society for Promoting Christian Knowledge," which Society includes, by right, among its members all the archbishops and bishops of the established Church, and Mr. Palmer himself. Surprised and confused, he was compelled to say: "If the Catechism of the Church of England taught that doctrine, I would not remain in her communion. But Crossman's Catechism is not the Catechism of the Church of England!"

A few days later, Mr. Palmer received from his friend a reasonable, but singular reproach; we transscribe it in his own words from a document written by himself.

"The day following the festival of the Assumption, August 16, Mr. Dupont told me that being seated as Administrator of the Church on a bench in the nave of the cathedral, his eye fell upon me as I passed before the altar after Vespers, and he noticed that I had not made a genuflection to the Blessed Sacrament. He could only conclude that this indicated a want of faith. 'You say that you believe as I do in the real presence, and you did not bend your knee! Ah!' he exclaimed, 'you have not faith.' To all the explanations and excuses which I offered, he persisted in repeating. 'You did not bend your knee! You do not believe!' He then quoted a passage from St. John Chrysostom, in which this father speaks of an old man of his acquaintance who had been favored with revelations, and who affirmed that on one occasion he had seen angels bowed before the altar, adoring God really present. And for my part, adds St. Chrysostom, I believe it. I told him I was not disposed to deny it. 'But,' replied Mr. Dupont, 'you do not bend, although angels adore!' Among other things I told him that I had not the presumption to join in religious ceremonies in Catholic Churches; for I was regarded as excommunicated, and my presence only tolerated. 'Ah!' he replied, 'the laws of men are nothing in such cases. But far from believing, you call us idolators because we bend before the Host.'"

These remarks made a deep impression upon Mr. Palmer. With admirable docility, and an entire freedom from human respect, he profited by the lesson given him relative to genuflections before the Eucharist. "Not long after the above conversation," he says, "two Anglican ministers, Fellows of Oxford, (one of them had been my professor,) making me a visit at Tours, reproached me for having knelt before the Blessed Sacrament in that very church, where I had scandalized Mr. Dupont by not making a genuflection." Mr. Palmer was seeking the truth with sincerity: he was converted and became a zealous and fervent Catholic. Passing through Tours in 1862, he had the happiness of praying with Mr. Dupont before the Holy Face.

Mr. Dupont continued in his letters the good work he had commenced in his conversations. His correspondence, on his first arrival at Tours, was considerable; by degrees his letters were entirely on pious subjects. He wrote with facility and clearness; his style was that of good conversation; his thoughts were developed naturally and without effort; the mode of expression is often sprightly and original, enriched with quotations from Scripture, and associations of dates and circumstances furnished by his excellent memory. The number of letters he wrote was prodigious. Unfortunately, many which would have possessed a peculiar interest for us were destroyed; but those which have been preserved are charming: they reflect the qualities of his beautiful soul and loving heart; wise counsels and pious sentiments abound, and not unfrequently they are animated with a celestial enthusiasm.

Chapter V

His Vocation — His Relations With Sister Saint-Pierre — La Salette.

WITHOUT HAVING the character and mission of a priest, Mr. Dupont exercised the apostleship by his letters, conversations, and charitable intercourse with others. Several of his friends were astonished that he remained a secular without elevating himself to a more evangelical and perfect state. A holy missionary of America, who was well acquainted with him, and with whom he kept up an active correspondence, judging by his letters inflamed with divine love that he might yet devote himself to the function of the priesthood, and become an apostle of the new world, proposed it to him. Mr. Dupont refused humbly and frankly. He did not consider himself worthy of the vocation to the missionary life; he admires it in those who have received it; he envies them; but our Lord has not said to him: *"Sequere me."* "Follow me." "Besides," he adds, "it is not necessary to expatriate oneself in order to find souls to save. He, Who alone gives vocations knows where to send his workmen. What concerns us, is to beg our dear Lord to send laborers to the harvest of souls in France, that the reign of God may be established, and that France may be blessed with sons ready to march to the conquest of the pagan world beyond the sea." He will not then be of the number of those conquerors whom he admires; he is not called to the apostleship of the priesthood; but another vocation is assigned him. Whilst remaining at Tours, in the bosom of his family and in the secular state, he will become one of those "laborers" in the Lord's vineyard whom he asks for France; it is in France, in his own country, that he will contribute, in his way, to extend the "reign of God," of which he so ardently desires the increase.

The apostolate which Mr. Dupont was destined to exercise in our midst was that of reparation. Without knowing it, without even suspecting it, he was already, as if instinctively, preparing for it in prayer. Not satisfied by uniting with the Church in the recitation of the breviary, he associated himself with holy souls in imploring the salvation of France and in acts of reparation for the scandals which were committed.

Among these scandals, one particularly afflicted him. It was that of blasphemy. Perhaps in our days the habit of gross blasphemy, which consists in continually pronouncing with irreverence the adorable and holy name of God, has somewhat diminished, at least in the higher classes of society. But it was different at the period of Mr. Dupont's life of which we are now writing. After the revolution of 1793, this ignoble and horrible habit pervaded all ranks and even tainted the conversation of literary men. It was not uncommon to hear very small children uttering frightful oaths and blasphemies, even in the presence of their parents. It was allowable in certain salons in which was assembled a revolutionary, Voltarian, and impious society. This will furnish an explanation of the holy audacity displayed by Mr. Dupont in his efforts to combat this habit. Whenever a word which directly attacked the Divine Majesty fell upon his ear, he was moved by a virtuous indignation. He was restrained neither by personal considerations nor by human respect. Zeal for the outraged glory of God urged him to acts which none other would have dared to permit himself, but to which the efficacy of his prayers, and the benediction of heaven always attached a special grace of reparation, and, not unfrequently, a striking conversion.

Once, when travelling, he took his seat beside the driver who uttered a blasphemous expression. Mr. Dupont instantly dealt him a heavy blow. Surprised and indignant, the driver stops his horses and demands an explanation of the insult offered him. "Unhappy man," replied Mr. Dupont, "it is *you* who have insulted me. You have outraged my Father! Who gives you the right to insult my Father in this manner?" "Your Father," said the blasphemer, astounded as much by the remark as by the blow. "Yes," continued Mr. Dupont, "God is my Father and your Father; why do you outrage Him?" And then with the eloquence of his heart and the vivacity of his faith, he endeavored to make him comprehend how unworthy it was of a Christian to blaspheme the thrice holy God. The poor man, confused and ashamed, alleged as his excuse, his deplorable habit and promised to amend. By the time they had reached the end of the journey, they were good friends. Mr. Dupont, on parting, presented him a five-franc piece, and invited him to visit him at Tours. He had the gratification of learning later from the driver himself that he had corrected his bad habit and was leading a Christian life.

On another occasion, when he was going in a diligence from Saint-Malo to Rennes, the postilion scarcely spoke without an oath. Notwithstanding the presence of two or three travelling agents, at each oath, Mr. Dupont repeated aloud a *Gloria Patri* in reparation. At last, unable to endure it longer, he caught the postilion by the arm and said to him: "Friend, cease, I beg you, to blaspheme the holy name of God. Each time you wish to swear, give me a blow instead; that would please me much better." We may judge of the impression made upon his auditors by the words of a man whose only thought was the glory of God. A good Religious, who was once in the coupé of a vehicle with him, relates that he paid the driver so much a league for refraining from blasphemy. As this practice was habitual with him, we shall know, only at the day of judgment, how many oaths he prevented.

When passing through the streets of a city he never failed to reprove blasphemers, although he was often repaid by insult and contempt. Once, however, he met an unfortunate man who was uttering terrible oaths. Mr. Dupont stopped and begged him earnestly either to be silent or give him a blow. "Why should I strike you, sir?" asked the man in astonishment. "Because it would be far less painful to me to receive a blow from you, than to hear you outrage the holy name of God." Impressed by his words, the blasphemer begged his pardon and promised amendment.

His zeal on this point suggested to him minute precautions which would hardly have occurred to another. One of his friends writes: "I was walking, on one occasion, with Mr. Dupont. He saw lying on the pavement a small stone; he picked it up and placed it against the wall, remarking as he did so: "Whenever we find a stone lying in the way on a street or road, we should always remove it, because it might cause a man or beast to stumble, and besides the injury it would do to them, the man might be irritated and tempted to blaspheme the holy name of God."

His devotion to St. Louis, king of France, arose partly from the idea of reparation, as he particularly honored in the prince the zeal of his justice in punishing and reforming blasphemers, and he prepared himself for the annual celebration of his feast by special prayers, called "The Forty Days of St. Louis."

This *union of prayers*, sent to Tours during the the course of the year 1843, was distributed to a few pious souls, and among others to Mr. Dupont, who accepted it with delight, and observed the practices enjoined. It commenced on the 16th of July, festival of Our Lady of Mount Carmel, and terminated on the 25th of August, feast of St. Louis. A copy of the prayers was not sent the Carmelites, and they had absolutely no knowledge of the devotion. It is important to remark this fact, because on the day following the feast of St. Louis, August 26, there occurred at the Carmelite convent, a remarkable, supernatural event, which was to be the commencement and origin of Mr. Dupont's grand mission of reparation.

There was among the Carmelites a young Religious, a native of Brittany, whom St. Martin seemed to have conducted to Tours by a special protection. She was a simple workwoman of Rennes, possessed of few natural endowments, but favored by God and enriched with the gifts of grace. Her name in religion was Marie de Saint-Pierre. Her amiable disposition and her sweet cordiality equalled the fervor of her piety and her simplicity. God did not long delay to manifest His designs over her. On the morning of the 26th of August, 1843, she sought the Rev. Mother Prioress after Mass, and throwing herself at her feet, said to her: *"Our Lord has just commanded me to say, and induce others to say as often as possible, the following invocation respecting the great crime of blasphemy. May the most holy, most sacred, most adorable name of God be praised, blessed, loved, adored, and glorified in heaven, on earth, and in hell, by all the creatures of God, and by the Sacred Heart of our Lord and Saviour Jesus Christ, in the most holy Sacrament of the Altar!"*

Now it happened that the 25th, the eve of this ineffable communication, was the last day of the forty days' devotion to St. Louis, of which we spoke above, and which terminated by the aspiration: *May Thy name, O Lord, be always and everywhere known and blessed!* It did not seem at all improbable, that the "union of prayers," which had not been made at Carmel, but in many cities and by a large number of pious persons, had hastened the establishment of the work of reparation.

This communication was the prelude of a series of graces granted to the humble Religious, having, for their object, the establishment of a confraternity destined to repair the crimes of blasphemy and the profanation of Sunday. The Sister had proved the truth of her mission by circumstances esteemed miraculous. Permission in the first instance was given to have printed a small pamphlet containing the prayers sent from Poictiers, under the title of *Association for the Extinction of Blasphemy;* at the head was a picture of St. Louis in prayer, and underneath, the aspiration: *May the name of the Lord be blessed!* These were republished at Tours with the approbation of the Archbishop, Monseigneur Morlot. As the publication involved communication with persons outside the monastery, and as Superiors, through prudential motives did not wish to appear in the affair, Mr. Dupont was selected to attend to the necessary arrangements. Monseigneur Morlot approved the choice, and wrote himself to Mr. Dupont upon the subject.

He permitted an act of reparation to the holy name of God to be added to the prayers of the Association. The associates were to pledge themselves never to utter a blasphemy, to exert the authority they had over others to prevent blasphemy, to make reparation, by a vocal or mental aspiration, for the blasphemies they might hear. In this we have the germ of the work of reparation.

The servant of God sincerely rejoiced at the encouragement thus extended by the pious Archbishop. On one of these pamphlets he wrote: *Signatum est super nos lumen vultus tui, Domine, dedisti lætitiam in corde meo. The light of Thy countenance, O Lord, is signed upon us: Thou hast given gladness to my heart*—and he added below: *St. Veronica, pray for us.* The devotion to the Holy Face commences to dawn.

Mr. Dupont became avowedly the distributor— according to his own expression—the pedler of the pamphlet of St. Louis. He conceived, at the same time, the idea of composing a Little Office in honor of the holy name of God. With this intention, he first collected all the texts referring to the divine name, which are scattered through different parts of the Scriptures. A selection of beautiful prayers analogous to the texts, enriched the collection as so many precious stones. Having completed this portion of the work, he chose from these passages of the Old and New Testament, a certain number which he arranged in the form of Psalms, lessons, chapters and versicles, presenting as a whole, a harmonious liturgical prayer appropriate to his design of reparation. As was his custom, he subjected his work to competent judges.

The Little Office of the Holy Name of God was issued with the approbation of Monseigneur Morlot. Each hour is preceded by a short explanation. The Latin text is followed by a French translation, carefully prepared by Mr. Dupont, who, to secure its correctness, consulted the most learned ecclesiastics. The little book was published by M. Mame, in the same volume with another entitled: *Association of Prayers against Blasphemy, Imprecations and Profanation of Sunday and Holy Days*. This latter work contains the statutes of the association of reparation, reflections on blasphemy and the profanation of Sunday, acts of reparation, aspirations and prayers. Thus arranged, the book was widely circulated, and prepared the faithful for another more important work which, in the designs of Providence, was about to be established.

This was the work of reparation urged by Sister Saint-Pierre. Three years had already passed since the pious Carmelite demanded it in the name of God. She declared that the exterior emblem would be the outraged Face of Christ; and acting on this idea, she had composed the Litany of the Holy Face and other analogous prayers. After many and various trials, intended to test the reality of the communications she professed to have received, her Superiors acknowledged them to be truly from the Holy Spirit, and they were desirous of carrying the project into execution; but none of them would venture to take the initiative. At last they arranged a pamphlet which contained the substance of the divine communications, and which was called: "Abridgement of the Facts Concerning the Work for the Reparation of Blasphemy." This pamphlet, intended for circulation among a few Carmelite houses and a small number of pious souls, was submitted in manuscript to the Archbishop, and was approved by him. Mr. Dupont, again placing his services at the disposal of the community, distributed these pamphlets among his friends.

One of these fell into the hands of Mr. Lebrument, a fervent Christian of Rouen. To assure himself of the reality of the facts related in it, he determined to make a visit to Tours. Convinced of their truth by the information furnished him in that city, he did not hesitate to interest himself actively in the success of the work, being resolved to forward it whenever Providence should throw the occasion in his way. An opportunity soon offered.

Passing through Paris on his return to Rouen, he met at the hotel a priest of his acquaintance, M. l'Abbé Favrel, vicar-general of the diocese of Langres, who informed him that his Bishop, Monseigneur Parisis, was at the same hotel, and invited him to pay his respects to the illustrious prelate, which he did that very day. During the conversation, the pious layman spoke of his visit to Touraine, related what he had learned from Mr. Dupont, and dwelt upon the necessity of the work of reparation. The Bishop of Langres was struck by what he heard. He admitted that, for some time, he had cherished the wish of establishing a similar confraternity in his diocese. He wrote immediately upon the subject to the Archbishop of Tours, who, as a measure of precaution, on account of the revelations made to the Carmelite sister, upon which he was unwilling to pronounce authoritatively at that time, left the initiative to Monseigneur Parisis. Thus empowered to act, his lordship of Langres, by an episcopal decree dated June 28, 1847, erected the confraternity in reparation of blasphemy and profanation of Sunday in a parochial church of Saint-Dizier, dedicated to St. Martin, and he deputed to Rome M. l'Abbé Marche, curate of that parish, to solicit in favor of the association the title of archconfraternity and special indulgences. Pius IX, who had been elevated to the chair of St. Peter two years previously, welcomed with a kind of enthusiasm the petition of the Bishop of Langres, and made, on that occasion, the remark which has been so frequently repeated: "Reparation is a work destined to save society." He granted the indulgences which had been asked, elevated the Association of Reparation of Saint-Dizier to the dignity of an archconfraternity, and inscribed his own name the first on the list of associates, a wonderful privilege, which was the seed of many benedictions.

The idea of repairing blasphemy and the profanation of Sunday, hitherto entertained in the secrecy of their hearts by a few pious souls, now became general. Parishes and individuals were registered by thousands, and the revelation made to the humble Carmelite and, through her, communicated to the Church, was the source whence has sprung all the works of reparation of our day.

In consequence of the facts above related, Mr. Dupont had frequent interviews with Sister Saint-Pierre. The fervent layman followed with ever increasing interest the action of God on this privileged soul. His candid and simple faith led him to unite cheerfully with the Sister in her cherished devotions, particularly in that to the Infant Jesus. Whilst the Carmelites remained near the cathedral, awaiting the completion of their new monastery which was being erected in the street of the Ursulines, Sister Saint-Pierre filled the office of portress, and Mr. Dupont went frequently to receive her commissions and to recommend himself to her prayers. She presented him little cases containing the Gospel which is read on the Feast of the Circumcision, in which is mentioned the name given the Child Jesus. The pious Sister, to honor the divine Infant, had made numerous copies of this short Gospel and had enclosed them in little cases prepared for the purpose. Mr. Dupont assisted the Sister both in copying and distributing the Gospels. They were generally named "the short Gospel of Sister Saint-Pierre." They were sent to persons who were ill, and remarkable cures, as well as great conversions, were obtained by those who wore them.

The Carmelite Religious expressed the highest veneration for the servant of God. She took an interest in all that concerned him. As the time approached when Henrietta was to make her first Communion, her father was extremely solicitous that she should be properly prepared for so holy an action. The Sister wrote to him: "I gladly accede to your request to address to the divine Infant Jesus for your daughter the touching prayer you have sent us, that this divine Infant may so dispose her young heart, that she may receive Him with perfect dispositions." The prayer referred to is one addressed to the Infant Jesus, copied by Mr. Dupont, on the back of a little picture blessed by Gregory XVI, and sent from Rome by Madame Barat, in 1843. The Infant Jesus is represented seated amid lilies, holding a dove in his hand, and beneath is the inscription; "The Lord Jesus received in Holy Communion by a pure soul." The pious Carmelite continues: "I am unworthy to offer your petitions to the Infant God; but I will beg Mary and Joseph to present my prayer, and to offer this dear child to the holy Child Jesus, that the day of her first Communion may be as the day of her betrothal with the heavenly and divine Spouse."

We see that Mr. Dupont's association with the Carmelites was familiar and intimate. When the community removed from Bauchereau street to the street of the Ursulines, Mr. Dupont, with the devoted kindness of a friend and benefactor, transacted all exterior affairs for them; he even became, so to say, their servant, going and coming from one house to the other, carrying in his hands statues and other articles liable to be broken. His house was the depot, during that time, for all articles belonging to the service of the chapel; the sacred vessels and the precious reliquaries of the convent remained sometime in his room, and, by a remarkable coincidence, rested in the very spot which is now occupied by the picture of the Holy Face.

In the meantime, Sister Saint-Pierre continued to beg of God by fervent prayer to accomplish, through the instrumentality of others, the designs which He had revealed to her; for she, a poor Religious, could do nothing, and she wished to remain unknown in her obscurity. There soon occurred in France a miraculous event of the utmost importance to reparation; an event which appeared to Mr. Dupont to be intimately connected with the divine manifestations vouchsafed the Carmelite Religious.

He writes of it in the following manner:

"In 1846, early in September, I went, on the day preceding my departure with my family to Saint-Servan, to receive from the Prioress of the Carmelites, any commissions she might have for Saint-Malo, where she had relatives. During the conversation, we spoke of Sister Marie de Saint-Pierre. I had a pencil in my hand and I wrote at once what the Reverend Mother communicated to me. 'The Sister has just told me that our Lord said to her: 'My Mother has spoken to men of my anger. She desires to appease it; she has shown Me her breasts and said to me: Behold the breasts which nourished you; permit them to pour out benedictions upon my other children; then full of mercy to man, she descended to earth: have confidence in her.'' I placed these lines in my prayer book," continues Mr. Dupont. "The words were mysterious, apparently linking the past with the present and the future. I did not attempt to fathom their meaning; I rested content in the somewhat vague conviction I had previously formed that the Sister was favored with confidential communications from our Lord. My conviction became stronger, when I received on the 22nd of October of the same year, a copy of the first letter written by the curate of Corps, relative to the apparition of the Blessed Virgin at La Salette on the 19th of September." Mr. Dupont considered the apparition as a confirmation of the words of Sister Saint-Pierre, which seemed to foretell it. He immediately forwarded to the curate of Corps, a copy of the notes he had taken in the parlor of the Carmelites. The curate replied: "I believed in the apparition from the first; I am now doubly convinced of its reality."

Mr. Dupont believed also. He was not in the least astonished when he heard an account of the apparition of the Blessed Virgin at La Salette; he admired the connection existing between that event and the communication vouchsafed to Sister Saint-Pierre. "How touching it is," he said, "to behold our August Mother confiding the sorrow of her maternal heart to poor little children! Was it not enough that she should have been sprinkled with the blood of her Divine Son on Calvary? Must the frightful stations of the streets of Jerusalem be renewed in our days by the blasphemies of an impious generation? What will become of us, if Mary can no longer restrain the arm of Jesus?"

An account of the miraculous apparition was communicated to the Carmelites of Tours by Mr. Dupont, and it created considerable sensation among them. Like their holy friend, they regarded it as a striking confirmation of the demands made by Sister Saint-Pierre on the part of God. The mission imposed on the shepherds of the mountain was, evidently, identical with that confided to the cloistered Religious. The Sister, therefore, when speaking of them, called them her two little trumpets. Hearing shortly afterwards of the erection of the archconfraternity, she exclaimed joyously: "My mission on earth is accomplished, now I shall die." She was not mistaken. She died July 8, 1848, offering herself as a victim for the salvation of France. She was thirty-one years of age.

Mr. Dupont assisted at the funeral obsequies and accompanied her mortal remains to the cemetery. From that time, he was accustomed to pray frequently at the tomb of the venerated Sister, and he took care that it should be kept in good order. When, seven years afterwards, the cemetery was removed beyond the city limits, Mr. Dupont took advantage of the circumstance to exhume the remains and restore them to the monastery. With pious care and religious respect, he collected the bones, and, to the great joy of the Mother Prioress and the Religious, he obtained the sanction of the authorities to deposit them within the enclosure; they were placed in the chapter-hall, where they now lie. True to his characteristic faith and influenced by his belief as to the necessity of reparation, Mr. Dupont never, for an instant, doubted the miraculous apparition at La Salette. He was one of the first pilgrims to the holy mountain. He visited it in company with a venerable priest of Grenoble, from whose account we copy the following:

"We went in the month of July, 1849, the year after the apparition. We found but two cabins on the mountain. At our departure from Corbelin, we numbered five. As there was at that time no railroad running to the place, we travelled in a stage-coach; the good *pilgrim* took advantage of every occasion to speak of the things of God. Like St. Francis of Assissium, he made use of creatures to rise to the Creator. Prayer and aspirations seasoned his agreeable and edifying conversation. On the road we passed a castle in which a miraculous cure had been obtained by a member of the family; Mr. Dupont proposed that we should say a prayer of thanksgiving for the favor granted by God to the individual, after which he related other wonders of grace which this recalled to his mind. It would be impossible to express the pleasure we derived from his charming conversations. At Corps, we were received by the Sisters of Providence with whom the two little children of the apparition had been placed. We were permitted to see and interrogate them without restraint. They accompanied us in our ascent of the mountain, and on the very spot of the apparition the children separately gave us an account of it.

At that time the stations of the Blessed Virgin were marked only by three small crosses, and the path she traversed was covered with grass.

"On the mountain, Mr. Dupont edified the pilgrims by his humility and faith. How often he kissed the ground hallowed by the footsteps of the Blessed Virgin! He followed, on his knees, the path she had traversed; he plucked a few blades of grass and gathered some little stones as a souvenir of the spot, and drank of the water of the fountain. How precious, but how short were the moments we passed on the mountain! We descended like the Apostles from Thabor, and the *good brother* said to me: 'Write in the note-book: The pilgrim who has travelled a hundred and eighty leagues says: I will return!' Writing afterwards to the good pilgrim at Tours, I reminded him of his promise; but he replied that he was the *pilgrim obliged to remain in one place and the servant of the Holy Face*, that his time was no longer his own.

"Mr. Dupont, during the pilgrimage, was the hero of our companies. He edified, he *astonished* by his Christian conversation; he was regarded as an apostle. When we were visiting the Sisters at Corenc, the Superioress assembled the community in their conference-hall, and the holy man, for nearly two hours, edified, charmed his auditors. Thence we went to the Grande-Chartreuse. The woods, the rocks, the grottos, but more than all, the penitential life of the Angels of the Solitude spoke to the heart of the *pious pilgrim*, who saw them for the first time."

We can readily imagine from the above unaffected narrative the edification given by Mr. Dupont during this journey. His amiable qualities and his eminent virtues were evident to all who were thrown in his society. Mr. Orcel, Superior of the grand seminary of Grenoble, frequently inquired for *that good Christian of the first century*. The curate of Corbelin wrote of him: "Since the Sunday when he served my Mass, I have felt increased devotion to the Blessed Sacrament of the altar."

CHAPTER V

On this journey, Mr. Dupont saw the curé d'Ars. The interview between the two servants of God was remarkable: it recalls that between St. Dominic and St. Francis of Assissium. Mr. Dupont tells us that he undertook the journey for the purpose of having a conversation with Fr. Viannay, for whom he had long professed great veneration. But how could he succeed in addressing him when a crowd of people, arranged in double rows, were already there, and were crowding upon his path as he left the church. Suddenly the curé d'Ars perceives the holy man of Tours, with whom he was not acquainted, whom he had never seen. He stops, goes up to him, fixes upon him his eyes beaming with kindness; then smiling, he joins his hands, and glancing upward, he says: "O my dear friend, how sweet it will be to us to find ourselves in heaven singing the praises of our God!" "I needed nothing more," added Mr. Dupont gaily; "I withdrew contented, preserving in my heart the words of the holy curé."

His first care, after his return from this pilgrimage, was to establish at Tours a sanctuary as a centre of the devotion to Our Lady of La Salette. The simple chapel of the Monastery of the Purification seemed to him suited to the purpose. He was particularly interested in the community. His confessor and friend, the Canon Pasquier, had founded it, with the intention of repairing the outrages committed against the Divine Majesty by those who profane the Sunday, and also to labor for their conversion by works of expiation and by prayer. The intention was pleasing to the servant of God. He had already aided the recent foundation by abundant alms; ties of friendship united him to the Superioress. At his suggestion and by his advice, she petitioned the ecclesiastical authorities to place the humble sanctuary under the invocation of Our Lady of Salette. As there was question of rebuilding it, Mr. Dupont presented a large sum, to facilitate the purchase of the ground and the enlarging of the building. When, in 1856, the whole was completed, he placed in the sanctuary, beside the altar, a picture of the apparition, which for the first time was exposed to the public veneration of the faithful.

Such is the commencement of the devotion to Our Lady of Salette among the people of Tours, and the origin of the novenas which are annually made previous to the 19th of September. In order to give permanency to this movement, the servant of Mary considered an association necessary. After conferring on the subject with ecclesiastics on whose judgment he relied, he decided to request the Archbishop, Monseigneur Guibert, to erect a confraternity. He returned a favorable answer to the petition, and by a decree of the 19th of September, 1857, he erected in the Chapel of the Purification the Confraternity of Our Lady of Reconciliation, which was afterwards affiliated to the archconfraternity of the same name established on the holy mountain.

The Chapel of the Purification, next to that of the Carmelites, was the one most frequently visited by Mr. Dupont. He often heard Mass and received Holy Communion there; he never failed to be present on any special feasts of the monastery; he interested himself in a paternal manner in all the necessities of the house. For example, not long after the chapel was built, the stone cross surmounting it fell upon the roof. Mr. Dupont, on visiting the community, noticed it. He sent immediately for a mason, ordered a similar cross, upon which he directed the Heart of Jesus to be cut; the whole was executed at his expense.

The devotion to Our Lady of Reconciliation led to intimate and friendly relations between himself and the Religious of the Purification which lasted as long as his life. "A few weeks before his death," writes the Superioress, "he sent us a bottle of the miraculous water which he had brought with him from the holy mountain. The date is written with his own hand, and, although so many years have passed since it was drawn from the fountain, the water is perfectly clear and pure."

CHAPTER V

During his whole life, even when he was the most absorbed by the worship of the Holy Face, Mr. Dupont preserved a particular devotion to Our Lady of Salette. To his eyes, there was such a relation between the Face of Jesus covered with sweat, spittle and blood, and that of the Virgin of Dolors inundated by tears, that for him the two devotions were but one. "Our Lady of Salette," he would say, "seems to have united them by bearing a crucifix on her breast."

Chapter VI

His Daughter.

A few months after his return from La Salette, Mr. Dupont was subjected to a bitter trial, God, to purify his soul, demanded of him the sacrifice of what he held dearest on earth.

Henrietta, his only child, had attained her fifteenth year. Gifted by nature with great personal beauty, a brilliant intellect and graceful simplicity of manner, she was beloved by all who knew her. Her grandmother, Madame d'Arnaud, idolized her, denied her nothing she wished, and became excessively alarmed by her slightest indisposition. As it frequently happens under such circumstances, Henrietta took advantage of her grandmother's indulgent affection; whimsical and self-willed, she sometimes yielded so far to her childish caprices that even her father could not control them. Nevertheless, her heart was good and kind, and inclined to piety.

Mr. Dupont directed his attention chiefly to her religious education. She was not seven years old when he wrote as follows to a friend: "Henrietta gives fair promise for the future; she evinces uncommon talents, is very bright and comprehends quickly. I will do all in my power to instil into her solid principles of religion. I hope the child will correspond to my ardent desire that she may walk in the secure path of the evangelical counsels. I think it is difficult to be assured of salvation in any other. Already I dread for her the dangers of the world. But I confide in God: He will grant her the graces she needs."

On his arrival at Tours, Mr. Dupont had entrusted her to the care of Madame de Lignac, who was a second mother to the little girl. Unequal in disposition, Henrietta required an exceptional training. The prudent mistress, finding she could be touched by motives of faith and of piety which, while an infant in the arms, she had acquired from her father, skilfully profited by them to obtain, occasionally, from her little pupil generous efforts to overcome herself. The following charming incident is related by Madame de Lignac herself:

"One day, whilst she was still quite a small child, she asked me during Lent to relate to her the history of the life and death of our Saviour. I promised to gratify her, upon the condition that for two weeks she would be very good and obedient. Every day she came to ask if she had been good, and if the two weeks had nearly expired. At last the long desired moment arrived; I narrated to her minutely the life, passion and death of our Saviour. The child's emotion was wonderful; catching every word with the deepest attention, she wept bitterly, and exclaimed from time to time in astonishment and grief: 'What! did they really do that?'

"When she was seven years old, she was present at an instruction given by a reverend gentleman during a retreat. He said among other things:

'My children, preserve your innocence, and you will see what God will do for you.' The remark made such an impression on her, that she frequently repeated it, and her father, pleased by its salutary effect, loved to recall it to her mind."

We can readily understand how much this precocious piety delighted her father, and what pains he took to cultivate it. The father of one of the pupils called one day to request of Madame de Lignac the favor of seeing his daughter daily. "It is impossible, Sir; our rules forbid it." "But, Madame, I have it from good authority that you make an exception in favor of Miss Dupont, who sees her father every day." "That is true, Sir; Mr. Dupont assists every morning at our Mass and Communicates; after his thanksgiving, he passes through the parlor, where he blesses his child, without, however, addressing a single word to her. If you follow Mr. Dupont's example, the same permission will be extended to you and you will have the opportunity of seeing your daughter daily." This judicious reply was unanswerable.

Mr. Dupont did not neglect to solicit the prayers of Sister Saint-Pierre for Henrietta when she was preparing for her first Communion. So powerful an intercession could not fail to have effect in her regard. "She appears to be in good dispositions," said the father two days before that important event; "She begs our Lord to preserve her in that happy state of childhood which was the desire of all the saints."

The delicate health of his daughter was a cause of great anxiety to this devoted father, and he neglected no means which he considered serviceable for strengthening her constitution. He often took her with him on his journeys and pilgrimages, particularly when he went to Catholic Brittany. His pious friends and many ecclesiastics encouraged him in this course. One of them, the rector of the grand seminary of Tours, thus expresses himself: "You do well to withdraw Henrietta from the dangers of the world, and to take her to a province where she has only good example before her eyes. The simplicity of manner of the Bretons is far more estimable than the refinement of our civilization."

Mr. Dupont was of the same opinion. He gave the preference to Saint-Servan, where he went annually for the benefit of the baths. We learn from a Religious, who now resides in America at St. Mary of the Woods, in Indiana, the kind of amusements and visits he allowed his daughter. "Every year," she writes, "Mr. Dupont sent his only daughter, Henrietta, with her venerable grandmother to Saint-Servan to take the salt-water baths; he came later to take what he called the 'baths of faith.' He took pleasure in visiting those families of the city with whom he was on terms of friendship, and his daughter accompanied him. He watched over her very carefully, scrutinizing her least actions. He came frequently to our house, and my parents listened eagerly to his account of pilgrimages, conversions, miracles, &c., whilst we, at our age, found them too long and too serious; for, religious subjects were the sole topics of conversation. Even whilst waiting at the house of a near neighbor for the servant to open the door, he proposed to my brother to recite an Ave of his Rosary, which he had always in his sleeve, so that he might not lose a minute. He made every effort to keep alive in us the spirit of recollection with which he strove to inspire us, and I remember well how annoyed he was on one occasion when he discovered Henrietta amusing herself with us in some simple game of cards. She was then about fourteen years of age.

"Mr. Dupont 'walked in spirit,' to use his own expression, through the streets of Saint-Servan, picking up the pins he saw lying on the ground. When the bathing season was over, he carried all these pins to the Little Sisters of the Poor, in whom he was deeply interested. When Henrietta expressed a desire to see the Mount of St. Michel, a few kilometers distant from Saint-Servan, he required of her a promise that she would go as on a pilgrimage, and she was, consequently, obliged to observe silence during the entire journey. She indemnified herself on her return by relating to us all that had occurred on the way." "This dear child," observes the Religious who wrote the above, "was fond of pleasure and enjoyed life; she caused her father great anxiety; he feared the effect of contact with the world upon her impulsive, joyous nature."

Her talents obtained for her the first rank among the pupils of Saint-Ursule, as may be gathered from the following circumstance: In the month of August, 1847, there was a literary entertainment among the boarders: they recited in costume some scenes from Athalie; this sort of exercise was at that time customary at the Ursuline convent of Tours, and Madame de Lignac, with her refined taste and nice discernment, had selected for the occasion the finest verses of Racine. The representation was private. The Religious, the pupils, the curate of the parish and the ecclesiastical superior constituted the audience. Mr. Dupont was the only layman present; he was invited because Henrietta supported the part of Athalie. She wished to appear in a toilette suitable to a queen, and her father's condescension placed at her disposal a portion of her mother's wardrobe. The intelligent and graceful manner in which Henrietta acquitted herself of her part was commented upon; and the father was not insensible to this little triumph of his daughter.

His thoughts dwelt frequently upon the vocation of his dear child. In his heart he ardently desired to develop in her a taste for the religious life. But how could he cherish such a hope when he considered her natural temperament? The Superioress of the Monastery of the Purification tells us how, on one occasion, he gave expression to his earnest wishes. Mr. Dupont, accompanied by his daughter, called at the parlor to make a visit. Turning to her, he said: "Henrietta, pass through the turn what you have brought to these Ladies." The young girl uncovered a basket containing a beautiful white rabbit, which she offered to the Superioress. Mr. Dupont looked serious as he watched her placing the rabbit in the turn, and said a moment afterwards: "How happy I should be, my daughter, to see you also pass through the turn to remain in the convent."

As she grew older, his anxiety increased. "I beg you more earnestly than ever," he writes on the 7th of December, 1847, "to pray particularly for my daughter. She has entered her fifteenth year, and as far as I can judge, God has not yet said to her: 'The world is so dangerous, you must fear it! A life hidden in God is so sweet, you should aspire to it!' Pray then for her, pray much." The world appeared to him to be particularly dangerous in her case, as her rare gifts seemed to prepare for her what is called a brilliant future. Speaking in confidence to a Religious, he said that if to secure the salvation of a child so dear to him, it would be necessary for him to build a monastery, he would be happy to dig the foundations with his own hands and carry all the stones on his shoulders.

Several honorable families desired the hand of Henrietta for their sons. One of them made the formal proposal through an ecclesiastic who had his confidence. The match was suitable in every respect, advantageous, and such as naturally might prove acceptable to him. "On receiving the communication," says the ecclesiastic who was charged with the commission, "he became serious, and extending his arms with a gesture habitual to him, he raised his eyes to heaven with an expression I shall never forget, and which immediately suggested the thought that he was offering his daughter in sacrifice to God. What was my astonishment on learning a few days afterwards that the young girl was dying! Had he not, as another Jeptha, immolated his daughter?" Speaking himself of the circumstance and his emotion on the occasion, he says: "The proposition was to me like the thrust of a dagger." The parties persisted in the request; friends were solicitous for the alliance. "Now," said Mr. Dupont confidentially to a friend, "now I ascend Calvary!" The Calvary in store for him was a sudden separation from his daughter by death.

No father could love a daughter more tenderly and devotedly than Mr. Dupont loved Henrietta. Indeed, he often reproached himself for yielding sometimes, through an excess of affection, to her childish exactions. But there was one point in which, as a Christian father, he was inflexible: he never permitted her attendance at certain worldly amusements, particularly theatrical representations, which, even when not absolutely reprehensible, are always dangerous, by inflaming the imagination, and attracting the young to the deceitful charms of sinful pleasures.

It happened that Mr. Dupont once took his daughter to visit a relation in Paris. It was a visit of pleasure, a recreation during the vacation, and the young girl thought only of amusing herself and enjoying her freedom from school duties. The day after their arrival, during her father's absence, a member of the family indiscreetly spoke to Henrietta of a play which she could innocently attend, and which would afford her great amusement. The young girl clapped her hands with delight at the proposition, and with her natural impatience and eagerness, ran to meet her father on his return, to solicit his approbation of the project and his permission "to go," she said, "to the play." The father, whose conscience had often reproached him for his want of firmness in controlling his daughter's caprices, considered it a duty to refuse on this occasion, and, notwithstanding her repeated and urgent entreaties, he persisted in his refusal. He knew Henrietta's character so thoroughly that he justly feared, this first satisfaction, apparently innocent, contrasting with the simple and quiet pleasures in the bosom of her family, which she had hitherto exclusively enjoyed, might awaken in her heart a thirst for other more dangerous pleasures of the same kind, and arouse other sentiments which he might not be able to control. The young girl, although pious and habitually submissive, was chagrined by a refusal which was inexplicable to her. Her manner and conduct betokened for several days the depression of spirit caused by the disappointment. The striking effect produced by the privation of a dangerous amusement was a sort of revelation to the father; he foresaw more perils to his daughter in the world than even his parental solicitude had hitherto suspected. He renewed his sacrifice and said interiorly:

"If Thou foreseest, O my God, that she will stray from the right path, take her to Thyself, rather than let her live, loving the vanities of the world." Heroic prayer which was made with the faith of Abraham, and which God did not delay to grant!

An epidemic having made its appearance in the school of the Ursulines, Madame de Lignac was obliged to send all the pupils to their parents for a short time. Henrietta, with her frank, impulsive disposition, hailed the unexpected holiday with a transport of delight which she made no effort to conceal. "What a fortunate disease which gives us a week of holiday!" she exclaimed joyfully as she bade good-bye to Madame de Lignac. How little the poor child suspected what was about to happen! The holiday which she anticipated with so much pleasure, was to end for her in the grave. She left the convent at half-past four in the afternoon, and she was attacked the following morning by the fatal malady from which they hoped to shield her. She seemed, at once, to have a presentiment of her approaching death, and turned all her thoughts to God.

"She received the Holy Viaticum the eve of her death," says Madame de Lignac, "and I was present at the administration of the sacrament. After her thanksgiving, she reminded me of a remark made during a retreat, which had particularly impressed her. 'Do you remember,' she said to me, 'what the Father said: That all the gems of the earth are worthless when compared to the love of our Lord? Oh! he was right! What are they? Our Lord alone is all, all, all!'"

The virtue of Mr. Dupont, which had already attained a great perfection, arose during these days of anguish to a degree of heroism which elicited the admiration of those who witnessed it. "I should write a volume," says M. l'Abbé Regnard, "were I to attempt to relate all that I saw beside that death-bed, which edified and charmed the friends who were present."

This testimony is valuable, given by a holy, simple, upright priest, a learned man, possessing practical good sense, who, knowing Mr. Dupont intimately, was with him during the whole of his painful trial.

"After the last sacraments had been administered to the patient, her father recited aloud the prayers for the agonizing. He held the hand of his daughter in his, and with a sublime faith said: 'Depart, Christian soul, depart! Remain no longer on earth where God is offended, depart! Death is life; the world is death! Go, my daughter! You are about to see God! Tell Him all we are suffering at this moment. Tell Him our only desire is to do His will under this trial. I suffer; my heart is crushed by sorrow. But, my daughter, today I give you birth for heaven. We are, it is true, here on earth, the image of God, but an imperfect image; God completes and perfects us in heaven. Go, my daughter, and fulfil my requests. I am still your father, and by my authority as such I command you to present my petitions to God, as soon as you appear in His divine presence.'"

We shall see later what these requests were. Mr. Regnard continues: "From that time, his Christian faith and hope never forsook him. The following day I was praying beside the bed of death... She was in heaven... Her father approached and said to me: 'Father, let us pray together for my intention. My daughter has begged of God graces for myself and my family, and I have the intimate conviction that she has obtained them. We must now ask of God that we may make a good use of them. Grant us, O my God, to make a good use of Thy graces!'

"'Dear child,' he said to me weeping, but weeping gently, as though his tears were sweetened by hope, 'she was about to enter upon a combat. She desired to conquer and remain pure in the world, but she felt her weakness; she feared to be overcome, and she deserted; she escaped by flight! I do not view God in this blow as a judge, nor as a master. He is a father; He is the good gardener who descended into

His garden; He found a very beautiful and pure flower; he culled it, lest it should be withered by the storm.' 'In the midst of my grief,' he said another time, 'I feel in the depths of my soul a joy infinitely surpassing all the joys of this world. My daughter was created for eternity... She has attained the end of her creation... All is consummated!' When at the cemetery, the coffin was lowered into the vault, he stood at the bottom of the ladder; he laid his hand upon the bier, bade a last farewell to his child, making over her the sign of the cross."

We were unwilling either to interrupt or to abridge the above letter, written by a pious ecclesiastic, who was an eye-witness of what he relates. We now return to the commencement of the little girl's illness.

Mr. Dupont solicited the prayers of the different communities of the city for the preservation of a life so precious to him. Sister Saint-Pierre, in whose intercession he had great confidence, had, at his repeated request, prayed fervently for his intention; but she, several times, expressed her conviction that the child would not recover. The reason given by the pious Carmelite was, that this affliction would aid Mr. Dupont to advance in the path of sanctity and prepare him for the designs God had over him.

The recommendations imposed, in a solemn manner, by the father upon the dying girl touched the hearts of all who were present. Standing by her bedside and taking her hand in his, he said: "My daughter, you are about to appear before God, you will see Him, you will speak to Him. Before all else, you must present Him the petitions I now give you. I, as your father, command you to do so. Pray for your father, your grandmother, for the members of your family... (he enumerated them). Pray for all the kind friends who have taken charge of your education and your health... (he enumerated them, mentioning his servants among them). Pray for the inhabitants of this city, for your friends, companions and acquaintances."... Pausing a moment, he resumed with still more solemnity: "Pray for the excellent doctor who has taken care of you from your infancy, who has, with untiring devotion, exhausted his science in this, your last illness, without being able to relieve you; pray for him when you are before God." No words could express the impression made by these remarks, spoken with an accent of strong faith. Henrietta, who was perfectly conscious, listened to them calmly and in silence, making a sign of acquiescence. Doctor Bretonneau wept with the others, for all were deeply moved. The illustrious physician was as celebrated for his tender heart as for his medical skill; he esteemed and loved Mr. Dupont; and although powerless to save the life of his daughter, his friendship retained him near the afflicted father to the last.

The child was fully conscious when Extreme Unction was administered. At the conclusion of the ceremony, her father, who had been kneeling in fervent prayer, arose, and taking his daughter's hand, said: "Now, my daughter, that you have received so many graces, you are content?" "Yes, Papa." "You do not, then, feel any regret in leaving this miserable life?" "Oh! yes, Papa!" "And what do you regret, daughter?" "To leave you!" "Oh! no, my daughter, you will not leave me. We shall not be separated; God is everywhere. You will be in His presence in heaven, and you will see Him; I too, although here below, shall be also with Him, and through Him I shall be with you. Two walls separate us at the present moment. Yours is about to fall; mine will fall sooner or later; we shall be then united forever."

When she had breathed her last, Mr. Dupont turned towards Doctor Bretonneau with a heavenly expression on his face and said: "Doctor, my daughter sees God!" In a transport of superhuman joy, excited by the thought, he recited (others say he entoned) the *Magnificat*. Some in their surprise, who did not know him as he was, thought he had lost his mind. Doctor Bretonneau judged him correctly, and in relating the circumstance, he added: "He is the model of a perfect Christian."

The Christian, in truth, was in this case sublime, not only by the calmness of his humble resignation, but still more by the joy he experienced in offering to God what he held most dear and precious, his only, his beloved child, expiring in the spring-time of life, in the freshness of her youth and in the purity of her soul.

"I was at Mr. Dupont's during his daughter's agony," says Monseigneur d'Outremont, Bishop of Mans, who was, at that time, attorney for the prefecture. "I had been sent from her apartment on account of my youth, and I remained in the adjoining room. The father had just received the last sigh of his beloved child. He entered the room where I was, the tears streaming from his eyes. He embraced me and said: 'We must not weep as those who have no hope.' I saw him again the following morning. 'I slept,' he said to me, 'about an hour. In my kind of half-sleep, I seemed to put to myself this question of the Catechism: "Why were we created?" And the answer came naturally to my mind in sleep: "We were created that we might know, love and serve God in this world and be happy with Him in the next." This is the whole man... this is the term of his existence! I said to myself: My daughter was created to know God, to love God, to possess God... she has attained her end... why should I weep for her? I awoke at that moment, repeating with a great peace and consolation: My daughter was created for God! She has attained the end of her creation. Why should I weep for her?"'

When the preparations were being made for the funeral ceremony, Mr. Dupont left his apartment just as the corpse was removed from the upper room to be placed in the hall. He met it at the door. For a moment his feelings overpowered him, but quickly repressing his grief, he approached and pressed his lips upon the coffin, saying: "Farewell, daughter, we shall meet again."

His courage nearly deserted him when the time came to convey the mortal remains of the dear deceased to the grave. "I can see him now," writes a venerable canon, then vicar of the cathedral, who was present on the occasion; "he had withdrawn to a short distance from the coffin, but he now approached for the last adieu. He stood with his arms crossed upon his breast; his eyes resting upon the face of his daughter with an expression of ineffable tenderness. But at length he was unable to restrain his emotion; tears flowed down his cheeks, and his frame was convulsed by the sobs he strove, in vain, to check.. The Christian, however, soon gained the mastery over the man. He fell upon his knees, remained awhile in prayer, then arose calm and strengthened by the few minutes' communing with his heavenly Father. 'I was near yielding,' he said, 'and yet my daughter is not now as far removed from me as she was before. Two walls separated us and prevented our union: hers has crumbled; mine will fall ere long, and we shall be forever reunited.'"

From that time, his faith and submission never faltered. "As soon as I heard of Henrietta's death," says Madame de Lignac, "I went to see Mr. Dupont; I found him wonderfully calm and resigned. He was seated before a desk on which lay the Holy Scriptures, and was reading such passages, as might best fortify him under his terrible trial. Numerous visitors called to express their sympathy with him in his affliction. He would point to his daughter's coffin and repeat the text of the Gospel which has reference to the glorious sepulchre of the risen Redeemer: 'She is not here. Why do you seek the living among the dead?' *Quid quæritis viventem inter mortuos?* And again he would say: 'God gave her to me, God has taken her away; blessed be His holy name!'"

He said to Monseigneur d'Outremont: "A few days after Henrietta's death, on opening the Gospel to make my meditation, my eye fell upon the passage in which St. John relates how Mary Magdalen, at the sepulchre, had taken our Lord for the gardener. It was a striking text, and I immediately made the application to my daughter. Our Lord was indeed a good gardener in her regard. Gardeners, on the approach of winter, place in hothouses their most delicate and valuable flowers: in like manner our Lord called to Himself my dear Henrietta at the moment when, like a delicate flower, she was about to be exposed in the world to the icy blast of the passions; He wished to preserve her, and He sheltered her in the hot-house of His paradise." This evangelical figure furnished his triumphant faith with many beautiful and sweet thoughts. As a memento of her, he designed a little engraving in which our Lord is represented under the emblem of a gardener plucking a flower from his garden.

Throughout the remainder of his life, Mr. Dupont thanked God for having called his daughter to Himself at an early age. Conversing once with a lady on the extravagant style of dress indulged in by the women of the present time, and deploring its excess, he added: "Oh! how I bless God for having removed my daughter from the world in her youth!" He particularly took pleasure in the thought that she had died before being contaminated by contact with the world. "Do you remember," he wrote to a friend, "the anguish of my soul when I pictured to myself the dangers that would surround my child? I ardently desired to secure her happiness. Is she not happy today? When I closed her eyes, I comprehended that true paternity dates only from the moment when we can say to God: 'Here is my child!' Now, I am convinced that Henrietta, clothed in the white garment of innocence, and fortified, moreover, by the sacraments of the Church, has already seen my donation accepted! How happy are those fathers whose children precede them to heaven! How many graces are obtained by innocence kneeling before the throne of God! If in the old law, parents were inconsolable when the death of a child deprived them of the hope that the Messiah might be born in their family, under the law of grace, a father has the ineffable consolation of reflecting, that his virgin daughter becomes forever the beloved spouse of Jesus. How true it is then that we have no cause to grieve like those unfortunate men, who have no hope beyond the tomb. The tomb! Since the resurrection of our Lord, the tomb is the cradle of eternity." "Do you know," he said to a friend one day, "the pretty thought I had in regard to Henrietta? She has been six years in heaven; now the day of our death is truly that of our birth; my little girl is, therefore, six years older than I; she will be the elder in paradise. Imagine," added he, rubbing his hands with delight, "the effect that will have in heaven, should I live several years more. She will be as my mother, and I shall be as an ignorant little child."

His great consolation was to visit her grave. "There I seem to be with her again," he would say. "I speak to her, I interrogate her about heaven. Oh! how much I suffered the first time I knelt upon her newly-made grave! All was over, I was alone! No one with me... I said to her: 'Henrietta, I am going to ask something of you: remember the prisoner who is condemned to death and who refuses to be consoled.' That was the first favor she obtained for me; since that time whenever I have anything difficult to accomplish, I put it in her hands."

He placed above her grave a simple and unpretending monument; at the head, is a cross on which is carved the one word, Henrietta; at the foot, is a white marble prie-Dieu turned towards those who pass, as if to invite them to kneel and pray. It was the end of all his solitary walks. He was careful that flowers should bloom, at all seasons, around the cross. He loved to gather them and send them to his friends in memory of their affection for Henrietta.

The least article which had been used by his daughter, was valued by this Christian father. She had drawn whilst at school with the Ursulines a beautiful picture of the Guardian Angel; he had it photographed and distributed copies among his relatives. Nine years after the death of his child, being told of the edifying death of a young Religious, he exclaimed: "On the same day, another angel took her departure for heaven!... This should serve as a warning for us. Let us, in earnest, devote ourselves, like the Saints, to our great affair, that we may one day be united with them in the Holy of Holies." He writes to one of his goddaughters as follows: "Reflect seriously upon Henrietta's happiness. Let us belong entirely to God. Time is short; every minute is counted." Thus we see in Mr. Dupont the grandeur and energy of a lively faith united to the utmost tenderness of heart.

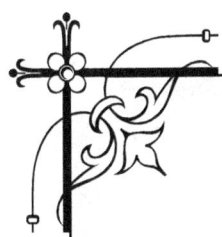

Chapter VII

Mr. Le Pailleur and the Little Sisters of the Poor.

From the time that death deprived him of his beloved child, Mr. Dupont's life was characterized by additional fervor, and he advanced in the path of perfection. Hitherto, he had remained somewhat a man of the world; hereafter, we shall see him thoroughly detached from earth, and having no other relations with his fellow-beings but those inspired by zeal and charity. On the day that Henrietta was buried, he distributed, what he called her "trousseau,"—an abundant alms to all the communities of the city. A large portion of the dower he had destined for her, was consecrated to establishing the Little Sisters of the Poor. Mr. Dupont had, for a long time, been acquainted with their founder. Their friendship commenced in the following manner.

We have already said that for many years he was accustomed to go in the autumn with his mother and daughter to Saint-Servan for the benefit of the sea-bathing. In 1843, he made the acquaintance, whilst there, of a young vicar, who, in his zeal for the salvation of souls, was striving to form a community of Religious, whose peculiar object should be to take care of the aged poor of both sexes, and prepare them for death. This vicar was M. l'Abbé Le Pailleur, and the community he founded, was that of the Little Sisters of the Poor, at that time only a grain of mustard seed, but which, ere long, was destined to increase and become the spreading tree, whose wonderful branches and still more wonderful fruits are, today, the admiration of other countries as well as of our own. With the vivacity of his faith and his intelligent love of the poor, Mr. Dupont discerned, at a glance, the fitness and the eminently evangelical spirit of the new Institution. Invited by the vicar to visit the humble dwelling which saw the commencement of the work, he witnessed the prodigies of charity already accomplished in this asylum of the aged. He was deeply touched, and, thenceforth, he was inviolably attached to the new Congregation which found in him a devoted friend during his whole life.

The Little Sisters of the Poor soon became aware of his interest in their undertaking, and, in the difficulties which beset their path in the early days of their Institute, they often appealed to his generous charity. The Superior General, Sister Mary Augustine of Compassion, considered him as one of their greatest benefactors. Mr. Le Pailleur placed entire confidence in him, and imparted to him all the plans he had formed for the development of his work. He informed him, also, of a project he contemplated for the establishment of a society of missionary priests, to be employed among the peasantry.

A strange circumstance unexpectedly enabled Mr. Dupont to give important aid to this project. One of his friends, who owned land at Bougligny in the diocess of Meaux, died at Paris, his usual residence, having bequeathed to him all his property. This friend was Mr. Bordier, the fervent Christian who labored so earnestly for the instruction of the little Savoyards, and with whom he had been on intimate terms since their first acquaintance. Mr. Bordier had frequently told him that it was his intention to make him heir to all his possessions, and to confide to him after his death the expenditure of his fortune. Mr. Dupont always excused himself, alleging, as a reason for his refusal, that he had already too much to attend to in managing his own property. What then was his astonishment, on receiving from Mr. Bordier's lawyer a letter announcing to him the death of his friend, and, at the same time, communicating to him the intelligence that he was the sole heir to the property. He thus found himself, notwithstanding his former refusal, possessed of a large estate situated in the diocess of Meaux, yielding an annual income of twelve thousand francs. Mr. Dupont was well aware that, in bequeathing this fortune to him, it was Mr. Bordier's intention that he should enjoy it as his own private fund; he had even particularly requested, that if his friend preferred to expend it in works of charity, he would, at least retain a portion for himself. He was greatly embarrassed. He was, as it were, stunned when the news reached him, as he himself relates. "But," he said, "why did Bordier select me for his heir? What does Bordier wish me to do with his fortune? I do not need it." Then reflecting upon the affair he thought: "Evidently Bordier intends me to continue his good works! To which one of them should I devote it?" Fatigued, and uncertain how to act in the affair, he fell asleep without having found a satisfactory solution to the question. The following morning, he went to Mass, as was his custom, begging light from God as to the course he should pursue. He received the answer to his prayer the moment he Communicated. Scarcely had the Body of our Lord rested upon his tongue, when the two names, Bordier, Le Pailleur... Bordier, Le Pailleur... arose to his mind, inseparably united as though by an invincible power, and as if a voice from heaven directed him to aid the apostolic projects confided to him by the one, with the pecuniary resources so unexpectedly, but so opportunely, furnished by the other. So powerful was the impression made upon him, that Mr. Dupont did not hesitate to act in accordance with it. He wrote at once to Mr. Le Pailleur, to make known to him the fortune which had come into his possession, at the same time placing it at his disposition, if he still desired to execute the design of which he had frequently spoken. Mr. Le Pailleur accepted the offer made him by his friend, and after consulting God in prayer, they decided that the association destined to prepare missionaries to labor among the peasantry, should be established at Bougligny upon Mr. Bordier's estate.

It does not come within our plan to relate the circumstances connected with that work, which, ultimately, became an association of diocesan missionaries, under the name of Priests of Our Lady of Hope. We shall only add, that Mr. Dupont exhibited as much delicacy and generosity towards the relatives of Mr. Bordier, as he had evinced disinterestedness where he was personally concerned, and zeal in regard to the missionaries. The family of Mr. Bordier were so displeased on finding their expectations as to his property frustrated, that they attempted to invalidate the will. But as it was properly drawn up, and the testator had only used his undoubted right to bequeath his property as he wished, they could advance no reason of sufficient weight to annul the provisions he chose to make. After the members of the family discovered the disinterested and conciliatory spirit of the legatee, their sentiments changed in his regard, and they withdrew their opposition. Then, Mr. Dupont, having the incontestable right to dispose of the property as he chose, gave a portion of it to the natural heirs, who often expressed their gratitude for his kindness. He was equally admired in the diocess of Meaux, where his name was inscribed among those of the greatest benefactors.

The ties of friendship which united him to Mr. Le Pailleur became still closer and more spiritual, as we may judge from the following incident. Having successfully concluded a business transaction connected with the association

CHAPTER VII

at Bougligny, Mr. Le Pailleur had written hurriedly to Mr. Dupont, to inform him of the fact, and, expressing his gratitude, he added: "How good is God! Let us repeat it a thousand times." After having mailed the letter, Mr. Le Pailleur was forced, by important affairs, to undertake a journey which obliged him to pass through Tours. He set off and arrived, unexpectedly, at Mr. Dupont's about ten o'clock in the evening, fatigued, dusty, and hungry, after having travelled all day. Mr. Dupont, who had received the letter of his friend only a few minutes previously, animated by the sentiments of joy and gratitude it suggested, had knelt to offer a prayer of thanksgiving. Seeing Mr. Le Bailleur enter, he took him by the arm, and, wholly absorbed in the one idea, without a thought of the possible necessities of the traveller, he gently drew him upon his knees by his side and said to him: "You come just in time. I was repeating a thousand times; How good is God! *Quam bonus Deus Israel!*"

The man of adoration and divine praise had taken in a literal sense the words of Mr. Le Bailleur, and had at once commenced repeating the aspiration his gratitude had suggested. "Look," he added, showing the rosary he held in his hand to mark the number of his acts of praise, "I have already made five hundred. We will continue them together. It is as little as we can do in return for so great a favor." Mr. Le Bailleur acceded to the request, and the two repeated with the liveliest sentiments of gratitude and piety: "How good is God! How good is God!" until they completed the number of times specified. It was only after he had fulfilled this duty, that Mr. Dupont descended from the higher regions of faith and prayer, and noticing how absent-minded he had been, hastened to attend to the wants of his friend.

One of the fruits of this holy friendship, was the foundation of a house of the Little Sisters of the Poor at Tours. There were many difficulties to be overcome, but Mr. Dupont succeeded in removing them. Three Sisters arrived at Tours on the 30th of December, 1846, at four o'clock in the morning. The fatigue of the journey, the cold weather, would, certainly, have dispensed them from attending Mass the day of their arrival. "But," they said, "what can we do without Jesus? Where shall we find elsewhere the strength necessary to fulfil our duties in our new undertaking?" They were met, according to promise, by Mr. Dupont who accompanied them to church where they Communicated. After this, they breakfasted with Mr. Dupont, who esteemed it an honor, as well as a pleasure, to entertain them. They accepted his hospitality until the 6th of January, Feast of the Epiphany. That evening, in order to honor, in the poor, the royalty of Jesus Christ, they commenced their duties, and established themselves at Notre-Dame-la-Riche in a house prepared for them by the kindness of Mr. Dupont. One old woman was already there, sent to them providentially, as Mr. Dupont relates. "Passing through the city. I had the opportunity of inquiring concerning the Penitentiary where I had not been for several days. I met one of the guards and asked him: 'How are you getting on at the Penitentiary?' 'A great misfortune has just happened.' 'What! at the Penitentiary?' 'No, sir, in the house where I live.' 'But what is it?' 'It is the death of a young man.' 'How did he die? Suddenly? Did he commit suicide?' 'Oh! no, sir; he died after a long illness, four days ago. He was the only support of an aged mother; and now he is dead, what will become of her? Poor woman! She is eighty-four years old. I feel so keenly for her, that I mention her to you, although she did not ask me to do so.' My answer gave me no difficulty that day, as it was the one appointed for the departure of the Little Sisters from Rennes for Tours. I said to the good man: 'Recommend this woman to have great confidence in God, Who will soon afford her relief in her miseries.'" The poor woman was received on the Epiphany. The Little Sisters commenced their work of charity by giving their attention to this poor creature who went to them in rags and covered with vermin. She was not of an amiable disposition, and she furnished the community with many opportunities of practicing patience.

Mr. Dupont desired to accompany the Little Sisters to their dwelling where he had sent beforehand beds, wood, and provisions. Knowing that they were in need of many other things, he used his influence with his relatives and acquaintances to secure sufficient alms to provide for their daily necessities. Notwithstanding their poverty, which the aid thus obtained for them relieved only in part, they admitted many old women, all interesting to the Sisters by their different miseries. Mr. Dupont wrote on the 22nd of January, 1847: "There are seven old women at the home. All goes on well. They have begun to work, and thus they help a little for their support. God blesses the good work. The last poor woman received this morning, had had nothing to drink for four days, only a few dry crusts to eat, and was lying on a little straw more dead than alive, when she was made happy by the sight of a human face." He relates the entrance of another: "I could give you many affecting details of the good women received into this pious asylum. Last Saturday I went there in the evening. Supper was over and the old women were in bed. The Sisters proposed to me to enter and see the last one who had arrived just at supper time. We made no noise so as not to awaken them. We approached the bed and spoke in a very low tone. The poor old woman, who was eighty-three years old, sat up in the bed. 'Oh! you are not asleep!' 'I asleep! How could I go to sleep so soon on such a bed as this? I, who have been lying alone on straw laid on the ground! I asleep! Why the pleasure of being so comfortable will keep one awake all night.'"

Not long after the establishment of the Little Sisters, Mr. Dupont met one of the vicars of the cathedral; he stopped him and pointing to heaven said: "Would you believe it possible? The rich, the high-born of this world give large sums, they lavish gold and silver to purchase the service of domestics, and they are poorly served. And behold! the bare-footed poor, the diseased, are served... as God Himself is served!... And by whom? By Sisters! By the friends of God! By the Little Sisters of the Poor!"

In consequence of the inundation of the preceding year, the year 1847 was a season of general distress and privation for every one. The Little Sisters of the Poor, placing their trust in Providence, refused none of the old people whom heaven sent them; but the house they occupied was so inconvenient that they were obliged to change their residence, and the 1st of July was the day appointed by them to go to their new dwelling. Mr. Dupont wished to be with them when they moved. He worked like a hired laborer and with so much interest, that his servant was obliged to remind him that he had not dined; as it was a fast-day, and he always fasted very strictly, he had remained without food until noon. After seeing all their poor utensils arranged in their new home, Mr. Dupont noticed that many articles were needed. He furnished a quantity at his own expense. When there was question, in 1848, of purchasing the house which the Sisters occupy at the present time, he showed the utmost zeal in conducting the negotiations. He had just lost his daughter, and the poor were to be his adopted children: the dower he destined for Henrietta, was devoted to the Little Sisters, the servants of the poor.

How kind he was to their house in Tours! He interested himself in their least necessities; he often visited the old people, always treating them with the utmost kindness: under every circumstance he appeared happy to render any service to the Sisters. He would often stop on the street the venders of vegetables, fruit or fish, and purchase their stock, which he would direct them to deliver to the Little Sisters. His countenance, on such occasions, expressed the delight he felt in giving pleasure to the old people and procuring them an agreeable surprise. If at any time he noticed they were in need of a useful or necessary article he would, at once, procure it for them. For instance, remarking one day, that the kettles were all of copper, he ordered others, fearing an accident might happen.

This devotion to the Little Sisters was exhibited under all circumstances, and sometimes it arose to heroism. In 1853 a contagious fever spread through the city. Seventy-five among the old people were attacked by it. Mr. Dupont visited them several times a day in order to give them comfort, and often performed for them the most menial services.

In 1854 Tours was attacked by the cholera. The house of the Little Sisters of the Poor did not escape the scourge. They were sorely tried on that occasion; in the course of a few days, they lost nineteen old men, one Religious, and a postulant. Their friend visited them as constantly that year, as he had done in the preceding one, although he exposed himself to the imminent danger of contagion. When ten Sisters were ill at the same time, and there remained only three to attend to the whole establishment, he begged alms for them, taking to them, besides his own offerings, the small coin he collected from house to house; and he continued this act of charity as long as the epidemic lasted.

He felt for the old people a tender affection which only charity could inspire. If he was seen, on certain days, directing his steps towards Notre-Dame-la-Riche, having the large pockets of his overcoat filled with cakes and candies, all knew he had prepared a pleasant surprise, a treat for the good old men and women of the Little Sisters. If, again, he was noticed picking up the pins which lay in his path, he would say pleasantly: "They are for our old people." Whenever he visited them, he had a kind word to say to each individually, and he spoke to them in general of "the good God." He listened patiently to the requests made to him, and supplied all their little wants. He rarely left the house without having bestowed an abundant alms. He was ingenious in devising means to amuse them, and often provided little entertainments for them. Although feeble and suffering in the latter years of his life, he went once a week to visit them; and when, at last, he was confined to his room, he would go to his window, which overlooked the garden, to assure himself that the fruits and vegetables were laid aside for the Little Sisters. The greater portion of the fine beans which he cultivated, were destined for the good old people who appreciated the kindness, and loved him as a benefactor and a father.

The happiness of this noble Christian was at its height, when, during the annual retreats, he beheld some of the old men resuming the practice of their religious duties, which they had neglected, perhaps, for many years. He always assisted at the exercises of the retreat, and he regarded it as an honor to serve them at table on the day of its conclusion. He never neglected to furnish for that entertainment a few bottles of his Martinique rum. On one occasion, when he was serving them with the clergyman who had given the retreat, his attention was attracted to a poor blind man recently received in the house, whose spiritual condition had caused the Sisters great anxiety. Despairing of salvation, he had talked of committing suicide. But he made the retreat, he was now at peace with God, he had fed on the bread of angels, and his heart was so overflowing with joy, that even when seated at table, he expressed his feelings aloud. "Is it then true, O my God," he said, "that Thou hast, this day, given Thyself entirely to me?" Mr. Dupont heard him, he was triumphant, he was in an ecstacy of delight. He knows not "how to thank God," he says, "for the wonderful graces imparted to this soul, which had been so rebellious."

Mr. Dupont continued during his whole life to interest himself in the Little Sisters of the Poor. Once in the depth of winter, he ordered, through his friend Mr. d'Avrainville, some beans to be forwarded to them from Nice. He wrote to his friend: "If the snow will permit the wagon of the Little Sisters to pass through the streets, your supposition as to the 'gala' on Christmas-day will be verified. They will thank you heartily at the Little Sisters for the bag which arrived safely from Nice, and they will add: 'May God reward you!' It is nine o'clock," he continues, "and the snow is still falling. The Little Sister caterer will not be able to come: but the opportunity of doing justice to your present, (Mr. Dupont himself had paid the expense), will soon offer."

He was ingenious in giving to others the credit of suggestions made by himself, and he considered a kindness done to the Little Sisters as a personal favor. He wrote to the same friend: "You made the mouths of the Little Sisters water, by telling them of a certain wonderful churn. As the poor churn they have been using, is now wholly past service, I beg you to send me one of the kind you mentioned: charge it, of course, to my account." A short time afterwards, he acknowledged the receipt of the churn and returned his thanks. The sprightly tone of the letter indicates his interest in the most trifling concerns of the community. "The Little Sisters accept the churn with gratitude, and they anticipate having some good butter to offer you when you next visit Tours. I hope our Lord will so arrange affairs for you that you will not defer, beyond next summer, the little pleasure the Sisters promise themselves in offering you the fruit of their work." In the meantime, he wishes to give him news of "the churn and its product." "Perfect!" he exclaims; "I know it by my own experience this morning. The butter sent me by the Sisters was excellent; and moreover, the churning proves advantageous to them. They buy six francs worth of milk a week, which, after it is skimmed, is still good; from the cream, they make three pounds of butter: butter is now selling in market at twenty-four sous the pound. I will send you, by the first opportunity, a pot of this butter that you, also, may pronounce as to its quality."

Thus, Mr. Dupont, in his affectionate charity for the poor, made himself little and simple with the little and simple. It was for that reason that he appreciated so highly the simplicity of the good Sisters, who, in his opinion, owed to this virtue the gift of intelligence of heavenly things. He wrote to his friend concerning his "Thoughts on the Love of God," of which he wished a second edition: "I intend it to be sent to the Noviceship of the Little Sisters, where they will be pleased to have it, because I have had occasion to read portions of it to Sisters who have passed through Tours, and they are very fond of such books. When you come to Tours, we will visit the Little Sisters, and you will see how clearly they comprehend the most elevated thoughts on the interior life. They owe this, not to their education, but to their incredible simplicity of soul."

On their side, the veneration the Sisters entertained for Mr. Dupont was such as they would feel for a saint. When he died, all expressed their enduring gratitude for the favors he had bestowed upon their Congregation, and for his affectionate and unfailing devotion to their houses and their poor. They continue, to the present day, to speak of him with the same reverence, the same filial affection, as when, during his life, he visited their old men and women.

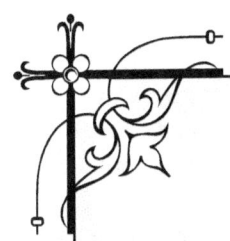

Chapter VIII

Various Works of Charity.

The peculiar work of the Little Sisters of the Poor, was not the only one which called into exercise the charity of Mr. Dupont. He joyfully availed himself of every opportunity offered by Divine Providence of doing a service to others, or of bestowing an alms.

As a member of the conference of St. Vincent de Paul, he made it a duty to visit the sick poor. There were certain families whom he regularly went to see; and it was, principally, the miserable condition and isolation of the aged relatives of these families, that determined him to obtain the services of the Little Sisters. Even when other duties prevented him from attending constantly the weekly assemblies of the conference, he never neglected to visit the sick and assist them in their own homes. He requested the physicians to make known to him the most needy and the most abandoned; when necessity required it, he served them with his own hands. We know of instances, in which he did not hesitate to render, for several months, services the most repugnant to nature, and to perform them with a courage, a perseverance, and self-abnegation, equalled only by the Saints of God. These charitable actions were the charm of his life, and, to interrupt them, required nothing less than the occupations which held him captive before the Holy Face, and, later, the infirmities of age which confined him to the house. He, nevertheless, requested to be considered as a member of the conference, "an honorary member, on the shelf," he said, with humility.

Another spiritual work of mercy had a peculiar attraction for him, visiting prisoners. The penitentiary of Tours, recently organized and regarded as a model of its kind, was naturally a field for his zeal. He offered his services to the chaplain, and was delighted to aid him, as far as he could, in the case of certain criminals whom he endeavored, in concert with the chaplain, to inspire with Christian sentiments. He frequently added pecuniary aid to his wise counsels and kind words, and he continued his good offices in their regard after their liberation from prison. We have read letters from several of these unfortunate beings, in which their gratitude is sometimes expressed in a touching manner. One among them writes: "Sir, I shall never forget during my whole life that once, when an unfortunate young man, abandoned by his friends, was a prey to despair, you charitably came to his aid, and as a skilful physician, administered to his broken heart the only remedy capable of restoring it to life. I owe you an eternal debt of gratitude, and when the difficulties I meet in my efforts to return to the path of rectitude, seem beyond my strength, I think of your charity, and I am encouraged to greater exertions."

Another young man, a galley-slave from the convict-prison of Brest, writes to testify his gratitude, and thanks him particularly for his kind words: "What a consolation it was to me to receive from your paternal kindness a truly apostolic letter, one capable of helping a Christian to endure a cruel martyrdom! The details into which you enter are more soothing to me than you can imagine. I can repay you only by blessing the hand which traced the lines, praising the heart which conceived them, and proclaiming everywhere that a thousand times blessed is the mouth which utters such words."

It even happened that God, rewarding the charitable care of this friend of the prisoner, granted miraculous favors to some of these unfortunate men. The following circumstance made a deep impression upon Mr. Dupont himself, and upon all who were acquainted with the circumstance.

A young man, named Adrien Bouchet, had been arrested at Tours with sixteen others, accused of having demolished the street-lamps during the riots which took place in the month of December, 1846, in consequence of the high price of flour. They were seized, upon the information furnished by an accomplice. Bouchet pretended to be innocent, declaring that, instead of being engaged in breaking the lamps, he was actually, at that very time, in bed. He was condemned, notwithstanding his protestations, to three months in the penitentiary; this threw him into a state of indescribable fury. The chaplain confided him to the care of Mr. Dupont, to calm him, instruct and prepare him for his first Communion, which he had not made. "On entering his cell," says Mr. Dupont, "I was met by a terrible odor, the cause of which had been explained to me by the guard. A little straw replaced the hammock usually furnished prisoners. Bouchet scarcely raised his eyes. I felt the most intense compassion for the condition of the unfortunate man, who told me that, from his childhood, he had suffered from a disease, in consequence of which he had been prevented from making his first Communion, from learning to read, or working at a trade; and that, being an object of horror to himself, as well as to others, he had been unable to support himself." We heard, elsewhere, that when he was a child, his comrades could not endure him near them; they called him by ignominious names; even at church, when he was sent for instruction in catechism, the curate had been forced to place him at a distance, apart from the other boys. In consequence of this same disease, the poor young man. infected the prison with so horrible an odor, that the guards of the penitentiary would place his food in the cell, and leave it as quickly as possible. "After four or five visits," continues Mr. Dupont, "I sought the physician of the penitentiary. 'I have already examined the condition of Bouchet,' he said to me. 'It is a disease without remedy.' At my urgent entreaty, he consented to go to the cell; he suggested nothing but a costly instrument to be procured when he should be liberated from prison."

It required all Mr. Dupont's courage, and his great love of God, to enable him to surmount the repugnance of nature to approach the prisoner. For several months, his indefatigable benefactor continued his visits, although he was always, during that whole time, received with rudeness and addressed in abusive language. At last, by dint of patience and unvarying kindness, he succeeded in touching the heart of the unfortunate man, and persuading him that he sincerely desired to benefit him. Bouchet consented to accept a medal. "I gave him," says Mr. Dupont, "a medal of St. Benedict, and having related several incidents for the purpose of exciting his confidence, I proposed to him to make a novena in honor of the great saint. When I visited him four days afterwards, I was agreeably surprised to notice a diminution of the disagreeable odor. 'I am better,' said the prisoner, as I entered. Circumstances prevented me from going again to the penitentiary during the novena which ended on Sunday. On Monday morning, as I entered his cell, Bouchet, radiant with delight, announced to me that he was cured. This was thirty-three days ago. The poor young man, impressed by the signal favor bestowed upon him, made his first Communion with great fervor and piety. He was released from the penitentiary nine days ago, and he has since conducted himself in the most satisfactory manner. I obtained board for him with a pious family at la Riche. The good Mother Superioress of the Little Sisters of the Poor kindly gives him two meals every day. He takes the third at my house. He goes to the Brothers for instruction. They are delighted with him. Yesterday he made his Communion for the intentions of the Jubilee."

The charity which was overflowing in the heart of Mr. Dupont, found expression in various ways towards all kinds of persons. We know a priest who was studying at the Seminary, and who was accustomed at the commencement of the vacation, to make a visit to the servant of God; he never left without having received from him a valuable pecuniary gift. When he was raised to the dignity of sub-deacon, Mr. Dupont wrote in humble terms requesting to be permitted to purchase his breviary.

A huckster woman was one morning passing through the street, pushing before her a hand-cart. Just opposite the chapel of the Carmelites, one of the wheels of her cart broke, and all her vegetables were scattered on the ground. Standing in the middle of the street, she cried aloud, lamenting the sad accident which had befallen her. Mr. Dupont was, at that moment, leaving the chapel where he had assisted at Mass; he kindly approached the poor woman, helped her to raise the cart and replace her vegetables. He consoled her by saying a few words of the goodness of God, and slipped into her hand, before leaving, a ten-franc piece, to compensate her for the loss she had sustained and repair the broken wheel.

One evening, he met a cart-driver who was leading a horse fastened behind his cart. The horse broke the rope and ran off. Mr. Dupont caught the animal and restored him to his master, who, without ceremony, requested him to hold the horse whilst he went to mend the rope at the wine-shop at the corner. Although Mr. Dupont suspected that the man would remain for another purpose, he readily consented, held the horse for more than an hour, and resented the abuse of his kindness only by saying with his usual gentleness a few jesting words to the man on his return.

An unfortunate woman was reduced to a state of utter destitution. A neighbor, who was deeply interested in her welfare, exerted himself to the utmost to secure assistance for her, but without success. At last he applied to a well-known Sister of Charity, Sister Angela, and begged her kind ministrations in behalf of his protegée. But the Sister, after paying one visit and making inquiries concerning the woman, thought it more prudent that she should take no further step in the affair. The good neighbor, impelled by his zeal, having heard of Mr. Dupont's kindness and his influence with the Sisters of Charity, called, to make known to him the circumstances of the case. Mr. Dupont received him with his usual cordiality, promised to speak of his protegée to Sister Angela, and accompanying him to the door, he saluted him politely, and placed in his hand, as he bade him good-bye, a twenty-franc piece, saying: "Make use of this for present necessities, until we can give greater help." An alms thus bestowed upon an entire stranger, made so deep an impression upon the man, that it influenced him to lead for the future a life of greater fervor in the service of God.

Among the sufferers who flocked to his drawing-room to have recourse to the Holy Face, were often those whose poverty was so extreme as to call largely upon his charity. He furnished them with food, gave them abundant alms, and it not unfrequently happened that some of them, after returning to their own homes, would importune him for aid.

His charity was great, and his generosity unlimited; but he carefully concealed them, and frequently conferred his benefits through the medium of others. A lady of rank, a Creole of his acquaintance, who had become reduced in circumstances, received from time to time remittances from Martinique, which she supposed were forwarded her from the products of her own possessions: they were a delicate offering from Mr. Dupont. One of his cousins in

CHAPTER VIII

speaking of him, said: "When Léon receives his revenues from the Colonies, he orders a carriage, takes the funds and goes on a short journey, and returns with an empty pocket-book; when asked by his mother where the money is, he replies: 'There is none left; we shall have more next year.'"

He was very prudent and discreet when necessity required precaution. He was notified on one occasion that a family in the city were reduced to the utmost poverty. One little girl had just died of consumption; her sister was ill, and the father, an incorrigible drunkard, did not even supply the family with food. Mr. Dupont had been informed that the wretched man would even search his wife's pockets in the hope of finding the means to gratify his miserable passion. "Here is a case," he said, "where alms should not be given in money." He requested a friend to pay the butcher and baker regularly, and these poor people were provided with food for several months, without knowing who was their kind benefactor.

At another time, having been applied to in favor of a workman, who needed tools, he had, at that moment, no means at his disposal. In the afternoon of the same day, however, a charitable lady having presented him twenty francs for the poor, he requested a pious woman to take the money to the workman. It was on a Sunday and the bell had rung for Vespers. The woman, depriving herself of the gratification of assisting at Vespers, went without delay to fulfil the duty of charity. Mr. Dupont approbated the promptitude with which she had acted, and related what had once happened to himself.

"Urged by an interior impulse to give assistance to a family, which, however, had not been mentioned to him, he found, on his arrival, that they were so destitute as not even to have bread to satisfy the cravings of hunger; and they were, humanly speaking, without hope of aid of any kind, as their poverty was such, that they could not obtain credit. He rejoiced at not having deferred the good work he was inspired to perform, and decided never to delay a charitable act to which he was interiorly impelled." He was careful to conceal, as far as possible, even from his servants, the alms he bestowed, which were abundant, not only in money, but in food and clothing. He would give away even the most necessary articles of his own wardrobe. Adele relates that his shirts disappeared by degrees, and when she saw a rent in his pantaloons, she was often obliged to say to him: "Sir, you must go to bed whilst I mend them; you have no others." He obeyed her simply and cheerfully.

His generosity extended even to trifling things, and upon occasions, he was thoughtful of minute details. Thus, as it was a custom with some families to prepare the traditional Christmas-tree, Mr. Dupont entered into its spirit, and devoted himself to amuse and interest the children, who so impatiently and eagerly looked forward to the festival. The tree was decorated chiefly at his expense, and he made it a point to be present at the distribution of gifts. He contributed ten or twenty francs towards the entertainment of the poor children who were feasted by the family on that day. Whenever he visited a friend, particularly in the country, or when there were children at the house, he, never failed to carry tarts, cakes, and candies, or bottles of Martinique rum. He provided these in large quantities, giving generously, and putting every one at ease by his cordial and affable manners.

Mr. Dupont extended a warm welcome not only to his intimate associates; his refinement and courtesy were attractive to strangers and Protestants, some of whom became his firm and constant friends. We may mention, among others, an excellent Catholic Irish family of the name of Straker, who remained some time at Tours. The father, of English descent, was a Protestant.

One of his daughters writes: "From our earliest childhood, my mother had taught my brother, my sister, and myself to offer constant prayers for the conversion of my

CHAPTER VIII

father. A secret presentiment seemed to urge her to do violence to heaven, to obtain the object of her ardent desires, and, although we knew Mr. Dupont only by reputation, we called upon him. He received us with great courtesy, inscribed my father's name upon the register of the Nocturnal Adoration, and assured us, with a confidence which seemed to have become inherent to his nature, that we might rely upon this conversion as a certainty. He turned over the leaves of his Bible, which was always open on a desk, and read us a text in confirmation of the promise he had just made us. As he talked, he became radiant with joy; he spoke to us of God, of himself, of his daughter, who had been dead two years, of the happiness he experienced in serving his Divine Master... We reluctantly left him after a visit of an hour; I felt that contact with this fervent soul had made upon my heart an impression, which would never be effaced. A few days afterwards, he returned our visit, and, although my father could not comprehend this language of faith, so entirely new to him, he began to frequent the cathedral of Tours, assisted at Mass, even in bad weather, studied Catholic books, and died in the bosom of the true Church. Mr. Dupont visited us frequently during the affliction caused us by the death of my father, testifying the sympathy of an old friend, rather than the courtesy of a recent acquaintance. The loss of my excellent father was a heavy cross to my mother, but the servant of God always succeeded in consoling her. 'You grieve,' he would say to her; 'you should rather be overpowered with gratitude. The body which perishes, is a wall which falls; your husband is nearer to you now than when he was in life.' 'But,' said my mother, 'his illness was so short, and he lived sixty-four years in Protestantism. He was converted so late in life.' 'Well, that only gives you additional assurance of his salvation. Three hours sufficed the good thief. Did not your husband die, pardoning his enemies, and at peace with every one? Were not his last words those of our Lord: "My

God, into Thy hands I commend my spirit?" How, Madam, can you permit yourself to doubt, or to waver in your confidence, when he used the very words of our Saviour expiring on the cross?' From that day the man of God testified an interest in my family which never flagged. My mother was forty-four years of age when she was left a widow with three children. Mr. Dupont's influence turned her heart to God; he persuaded her to receive frequently the sacraments, which hitherto she had approached only on the principal festivals of the year. His kind heart suggested to him many delicate attentions which were gratifying to my mother. On the 17th of March, feast of the patron Saint of Ireland, he would send her a bunch of clover and beautiful violets with a branch of hawthorn, which had bloomed miraculously on the tree planted by St. Patrick on the banks of the Loire.* He wished, by this delicate attention, to express to the widowed woman, that the apostle of her nation had conducted her to a hospitable land. The act appeared to me particularly beautiful, evincing a spirit of courtesy worthy of an ancient Christian cavalier; it was French refinement elevated by sanctity."

There were few families among his intimate friends who could not relate similar circumstances indicative of his charity, ingenuity, and delicacy. A Christian mother of Tours furnishes us an example of the same characteristics. She writes as follows: "I made the acquaintance of Mr. Dupont in 1849. I had several times visited his mother in company with one of my friends, who was intimate with her, and who frequently spoke to me of the virtues of this holy man. At that time, I was so little inclined to piety that

---

* This tree is a hawthorn which grows in the village of St. Patrick in Touraine. Every year it is in bloom in mid-winter. Tradition relates that the patron Saint of Ireland crossed the Loire, which was swollen by heavy rains, on his cloak, using his cane as an oar; having reached the shore, he planted the stick in the ground. The following day, although it was in the depth of winter, the stick had taken root, and it was covered with flowers. The miracle has been renewed every year since that time to the present. Every winter, Mr. Dupont had on his mantel a small branch of this hawthorn in bloom, which he took pleasure in exhibiting to his visitors. We have ourselves seen it frequently.

the thought of becoming acquainted with a saint, made no impression on me. He seemed to me just like other people, although my friend insisted that he had received me with particular cordiality. My first visit was followed by others; I was attracted by something indescribable, for which I could not account. I felt perfectly at home with him; I spoke little and listened eagerly. All was conducted in the simplest way; without appearing to do so, he instructed me in many things of which I was wholly ignorant. Not knowing what a saint was, I regarded him as a very good, pious man, who was especially kind to me. Wherever he saw me, he met me with a pleasant smile. Sometimes we would remain standing, so engaged in earnest conversation that we paid no attention to the passage of time. The holy man! He knew the good he was doing me, and I was as unconscious of it, as is the plant, of the benefit it derives from the dew of heaven. However, grace was accomplishing its work, and we had become true friends. I confided to him the state of my soul, I told him what I felt that God demanded of me; but it was only after a long time that I comprehended how valuable his counsels had been to me. He was the best director I ever knew. It was, I am convinced, through his prayers that I obtained the immense grace of the conversion of a member of my family very dear to me. He loved that soul for which he had prayed so fervently; he said to me several years afterwards in the playful manner in which he often spoke: 'He can teach us now, and we must bow before him.' In his own home, and when with a circle of intimate friends, he was bright and cheerful; but at the same time, his joy was moderate and gentle. When he visited us in the country, he always filled the carriage with packages of cakes and candies for the children whom he loved very much. The children, of course, loved him dearly in return; but the larger ones found his conversation on pious subjects very long; for, when good father Dupont commenced speaking of God, he never wearied. His charity assumed all forms. If any one was ill in the house, he found time, notwithstanding his numerous occupations, to call and make inquiries about the invalid. I was once confined a whole month to my room with the measles. No one ventured to visit me; we had, at that same time, four children ill with the measles. Mr. Dupont, however, would come several times during the week, and remain two or three hours in conversation. One of my little girls was very ill; the Doctor gave us no hope of her recovery; Mr. Dupont came daily and prayed by the side of her cradle, and at the very time that her condition seemed the most desperate, he arose from his knees and said: 'She will be better tomorrow.' The following day she was out of danger; it was certainly the effect of his prayers alone, for no application of oil had been made. I cannot recall, without emotion, his kindness to me, and the simplicity with which he accommodated himself to my capacity. On my observing to him that I knew nothing, and yet I comprehended all he said to me, he replied with his sweet smile by repeating the following verse of the Psalms: '*Quoniam non cognovi litteraturam, introibo in potentias Domini.* (Ps. lxx, 15.) Because I have not known learning, I will enter into the powers of the Lord.'"

These charming details sufficiently explain the particular veneration in which Mr. Dupont is held by certain families, and the confidence with which, in their own homes, they have recourse to his intercession to obtain favors from God.

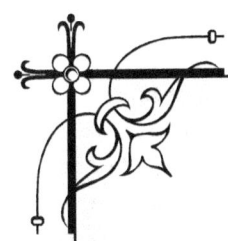

Chapter IX

The Nocturnal Adoration.

Mr. Dupont, in his letters, frequently promises his correspondents to recommend them to the prayers of the Nocturnal Adoration. We shall now make known the important place which this work holds in the life of the servant of God.

Established in Paris on the 6th of December, 1848, through the zeal of a recently converted Jew, the celebrated Father Hermann, the Nocturnal Adoration was commenced in Tours in February, 1849. Living as he did in the world, Mr. Dupont was eminently qualified by his fervent piety, his love for the Blessed Sacrament, and his intimate association with Father Hermann and other holy apostles of the Eucharist, for the foundation of this beautiful work. He embraced it at once and with delight, as a noble idea of expiation, "an idea cherished," he said, "by many men in France, who behold widespread evils and who equally comprehend the necessity of expiation."

But the idea was not entertained by others as readily as by himself. When he proposed to establish it in Tours, his friends regarded the project as rash, and were hopeless of success. As for Mr. Dupont, he did not lose confidence for an instant, and the undertaking prospered far beyond his hopes. Two months after its foundation he could write to a friend: "The beautiful thought of rendering homage to our Lord has been welcomed at Tours. The number of adorers now amounts to seventy-four, and we have the prospect of a great increase during the coming month. No words can express the happiness of these charming nights. The good work has brought us in communication with Christians full of fervor. His lordship himself is amazed at the rapidity with which the fire of devotion has spread from soul to soul."

This success was due to the zeal and popularity of Mr. Dupont; his charity and kind attentions to his neighbor, had made him a general favorite: he was universally loved and venerated. By his exertions, Tours was the first city after Paris in which the Nocturnal Adoration was introduced, and its requirement fulfilled by men. As the idea in his mind was, primarily, that of reparation, the servant of God was desirous that the pious vigils should commence on "the three nights of the days of dissipation and scandal which precede Lent." Mgr. Morlot, whose wisdom and prudent reserve were well known, received the new work with marked favor, and approved, without hesitation, the regulation presented to him by Mr. Dupont. It was intrinsically the same as that observed in Paris, modified, however, and adapted to the wants of the place.

The members were principally from the class of laborers and mechanics, at whose head were some members of the Conference of St. Vincent de Paul, and a few men belonging to families of the highest social position. Each night of Adoration was anticipated with pleasure as a feast, and it was not uncommon to hear workmen, at the conclusion of a day of hard labor, complain to the director of their division, that he had forgotten to notify them of their turn. A day laborer, living in the vicinity of Tours, walked two leagues to go and make his Adoration, after which, he would return the two leagues on foot. The night was terminated by a Mass, and, generally, those who remained in

Adoration approached the holy table; and not unfrequently, men were seen to amend their lives, that they might have the happiness of communicating once a month.

The order of exercises is given by Mr. Dupont in the following words: "We assemble, to the number of fourteen, at the feet of our Lord in the chapel of the Lazarite Fathers, who have also the kindness to allow us the use of a room, in which are placed a few camp-beds. There we converse together until the evening prayer, which is said before our Lady of Good Thoughts; there also, we take our repose before and after our hour of Adoration. Charts, designating the hour which has fallen to each, facilitate the awakening of the members who are successively called during the night. How short those nights are! How short, particularly, is the hour which falls to us for Adoration! Some pious books are placed near a lamp for the use of those, who desire the aid to their devotion. Very few take advantage of them. Some simply say their beads; the greater part kneel at the feet of our Lord, speak to Him, and listen to what he says to their hearts.

The latter find the hour extremely short. I have seen poor workmen, fatigued by the labor of the day, sleeping quietly, and I acknowledge that I rejoiced to have the honor of being near these friends of our Lord."

All the expenses incurred in the necessary arrangements were met by Mr. Dupont. The "camp-beds," as they were designated, consisted of two wooden supports, on which was placed a mattress, with a pillow and one or two blankets. As the work was commenced in winter, the room was heated by means of a stove, in which a fire was kept up all night. Mr. Dupont also sent a number of lamps. When the priests of the Mission proposed constructing a new chapel, Mr. Dupont conceived the idea of arranging a crypte, or subterranean chapel for the Adoration during the winter nights. He communicated his intention to the Superior, who consulted an architect, requesting him to draw up the plans. As, in order to carry out the project, it would be necessary to dig the foundation deeper, the expense would be increased by ten thousand francs. Mr. Dupont placed the requisite amount in the hands of the Superior, and the crypte, which is now seen under the chapel, was built.

His zeal in the cause of Adoration, made of this pious layman an eloquent preacher and an irresistible apostle. He visited his friends, sought the young men of his acquaintance, solicited their attendance, and inspired them with his faith and spirit of reparation. He engaged recruits from all ranks of society; from among workmen and soldiers, as well as from those occupying the highest positions, and from the midst of the most honorable families. He profited by a trial, a sudden affliction, to induce a father or a son to pass an hour in Adoration. He invited strangers in the city, persons unknown to him, chance visitors, to make the hour's prayer. His conversation in the room of their assemblies delighted all who were present. He amused, edified, and instructed them by turns; speaking without restraint, and with so much simplicity, unction, and fervor, that his hearers were inflamed with divine love and disposed to make any sacrifice for God. He had always some pleasant anecdote or consoling incident to relate; the members gathered around him, and became so absorbed in conversation that, at the end of the hour, it was necessary to remind them it was time to go to the chapel.

One of the priests of the Mission sometimes went to the hall, took his part in the conversation, and informed the members that, after prayers, he would be at the service of those who wished to confess. Mr. Dupont would immediately add the weight of his remarks to the proposition of the priest, saying a few words: "You hear the kind offer of the Father, the opportunity is favorable; let us take advantage of it." He would give the example of going to Confession, and there were few who resisted the proffered grace. He never absented himself from these assemblies. He himself distributed to each the hour of his prayer, as a general, when in face of the enemy, places the sentinels for the night, for the defence of the camp. He considered the nocturnal adorer before the Blessed Sacrament, as a soldier on guard, in the service of the Church, and for the salvation of souls. He was always on hand to supply the places of those who might not be punctual to the allotted hour. If he perceived that an inconvenient or disagreeable hour had fallen to the lot of an associate, who appeared chagrined, he would say gently: "I can arrange for you, this hour suits me, I will take it." He often continued in Adoration for several hours in succession. He remained during the entire time immovable, recollected, his whole attitude so expressive of faith and love, that he appeared seraphic to those who saw him. One of the associates usually said aloud the night prayers. Mr. Dupont reserved to himself, as president of the work, the reading of the offering, and his earnest manner made a deep impression upon his auditors. "I never heard him pronounce the formula," says a missionary, "without being moved to tears."

He was the soul of the work, and to his zeal must be attributed the number and fervor of the first associates. He employed a holy ingenuity to render the meetings agreeable to them, and to procure them a pleasant surprise. If there was to be Adoration in the evening of a day, on which a friend or a stranger of distinction visited him, he would induce him to defer his departure and accompany him to the chapel, to pass an hour before the Blessed Sacrament. In like manner, he secured the attendance of celebrated Religious, and of priests illustrious by their eloquence or virtues. It was thus the associates had several opportunities of hearing Fathers Eymard, Hermann, Chaignon, and many others. Through his influence and personal relations, he engaged in the work officers of the highest rank in the army, such as Colonel de Cotte, Commandant Taconnet and Captain Capdecoum. In assigning places, he dexterously made such arrangements as would convey a lesson to the eye and touch the heart. For instance, on one occasion during the prayer and the first hour of Adoration, the associates noticed Captain Capdecoum in full uniform kneeling on a prie-Dieu at the left; on the right, a young ecclesiastic; and between them on the uncovered flagstones, Father Hermann in the habit of a bare-footed Carmelite.

When the national guards were organized after the revolution of 1848, Mr. Dupont mounted guard as the rest, and profited by the occasion to make proselytes. The guards, when relieved from duty, have been seen accompanying him to pass the remainder of the night at the Adoration. Many persons remember having seen Mgr. d'Outremont, when he was attorney for the prefecture, making his Adoration in the uniform of a national guard. The zealous president also secured the attendance of young men, medical and law students, clerks and railroad employees. Among the last were some, whose duties left them but one night in the week free, and that, they would pass at the Adoration. A fireman, for instance, went regularly every week, and, after assisting at the Mass of 4 o'clock, he would say the rosary until it was time to resume his daily toil. We are told, likewise, of the heroic courage of a country school master, who, providing himself with a piece of bread and a gourd, was accustomed to set off at the close of school, and walk three leagues. He arrived in time for his hour of Adoration, passed the remainder of the night on a camp-bed, and, after assisting at Mass, he walked home, where his pupils always found him awaiting them for the morning class. For many years he imposed this sacrifice upon himself both in winter and summer, without regard to the weather.

Mr. Dupont particularly appreciated, in this association, the practice of frequent Communion. "Nothing touches me more," he writes, "than to see men who had neglected their religious duties, now rendering homage to God and joining the band of adorers of the holy Eucharist." His

CHAPTER IX

own ingenious zeal principally brought about this happy result. In his propagandism, he did not always apply to fervent Christians; he frequently aimed at enticing persons who neglected the sacraments, and by his charitable exertions, he would succeed in persuading them, first, to enroll themselves among the associates of the Adoration, and finally, to approach Confession and holy Communion. Sometimes, the return to a Christian life was effected in so singular and extraordinary a manner, that it was impossible not to acknowledge in it a powerful and peculiar grace. The father of a family, who had for a long time abandoned every religious practice, ardently desired to obtain the cure of an invalid son. "Come and pass the night with me," said Mr. Dupont, "we will pray together in union with all the associates." He agreed to the proposal, was present at the prayers, and made his hour of Adoration. In the morning during the Mass, seeing the associates approach the railing to receive holy Communion, he supposed that he, also, was obliged to Communicate; this he did, to the great surprise of one of the members who knew his previous neglect of his duties. On leaving the chapel, he questioned the man, who acknowledged that he had not been to Confession, and he inquired, with simplicity, if he had done wrong, and how he should repair the fault. The pious associate was embarrassed, supposing the act to be a frightful sacrilege: grieved and anxious, he hastened to refer the matter to Mr. Dupont who saw, at once, that the man had acted through an ignorance, unfortunately too common at that time. Convinced of his good faith, far from being disturbed by the Communion he had received, Mr. Dupont rejoiced at it, saying playfully that Satan had been caught in his own snares. "Take him to a confessor," he added, "and you will see that all is right." The man confessed with humility and contrition, and ever after led a Christian life. Mr. Dupont admired, in this instance, the conduct of God over the soul, considering in it a particular grace granted to the practices of the Nocturnal Adoration.

He refers frequently in his letters to the importance of enlisting youth in the work. "You cannot imagine," he writes to a brother member, "the consolation we have in the young men. It seems to me, that in acquiring the habit of frequent Confession and Communion, they are fortifying themselves to resist the dangers which will surround them in the world." In another letter he mentions a beautiful circumstance: "We number," he says, "among the associates three poor young men who never fail to make their hour of Adoration, and who are obliged to walk three, four and five leagues in order to come and adore our Lord. How their fervor shames those who have means of transportation at their disposal! Oh! if the rich would, or, I should say, could comprehend all the fruit to be derived from our dear work!"

He gives another charming example: "I hope R—— is well. (He speaks of a young soldier whom he recommended to a friend.) It is wonderful to see him resist the great corruption which infects barracks. God will reward him for his zeal. He travelled all last night, and did not lie down this morning. At nine o'clock he was at my house. I told him that one of his comrades had been begging of our Lord his restoration to health. 'Who is it?' he asked, even before I could finish the sentence, 'I will take him tonight to the Adoration.' Regardless of his previous fatigue, he passed the night there in company with his comrade, who suddenly experienced a great improvement in his condition; I think we shall have him, also, as an associate."

Officers of high grade in the army, when passing through Tours, would delay their journey one night in order to spend it with Mr. Dupont at the Adoration. Some would come from Paris, or from still more distant cities, to take their station before the Blessed Sacrament. Among these, the brave General de Cotte deserves a particular notice. He was in garrison at Tours when he was Colonel of Dragoons, and Mr. Dupont paid particular attention to him. These two servants of God became united in a firm friendship and they met frequently. The Colonel familiarly called his friend "General." By way of a courteous and pleasing jest, he took a fancy one day to render him publicly the honors due the title.

It was New Year's morning, 1850. Great was the astonishment of the inhabitants of Saint-Etienne street on hearing a flourish of trumpets, which they immediately recognized as the brilliant music of the Dragoons, so celebrated throughout the city. The windows were crowded; people ran out in the streets. The musicians stopped before Mr. Dupont's door. Mr. Dupont himself, hearing the unusual serenade, inquired what it meant. The leader of the band replied that it was "in honor of the General." "But there is no General in this neighborhood." "The order was given," answered the leader, "and I have made no mistake; we are at No. 8, before the house of the General... Dupont." Mr. Dupont laughed heartily and said: "It is a trick played me by de Cotte." He amused himself during the day by repeating the trick to his visitors who, in turn, complimented him playfully upon having so rapidly risen to the grade of "General." After Colonel de Cotte left Tours, he kept up a correspondence with Mr. Dupont, and occasionally went to pass a night with him in the chapel of the Lazarists.

The example of such men necessarily exerted a great influence. The salutary impression made upon the associates prepared them for the accomplishment of the most heroic sacrifices. We should not, therefore, be surprised that miraculous favors were the recompense. The following was the first of the kind obtained. Fr. Redon, Superior of the Priests of the Mission, was in want of four thousand francs to assist a worthy man who was greatly embarrassed in his affairs. He mentioned the case to Mr. Dupont, who said to him: "We shall meet this evening for the Adoration. We will enter your intention upon our register, and tomorrow, I hope you will have the money." His hope was realized. Fr. Redon, the following morning, said the Mass of the associates at 4 o'clock, and then took the stage which was to meet the cars to Orleans. It was a cold morning in winter, and enveloped in his cloak he, as well as the four passengers who occupied the stage with him, drove on in silence. As the day dawned and it became lighter, he noticed that one of the travellers looked at him fixedly; it proved to be an old friend, who, at last recognizing him, exclaimed: "I believe you are Mr. Redon." At the first relay his friend asked him to alight for a few minutes, and, taking him aside, said: "I am doubly happy to meet you, because, in addition to the pleasure of seeing you after a separation of so many years, you can do me a service. When my attention was attracted to you, I was revolving in my mind how I should dispose of a sum of money which I promised to employ in charity, if I succeeded in an undertaking. God blessed my work, and now I must fulfil my promise. You have so many good works on hand; suppose you take the money; you would know so much better than I how to apply it advantageously." The amount he gave him was exactly four thousand francs, just the sum Mr. Redon needed to relieve the embarrassment of the poor man. On his return to Tours, he informed the associates of the miraculous favor he had obtained. This was the first grace marked on the register with the sign of a cross; and, thenceforth, Mr. Dupont adopted the custom of designating by this sign the spiritual or temporal favors obtained by the prayers of the members.

Mgr. d'Outremont relates the following occurrence which he himself witnessed: "One of the associates had had his thumb terribly crushed, and the intense suffering had deprived him of sleep for several days and nights. The time came for us to kneel before our Lord exposed for Adoration. The wounded man, who knew his fellow-members were praying for him, repeatedly said to his wife during the evening: 'Have confidence; the associates are praying for me.' His faith was rewarded. About midnight he uttered an exclamation which startled his wife, as she feared he was worse. What was her delight and surprise to find him free from pain! 'I do not suffer now,' he said to her. After a short and fervent thanksgiving to our Lord and His Blessed Mother, he fell asleep and rested quietly the remainder of the night. From that time his wound healed rapidly, and the goodness of God so mercifully displayed increased our confidence and faith."

The evil spirit could not behold, unmoved, these triumphs of grace. We shall have occasion to mention some of his efforts to avenge himself on the servant of God, by whom, however, his malice was recognized and his snares discovered. A fire had been kindled, as usual, one very cold evening before the exposition of the Blessed Sacrament. The stove smoked in a most unaccountable manner, nor could they keep the fire lighted. Puffs of wind, blowing without any apparent cause, lifted even the ashes from the hearth. Mr. Dupont enters: "Oh! Oh!" he said with a significant gesture, "it is the 'old boy.' He is playing us an ugly trick. We will kneel down and recite a Pater and Ave, and then Vade retro Satana." They did as he requested, and, immediately, the smoke disappeared, the fire commenced to burn and gave no more trouble during the night.

There was a probability, at one time, that the property adjoining the chapel of the Lazarists might be purchased by a certain party, who proposed devoting the building to purposes which would prove an extreme annoyance to the community. The Fathers informed Mr. Dupont of what they had heard; he was alarmed on account of the Nocturnal Adoration. But his faith soon restored his equanimity; making the circuit of the wall, he threw some medals of St. Benedict within the enclosure. He also requested the Superior to allow him to examine the adjacent premises from the interior of his house. They conducted him to the sacristy, in which was a window directly opposite the building. He opened it and succeeded in throwing a medal to the very spot he wished to reach. "Well done!" he said, laughing heartily; "you may be at peace now; 'the old man' (the name he gave Satan) will have another occupation than tormenting you." His words were verified. The project which had alarmed the Lazarists was abandoned; they attributed the change of plans to the faith of their holy friend. The house became, ultimately, the property of a Religious community.

True charity is not limited in its zeal for the good of others; it dilates and strives to unite souls. Such was the character of Mr. Dupont's charity. Tours soon became too small a theatre for the exercise of his ardor in the cause of the Adoration. He undertook to establish it elsewhere, regarding the men assembled during the night in prayer before the altar as an army ranged in battle, wrestling with divine justice. "How true it is," he exclaims, "that the work of Reparation belongs exclusively to men! Who are the leaders of the conspiracy of earth against Heaven? By whom was lying philosophy invented? Who have taken upon themselves to propagate it? What would have become of civilization, if woman, for the past century, had not continued in prayer? Would not fire from Heaven have destroyed men and beasts, cities and villages? It is then time that men, who by a merciful Providence have been saved from the philosophical deluge, should unite in an effort for the faith. Since the day is devoted to temporal affairs, let us give the night to our good God, and let us become the friends and allies of Jesus, by rendering him the homage which is his due. Oh! if I were free to travel through the country, I would go from door to door appealing to men of good will, who are ready to open their hearts to our Lord at the first call of His grace." He actually practiced this at Tours, but his zeal extended far beyond the city in which he resided. "I have sent letters," he says, "to, at least, thirty different places. It is evident that the good God, like the father of the prodigal, is awaiting our repentance in order to pardon us. Let us, then, throw ourselves at His feet, and, as we are as poor as was the prodigal when he returned from his wanderings, let us offer, with our poverty, the infinite merits of our Lord."

He had friends and correspondents whom he inflamed with his own zeal and ardor for the work of the Adoration. They consulted him, confided to him their difficulties; he answered all, entering into details with regard to arrangements, in a manner wholly foreign to his natural disposition; but where the Nocturnal Adoration was concerned, he gave his time as readily as his money. When there was question of organizing this cherished work in adjacent cities or dioceses, he did not hesitate to go in company with some of the members from Tours, and unite in Adoration with the associates of the place, cheerfully rendering them every service in his power, animating their zeal by his presence and example. At other times, he would induce some pious souls to pass a night of Adoration with him, that they might understand how the Adoration was conducted at Tours.

The following incident related by himself, is an evidence of the manner in which he took advantage of the slightest event to attain his end. He was going to the baths of Neris, which had been ordered him by the physician as a remedy for gout. But nowhere did he lose sight of his dear Adoration. "On my way to this place," he writes, "a circumstance occurred, of which I could not, at the time, appreciate the effect. On the arrival of the train at Bourges, I engaged a place in the stage to Neris. I paid for my ticket, checked my baggage, and then went to a hotel to await the hour of its departure. I was in the yard of the hotel on the watch for the vehicle, which was a little behind time. I had entered into conversation with a soldier, when the stage stopped, took in three passengers who were quite near me, and drove off, without my being notified. I ran after it, but was informed that there was no vacant seat. There I was at six o'clock in the evening, detained at Bourges for twenty-four hours. The following morning, I called upon the Superior of the Jesuit Fathers. We talked of the Adoration. He showed me a lovely chapel which had just been constructed for the Fathers when in retreat. He offered it for the Adoration. We visited, together, several good Christians and spoke to them of the devotion: they would reflect upon it. And lo! the Father writes me: 'The work meets with favor, and we shall, ere long, be able to commence: we have placed our chapel at the disposal of the gentlemen. Come, and pass a day with us when you leave Neris.'" Thus, even when travelling, this lover of the Eucharist neglected no opportunity to advance the glory of God; he viewed in the most trifling event a design of Providence, which he forwarded with peace of soul and a tranquil confidence of success.

Mr. Dupont was concerned in nearly all the foundations of this work which were undertaken in various places. But he concealed, as far as possible, any part he had personally taken in their establishment. He preferred to act through the mediation of others. Sometimes he made use of officers of rank in the army. At Bayonne, for example, he called upon Mr. Rousset-Pomaret, Commandant of the Engineer Corps; at Brest, he was indebted to Mr. Cuers, a Captain in the Navy. He had correspondents at Marseilles, at Aix, and Toulon; he took advantage of the departure of a travelling agent from Tours for Spain, to introduce the Nocturnal Adoration beyond the Pyrenees.

It would be impossible to express the affection he bore that work. The holy man had thrown into it his whole soul. He never failed to celebrate the anniversary of its foundation at Tours, when the associates would pass three nights consecutively in Adoration; his zeal on those occasions was excited to additional exertion, and his heart was filled with an inexpressible delight. "This evening," he writes to a friend, "we shall be kneeling, at the same time, at the feet of Jesus. What a happiness! It is the anniversary of our establishment in 1849. Yesterday evening eight members presented themselves to supply the places of any who might, possibly, be absent; but all who were notified had responded to the call." In another letter addressed to a priest, he suddenly interrupts himself and says: "Apropos, let me tell you that we shall, as usual, celebrate, this year, the anniversary of our birth at Tours, and we shall pass in Adoration and reparation, the three nights previous to Ash Wednesday, which are generally devoted to dissipation. May God grant great graces to those who are recommended to the prayers of the pious associates!"

The feast of the Blessed Sacrament furnished him also with the opportunity of manifesting his zeal for the Adoration. "I am happy to tell you," he writes, "that several of our associates have requested permission to pass Thursday night of the Octave of Corpus Christi in Adoration. That is, moreover, the night upon which our Lord showed his heart to the Venerable Margaret Mary, and opened to us that new source of graces destined to secure the triumph of the Church in these latter days."

The nights of Adoration were his relaxation from the occupations of the day. In 1858, in the midst of the great fatigue resulting from the visits made to the Holy Face, he wrote: "For several days my work has multiplied in every manner. It is an inundation which is forever on the increase. Poor nature regrets to see her own weakness and insufficiency. Fortunately, I can have recourse to the Adoration; it offers a happy rest at the feet of the good Master."

It sometimes happened, however, that fatigue overpowered him, and he fell asleep during his holy vigil. He acknowledges this weakness in the following simple and ingenuous terms: "I fell asleep one night during my Adoration in the chapel of the Mission, so weak is poor human nature! On awakening, I perceived that my companion for the hour was asleep also. He was a poor laborer, wearied by his day's work, who was to commence another day of hard labor almost as soon as he would leave the chapel. I had not the courage to disturb his repose, being convinced, moreover, that his sleep was a more meritorious prayer than my watch. Confused and humiliated, I exclaimed: 'My God, my God! Behold what manner of guard is before Thee!' Ashamed of my weakness, I imposed on myself, as a penance, not to take snuff during the remainder of the time that I was to pass in Adoration. With increasing confusion I exclaimed again: 'My God, my God! How well Thou art guarded!'"

The above incident was related by a friend of Mr. Dupont, who had it from his own lips. It depicts to the life the charming simplicity of this devoted servant of the Eucharist. Humble himself, and full of charitable tenderness towards others, he considered that our Lord was more honored by a filial and respectful familiarity than by scruples and disturbance of mind.

He ardently wished that perpetual Adoration could be, at once, established everywhere. "When shall we see our Lord honored day and night in every parish throughout the Catholic world? Will it not be after the triumph which is to exalt the Church, and when the power of our Lord will have destroyed the impious league which now persecutes truth? I love to cherish the hope." At another time he would say: "What means shall we employ, to bring back to the Church those who have strayed from the right path? We may reply boldly to this question: The prayer of those who pray, and prayer in common, such as was so fruitful of benedictions in the first days of the Church. Assuredly, the best manner of prayer is to unite in one same thought at the feet of our Lord, to *adore* him, to make *reparation*, and *to expose to him our necessities*. Oh! what happiness would be in store for the present generation, if that idea could be realized throughout France!"

The Nocturnal Adoration, which continually occupied Mr. Dupont's thoughts, became the occasion of his forming many holy friendships which we may, not unaptly, call "his Eucharistic friendships." Of this number, we shall speak of Fathers Hermann, Eymard, de Cuers, and Captain Marceau.

Father Hermann, who became a bare-footed Carmelite under the name of Augustine Mary of the Blessed Sacrament, had preached in the cathedral of Tours in 1853. Mr. Dupont availed himself of his presence at Tours to interest him in the Adoration, and a close friendship, which circumstances tended to strengthen, sprang up between these two servants of God. The Rev. Father had promised to come to Tours, to baptize an infant for which his sister, Mme. Raunheim, was to be the godmother, and Mr. Dupont, the godfather. The child was the daughter of a mutual friend, Mr. Rosemberg, formerly a Jew, and like the celebrated Religious, a recent convert, and like him, also an eminent artist. The Bishop of Carcassonne, Mgr. de la Bouillerie, was aware of the arrangements which had been made for the baptism, and, as he intended about that time to visit his brother at Angers, he decided to stop at Tours and pass the night there, in order to complete the remainder of the journey in company with Father Hermann. Father Eymard, at that time occupied with the foundation of the order of Priests of the Blessed Sacrament, was also at Tours, and as a friend, had asked hospitality of Mr. Dupont. The devout servant of the Eucharist considered the occasion a most favorable one for bringing about a meeting between these three friends of God; he pleasantly called it "a little Eucharistic congress." The conversation turned principally upon the Nocturnal Adoration and the best means of propagating it. Mgr. de la Bouillerie, who was acquainted with Mr. Dupont only by the reputation of his sanctity, was much pleased with his conversation, and listened with great interest to the account of many cures which had been obtained before the Holy Face. The remark having been made by one of the party, that the Holy Face performed miracles: "Oh! yes, certainly," said Mgr. de la Bouillerie appropriately and wittily, "in our days, the Holy Face performs miracles; not the Holy Face of Angers, nor of Paris, but the one at Tours, the one in this house, the Holy Face of Mr. Dupont," insinuating that he attributed the miraculous favors obtained rather to the prayers of his host, than to the picture itself. The expression of the learned and pious prelate, which only echoed the sentiment of the public, was interpreted as he intended it, to the great confusion of the servant of God.

The ceremonies of the baptism were performed in the Church of the Ursulines. The next morning Mr. Dupont, as godfather, invited to breakfast all the members of the family, Mgr. de la Bouillerie, Father Hermann, and Father Eymard. When it was time for the Bishop of Carcassonne to leave, in order to meet the train going to Angers, Mr. Dupont proposed to his guests to accompany Monseigneur and Father Hermann to Port-Boulet, the fourth station. His proposition being gladly acceded to, he conducted his guests to the depot, engaged a special car at his own expense, and was thus enabled to converse, a few hours longer, with a sort of heavenly joy upon the inexhaustible subject so dear to his heart.

When speaking of Father Hermann, he said: "Let us hope that Father Augustine will augment the ardor of the flame already enkindled in the family of adorers, and that some sparks may ascend from our hearts to the throne of God, to implore the divine mercy for unbelievers." He saw, even at that time (1851), in the Nocturnal Adoration, a means of "combating the philosophical gangrene," a plank of safety "in the midst of the tempest which threatened the foundation of civil and political society."

Father Eymard, also, was on terms of intimacy with Mr. Dupont. He was frequently at Tours, called thither either to preach the *triduums* and retreats in the parish of St. Julien, or for different Religious communities. The servant of God considered it an honor to give him hospitality; he loved to converse with him and hear him preach; he admired the unction, simplicity and tenderness of his discourses; he venerated him as a saint, and was happy when he could engage him to speak at the Adoration.

The Holy Face seemed to smile upon this intercourse. Father Eymard suffered from palpitation of the heart: "He went to see Mr. Dupont, and after having been anointed with the oil which burns before the holy picture, he was completely cured." We have read the certificate, in which he himself asserts his cure, and in which he adds: "May the grace of God and His holy love make my heart palpitate, and consume it for his glory: I have no other desire."

This incident in the life of Father Eymard is worthy of remark. The miraculous favor for which he expresses his gratitude, was granted him at the period, when this ardent adorer of the Blessed Eucharist, after having been a Marist for seventeen years, urged by the desire of establishing the institute of the Priests of the Blessed Sacrament, had resolved to follow this second vocation, being fully pursuaded that it came from God. To carry out his designs, he needed strength and health; they were restored to him at Mr. Dupont's by the oil of the Holy Face. The pious founder was then free to abandon his heart to the demands of his Eucharistic love.

Father de Cuers, the successor of Father Eymard, is, perhaps, of all the laymen of his acquaintance, the one to whom Mr. Dupont expressed most fully his sentiments in regard to the Eucharist and the work of the Adoration. We may judge the character of the relations which existed between these two fervent Catholics, by the numerous letters which he wrote to Mr. de Cuers before he abandoned the world, to embrace the sacerdotal and Religious state, and whilst he was still an officer in the navy. Zeal for the extension of the Nocturnal Adoration was their animating principle, and it daily augmented the friendship which united them.

Captain de Cuers, when he was about to bid adieu to the world, urged his friend to resolve to do the same, and place himself under a Religious rule, in order the more perfectly to adore Jesus Christ in the Blessed Sacrament. Mr. Dupont replied to him on the 31st of March, 1854: "I wish, my very dear friend, that I could have the happiness of uniting with you and other friends of Jesus, when the opportunity may offer, of extending more generally the work of the Nocturnal Adoration. If I were at liberty to act, I would not delay visiting you for that intention, since the hearts to which you allude are in the country where you live. But, for the present, I am more tied than ever to the soil which gives me hospitality, and where I live, like the patriarchs, under a tent. But crowds flock to this tent to venerate the Holy Face, and to receive extraordinary favors.... I shall be more happy when it will be granted me, at least, to receive the body of our Lord from your hands whilst serving your Mass, if you will allow me that honor. I pray my guardian angel to procure for me this double favor."

Captain Marceau was, also, drawn to the pious layman of Tours by a kind of instinctive attraction. Their first interview occurred at a restaurant in Nantes; it is full of interest, and depicts in lively colors these two beautiful souls, and the secret of their strong friendship. Captain Marceau, in the uniform of a naval officer, was seated at table in one of the restaurants of the city, when a traveller, in the dress of a civilian, of modest, but dignified bearing, entered the apartment, approached the Captain, saluted him, and introduced himself as Mr. Dupont. Captain Marceau, who knew him only by reputation, arose, embraced him, and pushing aside his plate, commenced to speak with him of God, of the happiness which is enjoyed in His service, and of the devotion due from men to the interests of His glory. One hour, two, three hours pass; the two friends were listened to with curiosity and astonishment: human respect exercised a great influence at that period; few men were found who dared to acknowledge their faith publicly. Guests came and went, and still their pious conversation continued, until at last, they were notified that the restaurant was about to be closed for the night. Neither had noticed the flight of time; they had been perfectly oblivious of every thing around them. The recent convert had enjoyed with the pilgrim of Toura one of those charming moments which made him say: "How happy I am when I have the opportunity of spending hours in talking of the good God!"

From the very beginning of their acquaintance, these two souls were united together, like those of David and Jonathan, by a fraternal and unalterable friendship. They kept up an uninterrupted correspondence, and, as Mr. Dupont was engaged upon the composition of the "*Year of Mary*" he called upon the Captain to obtain for him, information concerning certain sanctuaries, situated in seaports which he could not himself visit. Capt. Marceau entered into his design with pious ardor and made the necessary inquiries.

When Mr. Dupont was devoting his attention to the work for the reparation of blasphemy, he proposed to his friend to unite with him in the effort to indemnify our Lord for the many outrages committed against His adorable name. Capt. Marceau warmly welcomed the proposition. "I am too happy," he said, "to make this act of faith, and to aid, if it be in my power, in the reparation of a disorder in which I took part for so long a time." Not satisfied with repeating the *Sit nomen Domini benedictum* every time he heard an oath, the Captain urged all persons over whom he had any influence, to repeat frequently this invocation. He became an apostle of the devotion of reparation, persuading as many as possible to join the association, and showed himself so zealous for the honor of God, that he succeeded in completely banishing from his ship the utterance of oaths and blasphemies.

Marceau felt that he needed a friend who would animate him to the practice of virtue, and fortify him in his good resolutions. Such a friend he found in Mr. Dupont. The letters of the holy man vivified his faith, and afforded him so much consolation and light that he begged for them with a kind of persistency: "I need," he said, "your good letters to animate and sustain me. One of my friends, whom you saw at Néris, says that you have an inclination to asceticism, which would terrify some persons. As for myself, I require your aid to correct the natural defects which were fostered by my education. It is, therefore, a happiness to me to find in your letters those details that teach me the religion of the heart, which I should not have without your aid."

Mr. Dupont having called him, "Sir," instead of, "friend," he complains to him of it. "Your letter with its heading of 'Sir,' startled me. I used this address to you, because it corresponded to the sentiments of respectful affection which I bear you; but permit me to claim the continuation of your friendship, your salutary advice and your fervent prayers."

Acceding to his wishes, Mr. Dupont spared him neither charitable reproofs, nor incentives to zeal. He particularly advised him to devote himself to the work of the Nocturnal Adoration, and he inflamed that ardent and generous soul with some sparks of the sacred fire which burned in his own soul for the Eucharist. Marceau derived from devotion to this august Sacrament the strength to overcome himself, and to gain the victory over others. His friends said to him on one occasion: "We do not know how you manage: your crew are always contented and happy, no matter how hard may be the work you command, and our sailors, on the contrary, complain, are ill-humored and passionate; we find it impossible to control them." "Gentlemen," said

Marceau, "I will tell you my secret; whenever I see that my men are discontented, I pass an hour or two before the Blessed Sacrament, offering the prayer for them, and after that, all goes on wonderfully well."

Mr. Dupont interested himself actively in the plan of the Captain to convey missionaries to Oceanica. He aided, pecuniarily, one of the party, and when he discovered, just as the vessel was about to weigh anchor from Saint-Nazaire, that a Religious destined for America had not means to pay his passage, he immediately obtained it for him.

A premature death deprived him of this friend, and he had not even the consolation of assisting at his last moments. "He died," he said, "from convulsions accompanied by a vomiting which exhaled a fetid odor." He relates, in regard to the corpse of his friend, two striking circumstances. "When I went to see the body of my departed friend, I kissed him on the forehead; but, ashamed of yielding to the feeling of repugnance occasioned by what I had been told of the odor accompanying the vomiting, I applied my lips to his half-open mouth, and I declare positively that I perceived nothing in the least offensive. I called the attention of those present, to the fact, and all agreed with me: at the same time, we could but admire the expression of happiness imprinted upon the features which had been beautified by death. After thirty hours had passed, there was no change, no odor. One of the eyes had opened, and a new charm was added to the lovely countenance." Ten days afterwards, the body was to be removed to its final resting-place. In order to prevent inconvenience to the assistants from the bad odor which naturally would be exhaled, the precaution had been taken of sprinkling the grave with quantities of chloride of lime. On the removal of the coffin, there was found in it an opening, sufficiently large to permit the shroud to be seen; it was fresh and untarnished. Mr. Dupont and one of the ecclesiastics approached the coffin, and examined the opening; they affirm that they perceived no disagreeable odor. They were both struck by the circumstance, and Mr. Dupont said, ironically: "It was worth while to take great precautions." He was confirmed in the opinion he entertained of the eminent virtues of the dear deceased, and of the happiness he was enjoying in Heaven. The affection of these two fervent laymen will remain for those who know them, the type of true and faithful friendship, such as is depicted in the Holy Scriptures, and such as exists only in hearts animated by the love of God.

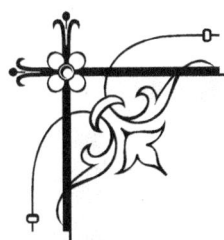

Chapter X

The Work of St. Martin.

Whilst Mr. Dupont devoted his life to works of charity, one illustrious model was always present to his mind, one important object was, more than all others, the aim of his prayers before the Blessed Sacrament. This model of charity was St. Martin; the object of his fervent and constant prayer, was the rebuilding of the celebrated Basilica of the thaumaturgus, which had been destroyed by the revolution.

When the pious Creole of Martinique fixed his residence at Tours in 1834, St. Martin no longer received the homage of the faithful as in former times. We have mentioned above how he had been drawn by an interior attraction to the corner of Descartes and St. Martin streets, where he would stop to pray; we have, also, spoken of the Stations of the Cross which he made at night, through the streets, in company with some friends. But few persons, however, participated in his devotion to the glorious patron of the city; still less, did they entertain a thought of reconstructing the ancient church formerly dedicated to him. Mr. Dupont, alone, cherished the unalterable hope. A simple and beautiful idea, inspired by charity and put at once into execution, was about to become the germ of the great enterprise.

Mr. Dupont had discovered that the old garments distributed to the poor were often rejected and sold by them, on account of their miserable condition. Hence he conceived the idea of making this distribution a separate work, under the patronage of St. Martin, in commemoration of the military catechumen dividing his cloak with a poor man. It was, no doubt, his devotion to the holy Bishop, and his desire to rekindle this devotion in the hearts of the inhabitants of Tours which inspired him with the charitable idea. It originated, also, in his supernatural respect for the poor, in whose persons he viewed our Lord Himself, and "Whom," he said, "he desired to honor whilst clothing the naked." At another time, he calls it "an unpretending work, which, quite naturally, should originate in Tours, but, which ought to be adopted in every city of France, because the incessant increase of luxury rendered it indispensable."

Mr. Dupont gives the following account of the organization of the Clothing Society: "A new work, having for its title, 'The Work-room of St. Martin,' has been added to those with which you are already acquainted. Our object is to form a society to receive old garments, which will be repaired in the best possible manner, and to purchase new ones, if there should be money in the purse. Pious work-women will devote themselves to the necessary mending, asking, in consideration of their services, only what is absolutely requisite for their support. Ladies, zealous in the cause, beg clothing and money, and sometimes aid in the sewing. A Board of Managers directs the Association." The Board was composed at first of the presidents and secretaries of the Conference of St. Vincent de Paul in Tours. The first meeting took place on the 6th of December, 1854, two days before the definition of the Immaculate Conception. At the preliminary assembly held on the 11th of November, feast of St. Martin, Mr. Dupont had been chosen a member, and, after the departure of the president, Mr. Bailloud, the united and persistent entreaties of his colleagues obliged him to accept the presidency. It was decided, at the same time, that the meetings should, in future, be held at his house, in the very apartment which has since been converted into a chapel, and which became the central point of all the plans devised for extending the public veneration of St. Martin.

From the very beginning, notwithstanding his office of president, Mr. Dupont, whose piety led him by preference to what is simple and unpretending, avoided long discussions, which he knew would prove fruitless, and he objected to multiplied practices. He relied more upon the efficacy of prayer than activity on his part. Like all other proceedings connected with the honor to be paid St. Martin, the Society for clothing the poor met with opposition in its commencement, and many difficulties were to be overcome before the regulations were approved. The man of God was contented with prayer, being fully persuaded that nothing would be accomplished if the Saint did not exert his power in their regard. Besides, it was necessary to make the trial of the efficiency of the Society. At the end of eighteen months they experienced the effect of the intervention of the holy protector of Tours; the obstacles were removed, and Mgr. Morlot approved the regulations of the Society under the title of "The Work of St. Martin to Clothe the Poor." Mr. Dupont, in concert with his friends, had drawn up the rule. He submitted the whole to the Archbishop, who examined it carefully, made a slight change in certain articles, and gave his final approbation. The rule, which is still observed even in the minute details, is very practical, and bears the impress of an enlightened charity.

The work became popular at once. In the course of the first year the president wrote to a friend: "During the past four months, we have distributed three hundred new garments. We have also had the consolation of knowing, by the legacies which we have received, that rich persons were pleased to find the means of assisting the poor." The honor rendered to St. Martin had likewise increased; for the members of the Board, whilst adopting every method to relieve the indigent, did not neglect the glory of their holy patron. They had already, in one of their meetings, expressed the wish that the novena made in preparation for his feast, should be more imposing than usual. Hitherto, the custom had been to make at the cathedral, during the nine days, only a short meditation with a few vocal prayers. The desire of the members was realized in 1856, when the novena was preached by a Capuchin Religious, the Rev. Father Bonaventure. The enthusiasm existing in the city, suggested to the eloquent Father, at the termination of his instructions, to propose to the people to erect a statue of St. Martin on the top of the tower of Charlemagne. The proposition was never carried into effect, but the popular sentiment was evinced by the pomp with which the ceremonies were conducted.

On the day of the feast, November 11th, Cardinal Morlot celebrated the Mass for the work of the Clothing Society, in the "Little Chapel of St. Martin." At the meeting held on the same day, an account of the present condition of the work was read by the director, M. l'Abbé Verdier, who, in the name of the Board, expressed the wish "to see collected the scattered stones of the Basilica, and to restore to the veneration of the faithful, the great thaumaturgus of Gaul." The proposition was warmly welcomed by the Cardinal. Thus the grave question of reconstructing the church of St. Martin, was, for the first time, broached publicly, and the desire which Mr. Dupont had cherished in his heart, and which had been for twenty years the object of his prayers, at last found an echo: the precious seed was not long in producing its fruit.

In the same year, 1856, Cardinal Morlot was at Rome. The members of the Board, having assembled on the 14th of December, upon business relating to their Society, agreed to apply to their venerable Archbishop, petitioning him to be their mediator with the Sovereign Pontiff and obtain from him a blessing upon their project of restoring the Basilica. Mr. Dupont requested that the letter to be forwarded to Rome, should be dated December 18th, the festival of St. Gatian, in order to secure for their undertaking the protection of the first bishop of Tours. The petition met with a favorable reception from the Cardinal, and the benediction was graciously bestowed by Pius IX.

Mgr. Morlot was transferred to the see of Paris, made vacant by the assassination of Mgr. Sibour, and was succeeded by Mgr. Guibert, who, from the very first, showed marked favor to the cause of the faithful who were so zealous to make reparation to St. Martin.

It was important, above all else, to discover the true location of the glorious tomb.

The members of the Clothing Society, among whom was the chief engineer of the Railroad, Mr. Ratel, made for that purpose a well directed and careful research. They met with every encouragement from their president, Mr. Dupont, whose mind often reverted to the remark made to him by the vegetable vender the first time he had gone to pray at that spot. Finally, through information derived from the city architect, they discovered in the archives of the prefecture a plan of the year IX, indicating the whole of the Basilica and the streets contemplated at that time. By comparing the plan with the actual condition of the locality, it was evident that the tomb did not lie beneath the street itself, as had been supposed, but beneath a row of private houses. It became absolutely necessary, in order to gain possession of this precious treasure, to purchase three of the houses. The members took measures to make this important acquisition without delay. They needed a broker to carry their plan into execution. Providence offered them one in the person of the Count Pedre Moisant, who had been recently admitted to the Board. This fervent and generous Christian presented a hundred and fifty thousand francs to aid in the purchase. The munificent donation decided Mgr. Guibert to abandon the idea he had entertained of restoring the worship of the blessed pontiff in the church of St. Julian.

But the work of God was destined to have its trials. The perpetual enemy of St. Martin seemed suddenly to arouse himself, to take his revenge by creating difficulties between the ecclesiastical authority and the Board. Differences of opinion existed, it is true, only on minor points; but they sufficed to arrest the progress of the work, and sometimes even to menace its entire cessation. In the midst of this anxiety which caused him much interior suffering, Mr. Dupont, we are told by his fellow-members, excited their admiration by his tranquillity, humility and faith. He was unwilling to seek light elsewhere than in prayer, nor any other help than confidence in God. Guided by his advice and stimulated by his fervor, the members of the Society undertook quietly and without parade several pilgrimages. Here, Mr. Dupont was perfectly at home. In his opinion, prayer and pilgrimages would bring all their designs to a successful issue, and the man of God was not mistaken. It was not long before Mgr. Guibert, addressing the people, and assuming the responsibility of the enterprise, said: "It is not I who have fixed the time... a voice has spoken from the depths of souls: its echo has been universal. I myself have been impelled by a mysterious force; I have not created it, I have only obeyed its irresistible power." On the feast of St. Martin of that same year, what transports of joy and hope filled the heart of Mr. Dupont, when from his seat in the cathedral he heard Mgr. Pie, the illustrious Bishop of Poitiers, in an admirable panegyric, exclaim at the commencement of his peroration: "To you alone, Monseigneur, it belongs to decide upon the time which Providence has decreed for this work of regeneration. But as soon as you speak, France, the whole world, will listen to your voice. Popes will hear you, bishops will hear you, priests will hear you, consecrated virgins will hear you, all Religious orders will hear you, the poor will hear you, future ages will hear you." It is impossible to describe the effect produced by these words upon the immense audience present in the Metropolitan church.

The work, notwithstanding, made no progress. The Board resolved, in accordance with the advice of Mr. Dupont, to make a pilgrimage to Ligugé, where a few Benedictines from Solesmes had taken up their residence in the monastery recently restored to them. All the members, with the president, repaired thither on the 14th of December. Kneeling in the cell where the great thaumaturgus, when a simple monk under the guidance of St. Hilary, had resuscitated a dead man, they demanded of him "to resuscitate his Basilica." In passing through Poitiers, they called upon Mgr. Pie, to thank him for the animating and consoling words which he had pronounced in the cathedral of Tours. The prelate, in bestowing his blessing, spoke to them in the most encouraging terms. Before leaving the city of St. Hilary, they wished to visit the ancient and beautiful church dedicated to him, and only recently repaired. They visited it on a day of some religious ceremony; the choir, as they entered, were singing the Psalm, *Cantate Domino*,—a Psalm which Mr. Dupont particularly liked. The circumstance did not escape the attention of the pious pilgrim. He stood a moment at the door, listened to the music, then, turning to his friends, he exclaimed in delight: "It is a good omen; they are singing *Cantate*."

Not long after this a public pilgrimage, suggested by Mr. Dupont and authorized by the Archbishop, was made to Candes. It was the first general pilgrimage from Touraine to the memorable spot which was the scene of our Saint's death. Many fervent Christians, as well as a large number of clergymen, took part in it. The servant of God could scarcely restrain his joy; he was not astonished; nothing in the order of the divine mercies astonished his faith; but he was in an ecstasy of delight. What a completion to the "pilgrim's" devotion so long practiced secretly and solitarily! He gives the following account of it to a friend, ascribing it to the sentiments excited by the victory of Solferino, at that time a cause of great rejoicing throughout France. It was in 1859. "On Sunday, the 28th of August, we made the pilgrimage to Candes; on Saturday, June 25th, the news from Solferino reached us. The members of the Society for Clothing the Poor were inspired with the thought that St. Martin, being a Hungarian, that is, an Austrian by birth, and a Frenchman by adoption, was, of all the Saints, in the most favorable position to say: '*My children, sheathe the sword!*'" The idea originated with Mr. Dupont himself. "Thereupon, we made a vow to go as pilgrims to Candes, in thanksgiving, if there were no more battles, and peace should soon be made."… "St. Martin caused two emperors to take the pen in hand, and we were engaged by our promise to make the pilgrimage in honor of our holy patron: *Digitus Dei est hic!* 'The finger of God is here.' I am not surprised, but happy…." He continues: "M. l'Abbé Besnard, Vicar General, presided over the pilgrimage, which was accomplished in the most pious manner. At the Mass, more than eighty men and twenty ladies received Holy Communion. We left Tours to the number of one hundred and sixty; all the people from the surrounding country attended the ceremonies at the church, filling its vast enclosure. You would not, on that occasion, have recognized the reserved and cold citizen of Tours. You can form no idea of the enthusiasm which was excited."

We add to the details given above a circumstance not mentioned in the letter, but the truth of which is guaranteed by a credible eye-witness. The one hundred and sixty pilgrims from Tours, having gone by the railroad, followed the right bank of the Loire. But as Candes is situated on the left bank, they were obliged to cross the river. At their disposal were only five or six small boats, which a boatman of Varennes had engaged to furnish. The means of transportation were insufficient; they succeeded, however, although with much inconvenience, in reaching their destination. The crossing of the river, on their return, was far more difficult. The number of pilgrims from Tours had been augmented by those from the vicinity, so that the small boats, filled with passengers, sank in the water to the very edges. A frightful accident seemed inevitable. Mr. Dupont, who was to embark among the last, was on the shore saying his beads, and saw all that passed. One of the directors of the pilgrimage approached him in great alarm, and, pointing to a boat which was nearly submerged, called his attention to the danger to which it was exposed. The servant of God, continuing to say his beads, answered only in these words of the Gospel: "Why do you fear, O man of little faith?" He embarked on that same boat, inviting his friends to accompany him. Notwithstanding their serious and well-founded anxiety, no accident occurred; several ascribed, without hesitation, their safety to the prayers and faith of Mr. Dupont.

This first general pilgrimage of the inhabitants of Touraine to Candes, was the origin of those which have since been made annually. It was, also, this impulse given by the name of St. Martin, which culminated later in those grand pilgrimages to Lourdes, Paray-le-Monial and other celebrated sanctuaries, which have been so fruitful of consolation and of hope for the future. Inspired and organized by Mr. Dupont for an object eminently national and French, it seems to have imprinted its character on all which have succeeded it, and it is but just to attribute the initiative to the pilgrim of Saint-Etienne street.

The work of St. Martin was not long in deriving particular benedictions from its influence. In a circular letter dated December 8, 1859, Mgr. Guibert announced his intention to replace the tomb of St. Martin on the spot it had formerly occupied. He asked the concurrence of his clergy in the execution of the "design of a few pious faithful who," he said, "had formed the project of purchasing, on their own responsibility, three houses situated over the site occupied by the tomb, in order to restore it to its original place, to return its precious relics, and to erect around it a chapel for the use of pilgrims." The Archbishop added that he could but approve the noble and generous project of these pious men, and that he had pledged himself to recommend their enterprise to charitable souls. He therefore authorized "every member of the Board of the Clothing Society" to make private collections in the city and throughout the diocess, reserving to himself the more particular permission for a public collection, when the time would come to enclose the tomb in a suitable sanctuary.

Mr. Dupont had gained a great deal. He accepted this public action of his Archbishop as a precious pledge of the realization of his dearest hopes. He derived consolation, also, from a little event, an account of which we give in his own words. "Everything induces us to believe that our glorious patron is lending his aid to this work of reparation. Among other proofs, we have the following: the very day that we took possession of one of the houses as a temporary place of meeting for the members of the Society, a neighbor offered us, as the first stone, a bass-relief taken from the Basilica of St. Martin, which represented our Lord receiving six pilgrims. This bass-relief, composed of two enormous blocks of hard stone, about six feet long, had been lying, for years, in the cellar of a grocer, the figures and the inscription being turned towards the ground. We eagerly cleared away the dirt which covered the inscription. Imagine our joy, as, letter by letter, the inscription become legible. At first, we were struck only by the sight of the six pilgrims and the first words of the inscription: *Peregrini sumus...* 'We are pilgrims.' But what was our delight upon discovering that the words were those of David, pronounced at the time that he gave his command to Solomon to construct the temple. This bass-relief, which is apparently a work of the 14th century, is now piously preserved in the temporary chapel of St. Martin. On examining it, we can readily understand the impression made upon the six members of the Clothing Society."

In the meantime, explorations had been made in one of the houses which had been purchased, and discoveries of different foundations furnished them with sufficiént basis by which to determine the axis of the Basilica, and, consequently, of the tomb also. A peculiar circumstance occurred at that time, of little importance intrinsically, but one which was regarded by Mr. Dupont and his colleagues as a presage of success. A draughtsman, in the employ of the Railroad Company, had been directed to go to the cellars and make a drawing of the masonry which had been uncovered. On his return after the completion of the work, he stated that, whilst he was engaged on the drawing, he heard a heavenly music, sweet and melodious. Supposing that he was deceived by his imagination, he left the cellar and asked the tenant of the house if he had heard any extraordinary music. Receiving an answer in the negative, he went into the street, but saw no one, nor discovered any cause to which it could be attributed. But as soon as he again descended into the cellar, the same enchanting strains commenced anew. He was convinced that they were supernatural, and he signed a written declaration of the statement which he had made, immediately after its occurrence, to a member of the commission by whom it was countersigned. Mr. Dupont considered the circumstance as a divine manifestation to man that Heaven was rejoicing: it was, he thought, the happy commencement of the great work of reparation.

In consequence of the discoveries already made, it was decided to arrange a temporary chapel above the cellar of one of the houses which had been purchased. The oratory was blessed on the 12th of November, 1860, the day following the feast of St. Martin: holy water, which had been blessed in the ancient Basilica and religiously preserved by a canon and his heirs, was used on the occasion. The Archbishop, surrounded by his Vicar Generals, the cathedral Chapter, and the curates of the city, celebrated the Mass, restoring in this holy place the sacrifice which had been discontinued there for seventy years. On the previous evening, Mr. Dupont, with the other members of the Board, descended into the cellar which lay beneath the oratory, and suspended from the ceiling a lamp which they lighted, and which has never since been extinguished. This first act of a reparation so long desired, was enthusiastically welcomed by the city and diocese. During the succeeding seven days, a large concourse of people crowded into the temporary chapel and the cellar. The faithful prayed fervently; they knelt under the lamp suspended from the ceiling; they kissed with devotion the red cross traced upon the wall in the supposed direction of the tomb. Some left wax candles to be burned; others, incense; flowers were carried to decorate the hallowed spot. It was calculated that twenty thousand persons, at least, had visited the place.

The servant of God followed the minutest detail with deep interest, and gave expression to his delight in his letters to his friends: "Our expectations," he writes, "were far surpassed at the benediction of the Chapel of St. Martin. During the Octave, the cellar was constantly filled with men in prayer. A hundred and eighty candles were kept burning, about sixty Masses were celebrated, and there were more than eight hundred Communions. Every one is impressed; all feel that something supernatural has passed in their midst." This was written a few weeks after the battle of Castelfidardo, and he adds: "Perhaps this is the signal of reparation. At least, we can, with a simple faith, cry unto Heaven and pray, like Zachary, that God will bring to an end the captivity of the Church, saying: 'Behold, O Lord, it is now seventy years.'"

In the meantime, the members had not been idle; they had energetically pushed their researches, and Mr. Moisant, who had already so generously contributed to the work, made another donation, in order to hasten the departure of a tenant occupying the cellar in which they anticipated finding the precious tomb.

All difficulties being thus removed, the explorations in the cellars were resumed, and, in order to work without interruption from the crowd of visitors, they walled up the doors giving access to the one, of which they had just obtained possession. A few workmen, with a superintendent to direct them, were thus enclosed in the cellar. They were to leave it, only by opening for themselves a passage through the wall into that part of the Basilica which had already been restored. The President, the members of the Board, and about thirty others, had collected there, to watch the progress of the work, which had been commenced in that place also, in order to aid, on that side, the workmen in the other cellar. They had conveyed a harmonium to the apartment, not, for a moment, suspecting the discovery they were about to make; but, as this spot was being explored for the first time, all were anxiously awaiting the result, and were engaged in fervent prayer. An ecclesiastic was seated at the harmonium, ready to touch it at the given signal; others were near him, prepared to unite their voices with his; among them a venerable pastor, the oldest clergyman of the diocess, who had performed the duty of choir-boy in the ancient Basilica. Mr. Dupont, serious and recollected, walked slowly from one wall to the other, praying in silence, stopping, at intervals, near the part of the wall which was to be pierced.

It was eleven o'clock in the evening. The work, although skilfully directed, had been long and hard, exciting, by turns, hope and anxiety. It had been decided to break through the wall at the spot marked by the red cross. In order to work in concert, and, particularly, to avoid the danger of deviating from the axis of the Basilica, upon which they knew the tomb rested, they had made a small opening in the wall so as to place the two bands of workmen in communication with each other. They were working earnestly, when, suddenly, those who were in the cellar recently purchased, noticed among the pieces which fell under the stroke of the hammer a few fragments of white stone. The superintendent examined them attentively, and saw that they were evidently of a more ancient date than the rest of the masonry. Cut transversely and hidden by a thick wall of more recent construction, there arose before him two small parallel walls of white gravel-stone, distant from each other about sixty-five centimetres, presenting at the top two arch-stones, the commencement of an arch no longer existing—crushed, no doubt, by the superincumbent modern wall. There is no hesitation in deciding that they are now looking upon the two parallel sides of the sepulchre or vault in which, after the ravages of the Huguenots, the ashes of the Saint had been collected, and in which his body had formerly been deposited. At the first sight of the white stones, the superintendent requested the work to be suspended on the opposite side. After a rapid examination, he made a sketch of the masonry now exposed to his view, and passed it through the opening in the wall to the commissioners, in order to receive further instructions. The preliminary examinations which had been made forced upon them the conviction, as soon as they saw the sketch, that the tomb of St. Martin had been found. Mr. Dupont announced the discovery to the faithful, who were kneeling in fervent prayer, anxiously and impatiently awaiting the result. The news was received with a transport of joy, and an intensity of emotion impossible to describe. One of the priests solemnly entones the Magnificat; it is continued by all present in alternate choirs in the two cellars on each side of the wall; never will those who participated in it forget the effect produced by that chant of thanksgiving.

CHAPTER X

After singing the *Magnificat*, the men resume their work energetically, but cautiously. The little monument is soon entirely disclosed to view, and they are satisfied that it is but slightly damaged; only the upper part is missing. The communication between the two cellars having been completed, the commissioners are able to visit and verify, in person, the important discovery so providentially accomplished. For, in effect, God permitted that on the 14th of December, 1860, the precise location of the tomb of His great servant, concealed during seventy years under profane buildings, should be discovered and restored to the piety of the faithful.

That was enough for Mr. Dupont. Fearful lest his unusual and prolonged absence might cause anxiety to his aged mother, who was unaccustomed to see him return so late, he hastened home. To her questions, he replied: "Rejoice, Mother, at last we have found it; we possess it!" The joy of the devout servant of St. Martin appears in all the letters written by him at that period. "I should have told you, my dear friend," he writes to one of them, "that we have been paying great attention here to the reparation of the Church of St. Martin. On a day observed as one of his feasts in the diocess of Tours, the vault, in which his venerable relics had reposed, was discovered, the discovery having been brought about by circumstances so manifestly miraculous, that all vie with each other in exclaiming: 'A miracle!'..." He wrote the following day: "Yesterday at midnight the explorations conducted us to the tomb of St. Martin, somewhat mutilated, it is true, but perfectly recognizable, and, this afternoon, several archaeologists have examined the spot and confirmed the discovery."

The news spread through Tours and the inhabitants were deeply moved. The spot was visited, not only by the Archbishop and numerous ecclesiastics, but also by the most learned laymen and the Society of Archaeologists, represented by its president, secretaries and other members of the Bureau. Mr. Lambron de Lignim, an erudite antiquary, who had found in the archives of Tours a curious verbal process of 1686, was also there. He proved satisfactorily to himself and his colleagues that the small vault of white gravel-stone, mentioned as the sepulchre of St. Martin in this important document, corresponded exactly, by its dimensions and form, with the small vault recently discovered. All present were convinced that the latter was, if not the sepulchre itself, at least the locality of that ancient and venerable monument. Many went further, and firmly believed that it was, not only the very place of the tomb which the Huguenots wished to destroy, but the original tomb built by St. Perpetuus, the same in which the body of the thaumaturgus was deposited sixty-four years after his death.

According to this view, the remains of the edifice of St. Perpetuus had become, in consequence of the accumulation of soil, a kind of vault completely concealed by the earth which covered it. The fury of the Huguenots was aimed, first, against shrines, then, against mausoleums, the altar and the ciborium. They destroyed all that was above ground, and it might, naturally, have happened that they did not discover the small vault hidden under the earth which thus escaped their sacrilegious devastations. Is it not wonderful that, by this providential disposition, the edifice of St. Perpetuus escaped the rage of the Huguenots, and that our century has the glory of restoring to the veneration of the Christian world the remains of that tomb in which the body of the thaumaturgus was enclosed for a thousand years? Such ideas as these charmed the beautiful soul of Mr. Dupont. He admired the hand of Providence in every detail we have related of the discovery. He traced coincidences which excited his gratitude, and inspired him with strong hope for the future.

Measures were soon adopted to enable pilgrims to venerate the holy tomb. The two cellars were cleared of the lumber, and temporarily arranged as a crypte, to which the crowd of visitors could obtain access; for the faithful flocked thither; priests and strange prelates went to celebrate the divine mysteries, and pilgrimages were organized in various parishes to visit the holy spot.

In order to give an idea of the decided change which had been effected in the usual social customs of Tours by the recent discovery, we will relate the following incident relative to the pilgrimage of an illustrious foreign lady, the Countess Marie de D——. That lady, a native of Peggau in Styria, near which place St. Martin was born, had left her home accompanied by her chaplain, for the purpose of making the four great pilgrimages of Christendom. She had visited Jerusalem, Rome, and St. James of Compostella, and on June 25, 1861, she arrived at Tours, wholly ignorant that the sepulchre of the patron of the city had, for years, been withdrawn from the veneration of the faithful. Alighting at a hotel, her almoner requested to be directed to the "tomb of St. Martin." He was told by those of whom he made the inquiry that they did not know what he meant, adding that there was not in the city even a church dedicated to St. Martin. The chaplain next proceeded to the cathedral to obtain information on the subject, and there he learned from an ecclesiastic how the "tomb" had just been discovered. The pious Countess was conducted to the temporary chapel, and she had thus the opportunity of satisfying her devotion and accomplishing her fourth vow.

From that time, the idea of rebuilding the ancient Basilica ceased to be considered strange and chimerical; by degrees, the project became popular, and the sentiment of the people found expression in practices of devotion and religious ceremonies on certain festival days, particularly on the feast of St. Martin; even the public organs of the civil administration concurred in giving vitality to the undertaking. The city of Tours, to material prosperity, wished to add the embellishment of art. Streets were being opened and extended, in order to afford a more convenient communication between the elegant buildings; new edifices were in process of erection which were considered necessary, not only to supply the wants of the citizens, but to increase the splendor of the city. Amid these desires of luxury and comfort, the thought of St. Martin had acquired the pre-eminence it deserved. All hearts properly estimated the importance of honoring the protector of the city in a particular manner, of consecrating a monument to his memory, of building an edifice to the ancient thaumaturgus, which would again, as in former times, attract a crowd of strangers and pilgrims to the city.

What kind of building should it be? Of what size? Every one answered these points according to his individual views; no one contested the principle. Mgr. Guibert, watching a favorable opportunity, took advantage of the issue of bonds by the city, for the purpose of raising funds to carry on the works of which we have spoken above, to propose the reconstruction of the Church of St. Martin, avoiding, however, the proposal of any particular plan. The municipal council appointed a commission chosen from their own members to examine into the case, and upon receiving a favorable report from the city engineer, they adopted, almost unanimously, the proposition of the Archbishop, tracing out themselves the portion of the ancient Basilica to be reconstructed on the existing foundations, and also the ground to be purchased, limiting to two million francs the amount to be subscribed before commencing work.

The success of this application to the Council was followed by a Pastoral addressed by Mgr. Guibert to the clergy and laity of his diocess, in reference to the reconstruction of the Basilica of St. Martin. Without deciding, as yet, upon the extent and proportions of the building, the prudent prelate indicated the principal points. "The new edifice," he said, "should be constructed upon the foundations of the ancient church, which are found to be near the

surface of the ground, in order that the tomb might occupy its former relative position; the Basilica ought to be connected with the tower of Charlemagne, which is in a perfect state of preservation; the whole edifice should present, by its size and beauty of construction, a monument worthy of the grand remembrances it is intended to perpetuate."
The Archbishop, at the same time, ordered collections to be made, and authorized an appeal to the Catholic world. "It is not for ourselves alone," he said, "that we desire to rebuild the sanctuary of St. Martin, but for the faithful of every nation. The work we are about to undertake is a national one, since its object is to glorify the most illustrious Saint of our country; but it interests, also, the whole church; for, there exists in the depths of my heart a presentiment that the restoration of devotion to St. Martin in its former fervor, will be the signal for the religious renovation of our own country and of many others." This presentiment of the Archbishop echoed the aspirations of other great minds, and particularly those so long cherished by Mr. Dupont. Therefore, we find him elated by joy and filled with gratitude. He writes on November 9th: "I will send you shortly the Pastoral of Monseigneur on the Work of St. Martin. The affair could not commence with greater prestige.".... "Let us hope that the awakening of devotion to St. Martin will be the signal of peculiar benedictions."

In his Pastoral, the Archbishop of Tours had nominated for the work of reconstruction a special commission composed of twenty-five members, among whom were the members of the first committee of the Clothing Society, and, consequently, Mr. Dupont was included in the number. At the first meeting, Monseigneur expressed his desire to commence the crypte as soon as possible.

The appeal of Mgr. Guibert to his colleagues in the episcopacy met with a prompt and favorable reply, as we learn from a letter of Mr. Dupont who writes as follows: "The work of St. Martin is progressing in the most satisfactory manner. Fifty-four bishops have responded favorably, and more than twelve have already issued Pastorals appealing to the piety of the faithful in behalf of the work of the reconstruction of the Basilica."

Satan could not behold without rage, nor leave unavenged, a success so easily obtained. An inexplicable opposition was suddenly manifested. First, the prefect, contrary to all expectation, refused his approbation to the decision of the City Council respecting the reconstruction of the Basilica. Then, defamatory articles were published against the members of the Clothing Society and of the Council; verses and songs to their discredit were circulated. Mr. Dupont was neither alarmed nor surprised. "The work of St. Martin," he said, "is vehemently combated by the worthy sons of the destroyers of his Basilica, but we do not falter in our hope, since the order to build comes from Heaven: *Tempus reædificandi.*" Attentively watching the progress of events, he continues to pray, and to advise pilgrimages as a means of conquering the evil spirit, and of triumphing over every obstacle. At his suggestion, and for this intention, a general pilgrimage to Candes was organized in the month of August, 1862. It met with great success, and one of its results was the decision made the following month, to render the access to the tomb easy for visitors, and to open it to the public.

A plan of a temporary church, capable of holding about fifteen hundred persons, had been drawn; it was adopted; and the new chapel, built to replace the small oratory which, for three years, had been the centre of the revived devotion to St. Martin, was dedicated November 11, 1863. Mgr. Guibert blessed it with great solemnity. However, many difficulties arose in consequence of the various plans proposed and urged upon the commissioners. Mr. Dupont, although alarmed, maintained a wonderful serenity and confidence. Instead of lamenting the state of affairs, or spending time in discussions, he humbly kept silence, contenting himself with encouraging his colleagues to persevere in prayer. When all their plans were endangered, or seemed about to fail, he would say: "We must have recourse to the powerful remedy;" and he would propose a pilgrimage. The remedy always proved efficacious. Then, the holy man, in a transport of joy, would raise his eyes to Heaven, and exhort his friends not to distrust Providence, but to await with confidence the hour of deliverance. *Expectans expectavi*, he would say: "*With expectation I have waited for the Lord.*"

"The calm and resigned attitude of our president," says one of the commissioners, "was not only an example to us, but it was the best means of advancing the work. We owe our success entirely to him, his influence, and his prayers."

Mr. Dupont, whose devotion to St. Martin was animated by an unbounded confidence, exulted in the evidence of big powerful intercession furnished by the two following incidents, which occurred in the temporary chapel.

During its construction, a portion of the scaffolding gave way, precipitating to the ground one of the masons, who was buried under the stones and lumber. He was taken out crushed and dying. He had worked for the discovery of the tomb with a strong faith and ardent zeal; and so efficacious were the prayers addressed to St. Martin by the servant of God, that he was restored to health the same night, and resumed his labors, as usual, the following morning.

The other incident regards Madame Viot-Otter, a pious and venerable lady of Tours, an Englishwoman by birth, sixty years of age, a great friend of Mr. Dupont. Whilst showing the sepulchre of the Saint to an illustrious foreigner, the Marchioness of Lothian, well known in England for her devotion to every Catholic work, she fell into a deep opening, made by the removal of a staircase which had been used by the public. She arose immediately without having received even a bruise; her miraculous preservation was attributed to the protection of St. Martin.

An equally visible protection of St. Martin enabled the commissioners to purchase certain houses near the precious tomb, which they would require later for the construction of the Basilica. In a fortnight, a number of these houses were bought by them for the sum of five hundred and fifty thousand francs. The operation was conducted with such celerity and secrecy, that the intervention of the good angels and the power of the thaumaturgus were evident. From the following passage which occurs in one of his letters, we can judge the joy experienced by Mr. Dupont: "The affairs relating to St. Martin have advanced incredibly during the past week. A worthy man bought, at a low price, all the houses which cover the ground occupied by the ancient Basilica. The Archbishop had simply said to him: 'Go and buy.' The enemies of St. Martin were struck as by a thunderbolt."

The following year, 1865, a magnificent relic-case, presented by Mr. Moisant, was placed above the tomb where it still remains. Within it, was deposited a relic consisting of a fragment of a bone of St. Martin. Thus was the glorious sepulchre properly honored; and, from that time, the people have visited it in crowds, including, among them, all the celebrated men of our day. Illustrious prelates, Religious, priests of every order and from every country, have there celebrated the holy mysteries. The Prussian invasion and the siege of Paris, brought the provisional government to Tours, and the tomb of St. Martin became the centre of uninterrupted prayer, where the faithful had recourse to God in their necessities.

At the close of the war, Mgr. Guibert was elevated to the See of Paris, and Mgr. Fruchaud succeeded him in the See of Tours. Carrying out the intentions of the new prelate, the commissioners of St. Martin directed one of our most skilful architects to draw a plan of the Basilica, reproducing, as nearly as possible, what the ancient Basilica must have been in the eleventh century. This plan, highly praised by connoisseurs, obtained in 1875 a gold medal at the Exposition of Fine Arts. At present, it is at the archiepiscopal palace, where, although it is only a sketch, it excites the desire and hope of all who contemplate it. Mgr. Colet, entertaining the same views as his predecessors, forwards indefatigably the preparations for reconstruction, and appears desirous of commencing operations as soon as circumstances favor the undertaking. The members of the Clothing Society are actively engaged in forwarding the work. As long as Mr. Dupont lived, the meetings were held at his house. When compelled by age and infirmities to keep his room, he aided his fellow members by his counsels, strengthening their resolution to continue the work, and animating their confidence in its success.

We wished to relate under one head the influence exercised, in various ways, by the servant of God over the project of the reconstruction of the Basilica of St. Martin, which at present so justly attracts the attention of the Catholic world. It is evident that Mr. Dupont was the first one who entertained the thought seriously and efficaciously; from his arrival at Tours until his death, he never ceased to act, to speak, to pray for this intention with the imperturbable confidence of his faith and the persevering ardor of his charity; it was in his drawing-room and in his presence, that were successively presented, discussed and prepared the different plans relating either to the discovery of the tomb and the foundations of the ancient Basilica, or to the construction of the future Basilica. If then Touraine be honored, and France regenerated by this work in the manner we hope, the happy result should be attributed to the influence and prayers of this pious layman, raised up by God to be the type of a true Christian in modern times.

We should not overlook the prevailing idea which governed Mr. Dupont's action in this holy enterprise,—that of reparation. With some it was a question of architecture and religious art; others considered it with a view to public utility, local interest, or national glory. Whilst the man of God did not exclude these considerations, chief and above all others, was the act of expiation. A satanic outrage, a sacrilegious crime had been committed against the majesty of God: to repair this crime, it was necessary to rebuild what had been destroyed. Therefore, he ardently desired to see erected, not a modern church, beautiful and spacious, but a Basilica reposing upon the foundations of the ancient one, possessing, if not the same form, at least proportions analogous to its imposing grandeur. It was thus, he thought, that the present generation would expiate the crime of their fathers, would offer a just homage to our Lord, and would conquer the perpetual adversary of St. Martin on the very spot, of which he believed himself the invincible and tranquil possessor.

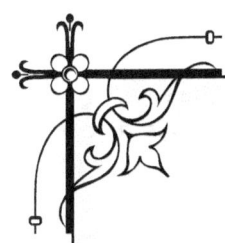

Chapter XI

Satan and the Medal of St. Benedict.

In the school of St. Martin Mr. Dupont had learned to combat the enemy of mankind by the arms of faith and prayer. A peculiar and strong hatred for Satan, manifested in every manner and on all occasions, was a special feature in the character of the servant of God. Like the holy Bishop of Tours, he considered Satan as the great adversary of all good, the perpetual and bitter enemy of God and man, whom we should pursue and thwart, without ever wearying, or relaxing in our efforts. His eminently supernatural and Christian instinct, and his assiduous study of the Scriptures, discovered to him the more or less direct action of the demon in numerous circumstances where it was concealed from others.

A diabolical influence was particularly evident to his discernment in the progress of the revolution. The Voltarian and revolutionary spirit, as understood by him, was Satan rendered visible and active. At a certain period, when the revolution seemed to triumph, he said: "We should pray fervently that Satan may not become master of the situation." He was not, consequently, surprised at the Satanic fury exercised in our day: "The necessity of devoting ourselves to the cause of our Lord," he said, "becomes daily more imperative, because the efforts of Satan are visibly more energetic. The wretch comprehends that the Church will rise victorious over the sea of iniquities composed of modern heresies, and his cupidity knows no bounds; he would wish to swallow at one gulp the present generation, so well instructed how to advance under his infernal inspiration." In his conversations, he strongly recommended, particularly the young, to distrust the devil; "because," he said, "he thrusts himself everywhere: in a game of cards, in a guitar, in a ringlet, in a spoonful of soup, &c..."

In the least obstacle to devotion to St. Martin, he discerned a trick, a snare of the evil spirit. He entered the chapel one day just as the sacristan, the sexton, and a priest were standing, in low conversation near the poor-box, which they wished to open. Each had tried, in vain, to turn the key. Mr. Dupont approached, and they mentioned their difficulty to him. "It is a trick of Satan," he said, shrugging his shoulders; taking the key he plunged it into the holy water-font, and handing it to them, said, "Unlock it now." The key turned with perfect ease, and the box was opened. He had applied the means indicated by St. Theresa, who declares from her own experience, that how powerful soever the demon may be, a little holy water used with faith and humility suffices to baffle his snares and put him to flight.

He beheld with sorrow this fatal influence in the corrupt press. "Of a certainty," he said, "the cause of all the scourges which desolate the world, may be traced to the pen, which Satan has enlisted in his cause." He, therefore, encouraged Catholic writers to become the champions of the Church. "When St. Michael," he says, "took his sword in hand to combat Satan, he, undoubtedly, obeyed the command of the Sovereign Master. The struggle still continues, and, from age to age, the good God raises up defenders of His glory. Honor to those who are called to do battle in His cause in the nineteenth century, when hell, perceiving that the number of the damned is nearly filled up, redoubles its fury against the elect!"

Then addressing particularly one of these valiant writers, he says: "Honor be to you, my dear brother, and victory likewise! Armed with faith, you can have no fear of the battalions, the legions, in array against you... Be courageous, since the head of the beast reappears notwithstanding his wounds. Oh! how long eternity will be to him, when the hour of his 'repose' in the abyss will have come! For, at the present moment, he enjoys himself, in his own way, in such men as Garibaldi and Renan." (This was in 1864.) "May the Lord strengthen your arm, and uphold it, as He upheld the arm of Moses, to enable you to strike well-directed blows against the wicked beast which rules, with sovereign sway, over our century sunk in sensuality and luxury."

He thinks, moreover, that it is useful that Satan should be represented to men such as he really is. "Our good God," he writes to the same friend, "has raised you up in an opportune time to unmask the devil to His children. It is a great grace granted at this time, when men deny the existence of the evil spirit and thus advance his interests. St. Paul says the Jews would not have crucified Jesus Christ, if they had known him: have we not reason to believe that Satan would have fewer followers, if he were better known? Use your speech as David used his sling against Goliah."

The rage of Satan thus let loose in the world, far from exciting Mr. Dupont's anxiety for the future, only increased his confidence. He beheld in it, simply, a proof of the fury of hell aroused by certain unexpected manifestations of Catholic faith. "The rage of the demon," he says, "is evinced by the malignity of his dupes; it is a sign that our Lord is granting us graces capable of regenerating the world. The evil is so great that God alone can give the victory to His Church, and give it in so striking a manner as openly to confound his enemies."... "It is evident that our contest is not against flesh and blood, that is, not against Mr. such-a-one, but against the infernal spirit, that it is against 'the beast,' the wicked beast, who lost only his sanctity by his fall: his power is still very great." He adds: "His chain is long just now, but I hope he will soon receive the order to return to his kennel."

In order to overcome the demon, he advised, above all else, faith and prayer. "The halter of 'the beast,'" he says, "is extremely loose, and the 'knave' takes advantage of it. It is time to raise the hue and cry against him, and say to him: Avaunt!... If he shows no sign of obeying, as obedience costs him much, then bearing in mind the words fulminated by our Lord, cry out: *Vade retro!* If we were always animated by a lively faith, we should often inflict great torture upon him, when he places obstacles in our way."

But in order to overcome or drive away the demon, he had a method peculiar to himself, which characterized him in an amusing manner. His idea was to "humiliate" this proud spirit, and with this intention, to treat him with the contempt he deserved. He considered no epithet more contemptuous and humiliating than the one given him in the Scriptures: *Antiquus serpens*, "the old serpent," because it recalled his first crime and the period of his fall. Applying this word then according to his idea, he called Satan "the old serpent," "the doting old man." "We are thus certain," he would say, "of putting him to flight, covered with shame and filled with rage. That word rouses his fury. In proof of the truth of this, make the experiment. If you are tempted, call him by that name. Say: 'Oh! oh! old man, I know you; away with you!' The old man is proud; he does not like that sobriquet; it is a kind of insult which torments and drives him away." He ridiculed "his horns, his nose, his tail." After reading a small book in which the devil was combated in a bright and witty manner, he said: "The old man will, hereafter, have his nose as long as his tail."

Comparing Satan to "a furious dog," he amused himself by describing him, seated on the ruins of St. Martin, as a large, plump animal enjoying for a long time a peaceful sovereignty; then he depicted the rage to which he would

CHAPTER XI

be aroused, when he would be driven in shame from a spot where he thought he should always remain the master. The very idea would make Mr. Dupont laugh heartily.

This comparison of "mad dog," or "chained dog" applied to the devil, pleased him, and he repeated it frequently. He had taken it from the Psalms: "Deliver, O God, my soul from the hands of the dog." "May our Lord be pleased," he writes to an author, "to impose silence on him whom you name so properly 'the knave,' and whom you abuse so charmingly. But he cannot bite beyond the length of his leash." "God grant you increased strength," he writes to the same friend, "that you may be able to force Satan to disgorge his prey! Prayer alone can make him loose his hold. The old enemy is powerful when the Master does not present Himself: witness the swine at the lake of Genesareth."

Satan was often the subject of the playful conversations in which Mr. Dupont indulged with intimate friends. On those occasions, he would jeer him, apostrophizing him in a contemptuous and ironical manner, using in his regard burlesque expressions and figures of speech. He would call him "the old liar," "the beast," the "amphibious animal," "the hog." Sometimes he represented him as biting his tail from rage and spite, and again as smoking it for a cigar: "This beast, this hog, sucks his tail. Why does he like to do so?"

The reader is, naturally, astonished to find such expressions in the mouth of a man so refined in his tastes, and so polished in his manners. He himself gives an answer. "Let us not hesitate," he said, "to think evil and to speak evil of the devil: he is the father of all evils, and we can only be on our guard against him through divine inspirations. Besides, in order not to think or speak evil of him, we must necessarily deny his existence, and this is what is done seriously by his dupes."

As for himself, he has no intention of sparing him in any manner. "We must," he says, "combat to the death the 'amphibious monster,' if we may thus name a creature which lives in hell, and can live on earth at the same time. As we cannot descend into hell to chain him there, let us go to the Heart of Jesus, and seek for arms with which to combat him on earth."

Seeing Satan thus abused by Mr. Dupont, we might be surprised that this wicked spirit did not seek to revenge himself by endeavoring to injure him, as he did St. Martin and other saints. A few lines jocosely written by the servant of God, brought to our knowledge the following circumstances. Hearing that an accident had happened to one of his friends on the 29th of April, he wrote to him: "I would wager that Satan had the idea of injuring both of us: during the day of the 28th, on hearing of the triumph of grace in a remarkable conversion, I laughed at the 'evil one,' saying that he was then, no doubt, like the hogs which are being sent from the slaughter-house to the butcher, on his back, with his paws in the air! However it may be, on the following night, I had a horrible nightmare. What terrified me was an ox, having on his forehead above his eyes a blasphemous label. The animal was rushing upon me, and I plunged into a deep hole to avoid the abominable label. But the hole proved to be the brick floor of my room, and I found myself lying on my right side, a singular circumstance for which I could not account; for, it would seem an impossibility that I should not have fallen on my left side. Now, what convinces me that Satan had a hand in this fall, is that on being suddenly awakened, and finding myself on the ground, I kissed the floor and said: 'My God, I thank Thee.' My right side was skinned; but I suffered no other inconvenience."

The other incident was mentioned to us by a reliable and intelligent layman. "Mr. Dupont spoke to me," he says, "several times of the struggles he had with Satan during the nights of the Adoration. On one occasion, particularly, he said he was lifted from his bed by his infernal enemy, and whirled in the air, and then dropped across the bed."

CHAPTER XI

The Nocturnal Adoration being a work of faith, sacrifice, and love, it appeared to Mr. Dupont to be one of the most efficacious means of overcoming this adversary. "I am not surprised," he wrote to a friend, "at the efforts of Satan to prevent our correspondence, since it is particularly devoted to bringing him to shame, and to mitigating the effects of his rage. He must have changed in a wonderful manner his habit of sitting with 'his paws crossed,' when he saw you taking time from your sleep to send petitions to the Nocturnal Adoration. It is, moreover, during the night that he concentrates his forces, because, on the one hand, his children then abandon themselves to every disorder, and on the other, Christians, after having made the sign of the cross, repose under the guard of their good angels. The poet described our enemy when he wrote: *Nox apta criminibus:* 'The night favorable to crime.'" He wrote on another occasion these beautiful words; "Let us advance in the love of God, and Satan will be forced to fly: he can live at his ease only in the fire of hell, since he replaced charity, by hate, in his heart."

He recommends, as a help to overcome the temptation to slander, the practice of touching the fingers to the tongue whilst they are still moist with the holy water, with which we have made the sign of the cross upon leaving the church. "The evil spirit will allow, at least, a short time to pass without attempting to rest upon it."

However, the weapon he employed the most frequently against the demon, was the medal of St. Benedict.

After having secured the most authentic design, he had a number struck off, and he became the zealous propagator of the devotion, and a generous distributor of the medals. He purchased them by thousands, of different materials and various sizes. He had them always in his house and about his person, in order to give them to visitors or to those whom he might meet.

When Dom Pitra went from Solesmes to Rome at the request of Pius IX, from whom he soon received the purple, Mr. Dupont, being well acquainted with this worthy disciple of Dom Guéranger, thought he had a favorable opportunity of forwarding to the Holy Father one of his precious medals: it was of gold, and accompanied by a little book on the origin and effects of the medal of St. Benedict. Cardinal Pitra personally presented the medal to Pius IX, to the great satisfaction of Mr. Dupont. A few days afterwards a violent water-spout broke over the Vatican; all the lamps and panes of glass in the palace were broken, with the exception of those in the room where Pius IX was at the time. So great was the damage, that the king of Bavaria, who was at Rome, considered his offering a large one, when he repaired the injury done the building at his own expense. "Ah!" wrote Mr. Dupont, "the coincidence between the medal and the water-spout is not without its significance, and we, who know the value of the medal, can rejoice in its efficacy on this occasion."

This fervent Christian never went on a journey without taking with him a quantity of these medals, to use either for himself or others. He was one day in a stage-coach, crowded with passengers, when it was nearly upset in a street, from which a portion of the paving had been removed. All were astonished at having escaped a danger which appeared inevitable; as for Mr. Dupont, he exhibited triumphantly to his travelling companions a medal of St. Benedict, to which he attributed their preservation.

In 1839, a celebrated magnetizer, who had been very successful in several cities of France, stopped in Tours to give an exhibition. He was accompanied by a young girl, a somnambulist, who was very profitable to him. The exhibition was to take place in a very large and ancient church which had been sold during the revolution. Mr. Dupont, having heard these details, went to the Carmelite convent, and asked to see the prioress, Mother Mary of the Incarnation.

"Will you help me, Reverend Mother," he said, "to play a trick on the devil?" "Very willingly," she replied. Mr. Dupont informed her of the proposed meeting not far from the monastery, and gave her a medal of St. Benedict. It was agreed between them that, in the evening at the hour appointed for the exhibition of the magnetizer, the prioress of the Carmelites should suspend the medal outside the window of her cell, which faced the place where the meeting was to be held. The plan thus formed was carried into execution, and Mr. Dupont and the prioress continued in prayer. What was the result? A large crowd, attracted by curiosity, had collected to witness the performances of the magnetizer, but they were entirely disappointed in their expectations. The clairvoyant could see nothing; the action of the magnetizer had no effect over her. The magnetizer was astonished; as they had in their possession money belonging to the public, they announced an exhibition for the following evening, ascribing their failure to the indisposition of the somnambulist. Mr. Dupont and the prioress of the Carmelites continued their anti-satanic plan and the prayers to St. Benedict. Again, the failure was complete. The following day, the magnetizer left Tours, to the great joy of Mr. Dupont, who, rubbing his hands with delight, rejoiced at the victory won by St. Benedict over a tool of his old enemy.

The servant of God was accustomed to throw medals in the foundations, or around the walls of certain edifices, from which he wished to expel Satan. How many he threw in the cellars and houses near the ruins of St. Martin! In order to secure possession of the property judged requisite for the reconstruction of the Basilica, it was necessary to act with great prudence, lest the proprietors should discover the importance which was attached to the purchase; other difficulties of various kinds arose. Mr. Dupont was careful to drop medals in the cellars, or to conceal them in the walls. The effect of the power of St. Benedict was soon visible; the agreement was made, and the purchase concluded, generally to the advantage of the commissioners.

A house was being built in the suburbs of Tours upon which the laborers worked on Sundays, to the great scandal of the neighborhood. Mr. Dupont, passing by one Sunday, witnessed the profanation. He threw a medal of St. Benedict into the masonwork. The following morning, the laborers were stupefied upon finding that the whole house had fallen.

The municipal council of Saumur decided in 1840, by the suggestion of the city engineer and under pretext of widening the street, to cut off a large portion of the ancient sanctuary dedicated to the Blessed Virgin, under the title of Notre-Dame des Ardilliers. In pursuance of this plan, they commenced the construction of a partition-wall to run the whole length of the church. The chapel of the Blessed Virgin, the object of so many pilgrimages, was thus sacrificed to a highway. The wall was already raised to the height of twenty feet, and the church, encumbered with materials, was ready for the workmen. Mr. Dupont, passing through the city as a traveller, was, at first, shocked and indignant at such a profanation. Soon, however, becoming calm and confident, he said: "No, no, this shall not be!" He proposed to his companions to attach a medal of St. Benedict to the statue of our Lady, which had been temporarily placed on the opposite side. He did this with the serenity of faith which was characteristic of him. A few days afterwards, the engineer, who had suggested the wicked thought of mutilating the house of God, died suddenly. His successor, on examining the wall upon which they were engaged, directed the laborers to suspend work immediately; he was struck by the inutility of a mutilation so odious in itself. The following day, he presented a report, adducing conclusive reasons to the municipal council, who, being better informed, empowered him to order the demolition of the wall, and the restoration of the church to its original state.

The ancient image, consequently, was replaced in its former position where it still remains. The circumstance was much talked of throughout the country, as the sudden death of the city engineer appeared as a chastisement from Heaven: this caused some to say that the good Mr. Dupont had terrible moments, and that sometimes "he killed people."

The man of God employed the medal, most willingly, to obtain the conversion of sinners. In 1854, a wicked and blasphemous woman was admitted into a charitable institution. Every one thought she was possessed by the devil; she never left her bed, in which it was supposed she kept concealed. Certain charmed articles influential in maintaining her evil dispositions. There was question of making some repairs in the dormitory, and one day they took advantage of it to lift the paralytic suddenly from her bed, and, notwithstanding her cries, to remove her to an adjoining apartment. The Sisters, upon examination, found under the mattress a bag filled with suspicious articles. They substituted for the bag a medal of St. Benedict given by Mr. Dupont. The woman, without being informed of what had been done, was taken back to the dormitory. But she had, no doubt, learned it from the evil spirit; for, no sooner did she approach the bed, than she became furious in her rage, reproaching the Sisters for having removed the bag. But she was no sooner laid upon the bed, than her cries ceased suddenly, and she was unusually calm. For the first time since her entrance into the house, her features, which had been always horridly contracted, assumed a peaceful expression. The unfortunate creature asked for a priest. A few days later, the infirmary, arranged as a chapel, brilliant with lights and adorned with flowers, received our Lord, Who came to visit a poor soul, now freed from captivity, and rejoicing as a bird, which has escaped the snare of the fowler. From that time, she continued until death to be an object of edification.

The following conversion is no less striking. We give it in Mr. Dupont's words. "Yesterday afternoon, March 14, 1859, I met a priest who expressed great anxiety concerning a young man of seventeen years of age who had returned ill from Paris, and who, in the opinion of his physicians, could not survive many days. The priest had three times called to see the young man, but had been refused by the family. I spoke to him of the medal of St. Benedict, gave him one, and advised him to make another effort. In less than an hour, we had gained the victory. The priest was refused admittance; he shows the medal, saying that it is for the patient. 'Ah! that makes a difference; come in, Sir.' At the sight of the priest, the young man covers his face, but uncovers it as soon as he hears him say: 'Accept this medal, my dear friend,' and he immediately commences his Confession with every evidence of sincere contrition." "On the same day," continues Mr. Dupont, "at eleven o'clock in the evening, a poor old woman, who had never, during her long life, performed a religious duty, lay in her death-agony. She was urged to make her Confession, but refused. A medal of St. Benedict was given her, and she at once asked for a priest. Those who were attending, hastened to procure her the consolation she desired; she was eager for the arrival of the priest. 'Will he give me my God in Holy Communion? How long he stays!' She confessed, but her condition did not permit her to receive the Viaticum. Extreme Unction was administered, for which she expressed her gratitude. Two hours afterwards, she expired, repeating over and over again with remarkable faith: 'I wish I could have received the good God.'"

The most violent passions, the most inveterate vices, yielded to the powerful influence of a medal given by Mr. Dupont. "A woman," he relates, "came to me one day, weeping bitterly, and said: 'My son-in-law, imagining that his wife has been guilty of a serious fault, has treated her very cruelly for the past three months. He has ceased to work, walks about all day doing nothing, and threatens continually to kill her, even if he should, in consequence, die on the gallows.' As the woman seemed animated by sentiments of religion, I gave her several medals of St. Benedict, advising her, as well as her daughter, to keep one about her, and, without the knowledge of her son-in-law, to immerse one in his drink. I also suggested to her to make a novena, and approach the Sacraments in honor of St. Benedict. She went away full of confidence in St. Benedict, and returned after a few days, to communicate to me the good news of the happy change operated in her son-in-law. She had followed my instructions, and she was not long in obtaining the object of her petitions. The poor man had become tranquil, and had resumed his daily duties."

The following fact is well known in Tours. In 1852, a woman in great distress, confided her sorrows to the servant of God. Her husband, although in other respects a good man, had contracted a miserable habit of drinking to excess. All the earnings of both husband and wife, were invariably expended by him as soon as received, and the family were reduced to a deplorable state of misery. Mr. Dupont gave the woman a medal, recommending her to touch with it the wine which her husband would use, whilst she herself was to drink only water. Hardly had the man tasted the wine, when he exclaimed: "What have you done to this wine? it is execrable." As the woman protested it was the wine usually served, he said angrily: "I will indemnify myself for this." He left the table and went to the tavern, from which he had not formerly returned until very late at night, and always under the influence of liquor. In a quarter of an hour the man entered and said to his wife: "This is a plot you have laid against me; the wine at the tavern is even worse than yours; I would rather drink water." He passed a quiet night. From this day, water became, of necessity, the drink of the former drunkard. The wife, who was a good Christian, did not confine her efforts solely to the correction of her husband's habit of drinking, and she succeeded in persuading him to resume the practice of his religious duties.

Such was Mr. Dupont's estimation of the supernatural power of this medal, that he did not hesitate to use it even upon animals, when he suspected a more or less direct action of Satan over them. We will give the following instance. A score of hens, comfortably housed, well fed, and properly cared for in every way, had not laid a single egg for several months. The Sisters of the community where this occurred became impatient, and killed several of the hens, but found no eggs in any of them. By Mr. Dupont's advice, they placed a medal of St. Benedict in the henhouse; four days passed, and they found one egg; the next day, two. "Since then," they write to Mr. Dupont, "the hens have done their duty every day." The singularity of the incident caused him much amusement. He refers to it, at different times, in letters to his friend, Mr. d'Avrainville. "I hasten," he writes, "to send you news of the hens. Since Satan has taken his departure, they give eight eggs regularly every day; there are sixteen of them. It is very comical. The Sisters have promised to send me some eggs. And I intend, if a good opportunity offers when I receive them, to share them with you."

Mr. Dupont had correspondents and agents in every direction, for the distribution of the medals.

From time to time, he would forward packages of them, and he inspired his friends with the faith and zeal which animated him. Thus, an individual wrote to him, we do not know from what place: "I always wear, as you advised, a medal of St. Benedict, and I distribute a large number. I directed some to be thrown into the flames during a great fire, and it was immediately extinguished. My mother, a lady, and myself, knelt and said the Litany of the Blessed Virgin and three invocations to St. Benedict; the fire originated in a manufactory, and it was raging with great violence; when we arose from our knees, the flames had subsided. We knelt and repeated the same prayers in thanksgiving. We did not know the persons whose building was on fire; the gentleman, who cast them into the flames, told me on his return: 'I threw your medals, and the fire was immediately extinguished.' We saw in this, the effect of St. Benedict's intercession."

The confidence of the servant of God in St. Benedict's medal was unbounded. At the time of the great inundation of 1856, which proved so disastrous to the city of Tours, when there was danger of the bursting of the levee, and the inhabitants were in terrible anxiety, the engineers sank, at the weak point, boats loaded with sand and stones. Mr. Dupont was present: shrugging his shoulders in his habitual manner, he said: "That will not arrest the force of the water." Returning alone a little while afterwards, he threw a handful of medals in the same place, and retired perfectly satisfied as to the safety of the city, which, in reality, escaped the flood, owing to the resistance of that portion of the dike. In conversation with an intimate friend, he once said that if he had a medal of St. Benedict in his hand, he could stop a locomotive if it were dashing upon him at its highest speed.

Mr. Dupont had committed to writing a number of facts similar to those we have related above. His manuscript terminates with these words: "Is it not time that we should acknowledge and proclaim, at this period when Heaven is pouring out graces so abundantly, the value of the medal which seems given by Providence, to clear the earth of the demon, the only obstacle to grace?"

He considered the virtue of the medal to reside principally in the words spoken by Jesus Christ in the desert: *Vade retro, Satana*. In support of this opinion he quotes what our Lord said to St. Gertrude: "The most precious relic I have left upon earth, is the words pronounced by me." With Dom Guéranger, he attributed a great influence also to the cross on the medal and the impression of St. Benedict. "To this great patriarch, was reserved the privilege of teaching us how exalted must be our faith, how entire our confidence, to enable us to say with effective force: 'Get thee behind me, Satan.'"

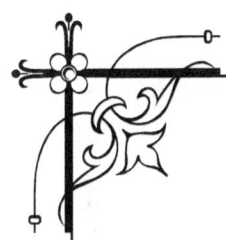

Chapter XII

The Holy Scriptures.

Mr. Dupont, even in his youth, loved the Holy Scriptures. The earliest letters we possess from his pen, contain frequent quotations from the sacred text. The facility and fitness with which he made use of them, in conversation, proved that he read the Scriptures so frequently as to have become familiar with them, and to have learned them almost by heart. We have known few ecclesiastics, even among the most erudite, who were as well versed in them as he was. He not only quoted passages from memory, but he loved to comment upon them, and this he did in a manner peculiar to himself, not by way of explanation, or interpreting as a theologian, but with an ingenuity, a charming apropos, and sometimes, with an elevation of sentiment and a broadness of view, not unworthy a Father of the Church.

In the middle of his room there stood, for his own particular use, a large desk like a church pulpit, upon which at all times lay open two folio Bibles, one in Latin, the other in French; he searched them, by turns, in order to find the exact words of a text which he wished to employ in his correspondence, conversations, or meditations. He was so perfectly familiar with the different parts of the Bible, that his finger rested immediately, and without hesitation, upon the passage he had in his mind. He explained the Old and New Testament, the one by the other. That was his method of studying the Scriptures. He rarely had recourse to commentaries, not through contempt, but from the natural turn of his mind. He compared different texts. He discovered in them relations, analogies with the events of the day, coincidences, by which his soul was moved to wonder and gladness; his conversation and letters sparkled with the beautiful thoughts, and glowed with the pious sentiments he thence derived.

A conversation with him did not long continue, before he found the opportunity of quoting a passage from the Bible. He did so, without affectation or formality, with an unction, a fervent love, which touched all who heard him. He seemed to feel, to taste the words of the text; he pronounced them with respect and devotion; he would repeat them over with an ever-increasing admiration and enthusiasm. This, above all else, impressed laymen and ladies of the world when visiting him. A word, spoken as it were by chance in conversation, would recall a text; then he would go to his desk, turn over the leaves of his Bible, and comment upon it in so interesting a manner, that one would willingly have remained for hours listening to him. A Christian mother of Tours who made the above remarks, adds: "When one of my daughters, who was still quite young, would see me about to enter Mr. Dupont's house, she would whisper to her father: 'Please do not go in, mamma will commence the Bible with Mr. Dupont, and they will never finish.'" A lady, a neighbor of the servant of God, writes of him in terms of the highest admiration: "I cannot express my regret, I may say, my remorse, for not having taken notes of all I saw and heard of Mr. Dupont. How often, on entering that room which has been the scene of so many marvellous events, I have found him standing before his Bible, and have heard from his lips remarkable interpretations of the Holy Scriptures! M. l'Abbé Boullay, a competent judge, because well-versed himself in the study of the Scriptures, said to me of Mr. Dupont: 'He has a clearer intelligence of the Bible than any one I know.'"

Although every portion of the Bible was familiar to him, there were certain personages of the Old Testament whom he regarded in a particular light, and for whom he professed a kind of enthusiastic admiration. One of these was Nebuchodonosor. This prince appeared to him clothed with extraordinary grandeur. He represented the abjection of man before God. After his trial, Nebuchodonosor lifts his eyes to Heaven and cries out: "All the inhabitants of the earth are as nothing before God." "I see him yet," relates an eye-witness, a celebrated writer, "and he never impressed me more than on that occasion. It was after dinner. He stood before his desk; the Bible was open at the Prophecies of Daniel. He tried to read, but it was too dark. Addressing his faithful friend, he said: 'Give me a light, d'Avrainville,' and he read in a tone of deep humility these words of Nebuchodonosor: 'I lifted my eyes to Heaven and my sense was restored to me: and I blessed the Most High, and all the inhabitants of the earth are reputed as nothing before Him.' At that moment Mr. Dupont was majestic. The words of Scripture, making evident the nothingness of man and the sovereign dominion of God, had found in him a living echo."

Not less ardent was his predilection for Job. "Job," he said, "may be considered as the perfect type of our Lord. He prays for his false friends who had drawn upon themselves the anger of God, and obtains their pardon. '*Here indeed the just suffers for the unjust.*'" One of his habitual visitors says: "Once when I went to see him as usual, I had hardly saluted him, when, without noticing my salutation, he apostrophised me with the words: 'Do you ever pray to the good man, Job?' The question appeared to me at first somewhat odd. I answered: 'I must confess that I have never thought of him. And yet, with my violent irascible temperament, I ought to have invoked him to obtain the patience I so greatly need.' He replied: 'You are wrong not to invoke him. Read.' Taking me to his Bible, he read me the following words from the Book of Job: 'Go to my servant Job and offer for yourselves a holocaust, and my servant Job shall pray for you: his face I will accept that folly be not imputed to you.'

"'You see, my friend, that God promises to hear the prayers of Job; he has promised this to no one else in the holy books. Consequently we should pray to Job. We do not lose our time when we pray for others. It is when he prays for his friends that Job is delivered.'"

His warm heart sought to communicate the light and spiritual joy he found in the word of God. He recommended particularly the reading of the Epistles of St. Peter and St. Paul. "There is," he said, "an ineffable sweetness in reading these Epistles, when we remember that they are addressed to each of the faithful individually. It was in reading lately the First Epistle of St. Peter, that this thought particularly impressed me. In effect, our Lord said to his apostles: *Teach all nations...;* and behold them writing letters for those whom they cannot reach by the spoken word."

An intelligent and well-educated lady, who has a particular love for the Holy Scriptures, attributes her taste for them to Mr. Dupont. "I had been living only a short time in Touraine," she writes, "when having the misfortune to lose my husband, I determined to relinquish the worldly life I had hitherto led, and to devote myself to good works. But I was much embarrassed as to the means of carrying my resolution into effect; I was about to enter upon an untried path, and I needed a guide. Fortunately, I heard of Mr. Dupont, and from my first interview with him, he comprehended my difficulties and my aspirations for a more perfect life, and he gave me the most salutary advice. We had exchanged only a few words, when he opened his Bible and read, in a grave and impressive manner, different passages from St. Paul upon the duties of a Christian widow, imparting great unction to the holy words. For several years, I had the happiness of frequent conversations with him, during which he would often have recourse to the Holy Scriptures. He took particular pleasure in reading to me from St. Paul, whose Epistles I have, consequently, relished exceedingly, although previously I was not familiar with them."

Mgr. d'Outremont was once complimented upon his happy application of certain passages of Scripture, commented upon by him in the style of the homilies of the Fathers. The prelate replied: I am indebted to Mr. Dupont for this method of interpreting the Scriptures. When I was Vicar at the cathedral, I visited him frequently, and our conversations turned entirely upon the Bible. He inspired me with a taste for the study of the Scriptures; he was my director and my teacher. Numerous interpretations and ideas of different texts, have remained impressed upon my memory; they recur to my mind when I am preparing to speak, and I am glad to make use of them."

In fine, the veneration of this fervent layman for the word of God, found exterior expression in an act of homage, which is one of the most remarkable of his life, and the most indicative of his character. Among the great Christians who have professed a special love of the Holy Scripture, Mr. Dupont is the first, and, to our knowledge, the only one whose devotion has gone so far, as to honor it by burning a lamp before it day and night, as before the Holy Eucharist. We see in the lives of the saints that some read the Scriptures on their knees and with uncovered heads; others carried it respectfully about their persons, whilst others placed it in cases fastened with ivory or silver clasps. We are not told that any of them conceived the thought carried into effect by Mr. Dupont. The idea of lighting a lamp before the Sacred Scriptures, is an idea of faith peculiarly his own, an idea of reparation, to expiate the crime of blasphemy so commonly committed in our days by unbelievers, impious men, and ignorant Christians, who either deny the divine origin of our holy books, or who regard them as a purely human composition. "The Holy Scripture," he would say, "is the Face of God; before that Face, as before the Divine presence, fire should burn day and night... I see Jesus Christ entire in each word of Scripture. Jesus Christ cannot be divided."

The period at which he realized the thought, should be recorded in his life as a memorable date. It was the 29th of March, 1865. He did it without show or parade; it was remarked only by his most intimate and most observant friends, and in a letter he refers to it with simplicity. Having occasion to write to some one that same day, he concludes with these words: "Let us repeat together this charming verse of the 118th Psalm: '*I entreated Thy face with all my heart: have mercy on me according to Thy word. Deprecatus sum Faciem tuam in toto corde meo; miserere mei secundum eloquium tuum.*' Now, my dear friend, it is only today, when for the first time I placed a lamp before the Holy Scriptures, that I noticed the appropriateness of that prayer. The lamp is on the corner of my desk, directly in front of my large Bible, and I, miserable creature, am between the two lights which burn in reparation of blasphemy."

There were two lamps. One of them burned before the Holy Face, the other, before the Holy Scriptures; and the man of prayer and reparation was there, between the two, burning with love for God and his neighbor. That was the place assigned him by God, and he desired no other. He occupied the place in person as well as in spirit, seated at a square table between the two lamps, between the Holy Face and the Holy Scriptures, always, either on his knees before the Holy Face, or seated at that table. We might say that Mr. Dupont was there also, entire and without division. The Scriptures, the Holy Face, they were his life.

He provides for his Bible in his will, expressing the desire that it should still be honored by a lamp. He bequeathed it upon that condition. By a concurrence of providential circumstances, his wish has been realized far beyond his expectation. In the very room where he so long venerated it, his dear Bible, the same he used in life, is open on the same desk; a lamp still burns day and night in its honor. This lamp is the pendant of that which is lighted before the Holy Face, and, with the one which hangs before the Blessed Sacrament, it gives a peculiar aspect to this little oratory, well suited to aid the piety of fervent souls, and to dispose them to sentiments of reparation.

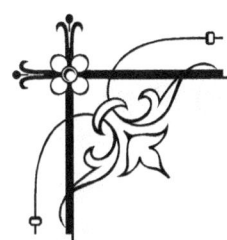

Chapter XIII

Commencement of the Devotion to the Holy Face.

In pursuing thus far the history of Mr. Dupont, we have been forced, by the nature of the materials, to present one after the other, in so many separate chapters, the different works of piety and zeal by which the servant of God was the most constantly occupied. It may seem that his life was divided, and, as it were, distributed on many different subjects at the same time, without connection and without any precise aim. This is far from being the case. There was one special, unique object from which his mind was never diverted,—the idea of reparation. It took a firmer hold on him day by day. This grand idea is about to assume a new form, to take entire possession of him, and to make him commence, if not found, a work of salvation wonderfully adapted to the wants of the Church and of France.

We have seen the relations established between Mr. Dupont and Sister Saint-Pierre in regard to the work in reparation of blasphemy. The pious layman had been made acquainted with the revelations successively made, on this subject, to the virgin of the cloister. He was particularly struck by the means of reparation pointed out by Jesus Christ to his servant, namely, the worship of his dolorous Face. As this included the love of our outraged Lord, and, at the same time, an idea very dear to him, Mr. Dupont took particular interest in it, and received with avidity the least details of the revelations made to the humble Religious. The latter, in obedience to Superiors, wrote, in the form of letters addressed to the Mother Prioress, the celestial communications as they were made to her. The Prioress never omitted to make them known to the man of God, who studied them attentively, and always derived from them additional light upon the work by which he had long been piously occupied.

On the 11th of November, 1845, Sister Saint-Pierre wrote: "Our Lord transported me in spirit to the route leading to Calvary, and portrayed vividly before me the pious office rendered Him by St. Veronica, when with her veil she wiped his sacred Face, defiled with spittle, dust, sweat, and blood. Afterwards, this divine Saviour gave me to understand that the impious renew at present, by their blasphemies, the outrages inflicted upon His Holy Face, and I comprehended that all these blasphemies, hurled by the impious against the Divinity, Whom they cannot reach, fall, like the spittle of the Jews, upon the Holy Face of our Lord, Who became a victim for sinners. Next our Lord taught me, that in performing exercises for the reparation of blasphemy, we render to Him the same service as that rendered Him by the pious Veronica, and that He regarded the persons who honor Him in that manner, with the same favor as he did that holy woman at the time of His Passion."

These ideas, developed by a series of revelations during several years, made a great impression upon Mr. Dupont. He saw at a glance all that was practical and opportune in the worship of the Holy Face, under this point of view. At all times, the divine Face of our Lord was undoubtedly honored by faithful and devout adorers; but that which is new in the devotion and peculiarly appropriate to the necessities of our times, is its being made the exterior and sensible sign of works of reparation, which the whole world, and above all, France, need so much. It was this that delighted the soul of the servant of God.

He was particularly charmed by the following words: "In proportion to the care which you will take in repairing the injuries inflicted on My Face by blasphemers, I will take care of yours, disfigured by sin. I will renew upon it My image, and I will restore the beauty which was communicated to it in the waters of baptism." "There are men on earth who can restore the health of the body, but I alone, can restore to souls the image of God. Behold then the grace I promise to all who devote themselves to offer to My adorable Face the honor and adoration which are due to It, with the intention of repairing, by this homage, the insults It receives from blasphemies." "And our Lord pointed out to me in the apostle, St. Peter, an example of the virtue residing in His Holy Face. That apostle, by his sin, had effaced the image of God in his soul, but Jesus turned His Face towards the faithless apostle, and he became penitent: Jesus looked at Peter, and Peter wept bitterly. This adorable Face is as the seal of the Divinity, which has the power of reproducing in souls which apply to It, the image of God."

One of the last communications made to the Carmelite is the following: "Our Lord made known to me that the impious, by their blasphemies, attack His Holy Face, and that holy souls glorify Him by the praises they render to His name and His person. There is, in effect, something mysterious on the face of a man who is contemned. Yes, I see there exists an intimate connection between his name and his face. Behold a man distinguished by his name and his merits, in the presence of his enemies. They will not raise their hands to strike him; but they overwhelm him with injuries; they insult him by opprobrious epithets, instead of using the titles of honor which are his by right. Notice the face of the man thus outraged. Might you not say that all the injurious words which proceed from the mouths of his enemies, rest upon his face and make him suffer a real torment? That face burns with shame and confusion. The opprobrium and ignominy inflicted upon it, cause more suffering than actual tortures in other parts of the body. Behold here a faint picture of the adorable Face of our Lord outraged by blasphemers and impious men. Imagine to yourself this same man in presence of his friends, who, having heard of the insults which he has received from his enemies, are eager to console him, to treat him in a manner becoming his dignity, and render homage to his great name by addressing to him honorable titles. Do you not see the face of this man reflect the happiness conferred by these praises? Glory reposes upon his brow and makes his countenance radiant. Joy sparkles in his eyes, a smile parts his lips; in a word, his faithful friends have chased away grief from that face outraged by his enemies; glory has replaced opprobrium. This is what the friends of Jesus accomplish by the work of reparation; the glory which they render to His name reposes upon His august brow, and rejoices His Holy Face."

The conclusion drawn by the Sister from all that our Lord revealed to her, is thus summed up: "This work has two objects: the reparation of blasphemy and the reparation of the profanation of Sunday by servile works; consequently, it embraces the reparation of outrages against God, and against the sanctification of His name. Should devotion to the Holy Face be united with this work? Yes, It is its most precious ornament, since our Lord has made a present of His Holy Face to the work, that it may be the object of the devotion of the associates; they will become all-powerful with God by the offering which they will make Him of the august Face, Whose presence is so pleasing in His sight, that it infallibly appeases His anger and draws down upon poor sinners His infinite mercy. Yes, when the Eternal Father looks upon the Face of His beloved Son, which was

CHAPTER XIII

disfigured by blows and covered with ignominy, the sight thereof moves Him to mercy. Let us endeavor to profit by so precious a gift, and let us beg our Divine Saviour to hide us in the secret of His Face during the evil days."

Mr. Dupont, who was kept informed of all that was passing, failed not to notice particularly the contents of these letters. Written by a Religious, formerly a poor workwoman of Brittany, without education or instruction of any kind, he discovered in them every mark of divine inspiration, and we can readily imagine the effect they produced upon him. On the 8th of July, the pious daughter of St. Teresa had been dead three years, but the holy man of Tours continued to venerate her memory, and as far as was in his power, communicated her ideas and propagated the work of reparation. A circumstance, simple in itself, was about to give form to these sentiments, and transform them for him into a work of practical and daily devotion.

The Lent of 1851 was drawing to a close. The Prioress of the Carmelites, who knew his sentiments, thought she would confer a pleasure by sending him two engravings representing the Holy Face, copied from that impressed upon the veil of Veronica which is preserved in the Vatican. She had received them from the Prioress of the Benedictines of Arras, with whom she had corresponded for several years. These precious pictures came from Rome, and were being distributed by the zeal of the said Religious, who had taken a deep interest in the revelations of Sister Saint-Pierre. Profiting by an opportunity, they had ordered from the eternal city a certain number of these pictures with certificates attached. At the request of the Prioress of the Carmelites of Tours, they sent some for different persons, and two, especially intended for Mr. Dupont. Both were forwarded to him on Palm Sunday. The following day, Monday in Holy Week, he sent them to be framed; they were returned to him on Wednesday morning. The more beautiful one, the one better framed was presented to the Work of the Nocturnal Adoration; it still hangs in the parlor of the Priests of the Mission. He kept the other, which was slightly damaged by a fold in the material which crossed the left cheek of the Holy Face; by this it can readily be distinguished from others and identified. He selected for it a simple frame of black wood.

A miracle that occurred at Rome in connection with the veil of St. Veronica at the Vatican, of which the servant of God had been informed, increased his appreciation of the precious facsimile of which he had become possessed. The following is an account of it as given by Mr. Dupont in a letter to a friend: "In the month of January, 1849, during the exile of Pius IX at Gaëta, public prayers, by order of the Holy Father, were offered in all the churches of Rome, to implore the mercy of the Omnipotent on the Pontifical States. On this occasion, they exposed in St. Peter's the wood of the true cross and the veil of St. Veronica. On the third day of the exposition, the canons appointed to the charge of the precious relics, noticed in the Holy Face, the impression of which on the veil is so faint as to be scarcely visible, a remarkable change. Through another veil of silk which covers it, and absolutely prevents the features from being distinguished, the divine Face appeared distinctly, as if living, and illumined by a soft light; the features assumed a death-like hue, and the eyes, deep-sunken, wore an expression of great pain. The canons immediately notified the clergy of the Basilica; the people were called in. Many wept; all were impressed with a reverential awe. An apostolic notary was summoned; a certificate was drawn up attesting the fact; a copy of it was sent to the Holy Father at Gaëta. For many days this prodigy, which lasted three hours, was the sole topic of conversation at Rome. On the evening of the same day, some veils of white silk, on which is represented the Holy Face, were applied to the miraculous veil. These veils have been sent to France."

CHAPTER XIII

In writing shortly after the reception of the two pictures sent from Arras, Mr. Dupont seems to insinuate that they might be from among those which touched the veil of Veronica on the very day of the miracle. It is certain, at least, that the custom of sending to France certified copies of the veil of Veronica, was introduced after the event related above, and, therefore, the one possessed by Mr. Dupont was really among those which were first forwarded from Rome. He attached a great value to it, and took particular interest in the miraculous event, which was either the immediate, or remote cause of the distribution of the pictures.

We shall now hear him relate the first use he made of the picture after it came into his possession. "I placed it," he says, "in my room on the left side of the chimney-piece, above a small chest of drawers upon which I could conveniently put a lamp, and with it, several small pious pictures. It was Wednesday in Holy Week. I had hardly arranged the whole, when my heart was touched by a sudden emotion. 'Can a Christian,' I said to myself, 'expose in his house this image of the divine Face of the Saviour of men, during the great week of the Passion, without offering some exterior mark of respect, adoration, and love?' Certainly not; this shall not be. And from this came the thought I had of burning a lamp before the Holy Face, my intention being, however, only to continue it during the remainder of Holy Week. I immediately acted upon that idea, but soon there arose another. The room was the one in which I was accustomed to receive my visitors, as well as those who came upon business; in it was my desk. I considered that every one would inquire why a lamp was lighted in the daytime. I reflected upon the answer I should give, and I was satisfied with the one which occurred to my mind. Yes, I said to myself, that is the very one. I will answer, as follows, whoever may ask me why I burn a light in the daytime: 'I do so, in order to teach those who enter here, that when the business which brings them is terminated, they must either speak of God, or withdraw.' And I concluded to write the following words on a card, which I placed on my desk, to make use of it as circumstances might require: 'Every one is free to do as he pleases in his own house; in my house, those who come must either retire after concluding their business affairs, or speak of the things of God.'

"That day and the following passed, and no one made the inquiry I had anticipated. Some did not appear to notice the lamp; others considered it a pious idea. On Good Friday, a travelling agent forced his way into my apartment, to solicit an order for Bordeaux wine. I returned to his question the answer I had prepared, and he was so surprised that I was obliged to repeat it a second time. This gave me an opening to speak to him of religion. He remained listening to me for more than an hour, and, having entered my room careless as to religion, he left me almost converted, and taking with him some of the water from La Salette. I do not know what became of him.

"On the following day, Holy Saturday, our Lord commenced to make known his intentions. I received a visit from a very pious person, Miss X——, with whom I was acquainted, and who was suffering with her eyes; on entering my room she complained of the sharp pain in her eyes, caused by a piercing wind, which filled the air with dust. She wished to see me upon business. As I was engaged in writing, I requested her to pray before the Holy Face, whilst waiting for me a few minutes. She profited by the opportunity to ask her cure. I soon joined her, knelt by her side, and we said some prayers together. On rising I said to her: 'Put some oil from the lamp upon your eyes.' She dipped her finger into the oil and rubbed it on her eyes; as she turned to take a seat, she exclaimed in astonishment: 'My eyes no longer pain me!' When she left, she took with her a little of the oil, because she was going to Richelieu, her usual residence."

He relates afterwards that on Tuesday of Easter Week, a young man of the city was sent to him on an errand; he had a sore leg, limped, and walked with great pain. The servant of God anointed the leg with oil from the lamp, saying a prayer to the Holy Face. The young man was immediately cured, and was able to run, with perfect ease, around the garden. "Another and very consoling event, which is not generally known in the city," observes Mr. Dupont, when telling of the cure.

At the end of the Holy Week, he intended to extinguish the lamp. "But," he says, "as often as I was about to remove it, my feelings were opposed to doing so, and I left it. Then came the month of Mary: I had an additional motive not to discontinue the little devotion, which I knew was not in opposition to the spirit of the Church. We next entered into the months consecrated to the Sacred Heart and the Precious Blood, and, from that time, consolation super-abounded. More than twenty persons had been relieved in serious illness. The cures that had been effected, were repeated from one to another. We then began to recite before the picture the Litany of the Sacred Face, composed by the poor workwoman of Brittany, known as Sister Marie de Saint-Pierre. Prodigies were multiplied; I cannot undertake to enter into a detail of the cures obtained by the use of the oil: cancers, interior and exterior ulcers, cataracts, deafness, &c... and many cases of them. From the 2d of December to the present time, May 3d, I have given more than eight thousand small phials of oil. Day by day the crowd increases; sometimes on Saturdays, more than three hundred persons arrive; the other days of the week, not so many. The proof that grace is acting on souls, may be seen by the fact that all understand that the novenas of prayers and of anointing with the oil, conclude with Confession and Communion."

"I will conclude here the recital of facts," says Mr. Dupont. Writing familiarly to a friend, he adds: "They have established a kind of pilgrimage to Saint-Etienne Street: *Infirma mundi et ignobilia et ea quæ non sunt... elegit Deus.* 'God hath chosen the mean things of the world, and the things that are contemptible, and things that are not.' I allow myself the liberty of saying to our Lord: 'Why have you chosen the house of the poor pilgrim of Saint-Etienne Street to operate such wonders?' Alas! so many others will say the same thing with a shrug of the shoulders."

Before relating the result of the pilgrimages and the miracles which were performed, it will not be without interest to learn whence the idea of anointing with oil came to the servant of God.

Whilst he was engaged in his compilation of his *Année de Marie*, a notice was sent him of Notre Dame de l'Enfantement, which is particularly honored at Rome in the church of St. Augustine. He noticed that the oil from the lamp, which always burned before the Madonna of that church, was used for anointing the sick, and that very many persons had been recompensed for their faith by a miraculous restoration to health. The fact made an impression upon him, particularly when he reflected upon the case of one of his neighbors whose lungs were diseased. He said to himself: "Is not the Blessed Virgin as powerful in France as in Italy?" Moved by this reflection, he went at once in the rain to the extreme end of the city, to procure some oil from the lamp which he knew was lighted before Notre Dame des Miracles. He found, on entering the chapel, that the lamp was extinguished for want of oil. He gave a piece of twenty sous to purchase oil, and requested to have the lamp lighted. He took with him, on his return, a small phial of the oil, carried it to the consumptive lady who, after being anointed with it, improved rapidly. In a fortnight, she was perfectly well; and the physician, although an unbeliever, certified that her lungs were entirely healed.

This occurred in 1840. He acknowledges that his thoughts, subsequently, dwelt often upon "the practice of lighting a lamp before the images of Mary." Now in 1851, just as he has carried into execution his pious design relative to the Holy Face, he learns that the celebrated Madonna of St. Augustine has been crowned at Rome. Rome seems, by her example, to authorize what he has done, and to serve him as a guide in the course he should pursue. The servant of God has clearly thus explained his motives, and we can but admire the ways of Providence in his regard. Every thing comes to him from Rome. The venerable picture, the object of his devotion, the idea of honoring this picture by a lamp, the practice of anointing with oil from the lamp for the cure of the infirm: these three holy things come to him directly from the eternal city, the centre of light, the source of grace.

The worship of the Holy Face, which was for the future to fill up the life of Mr. Dupont, evidently associated this grand Christian with the mission of Sister Saint-Pierre. The humble Carmelite had been the first to present the adorable Face of our Lord as the exterior sign, and the special means of reparation. From the very beginning, the pious layman regarded the miraculous cures which took place in his room, as striking manifestations of the will of God in this regard.

Among those which occurred during the first year, we will relate the following, which caused a great sensation in the city. A woman from Neuillé-Pont-Pierre, who was afflicted with a cancer, went to Tours, to receive treatment at the Petit-Hôpital. She underwent a painful operation, but, not long after her return to Neuillé, the disease returned with additional violence; the wound reopened with considerable discharge, and her acute sufferings prevented her from doing any kind of work. She visited Mr. Dupont, who advised her to make, with her husband, a novena to the Holy Face. At the end of the nine days, the wound was healed, and she was entirely free from pain.

A young girl of Chinon was suffering from a cancerous tumor, as large as the head of a small child, and was lying, as the physicians declared, at the point of death. A phial of the oil having been procured for her, it was applied to the diseased part, and a novena to the Holy Face was commenced at the same time. The next morning, the physician was astonished to find his patient better; she had slept well, and the tumor had diminished in size: it continued to decrease during the succeeding days. The girl had promised a visit to the Holy Face, and as soon as she was able to be moved she went to Mr. Dupont's. On entering his room, she was pale and suffering, the tumor being still as large as a nut. After she had been anointed with the oil, and had recited the Litany of the Holy Face, the tumor disappeared entirely, and she no longer experienced any pain. She had recovered her strength, and she walked some distance through the city before going to the railroad to return to Chinon.

The restoration of Doctor Noyer, a celebrated physician of Paris, is no less wonderful. The invalid hastily entered Mr. Dupont's room, and presented him with a letter of introduction from one of his friends. The servant of God opened the letter in his presence and commenced to read it aloud. After awhile, he hesitates, he stops. He was informed by the physician who wrote the letter that the gentleman presenting it, was so seriously affected that he could not live more than three weeks. Seeing this hesitation, Doctor Noyer said, "Do not fear to continue, I know what has been written to you,—that there is no hope of my recovery." "That is true," replied Mr. Dupont; "but have you faith?" "Certainly, I have." "Then, we will pray together." It was with good reason that his brother-physicians had pronounced his disease incurable, and his death, imminent; for, he was in an advanced stage of consumption, one lung being entirely gone. He was then on his way to Pau for the benefit of the milder climate. The two knelt in prayer; Mr. Dupont anointed his chest. The invalid, full of confidence, requested a few drops of the oil to drink: he

CHAPTER XIII

was instantaneously cured. On his return to Paris, he kept up a correspondence with his benefactor, sent his patients to him, and, during the remainder of his life, never failed to make annually a pilgrimage of thanksgiving to Tours.

Two things contributed to increase the number of these miraculous cures in distant places; the distribution of the pictures of the Holy Face, and the presentation of small phials of the oil. It will not be out of place here to describe these two means of propagandism, which created for Mr. Dupont two real occupations in his holy life. As early as the year 1846, long before he placed the venerable picture from Rome in his drawing-room, we know he was zealous in recommending certain representations of the Holy Face, as emblems of the work of reparation. When the facsimile of the veil of Veronica came into his possession, be had a photograph taken of it immediately, and from this, he directed small engravings of the Holy Face to be struck off. These were placed at the top of small sheets of printed prayers, and distributed in every direction. He devoted himself to the work with his characteristic zeal. He wrote in 1854 that twenty-five thousand had been stamped by the lithographer. The lithographer has informed us that, since that time, the number of these engravings of the Holy Face, has amounted to hundreds of thousands. He often sent thousands in packages addressed to persons of every condition and rank.

Another occupation connected likewise with this cherished devotion, was equally delightful to him. We refer to the distribution of the phials of oil. "Would you believe," he said in 1854, "that, by a rough calculation, more than sixty thousand phials have either been given away to persons before the Holy Face, or forwarded to a distance? The oil is sent for in every direction, and we have, daily, additional proof that the homage rendered to the Holy Face is agreeable to our Lord." "I have received from England to-day (February 1, 1857) an account of the cure of a cancer.

The individual was a Protestant lady, whose son, having entered the true Church, came to pass some time at Tours, until the anger of his father, a Protestant minister, should subside. He took with him several phials of the oil, and he now requests more to be sent to him; he relates very many graces obtained."

The man of God made a serious occupation of the forwarding of these phials; he arranged them himself and mailed them at his own expense; when occasion required it, he sealed and tied up the package. It was a curious sight which amused his friends to behold him devoting his leisure hours to these minute arrangements. Visitors would find him seated in a corner of his drawing-room before a table, on which was a number of small bottles in rows, filling them, by means of a little funnel made for the purpose, with oil taken from the lamp of the Holy Face, preparing, and cutting the corks. The selection and quality of the corks were not in his eyes unimportant matters, as these were to protect the oil from the risk of being spilled. The packages were sent by mail, as the laws regulating the post-offices were not so rigorous as at the present time. Mr. Dupont forwarded them, in that manner, not only to all parts of France, but we may say, to all countries in the world, to Poland, England, America, and even to Calcutta, and China. His friend, Mr. d'Avrainville, who resided in Paris, furnished him with the phials and corks. Their correspondence on the subject was often witty and amusing. This friend always had on hand a provision of small phials of oil sent him by Mr. Dupont, in whose name he distributed them in different directions; his house was a kind of emporium, and both were equally anxious to keep it well-stocked. These little phials became the cause of numerous conversions and cures, which rejoiced the heart of the servant of the Holy Face.

It would be impossible to relate all the events considered miraculous, of which Mr. Dupont's house was the scene.

CHAPTER XIII

They would fill volumes. However, as these events are so intimately connected with him, and occupy so large a place in his life, we cannot pass them over in silence. We shall, therefore, select some of the principal ones, preserving, as nearly as possible, the words of the witnesses from whom we heard them directly, or the text of the written documents which we have in our possession. The witnesses are grave and sensible persons of undoubted veracity; the documents have all the marks of perfect authenticity.

"In 1855," writes a priest of the Mission, "I held the office of Vicar of the cathedral. I was in Mr. Dupont's room when a woman, who had been lame for twenty years, and who used two crutches in walking, entered. The good old woman went into an adjoining apartment, and, having applied the oil from the lamp to her knees, returned to the drawingroom, where about thirty persons were assembled. All knelt and answered aloud the Litany of the Holy Face, recited by the Superioress of the Sisters of Charity. At the conclusion of the Litany, Mr. Dupont inquired of the old woman how she was; she replied that she was a little better. 'Have faith,' said Mr. Dupont to her, 'continue your prayers, and if you have confidence, you will be cured.' His words were verified: in a quarter of an hour, the woman was perfectly well. I was present during the whole time."

A lady, carrying in her arms a child about seven years of age, ill, and unable to walk, arrived by the railroad at Tours. She inquired of the conductor Mr. Dupont's direction. The employees at the depot were accustomed to such inquiries, and were so kind to strangers going to Mr. Dupont's, that often they would, themselves, act as guides to the pilgrims. And so it happened on this occasion: the conductor accompanied the lady to the house of the man of God, aiding her to carry her afflicted child. They arrive and kneel in prayer before the Holy Face. Mr. Dupont examines the child, and asks, "why he has no shoes." The cause was too evidently the deformity and swelling of the feet. "Because he cannot put them on," replied the mother. "Go and buy shoes for him," said Mr. Dupont, "at such a number, such a street." The mother obeyed and went out. In the mean time, the servant of the Holy Face anointed the feet with oil. When the mother returned with the shoes, the child could put them on without difficulty; he was cured." We heard the circumstance from the conductor himself.

Another person vouches for the truth of the following: "I arrived, on one occasion, at the time of the usual prayers. A young man from the country came in, bringing a letter from the mayor of the commune: his right hand was as inflexible as a bar of iron; he could neither close, nor bend it; and, for two years, he had been incapacitated from doing work of any kind. Mr. Dupont, placing the hand in his and examining it, pronounced these words: '*Oh! oh! this hand must close*' I trembled with emotion as I thought to myself: Will it really close? Mr. Dupont directed all to kneel down, saying: '*Come, it will be necessary to pray fervently.*' We recommenced our prayers, and the anointing was repeated ten times before the favor was obtained; little by little, the hand, which was at first stiff and inflexible, was bent and finally closed. After each anointing, Mr. Dupont took the hand, placed it in his, examined it, and encouraged those present to persevere in prayer, repeating each time: '*This hand must close.*' His words excited the confidence of all. I never saw him pray with so much fervor. When at last he saw the hand close, he sent the young man into his garden, to satisfy himself that he could work; they gave him a shovel, and he dug the earth with ease and without fatigue; he was cured. From those who witnessed this scene, there ascended a chorus of praise and unspeakable thanksgiving to the adorable Face of our Lord."

A boy, about seven years of age, was attacked by a disease, which had already carried off several of his sisters and brothers. For three consecutive months, he had endured intense suffering; he was so weak he could not stand. His father, a man of faith, seeing the inutility of resorting longer to human remedies, carried the child to Mr. Dupont. After the recitation of the prayers and one application of the oil, the young invalid was able to stand up. After a second anointing, he began to walk, and the third restored to him the strength, agility, and appetite which he had not enjoyed for three months. He ran about swiftly, and without experiencing the least pain; he rushed into the garden, where hunger, and the mischievousness natural to his age, urged him, as he acknowledged later, to pull stealthily some fine cherries, hanging rather high on the tree, which his infirmity would have prevented him, a short time previous, from even desiring to touch. On his return to the drawing-room, he ate with appetite a large slice of bread, and he never afterwards suffered from the same disease. This child grew up, became a priest in this diocess, and, in order to render homage to the servant of God, he now publishes this wonderful instance of the divine mercy.

Mr. Baranger, dean of Ligueil, related to us the following circumstance, which attests, at the same time, a miraculous cure and the conversion of a soul. "In 1856, a stranger of fine appearance and polished manners called to see me, and inquired if I was acquainted with Mr. Dupont. 'Certainly,' was my answer. 'He has converted me,' he said, 'and I have come to request you to hear my Confession.' He then related what had happened to him. Passing through Tours, he noticed in a street near the railroad a number of persons directing their steps to a certain house. He asked what took them thither. He was told that a gentleman, who lived there, performed miracles. On hearing this, curiosity induced him to enter with the others. It was Mr. Dupont's house. On seeing him, the servant of God saluted him politely and said: 'To what do I owe the pleasure of your visit?' The traveller related to him simply what had taken place, and what he had just been told. 'Yes, sir,' resumed Mr. Dupont; 'miracles have been performed here, and, by the goodness of God, they occur daily.' Upon seeing the astonishment of the visitor, he added: 'It is no more difficult for a Christian to obtain a miracle than to obtain a dish of peas from the shop at the corner; it suffices to ask; and, if you choose, you shall see one. Here is a woman who is nearly blind; we are going to pray for her, and I hope her sight will be restored.'

"'I knelt,' continued the traveller, 'with the others who were present, and I united with them in prayer, although ten years had passed since I had made an act of religion. The eyes of the blind woman were anointed. She said that she was unable to read a single word in a book which was handed to her; but, after having been anointed several times with the oil of the Holy Face, she began to distinguish the persons in the room; by degrees, her sight became better, until, at last, she was able to read.' Touched by what he had seen, and moved particularly by the words of Mr. Dupont, the stranger could not resist the inspiration to make his peace with God. He sought a priest to whom he made his Confession with every evidence of sincere repentance. This proved to be, in his case, the commencement of a complete conversion; at least, I know that for years afterwards he frequented the sacraments."

"A young girl of La Vendée, affected with a lachrymal fistula, had gone to Tours to consult a celebrated oculist, who judged a painful operation to be necessary. A friend took the girl to Mr. Dupont, and on her return to the oculist, he said no operation was required, as she was nearly relieved. Her complete cure was effected by the use of the oil of the Holy Face."

A lady (1851) certifies her cure in the following words: "I had been ill for two years, during which time I was unable to speak, and I had been given up by several physicians who pronounced me incurable. I went to prostrate myself before the Holy Face, and after the application of oil to my throat and forehead, I commenced to say the Litany:

at first, I could speak only in a whisper; but when I came to the *Agnus Dei*, I was able to say the remainder aloud. It would be impossible for me to describe my emotion; I could hardly believe in the reality of the miracle; my feelings overpowered me, and tears fell from my eyes. I sang the *Magnificat* in thanksgiving. My strength was immediately restored to me; the circumstance was so extraordinary that very many visited me through curiosity. The physicians themselves were compelled to acknowledge that the hand of God alone could have effected my cure."

A mother relates in a letter to Mr. Dupont, the cure of her daughter: "My little Marie had fallen from a swing and injured herself seriously, but she contrived for two months to conceal the circumstance from me. It was only when the poor child, overcome by pain and the swelling in the left side, asknowledged to me the truth, that we comprehended the extent of the injury. The remedies applied proved ineffectual. The little sufferer continued to grow worse daily, so that, at last, she could neither take a step, nor eat a mouthful of food without real torture. The child who had, hitherto, been the personification of joy and happiness, lost all her gayety, and the color faded from her cheeks. Such was her condition, when we decided to go to Tours, for the purpose of consulting the celebrated Doctor Bretonneau. The journey was accomplished with intense pain to the poor child, who, although dying from hunger, was unable to eat. After we had waited six hours, the doctor was at leisure to see my daughter; but before pronouncing decisively upon her case, he wished to make a second examination, and appointed the following day at half-past eleven. As he had been detained, and had not come at two o'clock, I could no longer endure the sight of the sufferings of my little Marie, who was not in the least relieved by the use of morphine which had been ordered. I, therefore, took her to you, sir; you prayed and anointed her with the oil which burns before the Holy Face of our Lord. The first three unctions produced no effect; but after that, as you prayed, the pain diminished in intensity, and, in a few minutes, the child declared she no longer suffered in *the least*. To test the reality of what she stated, I pressed with *great force* upon her side; the dear child laughed and said: 'Oh! mamma, you do not hurt me at all;' she could not before endure the pressure of her dress. However, I was not certain that the cure was complete; for Marie had suffered so much when eating, that I wished to make the trial at once of her condition in that respect. You had the kindness to send for bread and preserves; she ate with the avidity of a child who was very hungry, but without inconvenience. From that moment, my little Marie has been entirely free from indisposition of any kind. The family, on our return, could scarcely credit the good news; her grandparents shed tears of joy and gratitude. I know young libertines and unbelievers who do not doubt the miracle, and who desire to send many invalids to you."

Dom Guéranger had the thought one day to send a novice, who was suffering, to his holy friend, and command him to cure him. "I apply to you in behalf of our brother Boutin, who has a serious affection of the lungs: help him to obtain the favor he begs; his faith is simple; be sure to return him to me cured." The faith of the one and the obedience of the other were recompensed. Five days afterwards, the illustrious abbot wrote: "Our brother Boutin returned cured; this appears to me evident; however, before a positive decision, we must wait until the end of the novena." The novena being finished, he wrote: "Our brother Boutin has been entirely cured."

The cure of Captain Cléret, a relation by marriage of Mr. Dupont, was accompanied by circumstances so extraordinary that we cannot resist the desire to relate the principal facts. During the Crimean war in 1853, Captain Cléret was second in command on board the frigate *Jéna*, stationed at the port of Toulon, and appointed to convey provisions to the army. On the 24th of June, he was seriously wounded on board his ship during some evolutions at sea. While he was engaged in superintending the tacking of the ship, his foot became entangled in a rope, he was thrown down, and, but for the prompt action of the crew, who disengaged him from his perilous situation, his leg would have been crushed. His wound was serious. The attention bestowed upon him gave every reason to anticipate a speedy recovery; but after a few days, inflammation set in, and the patient was transferred from the vessel to the hospital, where the surgeon-in-chief reported that erysipelas of the most malignant kind had been developed. The swelling was extending to the knee, and none of the remedies used availed to check its progress. Symptoms of dysentery excited grave apprehensions lest gangrene existed in the intestines. The amputation of the limb was rendered very perilous by a burning fever. Nevertheless, several physicians were of the opinion that, although there was scarcely one chance out of a hundred that the amputation could be successfully performed, the operation should be undertaken, as it was the only hope left them of saving his life. They feared that Madame Cléret, who had been summoned by telegraph from Brest, might not arrive before her husband's death. As soon as the news of his illness reached her, she left Brest, and after many incidents on the journey, she gives the following account to her sister:

"On my arrival at Tours, I was grieved to find I could not proceed at once to Toulon, and I asked the agent at the depot if he could not remove my trunk, and allow me to go on in the next train. He consented very kindly to my request, and I thought I would pass with Léon the three hours I should be detained. (Mr. Léon Papin-Dupont, her relative.) When I entered, I found him engaged in conversation with a Polish princess; he was astonished to see me, and asked me where I was going. I told him I was on my way to Toulon, where my husband was ill; not to inconvenience him, I went up stairs to see my aunt, but returned after awhile to Léon. We had scarcely a moment alone; four persons from Blois arrived asking for prayers. Léon told me of the miraculous cures obtained by praying before the Holy Face, and the persons present confirmed what he said. When he had anointed them with the oil which burns before the sacred picture, we all knelt down to recite the Litany of the Holy Face, and Léon said to me: 'I am going to pray more particularly for your husband.' I was greatly touched by what I saw, but when I heard Léon say: 'It is possible, Antoinette, that your husband will be better from today; as soon as you arrive, write to me; tomorrow evening at the Nocturnal Adoration we will pray for him, and the general Communion of the next day will be offered for him,...' I experienced a confident hope of his recovery, which did not diminish during the remainder of the journey. When we were alone, he told me of several miracles. His great faith does good; when I left him, I felt better. He wanted me to remain longer, but my time was short, and I went to the depot."

She arrived at Toulon. "There," she says, "at the first gate of the city, a gentleman inquired if Madame Cléret was in the cars: I advanced immediately, 'Madame, your husband is much better.' His manner told me all, and I replied: 'Has he, then, been very ill?' 'Very ill, Madame, but I assure you he is much better.' We set off together, aud he related to me (this was on Friday), *that he had become unexpectedly better, that there was one night which the physicians called the miraculous night; that all thought it impossible to save his leg, and indeed had little hope of his life; that as to himself, upon calculating the hour of my arrival, he thought I would be in time to see my husband before he died.* These details impressed me; I thought of Léon. 'Have the kindness to tell me on what day and what night the change for the better occurred.' 'On Monday evening, he was slightly better, and on Tuesday, he was out of danger. Imagine my feelings! *It was on Monday that Léon said to me: 'Your husband will better today.'* I was overpowered with emotion on meeting my husband; he was frightfully changed. The priest was with him. I could restrain myself no longer, and I related all that had passed. *These gentlemen are as impressed as I am, and they declare that I owe to a miracle, not only the life of my husband, but the preservation of his leg.* I wrote immediately to Léon; I also told you of it; you have not answered my letter. *Perhaps you are incredulous! As for myself, that is impossible."*

It was not less impossible to Captain Cléret to be incredulous. Perfectly convinced of the great miracle operated in his favor, he wished, in order to render glory to God, not only to relate in conversation to his friend the fact as here given, but also to forward to him the confidential letter we have just read.

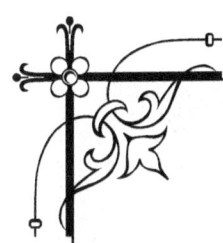

Chapter XIV

SECOND PERIOD OF THE DEVOTION TO THE HOLY FACE — CERTIFICATES.

In the midst of the emotion caused by the miracles operated in Mr. Dupont's room, what were the sentiments of the one to whom they were attributed by public opinion? It is an interesting inquiry. The answer is given by himself. "When any of those circumstances occur which are esteemed miraculous, my thoughts naturally turn to you, to Rome, and to God." He wrote thus to the Prioress of the Benedictines of Arras, to whom, we may remember, he was indebted for his picture of the Holy Face. He adds: "That is the proper way of proceeding, is it not? And I remain in that kind of confusion which must accompany those whom the people regard as instruments." "Our Lord," he says at another time, "blesses more and more those persons who undertake novenas in honor of the Holy Face, and desire in their hearts to repair the outrages committed against the holy name of God." The idea of reparation! That is the dominant idea in his mind; to that he refers all the miracles of grace which are operated.

He was urged to record them, that God might be glorified. He replies as follows: "It would be extremely difficult for me, amid the multitude of my occupations, to find time to give a detailed account of the wonders daily accomplished before the Holy Face; besides, I do not think I have a mission for that. I content myself with collecting the certificates which are forwarded to me. There would be matter for a large volume, even omitting such accounts as are not sufficiently detailed. Should I, at any future time, be asked for these attestations, I shall not delay to resign them to the proper authority; on the contrary, I would give them willingly, because I should thus be relieved from the anxiety attending the safe keeping of the papers. Moreover, they would recall to memory the writings of the venerable Sister Saint-Pierre: they would give an impulse to the movement which is already inspiring thoughts tending to the work of reparation of blasphemy. It would seem that the time had come, when men should know the intentions of God, should fear the chastisements of His justice, and should take refuge in the Heart of Jesus ever open to mercy."

Mr. Dupont awaited this moment in tranquillity and peace, but he would never consent to use the press as a means of propagating the work of the Sacred Face. A friend urged him to publish a circular upon this work, that he might abridge the overwhelming correspondence to which he condemned himself, in order to give repeated explanations. "It is true," he replied, "I am overwhelmed, but I do not think I am in a position to publish such a circular, although it would relieve me of heavy work. The public should not concern itself as to what passes here. So long as it pleases the good God to grant some little success to the work of the Holy Face, His providence will allow the 'miserable pilgrim' to perform his small duties." He had no less repugnance for the publicity acquired by means of pamphlets or books. A priest of the Mission, at that time Superior of the House at Tours, related the following: "A pious layman, a distinguished savant and celebrated writer, came to see me one day, after leaving Mr. Dupont. 'It is not fitting,' he said, 'that such prodigies of grace should remain unknown to the world; the glory of God and the good of religion are involved in it. There is subject matter for a beautiful book, having for its object to make known this holy man, and the work he has so zealously and so successfully embraced; I will undertake it.' 'Wait,' I said to him; 'the project, although good in itself, demands consideration; in such matters, ecclesiastical authorities must be consulted, and their approbation obtained; but it is chiefly important to know if Mr. Dupont himself would consent.' 'There can be no doubt of his sentiment on the subject,' he replied, 'as there is question of bringing before the people that which is the dearest of all things to his heart,—devotion to the Holy Face.' I went to see the servant of God with whom I had been brought into frequent and intimate intercourse by the work of the Nocturnal Adoration. 'I have good news for you,' I said abruptly: 'I know a pious and distinguished author, who proposes to write a book concerning the events which transpire here before the Holy Face.' At these words, Mr. Dupont,—I can see him now,—throwing himself back in his chair in a manner habitual to him, folding his arms, and raising his eyes to heaven, said energetically, in a tone of displeasure, and with a dignified air that I shall never forget: 'I declare positively that, on the very day, I hear that writer has published one word about me, I will close my house, leave Tours, and I will never return to it again.' The decided way in which he pronounced these words, and the expression of his countenance impressed me the more, because I thought I should confer a pleasure, by informing him of a project having for its object the manifestation of the miraculous power of the Holy Face. His humility taught this grand Christian that such were not the means to glorify God. The author, on being informed of what had passed, abandoned his intention."

On no account would Mr. Dupont have wished to attract attention to himself personally, or to lead any one to suppose that the favors obtained at his house were referable to him in the least degree. How often, when receiving in his drawing-room worthy people from the country, who, with simplicity and confidence, asked him to cure them of their maladies, has he exclaimed in a grave and severe tone: "Do you take me for a physician? I am nothing. God is good and all-powerful; kneel down and we will pray. If you have faith, you will obtain; others, worse than you, have obtained because they prayed with confidence..." At the same time, a certain expression of dissatisfaction and vexation upon his countenance, notified them that if they desired to please him, they were taking a false step by appearing to appreciate his virtues, and to rely upon the efficacy of his prayers. But he protested in vain; the miracles of the Holy Face were attributed to his intercession; and from every direction, there were sent him, under the form of attestations and certificates, letters of admiration and gratitude, in which praise of himself was mingled with the homage rendered to God.

What did he do? His course of action from the beginning was modest and prudent. Believing sincerely that he had no part in the miracles, referring all to the glory of the Holy Face, and to the work of reparation, he considered these documents as valuable evidence, as important testimony of sufficient weight to convince ecclesiastical authorities, when they should think the time had come to order an investigation. He regarded himself only as the depositary of them, not the proprietor. They were papers which Divine Providence deputed him to collect, and which were entrusted to his care. With this view, he accepted the certificates which were left with him upon the spot, after an instantaneous cure, or which were sent from a distance after a complete cure had been obtained. He verified these documents, and when occasion required, wrote brief notes upon them; he even requested them, reminding the individuals that it was their duty to render glory to God. It was not long before they lay in piles upon the shelves, and in the drawers of his desk. He cheerfully gave the most recent and most interesting to be read by his friends as a new incentive to their piety, or by strangers, to animate their faith. He would make them the subject of conversation, but quite simply, without parade or show, with an air of tranquil joy and quiet admiration; most frequently he would only point to them, indicating by a significant gesture, that they were awaiting the examination and decision of the competent authority, whenever it might be considered advisable to relieve him of the responsibility. As to taking steps for this purpose with the ecclesiastical superiors, in order to hasten the investigation, or prepare the way, none dared propose it to him, so well was it known that both by natural disposition and virtue, he was opposed to any step of the kind.

At least, would it not be advisable to arrange in a certain order this mass of papers which were sent from all parts of the country, and not leave them heaped pell-mell on his shelves? The question was asked the servant of God. Moreover, was it not necessary, at times, to give a certain form to the certificates, and draw up reports based upon the verbal depositions and written notes of the invalids and of eye-witnesses?

In consequence of his natural temperament and his constant occupations, Mr. Dupont was not the person to impose upon himself this kind of work,—a work, nevertheless, very important for the object he had in view. A friend offered to do it for him. This friend was Mr. d'Avrainville, his countryman, accustomed in the bureau of the navy department, in which he held a situation, to classify documents and write reports. He kindly offered his services to the servant of the Holy Face, to aid him in the "department of certificates," and the offer was accepted with joy and gratitude. From time to time, Mr. d'Avrainville came from Paris to put in order the writings and to arrange "the rubbish," as Mr. Dupont said, without adding or omitting anything, carefully preserving for these papers of every style, coming from persons of every rank, the traditional consideration with which the employees of a bureau guard the minutes confided to their care.

It was to this friend that the holy man bequeathed, by a codicil in his will, the entire collection of papers that, after his death, they might be delivered to those having jurisdiction over such matters. The trust was faithfully fulfilled. Arranged finally by other conscientious and intelligent friends, the precious documents are, at the present time, in the hands of the diocesan authority; and it is from them that we have been permitted to select the greater portion of the narratives we have given, relative to the miraculous cures which took place in Mr. Dupont's room. We shall continue our selection from the same source, and we will now relate the principal facts of this kind, comprised in what we call the second period, from 1856 to 1860.

A child, about eleven years of age, deformed with a hump-back, ill, and the back covered with blisters, was taken from the hospital to Mr. Dupont's. After the prayers were said, he requested Madame It——, who was present at the time, to retire with the child into the adjoining room to apply the oil. He never himself made the unctions on a female, unless it were on the forehead. Madame R—— was thus able to see the terrible affliction of the poor young girl. She had an enormous hump covered with blisters and plasters, because of a fearful ulcer, which the pious lady anointed with the oil, the best way she could, but not without repugnance. The servant of God redoubled his prayers. The unctions were repeated three times. After this, he resumed his writing, and Madame R—— began to read. During this time, the young girl walked slowly up and down the room, holding a crucifix in her hand and praying fervently. Every time she passed Mr. Dupont, who was seated at his desk, she politely bowed her head in salutation. She was a courteous, amiable, and very intelligent child. "Is it an imagination, an illusion?" said Mr. Dupont suddenly, as he raised his eyes and looked at the child; "it seems to me that the hump has disappeared. Take her," he said to Madame R——, "into the next room, undress her and examine the back." Madame R—— did as he directed, and as she opened the dress, the blisters, plasters, all the dressings of the ulcer fell to the ground. There was no hump on the back, nor the least appearance of the wound remaining; the child was no longer deformed. "Is it an illusion? Do our eyes deceive us?" said Mr. Dupont and Madame R—— to each other. They sent for Mr. Dupont's mother, Madame d'Arnaud, without telling her what had just happened. "Look at that poor little deformed child," they said to her; "see the hump on her back." "Deformed! a hump on her back!" said Madame d'Arnaud; "what do you mean? She is no more deformed than you or I." "She was, awhile ago," they say to her; "but she is so no longer; our eyes do not deceive us." Her clothing had become so large, that they were obliged to fasten it in folds to enable her to wear it.

On some occasions, prayer alone, offered by Mr. Dupont, sufficed to obtain wonderful cures. In 1856, one of his goddaughters, Marie R——, only five months old, was ill with fever, diarrhœa and vomiting. Her condition was such that they were obliged to watch her day and night; and the first inquiry made by the physician on entering the house was: "Is she alive?" At last, finding her very low, the doctor simply prescribed a mustard plaster, without anticipating any benefit from it. But, contrary to expectation, the infant passed the night without fever, diarrhoea, or vomiting, and the doctor, instead of finding her dead, as he expected, noticed so great a change for the better that he pronounced her out of danger. So surprising was the improvement, that he inquired for how long a time they had applied the mustard plasters. He was told they had not been removed at all. He hastened to remove them himself, attributing the reaction to the mustard, and to the blisters which he expected to uncover; but what does he see? The limbs of the infant are not even reddened; by some unaccountable mistake, instead of using the mustard which he had ordered, the nurse had made a flaxseed poultice. There was but one explanation of the extraordinary circumstance which could be given. About the time they applied the supposed mustard plasters, Mr. Dupont had called. He had prayed beside the child, and, upon leaving, he had said to the parents with emphasis: "Do not despair of her cure." The physician did not hesitate to recognize a supernatural power in the sudden change. The visit and the prayer of Mr. Dupont without an unction, or other exterior sign, had obtained the cure. Impressed with the truth of this idea, the parents always preserved a reverential gratitude towards Mr. Dupont; they honored him as a saint, and the child, miraculously saved from death, is now a Religious in a monastery of the Visitation.

The following anecdote was communicated to us by a Benedictine of England. Mr. Peter Swing, a student at the College of Downside, being attacked by an affection of the eyes which obliged him to suspend his studies, accompanied his family to Tours. There was no exterior evidence of defective sight. He went to the house of Mr. Dupont, who approached him, as he entered, and, to his astonishment, placing his hand upon his eyes, said: "Sir, the sight you came here to seek, will be restored to you." The young man became deadly pale on hearing revealed to him what he had mentioned to no one. He, in reality, recovered his sight and resumed his studies at Downside, in England.

A reliable person narrates the following: "I heard from Mr. Dupont himself what I now repeat to you. I went to visit him, and I was scarcely seated when he said to me in his inimitable tone of tranquil joy; "Something singular has happened; it is a charming circumstance. A short time ago, a lady came and asked permission to pray before the Holy Face, requesting me to unite with her to obtain the conversion of her brother, an officer of high rank, at that time in garrison in a northern city. We recited some prayers, after which I spoke to her a few words of encouragement, and urged her to have confidence in the success of her petitions. I looked at her, and suddenly, an idea struck me. 'But, Madam, there is something defective in your eyes, (she squinted); take a little oil and anoint them.' 'Oh! sir, that is of no consequence at my age, ... and I have lived thus up to the present time.' I insisted: 'it is so simple and so well to ask of God even trifles.' She consented and used the oil once; we prayed, and, after a second unction, she arose perfectly cured. We thanked God, and now she was full of confidence, sure of obtaining the desired conversion. She recommended herself to the prayers of the Adoration, and I promised to inscribe her petition upon the register. Yesterday morning, I received a letter from her. On her arrival, her brother regarded her with astonishment. 'Ah! you have had an operation performed?' 'Not at all.' She related to him what had passed; he was so impressed that he has received the sacraments."

A priest from Normandy, the curate of an important parish, had been suffering for nine months from an extinction of voice. He was obliged always to carry about him a slate, as it was his only means of communicating with his friends. He went to Tours. Mr. Dupont anointed his throat with the oil which was burning before the Holy Face, and then began the prayers for the restoration of the invalid. Having finished the prayer, he requested him to speak. The priest replied in the lowest whisper that he dared not attempt it, because the effort to speak louder, deprived him of the power of uttering any sound whatever, and, moreover, resulted in acute pain of the throat. Mr. Dupont insisted. "You are a priest, sir, and you know better than I, who am a layman, the faith that is required, the faith that moves mountains. Try to say: *Sit Nomen Domini benedictum!* The good curate endeavored to articulate these words. He succeeded in making his voice heard, but it resembled that of a ventriloquist. They then said the Litany of the Holy Face and other prayers, which he was able to answer in a loud voice. The longer he continued to speak, the stronger his voice became, until, at last, it acquired its natural tone. 'Sing the *Magnificat*,' said Mr. Dupont; and immediately he sang the *Magnificat* in a strong and loud tone. The following Sunday, he preached at high Mass, and related to his parishioners the facts above stated. He left his slate at Mr. Dupont's, in testimony of his gratitude. For a long time, it lay on the chimney-piece of the servant of God, enclosed in a frame covered with glass. At the present moment it is among the "*ex votos*" in the oratory of the Sacred Face.

Besides the certificates of which we have spoken, there was another kind of *ex voto* not less valued by Mr. Dupont: we mean the canes and crutches left in his hands by the infirm and lame who had been healed before the Holy Face. These were collected, tied in bundles, and placed in a small cabinet which opened into the drawing-room, and which has since been styled "the miracle room," a sort of museum, unique in its kind, presenting to the eye different objects which it is impossible to contemplate without a lively interest and intense emotion. To the pilgrim and the traveller, they offered indubitable evidence of the miraculous power exerted in that holy spot. They were of all forms, and of every quality, from the commonest stick and ordinary cane, to the pair of crutches skilfully stuffed and polished, each fashioned to suit the want of human infirmity; the greater portion of them had evidently been in long use. This strange and curious collection increased by degrees, as cures were operated and graces obtained. The account of it is simple and touching.

Almost every day, one, or several infirm persons present themselves with the hope of being healed. They are the cripple, the maimed, invalids attacked by gout, rheumatism, or paralyzed in different ways. One arrives dragging himself along painfully, leaning on crutches, or a stick;

another is carried in the arms of a parent, a servant, or a friend; others are supported as they totter along. Prayers are said, and the holy oil applied to the diseased, or paralyzed limbs; the prayer is heard, and faith is rewarded. The sufferer declares himself, either partially, or wholly relieved; the infirm recover their health; the lame walk; those who, a moment before, were incapable of moving, arise and move without help. To test their strength, they walk around the apartment, or, with overflowing joy, they run in the garden. Before leaving, in order to visit, by Mr. Dupont's advice, the different churches of the city, and to deposit, for the poor, in the box of each, an offering of thanksgiving, they place in the "room of miracles" the stick or the crutches which, in future, will be useless to them. The man of God attaches to each an inscription, containing simply a name and a date. It is an additional *ex voto* offering, another homage rendered to the power of the Holy Face; it is a palpable proof which none can contest, which will rejoice the good, fortify the weak, and inspire others with confidence in the efficacy of prayer. Later, they will furnish to diocesan authority matter for an official document which may be presented as evidence in favor of the work of reparation. They have been deposited by persons from different countries, and from all parts of France. In this manner the precious collection has been gradually formed. The facts we have thus grouped together and recorded in a general way, occurred successively, in public, in the presence of friends, strangers, pilgrims of every kind, going and coming during the whole time, all of whom could say: "I saw, I was present, I can assert."

"I saw," says Zépherin, the servant of Mr. Dupont, "a young girl of seventeen brought in a carriage from the depot, and carried in her father's arms to the drawing-room. I saw her instantaneously cured; she left her crutch before the Holy Face, and returned to the cars without any support whatever." The same servant relates many similar instances which he witnessed almost every day. He mentions, among others, a cripple, living near Tours, who was completely cured, and who left his crutch at Mr. Dupont's.

These miracles were, of course, much spoken of by the public, and they formed an inexhaustible subject of conversation. Very many were reported by the citizens of Tours, and circulated among the people. It would be impossible to relate so large a number; we, however, give an extraordinary one, for the truth of which we can vouch.

A worthy woman, well known in her neighborhood by the name of Mother Eugene, had been for a long time confined to her bed, from which she could arise only with extreme difficulty. The parish priest, on going one day to visit her, found her almost incapable of moving herself. What was his astonishment, the following day, when he saw Mother Eugene walk rapidly towards the confessional where he was seated, and kneel, without difficulty, to make her Confession, —Mother Eugene whom he had seen on the eve unable even to lift her hand! 'How did this happen, good Mother?' he said to her. She answered calmly: 'Oh! sir, I went to Mr. Dupont, and I am well now.' And then she told, as the most natural and simple thing in the world, that being urged by one of her neighbors who had been talking to her of the holy man, she arose, as best she could, aided by Mother Proust, another kind neighbor; she begged her husband for a crutch, and he borrowed one for her. She reached Mr. Dupont's in this condition. She was anointed with the oil, and she was immediately cured. "As a proof of your cure," said Mr. Dupont, "leave your crutch here." She did as he directed. On her return home, she related all to her husband. "Where is the crutch?" he asked. "What have you done with it?" It was a borrowed crutch which he had promised to return. In order to leave a perpetual memorial of the miracle, the husband ordered a new crutch, took it to Mr. Dupont and withdrew the other. This crutch, inscribed with the name and date, remains among the *ex votos*.

All these objects were held sacred by the servant of God, it mattered not from whom they came. On receiving them, he constituted himself their depositary and guardian in the name of the Holy Face, and in the interest of reparation. These crutches, these sticks remitted to him with so much emotion, with such transports of pure joy by poor sufferers cured before his eyes, under his hand, were venerated, we might say, nursed by him, as sensible proofs of the divine goodness; he exhibited them with an air of satisfaction and triumph. He took a jealous care of their preservation, was careful in preventing the inscriptions from becoming detached. From time to time he directed the servants to dust them; once or twice a year, he sent them to the neighboring baker's, that by being heated in an oven, they might be protected from moisture, and preserved from decay and from worms. By such precautions, he kept them always perfectly clean and sound.

During the Prussian invasion, when the ambulances established at Tours were crowded with the sick and wounded, they could think of no better way of supplying the wants of the unfortunate victims of our disasters, than by levying on the arsenal at Mr. Dupont's. It was a sacrifice for him; he made it, however, with his habitual serenity and charity; but his cherished stock was notably diminished. Many crutches and sticks, which were borrowed from him, were never returned. It would be impossible to estimate the exact number of those precious articles which disappeared at that time. Mr. Dupont computed them at sixty or seventy. After his death, all that remained were verified, collected, and put in order by two of his friends.

These curious *ex votos* now number one hundred and forty-six. Nearly all of them are arranged in order in the "room of miracles," which has become a part of the sacristy, and in the oratory on each side of the main altar, where they attract the attention of pilgrims. Those who deposited them, easily recognize them. Thus, on the 16th of November, 1876, a worthy man from Chissay, not finding us at the oratory of the Holy Face, sought us in the sacristy of the cathedral. He was accompanied by his curate and two villagers, the elder of whom said he had been a servant of Mr. Dupont, when he was staying with Mr. de Marolles at the chateau of Chissay. The other related to us, in presence of several members of the chapter, that in 1857 his leg was in such a condition that the physicians thought of amputating it. He went to Mr. Dupont by whom he was known; he anointed his leg three times; it was instantaneouly cured, and so perfectly that he was able to go, at once, to the cathedral and several churches, to offer the prayers of thanksgiving recommended by the servant of God; he waited a fortnight, and then returned before the Holy Face, to deposit the crutch which he no longer needed. It is still marked with his name. "Oh!" he said, laughing, "I recognized it very well in the chapel; it is on the right side."

On the 22d of November, 1878, a resident of Lignières, who had gone to Tours to celebrate the festival of St. Martin, entered, by chance, the oratory of the Holy Face; at the sight of Mr. Dupont's room transformed into a chapel, he was touched and astonished. Meeting with a priest of the house, he narrated to him how he had been formerly cured. "On this spot," he said, "I prayed with Mr. Dupont; here, he anointed my leg. I left my stick in testimony of my gratitude; where is it?" We examine those arranged around the altar, and then we pass into the "room of miracles;" the worthy man joyously recognizes his stick among the *ex votos* of this small apartment "There it is!" he exclaims. His name and the date of his cure is inscribed upon it: *January 11, 1873,—Martin Daveaux, of Lignières*. He had not seen the house since that time; but on entering, he recognized the porch and the hall, where Mr. Dupont had kindly taken leave of him, having accompanied him to the door with his habitual politeness.

Among the crutches and canes arranged in the oratory of the Sacred Face, an old, common umbrella is noticeable.

The inquiry as to the manner in which this strange *ex voto* obtained so honorable a place, is naturally made. It happened in the following way. Cardinal Morlot, while he was Archbishop of Tours, went to Paris at the invitation of the Saint-Saène family, in order to bless the marriage of Mademoiselle de Saint-Saène with Mr. de Musy. This circumstance threw him in the company of the brother of the groom, M. l'Abbé Musy, who, in consequence of an affection of the throat, had, for four years, completely lost his voice. The Cardinal invited him to go to Touraine, and told him of the miraculous cures obtained at Mr. Dupont's. The invalid went in May, 1854, and was instantaneously cured. The whole family, moved by gratitude, desired to go to Tours, to return thanks to the Holy Face. They wished, moreover, to obtain the cure of Madame de Musy, who was so far deprived of the use of her limbs, as to walk with great difficulty and pain. Several other persons joined the party; among them, a young workwoman of Paris, who was the victim of a terrible cancer. Mr. Dupont thus received about a dozen travellers: the usual prayers were said. In a short time, Madame de Musy was able to walk, and was decidedly better. They next turned their attention to the poor girl with the cancer. Madame Viot-Otter, who happened to be there, took her to the cabinet and made the unction with the oil; she repeated it six times without effect; the patient returned after each unction to pray before the Holy Face. After the seventh unction Madame Viot entered triumphant, saying that one of the openings of the frightful wound was healed; there were three. The second was healed at the eighth unction, and the third, at the ninth. Thus completely cured, the young girl could scarcely contain herself; she seemed intoxicated with joy. The following day, she was presented to the Cardinal, who could not withhold the homage due to the power of the Holy Face. These cures were widely known and talked about generally in all circles. A Mr. Malibran, a musician, persuaded his wife, an artiste also, affected with a throat disease, causing extinction of voice which prevented the exercise of her talent, to make the pilgrimage to Tours. She obtained her cure, and her grateful husband fulfilled his promise of going thither on foot. On the way, being overtaken by rain, he bought an old umbrella from a peasant. Having returned thanks to the Holy Face, he left the umbrella among the *ex votos* as a souvenir of his pilgrimage.

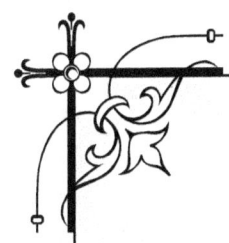

Chapter XV

His Correspondence.

WHILST PASSING his life before the Holy Face, in the midst of the infirm and afflicted who went every day to beg the aid of his prayers, and solicit from his hands unctions with the miraculous oil, Mr. Dupont was not less faithful to the daily labor of his vast correspondence with his acquaintances, friends, and all who had recourse to him by letters, for any purpose of faith or piety. His correspondence occupied a large place in his life. It contributed, as much as his good works, to procure glory to God by the benefit it was to numbers of souls.

He frequently received fourteen and fifteen letters a day. He answered all of them on the same day; he made this practice a law to himself. It is difficult to appreciate properly the additional amount of occupation this imposed upon him, and the various sacrifices which thence resulted. For a long time, he had renounced even dining out with friends; this, however, did not cost him much, as he himself acknowledges: "For twenty-three years (he writes in 1859,) I have not dined from home. I cannot express to you the pleasure I experience in realizing that I have been able to escape that tyranny." He had, likewise, given up every kind of amusement, and all games introduced into drawing-rooms; this cost him no more than the other, as he gives us to understand in certain remarks made in a letter to a friend: "I should be astonished, if you could discover any sign of real joy on the faces of those engaged in backgammon, and such other trifles invented to kill time. But the Holy Scriptures, in telling us that *time is short*, instruct us that we should not kill it, but make a good use of it."

These sacrifices were light, but nothing was more opposed to his natural disposition than the habit to which he subjected himself of replying, day by day, to the letters which were sent him, and remaining seated for hours at his desk, attending to his correspondence. He was to be seen taking notes, registering recommendations for the Nocturnal Adoration, or for the Holy Face, replying to persons who had written to him, and doing it all with a serenity of countenance, and an air of cheerfulness which never betrayed the extent of the sacrifice. The number of letters, the result of this incessant labor, was immense. We have in our possession only a portion of those which have been preserved, but these suffice to enable us to form a judgment of the others. All bear the impress of a holy originality, which stamps him as a supernatural man, a man of faith, living in the midst of our modern society, in a world apart, like a Christian of the early ages. Mr. Dupont appears in them just as he is. He is truly "himself;" we find his exquisite urbanity, his preventing and affectionate charity, his elevated piety, his active and generous zeal for the glory of God, the interest of the Church, and for her works; there is in them the same cheerful pleasantry as in his conversations, the same serenity of soul and imperturbable confidence in God; there is the same disposition, the same simplicity, the same forgetfulness of self and of his personality.

There is not a letter which does not contain a pious sentiment, either under the form of a remark, a reflection, or a prayer. Even his letters of business and pure civility, however short they may be, exhibit this characteristic. He frequently commences thus: "I salute your good angel," or the Blessed Virgin, or the saint whose festival was celebrated on that day. They conclude with such words as the following: "Let us love Jesus, in order that He may grant us the graces we need, to serve Him." "I salute you at the feet of Jesus and Mary." He rarely omits to quote in the body of the letter a text from the Scriptures, and if he refers to the political or religious events of the period, he views and judges them with the eye of faith. The motto he had adopted for conversation: "To speak of God, or to keep silence," seems to have been applied equally to his correspondence: "To write of God and the things of God, or to cease to write."

The nature of the subjects of which he treats is infinitely various, according to the impressions of the moment, the circumstances in which France and the Church are placed, or the persons to whom he is writing. He enters at once into their spiritual necessities and the dispositions of their souls. He is particularly interesting, when he undertakes by his letters and prayers to obtain the return to God of a friend, a countryman, or of one who is dear to him. With this in view, he enters into an active and continuous correspondence, from which no other occupation has power to withdraw him.

As long as time was at his disposal, previous to the commencement of the pilgrimages to the Holy Face, he would write at length upon a subject of devotion which attracted him, or on some religious news recently imparted to him, which caused him joy. His letters, at such times, would extend to four or five pages, or even more, written neatly and without erasures, from the abundance of his heart, and with the outpouring of his beautiful soul. In proportion as the visits of pilgrims call upon his time, his letters become shorter and shorter, concise, reduced to a few lines with many words abbreviated. At last, they were simple notes, in each of which sparkled in streams of light and fire, holy thoughts and pious words. Without being a scholar, he had real epistolary genius. His phraseology, although somewhat diffuse, at times obscure or unconnected, is expressive and graceful. His style is flowing, easy, agreeable, simple, elegant and correct; it is the language of a man of education and taste, stamped with a seal of originality and a vigor of expression which possess both merit and beauty.

To enable the reader to appreciate the servant of God in this respect, we will reproduce some of the letters written by him on different subjects during the period (1845 to 1860) when he was actively engaged in the works of St. Martin, the Nocturnal Adoration, and the pilgrimage to the Holy Face.

To Mr. Le Pailleur. December 8, 1845. "My dear friend, *quam bonus Deus Israel!* How good is the God of Israel! How wonderful is the attribute of goodness in God! God alone is good, said our Lord... But we must become good, as far as our weakness permits, since it was said that the good will be on the right hand, and the wicked, on the left. What a moment! I imagine that those who will have passed their lives in thinking and saying: 'How good is God!' will not be condemned to feel the weight of His justice during eternity. Pray then, I beg you, that these words, so sweet to the heart: 'How good is God!' may often be upon my lips to refresh them; pray that I may often have the opportunity of speaking them to the ears of those with whom I may be associated. My God, since faith comes by hearing, I understand that Thou must demand an account of idle words, and I humbly ask pardon for all those which I have either uttered, or listened to with pleasure. Ask for me of our good God the secret of loving, and the grace afterwards to impart it."

To a friend in Cayenne. April 8, 1848. "What will become of Europe, Asia, America, and the Colonies? God knows. What we know, my dear friend, is that 'all things work together for the good of the elect,' and in order to look calmly at the future, we need to advance, as far as possible, in the path of justice. A narrow way, because it is but little frequented, but assuredly a very pleasant way. The wicked, after death, will exclaim, howling: *Lassati sumus in via iniquitates et perditiones.* 'We wearied ourselves in the way of iniquity and destruction.' It is not necessary to have advanced far in life, to know that man takes more trouble and pains to damn than to sanctify himself. When, appealing to the Gospel, we say to some one: 'Do not deceive yourself, the present life is short; a throne of glory awaits in the life to come those who yield their hearts to this magnificent promise,...' too often, alas! these beautiful words are disdainfully rejected, and after having derided both the Holy Book, which contains the glorious Testament, and him who interprets it in favor of man redeemed by the blood of Jesus Christ,... the foolish man returns to the things of earth, and, as though it were not enough for him to wallow in the mire, he takes vanity in it. Fie! fie!"

To the same. October 7, 1848. "No doubt, my dear friend, the complaint you make, that you find few aids to piety in Cayenne, is well founded, but I should prefer to know that fortifying yourself against such an obstacle, you had made that very privation the corner-stone of a great spiritual progress. You would be as the tree beaten by the tempest, planted on a rock, which, for that very reason, becomes stronger and more hardy than the one which springs up delicate and slender, in the shade of a humid valley. Do you think that our Lord has no graces in store for those who practice to the letter the counsel: *Contendite intrare?* The possession of Heaven is worth the struggle, and I am convinced that the difficulties which we meet in the road, are levelled in proportion as we make use of them as stepping-stones to elevate ourselves to God.

"Hardly were they enlightened by the truths of faith, when the first Christians were ready to shed their blood in defence of these truths before proconsuls, and now among Christians, scarcely do we venture to say we are Christians. But a decisive moment has arrived: faith elevates itself, and God is not sparing of miracles. Truth alone can offer effectual resistance in the present crisis, which is the desperate struggle of all bad doctrines whose origin is the principle of a depraved reason, a principle, breathed into Luther, by the old liar, Satan..."

To the Superioress of the Visitation of Paray-le-Monial. May 9, 1848. "How many evidences are given at the present time to prove to people of faith that the hour for combat has arrived, and that our good Jesus is about to win for Himself, a second time, by the loving effusions of His Sacred Heart, the title of Saviour assumed by Him on Calvary, which the demon endeavors to tear from the hearts of men. And it happens that the successor of Pius IX has been prophetically designated by the glorious words: *Lumen in cœlo,* 'light in Heaven.' With what confidence then should we not consider the future! The contest may be terrible, but it will eventually be to the disadvantage of the impious, and, assuredly, many souls will be brought back to the love and fear of God. Let us live then in the sweet confidence that the Heart of Jesus, combating the *spirit* of the world, will gain a signal victory.

To a son on the death of his mother. December 12, 1857. "My very dear friend, the designs of Providence are merciful. You regret that you were unable to close the eyes of your mother; but who knows if your good angel and hers did not thus dispose circumstances, in order to secure a greater peace for your dear mother, at the moment when Jesus, Sacrament and not Judge, was about to introduce her into eternity? Is anything comparable to a death following closely upon holy Viaticum? We may well say then with the apostle: *Ubi est, mors, victoria tua?* 'O death, where is thy victory?' It not only opens the gate of Heaven to the deceased, but it becomes a balm of consolation to the survivors. We will pray that this balm may superabound in your hearts, particularly in your father's. On your return, we will consider together the happiness of those souls whose lives have been holy, and we will animate ourselves to follow their example, that we may not be, for those who survive us, a cause of sorrow."

To a wife on the death of her husband. October 3, 1855. "Madame, the trials of this life conduct us to the joys of eternity. This is the consolation which first presents itself to the soul, at the moment when a friend is taken from us, after having labored courageously at the work of salvation. It is in Heaven, and in no place else, that we must in thought unite with those who have happily terminated their pilgrimage. There is one sentence of the Gospel which will remain unchanged through centuries, always imparting peace to the wounded heart when, by slightly varying the sense, we apply to a deceased friend what the angel said to the holy women at the sepulchre: 'Why do you seek the living among the dead? He is not here.' No, he is not here in these mortal remains, which will await henceforth in the dust of the earth, the resurrection of the body. We must lift our eyes on high, and we never do so without experiencing either a great consolation, or entertaining the hope of being one day reunited to the object of our tears. How many things I could say to you! *Better is the house of mourning than the house of joy.* The Holy Scripture is explicit on this point.

"Be pleased to say to Mr. L—— that I am grateful for the sentiments of regard he expresses for me in your letter. His good angel will soon make known to him that the alms bestowed by his father, are singularly efficacious in abridging the distance between earth and Heaven. Nevertheless, we will pray at the Nocturnal Adoration for the venerable deceased. Permit me to subscribe myself in our Lord and at the feet of Mary, &c., &c..."

To a friend. Transports of fervor and divine love. May 17, 1851. It is true that the political situation is dark; but if the political horizon is clouded, the heavenly horizon is clear; we must be blind, if we fail to see the sweet dew of graces descending upon the parched earth. There are too many prayers ascending from earth to allow us to suppose that God will abandon us: too many holy souls are weeping, to permit us to fear the degrading chaos into which philosophy would drag humanity, contrary to its high destiny.

"Let us then weep with those who desire to save their brethren; let us love God, since He alone is good; let us also love each other since he has commanded us to do so, and, by obeying His holy law, we are certain of enjoying His holy love throughout eternity."

To the same. Love of our Lord and zeal for the salvation of souls. April 3, 1853. "Truly, my dear friend, what prevents us, who believe in Jesus and Mary, from running after them to the conquests of souls? We should weep incessantly at the thought of the terrible woes, towards which are rushing the impious, the careless, and, with them, the inert mass which more or less blindly follows the example of others. Was it not the tears of the sisters of Lazarus which made him come forth from the tomb, without their being able to take the least vanity from their mediation in the affair? Let us then weep over the spiritually dead, and Jesus, for the glory of God, may command many to come forth from the tomb."

To the same. Compliments of the New Year. January 15, 1855. "Had I been able to dispose even of a moment, I would, certainly, have written you at the commencement of the New Year. The Christian sentiment infused into it, relieves the idea of what is commonplace. There is, besides, a serious reality in the gift of another year for which we shall have to render an account. God evidently grants it to us, only with the intention that we should profit by it to do penance, and, through penance, to render ourselves worthy of *paradise at the end of our days*. Thus, those who content themselves with saying on the 1st of January: 'I wish you a happy New Year,' are generally indifferent as to the care of their salvation; and they need, at least once a year, to hear people of faith speak of paradise, in order to interrupt by such thoughts, the prescriptive right which Satan would claim over them."

The disastrous inundation of the Loire in 1856, holds an important place in Mr. Dupont's correspondence. He had regarded the one of 1846 as a serious warning from Heaven to his adopted country. He had thence drawn the conclusion, that in such circumstances prayer, persevering prayer, was a necessity.

Animated by the spirit of the Church, he wished to see his fellow-citizens profiting by this lesson of Divine Providence. Witnessing, on the contrary, the scandalous public rejoicing to which, after the inundation, even good people abandoned themselves, and which afforded just grounds to fear and foresee the political commotions of 1848 and the following years, the man of God was alarmed by what he called a satanic influence; he advised men to have recourse to the invocation of the holy name of Jesus, a practice of reparation by which he was, at that time, entirely preoccupied.

"Oh!" he said, "would that all at Tours could profit by the terrible warning! But behold, alas! balls and plays are arranged for the benefit of the victims of the inundation! Is not Satan merciless? His charity is to make men laugh, and every philanthropist must first amuse himself before aiding his unfortunate brother. The Holy Ghost has said: *The poor man is merciful*; but the lying spirit would persuade us that charity is in the heart of the *rich*; and then he ensnares the rich by the bait of pleasure, and they believe that they have performed a good work, when, after all, they have only insulted misfortune. This is one of the great evils of our age, and one of the most difficult to attack. But let us have recourse to our good Master. Let a holy distrust of self possess us at the sight of so many enemies, who wish to efface His holy name from our hearts. In order to resist this odious attack, let us have often on our lips the adorable name of Jesus. Are we not told that in His name we can do all things? What other help then do we need? Jesus! be to us a Jesus."

Mr. Dupont interpreted public disasters as providential and mysterious events, in which God, by a deep design of His wisdom, evinces both His justice and His mercy. It is from this two fold point of view eminently supernatural, that in 1856 he forms his judgment upon the sudden inundation of the Loire, by which the city of Tours was the principal sufferer.

In the midst of the catastrophe, the Prioress of the Benedictines of Arras and the chaplain wrote to make inquiries as to his safety. He replied immediately (June 10, 1856): "I am touched by the interest manifested by yourselves and the good people of Arras in our regard. It is undoubtedly true that Tours was in imminent danger of utter destruction. During the night of the 4th, it seemed certain that in less than an hour the whole city would be swept away like a straw, by the waters which, for several days, had been threatening to overwhelm us. We had never been in such danger. But our good God did not deal the blow. He did not wish to call, unexpectedly, thirty thousand souls before the tribunal of His justice."

Then in reply to the anxiety expressed concerning himself personally, he says: "One foot more, and the water would have entered my room. We were spared, and were consoled on finding that the water which was rising in the garden also, rose no higher from the moment that I yielded to the entreaties of two worthy men, and consented to elevate a little the stand which supports the lamp before the Holy Face."

These "worthy people," not having Mr. Dupont's faith, expected to see his room flooded, and, fearing for the holy picture, they persuaded him to elevate the stand. The servant of the Holy Face consented with great reluctance. What happened is not related by himself; it was too personal, but we can assert it upon the testimony of several eye-witnesses. When the waters of the Loire overflowing its banks, rose in continually increasing waves as far as Saint-Etienne street, Mr. Dupont, inspired by confidence and the spirit of faith, traced in his garden opposite the rise of the waters, a transverse line in the direction of the Holy Face in his drawing-room. The water, which was becoming higher as it progressed, stopped its course exactly at that dividing line. The house was not damaged in the least. Every one recognized in this circumstance a special mark of the divine protection.

Mr. Dupont exercised great generosity towards the sufferers by the inundation.

Notwithstanding the superhuman efforts to protect the quarter of Saint-Pierre-des-Corps from the waters, the whole faubourg and the surrounding country were submerged. Fortunately, a portion of the population had sought refuge in time, either in the grounds attached to Saint-Gatian, or in the gardens, and on the terraces of the archiepiscopal residence. It was a frightful night. In every direction, buildings and walls were falling with a loud crash. Those residents of the faubourg who had delayed to leave their houses, until escape was cut off by the waters, awaited the daylight in the most intense anxiety. Mr. Plailly, the curate of the parish, a man of intelligent zeal and active intrepidity, remained with a few courageous men as his companions in the centre of his parish, in order to lend aid wherever the necessity was most imperious. In this critical situation, while the whole city was a prey to the greatest alarm, Mr. Dupont went in a boat, at four o'clock in the morning, to visit the victims of the inundation. To kind words and charitable encouragement, he added the substantial help of provisions, money, and other important articles. Mr. Dupont was the first to go to the scene of the disaster; the second was His Eminence, Cardinal Morlot, who went in a boat to console and succor the unfortunate. The successor of St. Martin and the holy man of Tours, without previous concert, inspired by the same thought, met where charity called. Under such circumstances as these, Mr. Dupont considered, in the first place, the sanctification and spiritual good of souls; but he did not neglect the corporal wants of the sufferers, nor the duties of an enlightened charity.

His sojourn at the baths of Néris and of Bourbon l'Archambault furnishes, likewise, the subject of several interesting letters.

Mr. Dupont had an excellent constitution and robust health. His lofty stature and finely proportioned form, the serenity of his countenance which mirrored the peace of his soul, and the sprightliness of his conversation, evidenced a man sound in body and mind, equally well endowed physically and morally. But when, in consequence of the spread of devotion to the Holy Face, he condemned himself to a sedentary life, as contrary to his tastes as to his temperament, he suffered from severe attacks of gout and rheumatism, for which the physicians obliged him to try remedies. At first, they prescribed the baths of Néris. "Your letter of the 10th of May, my dear friend," he writes to a missionary (July 3, 1843), "found me at the baths, where I have been for the past week, by order of the physician, on account of rheumatism, which threatens to settle in all the principal joints. I am assured that twenty days at the baths will suffice to restore me. God knows. Does God will it? *Fiat voluntas tua*, that holy and sovereignly good will."

In going to the baths, he obeys the physician, he does the will of God, and we see the manner in which he sanctifies "the broad way," as he calls it, "along which he is compelled to drag himself with pain." "For our motto during the journey, we adopted," he says "these words of Father Avancini, *Assuesce non inania, sed divinia loqui, ut socium itineris habeas Jesum.* 'Accustom yourself to speak, not of frivolous things, but of God and divine things, that you may merit to have Jesus as the companion of your journey.'" Speaking of his sojourn at the baths, he adds: "I can scarcely meet with one here who is willing to make the agreement with me to speak only of God. Usually, people come to the baths only to *gratify* the beast; and the most wicked of all beasts derives great profit from this animal disposition."

As his malady had notably augmented in consequence of his continual and increasing correspondence, the baths of Bourbon were ordered him. His friends were surprised that he went to the baths, and did not have recourse to the anointing with oil, and the prayers he employed so efficaciously for others. "You must know," he writes to one of his friends, "that, before going to the baths of Bourbon, I asked our Lord to cure me of the rheumatism, which is of a nature to incapacitate me for work. Not having obtained my petition, which did not surprise me, I considered it my duty to seek natural remedies, submitting myself with my whole heart to the will of God."

We find him there again in 1862: "Here I am for twenty days to come, engaged in a life rather animal than spiritual. But I have scarcely more time than at Tours, as my correspondence follows me here." Without being entirely restored, he ceased going to Bourbon where, however, he left the reputation of a saint, as we may judge by the following extract from a letter written by a pious priest: "Oh! if you knew the good odor of virtue afforded by the 'holy man of Tours,' to the little city of Bourbon l'Archambault, where I was so fortunate as to live with him and study him closely for two seasons!" The citizens of the place, and the peasants of the surrounding country gave him no other name than "saint." "Is the saint here?" they would ask when they brought the infirm to him to be healed. A peasant woman one day led her child, who was club-footed, to Mr. Dupont, and asked him to cure her. The saint, in his humility, said to the woman: "It is not I who can cure your daughter; God alone has that power. Pray to Him with great confidence. Here is a little oil taken from a lamp which always burns before a picture of the Holy Face of our Lord; apply this oil to your child's foot, and, in the meantime, I will unite my prayers with yours." That time was not long: in a few minutes, the foot had assumed a natural form. Not able to contain her joy, the little girl, jumping four steps at a time, descended the two stories of the house. It would be impossible to describe the effect produced upon the inmates of the house by this instantaneous cure. The happy mother had, as she said, no trouble now, but that of getting new shoes and stockings for her child.

Perhaps the reader is curious to know what kind of life Mr. Dupont led during the season at the baths. It may be summed up in a few words. After taking the daily bath, and other remedies usually prescribed at such places of resort, he did not lose his time. He devoted none of it to anything frivolous, useless, or sensual. Every morning at half-past four, he was at church. "He was there," says the Superioress of the hospital, "at our meditation; he returned at three o'clock in the afternoon. He would go and converse with the curate; he would come to see us, and entertain the Sisters on some pious subject; he would visit the sick, the poor, the peasants of the neighborhood, in order to speak to them of God. His life was, in every respect, edifying, and in no way resembled that led by others who frequented the baths."

He did not exactly bestow large alms; but his charity was characterized by a delicacy peculiar to himself. When he met, or saw from his window, a woman carrying a basket of fruit or vegetables, he would stop her, buy her little stock, pay the price demanded, then, pointing towards the hospital, he would say: "Take them to the kitchen of the Orphan Asylum." When the Sister in charge of the kitchen inquired the price, the woman would reply: "You owe nothing; I have been paid: the grand gentleman who lives opposite sent you what I had." This happened so frequently that it ceased to excite surprise.

In the suburbs of Bourbon, there lived a poor man terribly deformed, and of the most repulsive appearance. Every one shunned him on account of his violent and disagreeable temper; his mother alone succeeded, although with great difficulty, in calming him. His name was Rollin. Mr. Dupont was told of the lamentable condition of the unfortunate man; he asked to see him, and was conducted to the house. By dint of kind attentions and gentle words, he tamed that passionate and savage nature, which gradually yielded to the influence of his goodness. The servant of God, moreover, declares openly that Rollin is his friend, and that he takes great pleasure in visiting and conversing with him. Rollin, for his part, is proud of his only friend. Religion soon crowns the work of charity. Faithful to the advice of his benefactor, he becomes reconciled with God and man. He died a few years afterwards with the sentiments of a true Christian. No one doubted that he was indebted to Mr. Dupont's charitable attentions for his happy death.

A season at the Springs has become in our days a requirement of fashionable life. In conducting thither the servant of the Holy Face, notwithstanding his repugnance, Divine Providence had His own designs. In his person was presented to those who frequent these resorts of leisure and pleasure, a model of the virtues which ought to be practiced by Christians. We know, moreover, that he was made the instrument of the conversion or the spiritual direction of many souls. Between the pious layman and unknown strangers, or passing visitors, there was often established a friendship or an acquaintance which led to a continuous correspondence, or which was the cause of graces miraculously obtained.

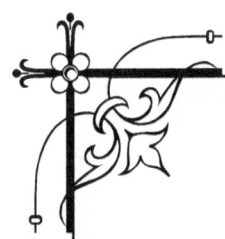

Chapter XVI

Death of His Mother, His Affection for His Relatives and Friends.

Until this time, Mr. Dupont's mother had been spared to him. This excellent lady remained with him after the trials and afflictions which befel her in her second marriage, and she placed in her beloved son, particularly after the death of Henrietta, all her joy and consolation.

She was, according to the account given by those who knew her, a woman of fervent piety. She rarely went out except to visit the church, and passed the greater part of her time in sewing for the poor. Her son bestowed upon her every mark of veneration and affection; he made no domestic arrangements without consulting her, and left in her hands the direction of his household. Knowing her sensitive nature, he was extremely careful not to oppose her, and, by his delicate and assiduous attentions, to spare her any vexation. On her account, he subjected himself to the most rigorous exactitude with regard to the hour for meals, and as soon as he returned home in the evening, he sought her at once, to avoid giving her cause of disquietude. His preventing kindness was exhibited, in every manner and at every moment, in the thousand details of home-life.

On her side, this beloved mother appreciated the virtues of her dear Léon, and she loved him tenderly; she provided for his wants, and watched over his health with a solicitude which, at times, was excessive, but which, nevertheless, Mr. Dupont respected through a sentiment of perfect and entire obedience. He was seen sometimes, when seated at his own table with strangers, to abstain, at the least intimation of his mother, from certain kinds of food which she imagined might be injurious to him, and send them away untouched. In everything else, Madame d'Arnaud left her son at perfect liberty. Far from interfering in his charities and good works, she would, on the contrary, favor them, and she often united with him in his plans to assist the poor. We will relate a touching instance. Mr. Dupont and his mother were informed that a friend, by a reverse of fortune, had met with a heavy pecuniary loss which destroyed his credit. They both decided immediately, and without consulting each other, to help to relieve him of his difficulties by a generous gift, and it appeared that each had fixed upon the same sum, ten thousand francs.

They lived thus together until 1860. But the time appointed by God to impose upon his servant the sacrifice of their separation had arrived.

Mr. Dupont gave the following edifying details of his mother's death a week after it occurred. "My good mother had the sweetest death one can imagine. It devolved on me to tell her that eternity was approaching; it was about two o'clock in the morning. 'I think,' she replied, 'that I shall soon die, but I have no fear; I have no fear!' These words, on her lips, were extraordinary; for, during her whole life, my mother had a great dread of the judgments of God. Her countenance was animated, her heart, full of charity, and her lips moved in fervent prayer. After the Angelus, which we recited together, as her pulse was growing weaker, I had the courage to tell her that she was about to enter into her agony; she said to me, with a gentle smile: 'You think I am dying?' and clasping her hands, she said aloud: 'Jesus, my Saviour, come!'

"How can I describe to you what passed during the five hours spent in contemplation of a blessed eternity? Her agony lasted but a minute. I had only time to place her hand on my head, to receive her last benediction; when I removed her hand and kissed it,... I saw that her eyes had closed naturally; she was, in the true sense of the term, plunged in a sweet sleep."

Nothing could be more beautiful and Christian than the manner in which such a son accepted the death of his mother. For several months, he speaks of it in every letter he writes to his friends. In every line, in the midst of the keenest sorrow and most tender regret, he gives expression to the supernatural sentiments by which he is penetrated. He makes it a duty to thank all his friends "who had prayed for his good mother," and he does it with affectionate warmth. A pilgrim to Notre Dame de Sénanque had applied the merits of his pilgrimage in suffrage to the soul of Madame d'Arnaud. "I thank you," he writes, "for the portion you have given me of the treasures of Notre Dame de Sénanque. My mother may, perhaps, have been enriched by it at the very time of her death." "I thank you," he writes to another, "as well as Madame X——, and the kind friends who have offered a Communion for my poor mother." He admits that the thought of his mother is never absent from his mind. "And yet," he adds, "she does not cause a distraction which interferes with my attention to business affairs. Death came to her in so gentle a form, that my heart cannot detach itself from the blessed scene."

Some time after the event, we were making him a visit, and we were alone with him, conversing upon the Holy Scriptures. Interrupting himself, he began to speak of his mother. The last words she pronounced had particularly impressed him, and the thought of them recalled another death-bed. He remembered having known a man who lived without religion, and who died, saying: "I am afraid." His mother, on the contrary, although sincerely pious, had always been exceedingly timorous; but at the approach of death, all anxiety fled; a smile rested upon her lips as she said: "I am not afraid," and breathed her last. The man, who had led a careless life died, saying: "I am afraid." The woman, who had lived in dread of death, gave up her soul to God, saying: "I am not afraid." The contrast made a deep impression upon Mr. Dupont, and as he nourished his faith with the Scriptures, he loved to apply to his mother the words which the wise man speaks of the strong woman living in the fear of God: "*She will laugh at the last day.*" He told us that his mother, during her whole life, had been tortured by scruples; "but," he added, "her obedience to her confessors, and her real fear of God merited for her peace of soul in her last moments. The fear of the Lord, then, is that precious pearl, to acquire which, we should sell all we have."

The death of Madame d'Arnaud had no influence in weakening the ties of devotion and affection which attached him to his native place, and to the different members of his family. From the time that he left Martinique, this faithful Creole kept up a constant communication with the island of his birth, which Christopher Columbus had consecrated by the name of St. Martin; he often spoke of it, always with pleasure, and in terms of praise; he extolled the products of its industry and the fertility of the soil; on this subject, he never wearied. To judge by his estimate of it, the rum of Martinique surpassed all other; it was even superior to that of Jamaica; and when occasion offered, to give force to his assertion, he furnished a practical proof to the friends who visited him, or whom he received at his table. Through his patriotic interest in the Colony, and not through natural taste or speculation, he informed himself of all that concerned the cultivation of sugar and the different improvements of which that industry was susceptible. The various questions relative to Colonial government which were being agitated, at that period, in the legislative body, and on which public opinion often conflicted, engaged his attention in a particular manner, and excited, by turns, his hopes and his fears. On many points he held views which were at variance with those entertained by others, and the wisdom of his opinions has been verified by succeeding events and by experience.

He was not indifferent to any religious, political, or commercial interests affecting the island. He willingly made them a subject of conversation, when he was in company with competent and well-informed men. It was almost the only profane digression which he allowed himself from his pious conversations. The disasters which fell upon the Colony, afflicted him sensibly. He was among the first to send aid from the mother country; he solicited assistance from his friends; he proposed and encouraged subscriptions. But under these circumstances, as in all others, he lifted his eyes and heart to the supernatural cause, and his first care on hearing of these misfortunes, was to have recourse to prayer, and to combat the spirit of evil with the arms of faith.

He was, therefore, desirous that his compatriots should be made acquainted with the devotion to the Holy Face of our Lord, and the many benedictions which thence accrue to the whole world. When he commenced to distribute phials of the oil, he did not overlook his native land, and many cures, so extraordinary as to be considered miraculous, were effected by its use. The collection of certificates contains several remarkable examples.

A priest of Martinique, M. l'Abbé Selièvre, related to us that in 1859, a wealthy landholder of the Island, a good Christian, a distinguished and intellectual man, had been miraculously cured of a deafness, which had not been, in the least, relieved by the many remedies prescribed by physicians. He was an old student of the College of Juilly. At the completion of his studies, before returning to the Antilles, he went to Tours to make a visit to Mr. Dupont, as a fellow countrymen, and was kindly received. Ten years afterwards, he was attacked by the infirmity of which we have spoken. His wife, a very pious woman, without informing him of her intention, sent for some of the oil of the Holy Face, and proposed to him to anoint with it, commencing at the same time a novena which was to terminate with Holy Communion. Although he respected the man of God and had confidence in his prayers, the gentleman acceded to the proposition, rather through condescension than from any hope of being benefited. Three Communions were offered by his mother, he made one himself; the unctions were continued during the nine days. At the end of the novena, he was perfectly cured, and never afterwards had a return of deafness.

When relating this to us, M. l'Abbé Selièvre added: "I have never seen Mr. Dupont, but I have frequently heard of him. You may form an idea of the reputation he enjoys in Martinique, by the remark frequently made of him in the island. Facing the sea on a mountain peak called "la Pointe du Carbet," a grotto is pointed out, in which lived during the reign of Louis XIII, a holy man of the noble family of Lestiboudois de Lavallée. He had gone thither from France with one of his brothers, to cultivate the sugar cane. He renounced all his possessions, and retired into a cavern which he never left, except on Sunday, to attend Mass; he lived there many years and died in the odor of sanctity. He was surnamed the "Hermit of Martinique." For some time, the idea was entertained of collecting testimony as a preliminary to the process of his beatification, but the project was abandoned, and it will, probably, never be proposed again. But it is a common remark among the Creoles: "If our hermit is not canonized, we hope, at least, that Mr. Dupont will be placed upon the altar."

The kindness of the servant of God extended to all who were united to him by family ties. They are unanimous in their commendation of the amiable qualities and rare virtues of their beloved relative.

During the first years of his residence at Tours, when he had more time at his disposal, he took pleasure in making a visit, in company with his mother and daughter, to the members of his family in the country. How happy he was, in return, to welcome them in his own home, and to extend to them a cordial hospitality! His house was to be to them as their own. Whether he was present or absent, he wished none of them to pass through Tours without going to visit him, either to remain or to refresh themselves, as suited their convenience. He received them in a warm and cheerful manner; was bright, frank, and joyous with them, and made no change in his exercises of piety, nor in the style of his conversation. He was always the man of faith and of prayer; neither family interests, nor the requirements of relationship, drew him from the supernatural atmosphere in which he habitually lived. Whether his company and conversation in these circumstances proved a source of heavenly benedictions, is the secret of God. We may, never-theless, conjecture that it was so, from the following incident related to us by one his cousins.

"Léon spoke to me often of the cure and conversion of a woman, whose tongue was eaten by a cancer. The cure was obtained by the prayers of a Carmelite Religious, who continued to repeat for that intention: 'Jesus, be to me a Jesus!' It was this invocation enclosed in a little case which Léon put around the neck of my little Raoul. I still preserve this case. Léon had it made, to attract the child who had been ill for several months, and refused to see any one. I had forbidden Léon to go into my room, because, on that day, we were fearing a dangerous return of fever. Léon persisted in going, and I remember saying to him: 'How obstinate you are!' I made haste to enter the room in advance of him, and I took Raoul on my lap. Léon followed me, crossed the room and seated himself on the other side. He said to

Raoul: 'Come to me? I expected to hear the child shriek. Instead of that, Raoul went to him, and climbed on his knee, although he saw him for the first time. Léon caressed him, and then hung this little case around his neck. He went down stairs and said to the family: 'Raoul is cured; there is no further cause of alarm; we will recite the prayer.' We discontinued at once the large doses of quinine which had been ordered him; his health was restored; and, to our joy and Léon's also, he became quite vigorous."

Among the members of his family, he counted the children with whom he had contracted a spiritual affinity in the sacrament of baptism, and they were very numerous. He estimated the number at forty. When any of his godchildren were mentioned, he would say: "he is one of my party." They belonged to every class in society; for, like Marie de Maillé, he cheerfully consented to act as sponsor, either to please a friend, or to oblige a stranger. Sometimes it happened that the parish priest could find no one to answer in the name of some poor, abandoned child; he would apply to Mr. Dupont, who never refused the request. He considered the choice of him as an honor, and he was careful to fulfil all the duties, and to acquit himself of a charge which, at times, proved very onerous. His godchildren were the objects of his constant solicitude. If their parents were either dead or absent, he acted as their guardian and father, received them into his house, gave them hospitality for weeks, or even months; he helped them in their necessities; for example, he often requested his friend, Mr. d'Avrainville, to remit sums of twenty, thirty, fifty, one and two hundred francs to some who were at a distance, and whom he knew to be in want.

On different occasions, he was sponsor for converts from Protestantism and Judaism. He was happy to perform the office, and was sometimes indemnified in the most gratifying manner. He speaks with enthusiasm in one of his letters, of the "last moments of a dear soul who returned to the bosom of the Church twelve years ago, and who repeated, over and over, with an uncontrollable joy: 'I am a Catholic, I am a Catholic!' I had the honor of being his godfather, and I am well recompensed by the sight of a death which is a signal triumph over the powers of hell."

Several of his godchildren are still living, and they preserve an ineffaceable remembrance of his wise counsels and his many acts of kindness. The same may be said of his servants, most of whom have survived him; they never weary when dwelling upon the virtues of their master, and upon the interest he manifested in their welfare on numerous occasions. Adele, particularly, who never left him after his arrival in Tours, says she had many touching proofs of his tender friendship. She was once dangerously ill, and Mr. Dupont lavished upon her the care of a brother or a father. He afterwards said frequently: "Adele has buried all who were near to me; she had a serious illness, but God has left her to take care of me to the last."

His attachment to his family leads us to speak of his delicate attentions and generosity to his friends; they were numerous, were from different countries, and different positions in life. All, without exception, extol the constancy of his affection and his preventing kindness. His relations with them were easy, agreeable, and marked by politeness and urbanity. Devoting his time entirely to the reception of pilgrims, and his daily increasing correspondence, he rarely left the house except to go to the church. "You know," he wrote, (May 31, 1866,) "that, for want of time, I see no one, unless the Little Sisters of the Poor, whom I visit once a week." But although he no longer visited his friends, he did not cease his kind attentions to them. Whenever he saw them, as for instance, on New Year's day, or on other festivals, he welcomed them warmly, and with every expression of joy; they rarely left him without having received some little gift, such as a picture, a medal, or printed sheets of prayers or pious ejaculations. He presented these simple articles to his visitors with a cordiality and an air of piety, that added to the perfume of holiness, and the aroma of good thoughts which were always the fruit of his conversations.

He was ingenious in devising means of rendering himself useful, or of conferring pleasure. Being told of a manufacturer of excellent razors, he wrote to Mr. d'Avrainville to buy him a pair for his own use. A month later he writes: "I am so pleased with the two razors, that I would like to offer a pair to Dom Guéranger the first time he comes to Tours. I therefore beg you to have the kindness to ask the cutler to select them, and add also a strap."

The "strap" reminds us of a singular means, which the excellent man had either learned or invented, of sharpening razors, and which, he said, he had always used with complete success. These straps consisted of small pieces of white wood smooth and well polished. He prepared them himself very carefully, in order to make presents of them, and he recommended them so earnestly that, not to appear disobliging, his friends consented to accept and try them. He sent one of this kind to Dom Guéranger, and we are told that the Religious of his community sometimes found him using Mr. Dupont's strap, and he declared that his razors had never cut so well.

As soon as the servant of God heard that any of his acquaintances were suffering, he hastened to propose, with the approbation of the physician, the use of his "sulphur cupping glasses." He would himself perform the operation, which he did with great dexterity, and, frequently, with wonderful success. We say "*his* cupping glasses," because the unusual size of the cups and the application of the vapor of sulphur, were his own idea. Moreover, he offered to do this little service with so much kindness and charity, he was so pleased when it was accepted, that the patient would have feared to pain him by a refusal.

What friend of his can say he never heard him speak of his famous "beans," nor ate them at his table, nor received a package of them from him? Had he a method peculiar to himself, a secret way of cultivating them? It is certain that none could be found in Touraine so savory to the taste, or so luxuriant in growth. They were sent originally from Nice. He ordered them of the best quality during a favorable season. He requested Mr. d'Avrainville to make the purchases for him, and his letters are filled with minute details, which give evidence of the zeal and delicacy that were evinced by this charitable man, even in trifles, when they had reference to his good works. The seeds which were forwarded to him served, first, for his own garden, and were, next, distributed to the different Communities of the city. He had always one, or several beds of these fine vegetables, the stalks of which were at the same time laden with blossoms, ripe, and dry beans, hanging in a marvellous profusion from high branches. The greater portion of these were destined for the Little Sisters of the Poor. As long as he lived, he superintended the cultivation, and distributed the yield which was considerable, and which furnished a welcome treat to the old people of the Sisters.

When the authorities of the city of Tours were engaged in the arrangement of a botanical garden, Mr. Dupont, always devoted to the interests of his adopted country, was not indifferent to this work of public utility. He imported from the colonies various exotic plants which could, with difficulty, have been otherwise procured.

He was as grateful for the kindnesses done to him, as he was generous, and desirous of rendering services to others. His course towards Mr. d'Avrainville is an example of this. He studies the means of giving him pleasure, and takes advantage of the slightest opportunity to pay him a little attention. "My dear friend," he writes to him, "the sight of some very fine peaches, which were sent us from Gascony, suggested the idea of forwarding to you a few bunches of grapes. They are not as nicely arranged as my mother and myself desired. There are eight peaches. My mother begs you to share the basket with Mademoiselle de R——." Not being able to go see his distant friends, he invited them to visit him. He offered them hospitality for several days or several weeks. Mr. d'Avrainville received one of these invitations nearly every year. His visit was arranged a long time in advance, and was impatiently anticipated. "I look forward with great joy, my dear friend, to our annual meeting. It is impossible for me to absent myself from home; but, like the good Samaritan, you will come to the poor traveller. You understand what I would add, if I knew how to return my thanks in a complimentary style."

In these invitations, he showed equal generosity and delicacy. "My dear friend," he wrote to him at another time, "it is absolutely necessary that we should meet before the Holy Face, and there speak to God. Do not be displeased, but I take upon myself all the expenses of the journey. Come spend a Sunday at Tours. You can easily do so." The few days which Mr. d'Avrainville passed in his house, eating at his table, praying in his oratory, walking in his garden, furnished him with a rest, a holiday which he required. To this intimate intercourse, we are indebted for many details of Mr. Dupont's private life which would, otherwise, have remained unknown. We will relate a little incident which, ludicrous and amusing as it is, will throw out, in strong light, his character, as well as the kind of reputation he enjoyed among certain persons. We give it in Mr. d'Avrainville's own words.

"Madame d'Avrainville and myself were seated with Mr. Dupont when he was opening several letters he had just received. We noticed, as he read one of them, that he was laughing immoderately. Having finished the letter, he said to me: 'My dear friend, you may guess a thousand, ten thousand times, and you will never hit upon the contents of that letter... It is an offer of marriage!... in order that the

CHAPTER XVI

individual may more certainly attain a higher perfection by the good example she will have!' A lady had really written him that, having heard of his many virtues and his great piety, and being very pious herself, she proposed a union with him, that she might more easily advance in the path of perfection, and cooperate in his charitable works; she informed him that she possessed an income of ten thousand francs, which statement could be corroborated by her lawyer, who was empowered to receive his reply. Nevertheless, she considered it her duty to inform him that, for several years, she had been afflicted with a tape-worm..." Mr. d'Avrainville adds: "Of his answer I only remember the following: 'That she had been misinformed as to the person whom she required to further her interests, as he had not time to attend to his own affairs, and moreover, since she said she was afflicted with a tape-worm, he must, in all charity and sincerity, advise her to remain content with that, as she would not be able to support two...?" Mr. Dupont never mentioned this circumstance to any one but Mr. d'Avrainville; he did not give the name of the individual, nor was the subject ever again broached between them.

He was admirable in his intercourse with persons in affliction. On occasions, a word from him sufficed to infuse the balm of consolation into a suffering heart, and to enkindle in it a ray of faith. A mother, inconsolable for the loss of her daughter, was once expressing her grief to him in extravagant terms. Calm and silent, he allowed her to pour out her feelings. Then folding his arms, and with an authoritative manner, which was so suited to him, he said: "Let us consider the circumstances for a moment, Madame. If, at this instant, it were in your power to resuscitate your daughter, and restore her to this world of imperfections and miseries, would you do it?" The mother was obliged to answer: "No." "Then do not mourn her death."

Without being a priest, he had the tenderness of the good pastor, and the active zeal of an apostle. What was said of our Lord might be said of him: that he was "the friend of sinners;" he manifested towards them a preference and a kindness, which sufficiently indicated his ardent desire to convert and to save them. He gladly made himself the servant of the father of the family, going through the streets and seeking the wandering sheep, to bring them back to the fold. His preventing charity was not limited in its exercise, and was ever on the alert to discover means of doing good. He would often stop, when passing through the streets in the evening, to assist some who had lost their way or been belated, to find their lodgings; these were children, workmen, strangers in the city, sometimes soldiers who should be at their barracks, but who, reeling from intoxication, could not, otherwise, reach them in time. His embarrassment was very great, one evening, on meeting an intoxicated soldier, when it was quite late. He began to reason with the man, urging him to return as quickly as possible, in order to avoid the punishment appointed by military rule to be inflicted in such cases. The soldier resisted all his solicitations. The holy man, listening only to the suggestions of his kind heart, gave him two francs, to induce him to consent; but the drunkard, overjoyed at having money in hand, insisted upon entering a neighboring tavern in order, he said, "to treat his benefactor." In despair, not knowing what expedient to adopt, and tired of the contest, Mr. Dupont requested the aid of a friend that lived near. He was an old soldier, who addressed the drunkard in such a manner as to force him, *bon gré mal gré*, to take the road towards the barracks. The servant of God asked him to follow the man, and prevent him from loitering on the way, and also to recommend him to the mercy of the superior officer. Full of interest in the case, he went, the next day, to inquire how the affair had terminated, and was delighted to find that the punishment inflicted had been very light. The result of his charity was the conversion of the soldier, who, being informed of the kindness exercised towards him, corrected his fault and became a good Christian.

His zeal for sinners made him appreciate the work of mercy performed by the Sisters of the Refuge. He felt a particular attraction for that community. He went there frequently, inquired into the wants of the house, and contributed, by his alms, to keep it in good condition. He placed in it penitent young girls, and he never lost sight of those whom he had confided to the care of the Sisters; he visited them frequently, to inquire about their progress, to encourage and counsel them. "We have sometimes seen him," says the Superioress, "kneel before young penitents who were tempted to return to the world, and entreat them to remain. At other times, when he could not influence some of them, either by reasoning or persuasion, to perform a penance imposed, as for example to kiss the floor, he would say: 'Very well, my child, I will perform the penance for you,' and kneeling, he would humbly kiss the floor."

It is not easy to record the kindness and preventing care which he lavished upon the sick and infirm who made a pilgrimage to the Holy Face. A servant in a community of the city was suffering from her throat; she had great difficulty both in eating and speaking. Full of confidence in Mr. Dupont, whom she knew, she arrived at his house just as he was going out. Pulling him by the sleeve, she said in the lowest whisper: "I was going to you, Sir, to be cured." He kindly returned, interrogated her, and asked if she could have the courage to drink a little of the oil burning before the Holy Face. She was willing to do anything, and swallowed a few drops of the oil which the servant of God presented to her. They began to recite the Litany. "All pain," she says, "left me, and as we advanced in the Litany my voice became stronger. 'Now you must eat,' he said, and I swallowed with perfect ease the food he offered me. As I was not entirely restored, he kindly said to me: 'You need more nutritious food; come here and we will take care of you.' I remained a month in his house. His mother, Madame d'Arnaud, attended to me, my health was reëstablished, and it has continued good for more than twenty years."

The same delicate and generous attentions were bestowed upon his workmen. He loved to give them pleasure, and never neglected an occasion of rendering them a service. When the provisional chapel of St. Martin was completed, there were twenty workmen of different trades who had been actively employed on the work. Mr. Dupont, in order to please them, arranged an agreeable surprise: he requested them to attend a Mass to be offered for their intention, after which he directed a good breakfast to be served them at his expense. Upon such occasions as these, he paid liberally, but he remained modestly silent, or spoke a few words without affectation. His kindness to the workingmen was based upon a supernatural intention; it would be, he thought, a means of bringing them nearer to God, and of conferring upon them a spiritual and solid benefit. Every one knew that this noble Christian had but one aim in these charitable actions, that of gaining souls to God and attaching them to the faith.

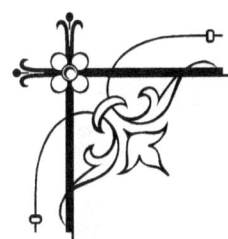

Chapter XVII

Third Period of Devotion to the Holy Face.

At the death of Madame d'Arnaud, Mr. Dupont was in the sixty-third year of his age, and the eleventh of his zeal in the cause of devotion to the Holy Face. His excellent mother, up to that time directed the household of her son; her society was a great happiness to him; she was a beam of light brightening his home with family joys. The sacrifice imposed upon him by her death, completed his detachment from earth. Henceforth, he will devote himself solely to the work which seems to be the mission entrusted to him by Divine Providence.

From 1860 to 1870, his life was passed entirely before the Holy Face; he appears during this period as if at the culminating point of his zeal for reparation and charity for souls. His whole time is devoted to prayer, the reception of invalids, and his correspondence. He contemplates this immolation in its fullest extent, and he voluntarily determines to accept it. His health is failing; he sees it, he feels it, he says so; but he resigns himself to the loss. God recompenses him, at first, by secret graces which elevate him to a degree of heroic perfection, and, afterwards, by numerous miracles of which he is more than ever the active assistant, if not the direct instrument and indisputable organ.

If we wish to form an idea of his solitary life and his duties, we must hear the account he gives of them in confidence to friends, either to beg their indulgence, or to excuse himself for refusing to render them certain services, which appear to him foreign to his mission. For example, the public festivals which were celebrated at Tours, either periodically or extraordinarily, attracted to his house a larger number of pilgrims and visitors, and increased his work to a great extent. Thus in 1864, he wrote to Mr. d'Avrainville: "I have rarely been so overburdened. Sixteen letters on my desk, four packages of oil to forward, and a great concourse of visitors. If you had been so kind as to pass the Assumption with me this year, as you did last year, you would have fallen in with the meeting of government officials, where all goes on quietly and smoothly, whilst I am overpowered with business." A few days later, he writes: "In addition to the official assembly, there is to be a fair for the next ten days, and that will bring me a prodigious number of pilgrims, and today, fifteen letters in the bargain… I am fatigued; therefore, I shorten my letter…" "You will find that I have grown old," he says on another occasion to his friend, "and, consequently, I am overpowered by the work demanding my attention. God tempers the wind to the shorn lamb. For myself, I can hardly manage my correspondence. Business rains down upon me from morning until night, and, therefore, the least undertaking requiring order or stability, is altogether impracticable to me. You cannot imagine, my dear friend, the nature and the number of my occupations arising from the devotion to the Holy Face."

To others, he writes nearly in the same strain, but it is to rejoice with them on account of the miracles which are made known to him. "You are not mistaken in supposing my correspondence is very extensive. Every day it augments, because our Lord continues to recompense the faith of those who put their confidence in the Holy Face. Could you believe that, since the 1st of January, I have received fifty-two certificates of favors obtained after the unctions with the oil? During all that time, eight is the lowest number of letters I have received on any one day." (April 11, 1863.) To a friend who is travelling: "For myself, I have no thought of going elsewhere, because the affairs of the Holy Face detain me, as it were forcibly, with a daily increase of work. Constantly, additional favors."

He finally abandons all pilgrimages, even that of Paray-le-Monial. "I have been urged," he says, (June 27, 1861,) "to go to Paray. I cannot, however, absent myself with impunity for four or five days, because of my correspondence, too voluminous for me to allow it to accumulate upon my desk, even for a short period. I repeat: Fiat! and that, with all my heart, in expiation of the little fruit I derived from the different pilgrimages which I had the happiness of making, when I was free to undertake them, and when I was of an age to offer other service to God than mere good will." But the sedentary life voluntarily accepted, although so contrary to his temperament and his habits, contributed to develop the malady which the baths of Néris and Bourbon had not entirely eradicated. He had frequent severe attacks of gout and rheumatism of the joints. In 1862, he again tried the waters of Bourbon, but it was for the last time. He was unwilling to absent himself in future; whatever might be the consequence, he would not neglect his mission. In his very infirmity, he saw the hand of God confining him to his solitude. "My lower limbs are only of moderate use to me, and as my suffering still continues, I must believe that there is no remedy, and that God wishes me to remain, more than ever, constantly before the Holy Face. And I add that I can truthfully say with the Psalmist: *Hic habitabo, quoniam elegi eam.* Here will I dwell, because I have chosen it."

Seated at his desk, or kneeling, with his eyes lifted to the venerated image of the Holy Face, he prays, he receives those who present themselves, he works. The concourse of pilgrims and of the infirm, is sometimes so great that the court in front, the porch, the adjoining grounds are crowded with people, baggage, and vehicles of every kind. One of his friends writes: "I can vouch for an incident, of which I was myself an eye-witness. As I was one day going to the depot at the time the train arrived, I saw one of the porters (they are forbidden to enter the enclosure in order to prevent them from importuning travellers,) make a speaking-trumpet with his hands, and call out in a loud voice: 'Are there any passengers for Mr. Dupont's?' The distance from the depot to the house of our Saint is very short; some of these rogues would drive the invalids around the city for the purpose of consuming more time, and thus increasing their pay. A pilgrim was, on one occasion, about to leave Mr. Dupont, in order, he said, to be at the depot in time for the departure of the train. He was informed that he had ample time as the train would not leave for an hour, and that five minutes would suffice to walk to the depot. Whereupon, the pilgrim told him that he had been a whole hour going between the railroad and Mr. Dupont's. He had evidently been driven around the city.

All the invalids who sought a cure did not obtain it; and among those who did, many, after some time, relapsed into their former condition. But for both, a greater grace was generally the fruit of their conversations with Mr. Dupont. They returned home edified, preserving a remembrance of this holy man which, under various circumstances, proved beneficial to them. This result was of frequent occurrence. It is particularly remarkable in the case of a noble lady who sent us in writing a detailed account of her visit. We present a portion of it; it will unfold to the reader the influence exercised by the servant of God over the souls of those with whom he had held correspondence.

"The remembrance of Mr. Dupont," she says, "was always associated in my mind with the idea of sanctity. I was in my sixteenth year, and my ill-health was a source of great anxiety to my family. I accompanied my mother and sister to Tours, and we were introduced to Mr. Dupont. He commenced by asking if we had been to Confession; on being told we had confessed recently, he replied: 'No matter, you must confess and Communicate, if you wish to obtain what you ask.' As we were strangers in Tours, he directed us to a confessor. He consented, however, to give us some of the oil from the lamp, and to pray with us. We returned twice to his house, and left Tours two days afterwards; my health had already commenced to improve, and for about eighteen months I was tolerably well. After that I relapsed into a worse condition than before; but my former confidence in obtaining a miraculous cure did not return; if I desired to see Mr. Dupont, it was rather to be edified by the sight of the saint, than to seek the health I had sought in vain elsewhere, and which God had always refused me. Even passing visitors, judging from his exterior, regarded him as a man entirely dead to himself, and living only for the love of God and his neighbor. To pass his life in the service of others, required a great self-abnegation; yet, he never exhibited weariness in receiving visitors, exhorting them or praying with them; all was done with unfailing sweetness and serenity. With what piety and recollection he said over and over again the same prayers! He always repeated them kneeling, and he wished the invalids to follow his example, notwithstanding the fatigue it might cause them. He would recite them several times for the same person when circumstances required it. And not a word escaped him to direct attention to himself; he seemed to have renounced all personality, and to live solely for the service of his Divine Master."

When the infirm were not cured, Mr. Dupont, without expressing any surprise, endeavored to discover the cause; he often found it in the want of faith and of confidence in the effect of prayer. He recognizes this distrust by certain signs, which would have escaped others, and which he points out with simplicity. Two ladies, who were going to the baths, presented themselves, on their way, as petitioners before the Holy Face: they did not obtain their cure. He remarked: "It is, generally, on returning from the baths, rather than when going to them, that graces are bestowed. It is said of the woman in the Gospel: *In medicos erogaverat omnem substantiam suam*; 'She had bestowed all her substance upon physicians?'" He does not complete the sacred text, which tells us that this woman, approaching Jesus Christ, touched the hem of his garment, was instantly healed, and merited to hear from the Saviour: "Thy faith hath made thee whole." Desperate hours are the hours of God. When we can no longer hope for aid from man, we turn to Him alone, and place all our confidence in His power and love. It sometimes happened that eminent and holy persons asked, without obtaining their cure. Thus, Mgr. Ségur went to Mr. Dupont at the commencement of his blindness; but God reserved him, to furnish the example of a prodigy more wonderful than the one he demanded.

Others, on the contrary, were satisfied with sending a letter, or even a dispatch, and their petitions were immediately granted. As the servant one day informed Mr. Dupont that dinner was on the table, he handed him a telegram. Prayers were requested for a child that was dying in a northern city. Mr. Dupont, who still preserved towards his mother the respectful deference of his youth, was unwilling to inconvenience her by his absence; he therefore laid the telegram before the picture of the Holy Face, saying as he did so: "Thou seest, Lord, that the case is urgent!" A few days afterwards, he received a letter of thanksgiving informing him that, at the very hour, a change had taken place for the better, and the child's life was saved.

In general, the miracles operated in Mr. Dupont's drawing-room, converted the invalids who simply witnessed them, as well as those who were more favored, into apostles of the Holy Face, and propagators of the devotion. The testimony of each added weight to that of the others. Every week, and almost every day, furnished new instances to the collection of certificates already accumulated in such numbers. We select a few of the more striking from the events of this period.

One of the most remarkable was the cure of Mademoiselle Hortense Dupin. We copy the certificate of the archpriest of the diocess: "I hereby certify that Mademoiselle Hortense Dupin of la Flèche, fifteen years of age, had been suffering for seven months from a malady, called by the physicians paraphlegia; having employed, without success, every remedy prescribed in such cases by practitioners, the doctor declared that no medical treatment could effect a cure. The young girl, for several months, had been unable to walk more than a few steps in ten minutes, even when leaning upon a stick and supported by a friend; at last, she lost all power of motion.

"On Thursday before Pentecost, Madame Dupin took her daughter to Tours, and had her lifted from the carriage into Mr. Dupont's drawing-room. Mr. Dupont united in prayer with the mother and child, gave some of the oil which burns before the Holy Face to the mother, directing her to anoint with it the knees and back of her daughter. The prayers and unctions were twice repeated on Friday, when Mademoiselle Dupin was able to walk with perfect ease around Mr. Dupont's room, whence she went to the cathedral, knelt before the altar of the Blessed Virgin, then visited the church of St. Julian, and returned to her hotel. The following day, on arriving at her own home in la Flèche, she sprang lightly from the carriage, and she has, ever since, walked without inconvenience or pain of any kind."

We shall now hear what Hortense herself writes on the subject to the servant of God. "Every one thanked God and pronounced my cure miraculous. The physician, who had attended me for seven months, was amazed on being told by a lady that she had seen me at High Mass, and that I walked without difficulty; he said it was impossible, and came at once to our house to ascertain the truth; he could scarcely credit the evidence of his senses, when he saw me walk. To many persons who questioned him, he replied, that I could have been cured only by the power of God, that no physician could have restored me to health, particularly in one day. My condition was so well known throughout the city, that every one sympathized with me and my parents; my cure has, consequently, attracted much attention. People came in crowds to see me, some, even from a distance of eight leagues. All who were infirm desired to be taken to you, and, although God did not will that all who went should be entirely cured, they have experienced some relief, as have those, also, who used the oil in their own homes. The curate of la Flèche and other priests were pleased to see me cured; but their pleasure was increased, when many persons, who had not been to their duties for years, and who had little confidence in prayer, decided to confess and Communicate before using the oil."

The great art of the servant of God, if we may apply that word to him, consisted in encouraging persons, and in communicating to them a little of that faith and confidence which obtain all things in prayer. Madame G——, a woman between fifty and sixty years of age, paralyzed in both limbs for eighteen months, having uselessly tried all the usual remedies, was, at her request, taken from the country to Tours where her son resided. Leaning upon two crutches, and provided with a folding-seat, she dragged herself along, as best she could, to Mr. Dupont's, having stopped, in her progress from the centre of the city to Saint-Etienne Street, at least twenty times to rest on the folding-seat. The unctions were made, but without effect. Mr. Dupont encouraged her, excited her confidence, and requested her to make a novena of prayers at home, giving her a phial of the oil. She suffered intensely in going to her son's. The following day she proposed returning to Mr. Dupont's. Her son, who had no confidence in the oil, had allowed her on the eve to do as she pleased; but he now decidedly opposed a second visit. "You were," he said, "excessively fatigued yesterday; you must not go today; say your prayers and anoint with the oil as much as you choose; but let it be done at home." Madame G—— submitted to so positive a refusal, particularly as it seemed reasonable; she said the prayers at home, and made the unctions; perceiving suddenly that she was better, she laid aside one of her crutches, attempted to walk without it, and found she could do so very well. "I am better," she said to her son; "see, I can walk with one crutch. I think I can even do without the other." Saying this, she laid it aside also, and walked with ease. "Now, my son," she exclaimed, "you certainly will not oppose my going to Mr. Dupont." Arriving without crutches, without support, feeling no fatigue, notwithstanding the distance, she related what had passed, and united in the usual prayers offered in thanksgiving. Having completed these, Mr. Dupont said: "You are now cured; but you must make a trial of your limbs. Visit in thanksgiving every church in the city." Madame G—— acceded to the proposition, and walked from church to church in the seven parishes; she performed the whole distance with ease, and without particular fatigue.

A young girl of Notre Dame-la-Riche was suffering with one of her feet, which was enormously swollen. Not being able to walk, she was carried before the Holy Face. As they commenced the prayers, she expressed aloud her desire and the object of her visit: "My God, if it be Thy will, grant me my cure." Mr. Dupont gently reproved her: "That is not the manner in which you should pray. You have not faith.... Say to God in a more positive manner: 'Lord, cure me!'... If you wish to be cured, you must command God." "Oh!" exclaimed the young girl, "I cannot do that, I cannot command God." "You have not faith," replied Mr. Dupont, "you must say: I wish to be cured! Cure me! We must have an unlimited confidence in prayer, and never hesitate to ask." "And yet," said the poor young girl, "it seems to me that I have faith." Exciting her faith by an increased effort, she recommenced the prayers. She was somewhat relieved, and was able to walk home, although not without pain. Encouraged by the unexpected improvement, and reproaching herself for want of faith, she said; "O my God, it is true that I distrusted too much Thy power and goodness in my regard.... I see it, I know it, Thou canst, Thou wilt cure me; I ask this favor of thee; grant it to me, O God! grant it to me!" She returned to the man of God, and left him radically cured. He had succeeded in elevating the faith of this person to the level of his own, to the level of that faith concerning which our Lord has said: "Amen I say to you, if you have faith as a grain of mustard seed— say to this mountain, remove from hence, &c." We have mentioned that the servant of the Holy Face preserved the certificates and the autograph letters, which attested the miraculous graces obtained in his oratory, but that he made an exception in the case of certain facts so striking and personal, as to alarm his humility. There are several of this kind properly authenticated, an account of which cannot be found, although the papers were placed in his hands. We have convincing testimony of the truth of the following incident, although there is no mention made of it in his papers.

This miracle was attended by remarkable circumstances. Mr. H. d'A—— had the kindness to send us, at our request, after a pilgrimage to the Holy Face made by himself and his family in May, 1877, a written account of the fact. "My wife," he says, "was in such a condition that she had been for weeks incapable of any movement whatever; she was lifted as an infant. So extreme was her weakness, that she could not even endure the scratching of a pen on paper, or the slight noise made in unfolding a newspaper. My father-in-law and myself considered her death as inevitable, a necessary consequence of her extreme weakness, even without any new complication; for a long time she had been unable to take any solid food. The case was desperate; the cure was complete. My father-in-law and my aunt, convinced that all human means were ineffectual, left together for Tours, to see Mr. Dupont. They had appointed Tuesday to visit him, but the cars having been delayed, they were forced to remain all night at Tours, and consequently to defer going to his house until the following day, June 5, 1867. As we were living forty leagues distant from Tours, we were entirely ignorant of the unforseen delay. At the moment we supposed that the pilgrims were with Mr. Dupont, we united our own with their intention, and recited the usual prayers to the Holy Face.

"This was on Tuesday, the 4th, the important day for us; but, as there resulted no improvement in the condition of the invalid on that day, and, as on the

5th, we concluded that our relatives, having terminated their pilgrimage, were on their return, we had nearly lost hope. However, on Wednesday, at the very moment when my father-in-law and my aunt were praying with Mr. Dupont before the Holy Face, the patient suddenly exclaimed in astonishment that she needed no support to her head, and could even raise her hand.

"The following day, on the arrival of the pilgrims, we recited the prayers of the Holy Face and applied the oil. She immediately expressed a wish to leave the bed, and moved her arms in a manner that, for the three past months, had been impossible. She arose, cast herself on her knees whilst making an act of thanksgiving, and did so without pain...

"I have, sir, given you herein a faithful account of an event which occurred ten years ago. But the remembrance of some events could never be effaced from the heart, even were one to live a hundred years."

This simple narrative exhibits in a strong light the greatness of the miracle, and the efficacy of the prayer of him who was the instrument in obtaining it. It also furnishes an explanation of the deep emotion manifested by these two noble pilgrims, when, accompanied by their children, they revisited the drawing-room of the servant of God, now transformed into a chapel. There they heard Mass and Communicated in thanksgiving, pronouncing with tears of gratitude the name of Mr. Dupont, reverently regarding him as a thaumaturgus and a saint.

The Countess de Vaux, in religion, Sister Teresa, Superior General of the Congregation of St. Louis, founded at Juilly by the celebrated Abbé Bautain, relates the following fact: "One of our pupils, Mademoiselle de L——, fifteen years of age, was the victim of a galloping consumption. Four days after the commencement of her illness, the physician of our Institution requested a consultation. A married sister of Mademoiselle de L——, a resident of Paris, brought a physician who made a specialty of lung diseases. After a thorough examination of the patient, he pronounced her case hopeless, adding that he scarcely thought she could live a month longer. Her sister proposed taking her home, but the physician declared that to move her would hasten her death, and all she could now do would be to prepare the family for the painful separation. On hearing the result of the consultation, instead of being grieved I rather rejoiced, as I recalled to mind that I had already obtained several cures by the oil of the Holy Face. After making the two physicians repeat in a decided manner that there was no hope for Mademoiselle de L——, I felt perfectly calm, and was convinced that she would recover. The physicians had no sooner departed than I applied the oil over the lungs, and commenced the usual prayers of the novena (five Pater and five Ave,) during which, as is always the case, her illness and weakness increased; in the same proportion did my faith in her recovery augment. On the ninth day, her expectorations were exactly similar to those on which the doctor had based his diagnosis of the case; on seeing them, he said: 'This is the last.' 'Oh! yes,' I replied, 'it is, in truth, the last.' On the following day, when making his usual visit to the patient, he found her free from fever and oppression. The young girl was very cheerful, and was taking a bowl of rich soup. 'How did this happen?' he asked in extreme surprise. 'Do not be offended, doctor,' I answered; 'but as you considered the poor child incurable, I consulted a skilful physician, the most skilful of all physicians.' I then told him of the unctions with the oil, saying: 'You see that even galloping consumptions cannot resist the great physician, the good God.' From that time, (1862,) Mademoiselle L—— has never experienced any lung trouble. She is now (October 30, 1878,) a Religious in our community: she desired to consecrate to God the life he had miraculously granted her in our house."

The infirm were very eager to present their petitions, but they were not always careful to acknowledge the graces they had received, or to offer a just tribute of gratitude to God for the favors He bestowed. The man of God considered an exterior act of thanksgiving to be a duty; and if that were omitted, he foresaw that the individuals would pay the penalty of their neglect. Thus, in a village not far from Angers, a consumptive woman, given up by the physicians, and too weak to move herself without assistance, was instantaneously cured. Shortly afterwards she was attacked by another disease. When Mr. Dupont heard it, he was not surprised. "So long," he said, "as she does not fulfil the duty of gratitude by sending a certificate, she will not recover." Twenty-five years had passed, and the certificate had not been sent. Very recently, with a view to obtain a cure, an attestation properly authenticated was forwarded, and, at the time we write, the individual, now nearly restored to health, has made a pilgrimage of thanksgiving to the Holy

Face, and has personally related to us the details of the miracle accomplished in her regard.

At certain periods the concourse of visitors was not so great. Mr. Dupont does not fail to remark it in his correspondence. "For the past month," he says on the 19th of January, 1864, "there have been very few pilgrims to the Holy Face, and I have not received a single certificate. I make no complaint whatever, I simply mention the fact." Two years afterwards, the 19th of September, 1866, he writes: "I am still at anchor in the spot you know so well; nevertheless, I see the number of pilgrims decreasing; this causes me no anxiety, as I feel my strength diminishing, and I must preserve sufficient for my correspondence, and forwarding the phials of oil, both of which require a moderate attention."

What caused the decrease in the number of visitors? In the course of time, novelty wore off; persons became so accustomed to the events which transpired in the drawing-room of the man of God, that they ceased to pay attention to them; fewer people went from curiosity; it was frequented only by pilgrims and invalids. And moreover, persons from a distance had recourse to him by letter, and requested oil to be forwarded to them, having had experience that, by these means, cures were often obtained. And should we not, also, read in this circumstance a particular design of Divine Providence, Who thus allowed his old servant to rest, and gave him the time to make a more immediate preparation for the final journey and the eternal recompense? However that may be, Mr. Dupont seemed neither pained nor surprised; he derived consolation from it, and even rejoiced that he was less besieged by persons, who lavished upon him honors which were painful and humiliating to him. As far as the glory of God and the good of souls were concerned, he knew, through the confidential letters that were addressed to him, that a supernatural action continued to be exerted in a secret, but not less efficacious manner. He was also fully indemnified by the pilgrimages to Lourdes, which were already rousing the masses of the people and assuming large proportions, in consequence of the wonderful cures effected by the use of the water. He even regarded this as one of the chief causes of the diminution of the number of visitors to his little oratory; it was, he thought, the adorable Face of our Lord impelling souls towards the Immaculate Virgin of Lourdes, in order that they might receive still more abundant graces. Mr. Dupont did not go to Lourdes. The state of his health and the devotion to the Holy Face, deprived him of this consolation; but the attention he gave the great event, which has rendered this place memorable, requires us to dwell upon it for a short time.

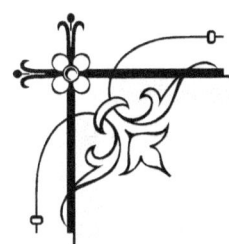

Chapter XVIII

Lourdes.

As soon as Mr. Dupont heard of the apparition of the Immaculate Virgin in the grotto of Lourdes, the hope of the speedy triumph of the Church over the powers of hell, which had been enkindled in his heart by the miracle of La Salette, revived in full force. "Everything conspires to encourage the thought that the Pyrenees will, in future, have no cause to envy the Alps. Undoubtedly, the apparition of La Salette is more than sufficient to make known to the world the value Mary places upon man's salvation; but, if it be true that she has again descended upon earth, what an additional cause for gratitude, and, withal, what ground for hope that the Church is on the eve of a grand triumph; for it is impossible to doubt that so great and repeated graces will subdue, and bring under obedience very many rebellious hearts. The evil is certainly great; but God can curb the malice of Satan; let us hope that the wicked beast may be put to shame, and that God may be glorified."

It was not long before he received a full account of the apparition from intelligent and well-informed persons. He immediately draws the contrast in his mind between La Salette and Lourdes: "At La Salette, Mary weeps; at Lourdes, she smiles. At La Salette, she wears on her garments the signs of the Passion; at Lourdes, can we not consider her white dress, her blue cincture, her radiant countenance, the emblems of joy? At La Salette, there is question of dreadful menaces, of scourges, as Pius IX read in the secret of the two children; at Lourdes, there is a simple recommendation to pray for sinners. What a sweet word is that! such a recommendation includes, in its very nature, the idea that God wills to pardon; how different His dealing with us when He does not wish to grant favors! For instance, He forbids Moses and Isaiah to pray for His people, *'lest they be converted and live.'* Moreover, at La Salette, Mary hides her hands when she speaks to the children (Mélanie told me so in 1847); at Lourdes, they are uncovered, she raises them, joins them, places them near her heart...; now hands are the symbol and the channel of liberality; the idea of liberality is connected with the hand: *Aperis manum tuam, et imples omne animal benedictine.* 'Thou openest Thy hand, and Thou fillest all animals with benediction.' Today then, Mary wishes to give; and she is rich enough to give lavishly. But she first makes a demand; she demands a sanctuary to be erected on the spot where she appeared, in order to perpetuate the remembrance of her visit of mercy. This fact should inspire us with peculiar confidence. She required no sanctuary at La Salette; but, as there is question of one at Lourdes, is it not because we are about to emerge from the period of demolition, and to enter that of reconstruction? *Tempus destruendi, tempus œdificandi.* 'There is a time to destroy and a time to build.' Mary would not direct us to *build,* if God were about to permit Satan to *destroy.*"

Elsewhere, he draws the following conclusion: "This second invitation, it is to be hoped, will induce us to enter upon the grand work of reparation foreshadowed by the definition of the Immaculate Conception. Then the surviving disciples of philosophy will direct their rage against the rock of Massabielle, whilst the children of the Church will draw from the miraculous fountain health and all kinds of graces. Their portions are indeed unequal, but the difference between them will be still more marked, when the figure of this world will have passed away. Then the exiles from their heavenly country will exclaim without ceasing: *Insensati...* (Wisdom v, 4.) But we, who believe it a misery to be separated from God in time and eternity, should devote ourselves, with our whole hearts, to such works as may help sinners to return to the good God. It is an undeniable truth that France and Europe would have turned their hearts to God, if the apparition at La Salette had been more generally believed and proclaimed. If the order to construct a chapel be obeyed, they will assuredly enter the path which leads to conversion."

Thus Mr. Dupont wrote twenty years ago. At the present moment, when we see the popular impulse directing thousands to Lourdes, it is a pleasure to follow the man of God as he reads the future.

He lived long enough to witness the commencement of the great work of reparation instituted at Lourdes. The events of the previous ten years justified his foresight, and filled him with joy. "The pilgrimages of this year," he said (April 12, 1873), "present us good grounds of hope for the future, with the more reason, as this external expression of Christian piety is becoming general, and extending among all the nations of Europe. If our fathers exclaimed at the time of the Crusades: 'God wills it!' we of the nineteenth century, with equal reason and confidence, may say: 'Mary wills it!' She everywhere wills, as a good Mother, to impel us towards Jesus." "Yes, it is in the order of things that Mary should lead us to Jesus. It is not for her individual honor that she is striving, when she says to Bernadette: 'Tell the priests to erect a sanctuary on this spot...; the people will come here in processions...' Mary knew well that thousands of souls would repair from the grotto to the Eucharistic banquet."

As to the numerous miracles effected in the name of our Lady of Lourdes, he had less cause than others to be astonished. Indeed, we may say that one of the first graces of this kind was obtained through his instrumentality. He narrated the fact himself: "I had a relative residing in the vicinity of Lourdes. I begged her to write me the particulars of what had taken place. She related to me in her first letter what had occurred up to the fifth apparition. I received this letter as I was about to go to the Little Sisters of the Poor; after reading it, I put it in my pocket, and, thinking of other things, I went to make them my usual visit. On arriving, I noticed that a Sister, whom I generally saw, was absent, and that her duties were discharged by another. I was told upon inquiry that she was suffering from a very severe toothache and a heavy cold. As I passed through the house, I met her; the poor Sister was in an agony of pain; she held her rosary in her hand. I said to her: 'My good Sister, after every decade of the rosary, repeat three times the invocation: "O Mary immaculate, who hast deigned to appear at Lourdes, cure me!"' The Sister continued saying her beads, and repeated the invocation; after I had made my visit the portress said to me at the door: 'Sister X—— is no longer suffering; the toothache left her whilst she was saying the rosary, but she still has a cold.' The next day I heard that she was relieved of the cold also."

Another instance of a similar kind was related to us by a Religious, the Superioress of the Daughters of Charity. "Mr. Dupont stopped at our house one day, as he passed on his return from the Little Sisters of the Poor. It was during recreation, and the Sisters collected in the parlor. It was always a great pleasure to the community to see the holy man and hear him speak of God. He entered smiling and very bright, holding in his hand a medal. 'Do you see this little medal?' he said, 'I have just received it from Lourdes, and it has already been the instrument of a miracle.' He then related what had passed at the Little Sisters of the Poor;

how one of the Sisters, who had been suffering intensely from toothache, had been completely relieved in an hour. Delighted and astonished, we wished to inspect closely the interesting medal; it passed from one to the other; each contemplated it, and reverently kissed it. There was seated among us our Sister Rosalie, who was so lame and feeble that, for two years, she had been incapacitated for duty, and consequently was unable, to her great sorrow, to visit the poor. 'Ah! Sir,' she said to the servant of God, 'will you let me place your medal on my foot, that I also may be cured, and be able again to visit my poor patients?' 'Certainly,' replied Mr. Dupont, 'here it is.' 'And what shall I do with it?' asked the Sister. 'What prayer shall I say? Must I commence a novena?' 'No, no,' replied Mr. Dupont with vivacity; 'there is no need of so much time; say simply: "My God, through the intercession of our Lady of Lourdes, my good mother, cure me, that I may visit my poor."' The Sister did as directed; she placed the medal on her foot and repeated the invocation. 'Now,' said Mr. Dupont, 'rise and walk around the room.' The Sister arose and walked, but it was with pain and difficulty. 'Are you cured?' asked Mr. Dupont. 'Not entirely.' 'Very well, apply the medal again.' A second time it was placed upon her foot and the prayer repeated; a second time she endeavored to walk, and still the cure was not complete. But encouraged by the slight improvement in her condition, the Sister made a promise, if she were entirely cured, to visit the Holy Face in Mr. Dupont's room. The next day, Sister Rosalie, who, for two years, had been unable to walk, went to Saint-Etienne Street alone, without support of any kind, and returned in the same manner, without experiencing either fatigue or pain. From that time she did not suffer from her limbs; she resumed her usual duties among the sick and the poor, continuing them until her death, a period of six years."

"This was not the only proof we had, during that visit, of the efficacy of the medal," said the Superioress. "A postulant, forty years of age, had recently entered the community; she had a gastric affection which caused frequent vomiting. Fearing this might prove an obstacle to her admission, she very improperly determined to conceal her malady from the Sisters; thus, no one was aware of it. Whilst the Sisters were passing the medal to each other and kissing it with respect, the postulant secretly took advantage of the opportunity to obtain the cure of an infirmity, which, by incapacitating her for continuous duty, would, in time, betray itself and cause her rejection. Pressing the medal to her lips, she said interiorly: 'O my God, by Mr. Dupont's faith in our Lady of Lourdes, cure me, that I may remain in this house.' She instantly felt that she was cured. She, however, waited a short time before mentioning the circumstance. As several days had passed without any return of the vomiting, and she was free from pain, she regarded her restoration to health as certain, and she came to me to acknowledge all. She begged pardon for having concealed her infirmity, but asserted that she was now perfectly well, thoroughly cured by the virtue of Mr. Dupont's medal. And such, in reality, was the case. The malady never returned, and, for several years, she fulfilled in our community, under the name of Sister Gabriel, all the duties assigned her."

We see clearly that, from the very beginning, there was a bond of union between the grotto of Lourdes and the oratory of the Sacred Face, between the marvellous apparitions of the Immaculate Virgin at the rock of Massabielle, and the graces granted at Tours through the instrumentality of the solitary of Saint-Etienne Street. There was another miraculous cure effected by the oil of the Sacred Face, which naturally finds its place in this connection. It is that of the historian of Lourdes, Mr. Henri Lasserre. The account of it was given by the celebrated author himself, in a letter sent to Mr. Dupont as a testimony of his faith and gratitude. We quote from the letter the important passages.

"I had enjoyed during my whole life," says Mr. Lasserre, "excellent sight. I was able to distinguish objects at a very great distance, and, at the same time, I could read a book, however near it was to my eyes. I passed entire nights in study, without experiencing the least fatigue. I myself was amazed at the flexibility, clearness and strength of my vision. I was, consequently, painfully surprised when, during the course of last June and July (1862), I realized that my sight was gradually failing, and that I was incapable of night work; at last, I was forced to abandon altogether reading and writing. When I attempted to read, the eye was so fatigued after three or four lines that I was compelled to desist. I consulted several physicians, particularly, two specialists, Doctors Desmares and Giraud-Teulon.

"The remedies prescribed did me no good; they even seemed to aggravate the evil. Such was my condition for three months, when, fearing the affection would become chronic, I was seriously alarmed. I suffered from great depression of spirits, which I concealed from my relatives and friends, who were as convinced as myself that my sight was permanently injured; we, however, mutually encouraged each other with a hope which neither party really entertained."

Mr. Lasserre then relates the miraculous cure effected by the use of the water of Lourdes, to which he had recourse by the advice of a friend. This restoration of sight, which was a great happiness to him, and which he regarded as a wonderful grace, did not continue long,—a circumstance, humbly called by Mr. Lasserre "a chastisement;" in our opinion, a permission of God, Who wished, together with the power of the Virgin of Lourdes, to manifest, in a striking manner, the power of the picture venerated in Mr. Dupont's oratory.

The pious writer continues his recital: "The Rev. Father Gratry, having been informed of my miraculous cure, wrote to me to inquire if it was true. In answer, I narrated succinctly all that had passed. Father Gratry was then at Tours, and I determined, in order to see him, to pass through this city on my return to Paris; other affairs demanded my attention, also, in that direction. Whilst in conversation with the illustrious oratorian, Mr. Dupont's name was mentioned by him, I do not remember in what connection; it was a chance remark. 'Mr. Dupont!' I exclaimed, 'I have desired, for several years, to become acquainted with him, and I often intended to stop at Tours, in order to visit him. Strange, that having formed the intention, some days ago, to come to Tours, and having been here since the morning, the idea of going to see him did not occur to me! I shall certainly not now lose the opportunity of being introduced to him.' For this purpose, I delayed, by several hours, my return to Paris.

"It is, indeed, worth the trouble to stop at Tours, or even go there expressly, to see Mr. Dupont. One fact will explain all: in his house, blessed by Heaven, by a simple unction he makes with a miraculous oil, are realized, to the letter, the celebrated sentence of the Gospel and the prophecy of Isaiah: Cœci *vidunt, claudi ambulant, leprosi mundantur, surdi audiunt.* 'The blind see, the lame walk, lepers are healed, the deaf hear.'

"When going to visit him, I had not the least idea of asking anything for myself. I hoped that, on my return to Paris, I should recover from my partial relapse, by using the Lourdes water; I was wholly averse to employ any other means than which had benefited me before, or to have recourse to other intercession. My only object was to know and see in his own home, the servant of God, of whom I had heard so much, and to beg the aid of his prayers for a great miracle in the moral order, the miracle of my perfect conversion.

"Mr. Dupont was at home when I called. I was detained a few moments in a large apartment situated on the ground floor. I looked around me, whilst the servant went to notify

CHAPTER XVIII

the master of the house. The furniture was very simple; at intervals on the walls, were hung *ex voto* offerings. Beside a desk covered with papers, upon a kind of stand in the form of a pulpit, I saw a large open book; I recognized the Holy Scripture. But my attention was principally arrested by one of those engravings of the 'Holy Face,' which represents the Face of our Lord such as He impressed it upon the veil of Veronica on the day of His Passion. Before this Holy Face a lamp burned, or rather, a taper, floating on a limpid oil contained in a crystal vase.

"The door opened, and Mr. Dupont entered.

"I strove to conquer my embarrassment. He inquired what service he could render me, and I told him my visit had no other motive than my desire to make his acquaintance; that I came to see him in consequence of what I had heard of all the wonders, the miracles, which, according to report, were accomplished in his house. 'Yes, Sir,' he replied, with a familiarity of language which struck me, 'it is now nearly eleven years since, in this room, before that Holy Face, our *Lord commenced to perform His miracles.* And He deigned to choose the house of a miserable creature like myself, in order that nothing could be attributed to the merit of the man, and to prove that He alone does all.'

"I requested him to relate to me on what occasion the wonders of which he spoke, first manifested themselves. 'I was far from suspecting,' he replied, 'that this room would become a place of pilgrimage, and that in it, would be effected innumerable miracles. But such was the design of God.'" Here Mr. Dupont related to his visitor what we already know of his idea of exposing the picture in his drawing-room, and of the first miracles it had effected. "'Since that time,' he continued, 'miraculous cures have not ceased. Not a day passes, that some wonder of the kind does not occur. The oil, when sent to foreign countries, is as efficacious there to heal the infirm, as in this place. Ah! Sir,' he exclaimed in conclusion, 'how great is God! how good is God!'

"'Yes, certainly,' I said, after a moment's silence, 'God is good. No one knows it better than I, no one has been more ungrateful to so kind a benefactor. I am not surprised at the miracles which are accomplished here, as I was myself formerly favored by a grace similar to the cures which are granted before that holy picture; but I proved unworthy of it, and I see that, at the present moment, the hand of God is about to precipitate me into my former condition.'

"I then related to him my history, my cure and my partial relapse, of which I explained the cause. He did not appear surprised. 'It often happens,' he said, 'that partial or complete relapses occur; and I have remarked that they generally proceed from two causes: either the individuals have been ashamed to testify to the miracle before men, or they have neglected to return thanks to God.' 'I have little human respect,' I replied, 'and I have not blushed to acknowledge the miracle by which I was favored; but I did not return thanks, and hardly was my sight restored, when I resumed my usual way of life.'

"'Every fault may be repaired,' said Mr. Dupont. 'We will now invoke the Lord, pray before that Holy Face, and anoint your eyes with the miraculous oil. Perhaps it will benefit you.' 'No,' I replied, 'I have been once cured by the Blessed Virgin honored at Lourdes; it is against her I have sinned; it is she, I hope, who will obtain my pardon and my cure. As soon as I return to Paris, I shall again bathe my eyes with the miraculous water. It is repugnant to my feelings to have recourse to any other intercession; it seems to me that I should fail in the homage I owe the Queen of angels, were I to invoke any power other than hers.'

"Mr. Dupont smiled and said gently: 'There is no jealousy in Heaven. Nevertheless,' he added, 'since such are your sentiments, here is a medal which was given me by Father Hermann; he immersed it himself in the water of Lourdes.

It has already been the instrument of several miraculous cures. Will you try it? Apply it successively on your eyes, and we will say together: "Holy Virgin show thyself as powerful at Tours as thou art at the grotto of Lourdes."'

"I knelt and did as he directed, but I experienced no relief. We repeated the same invocation several times, but always without effect. 'Ah!' said Mr. Dupont, without being the least disturbed, and lifting his eyes to Heaven as if addressing invisible powers; 'Ah! Blessed Virgin Mary, since thou refusest this cure, we will apply directly to thy Divine Son.' We prayed together a short time. Mr. Dupont dipped his finger in the oil which burned before the Holy Face and anointed with it my eyelids and forehead, under the eyebrows, wherever I felt the dangerous heaviness. No cure resulted.

"I dined with Mr. Dupont. After dinner, we recommenced the prayers, and he again applied the oil; but Heaven seemed deaf to our petitions. I experienced not the slightest relief. I attributed the failure to the right cause, and I acknowledged that I had deserved it.

"Mr. Dupont was pained; but, accustomed to deal with things in the supernatural order, his hope did not abate in consequence of the apparent rigor of the Divine Power. 'Do not be troubled,' he said to me; 'here is a phial of the oil which burns before the Holy Face of our Lord. We will consider the prayers and unctions of today, as the first day of a novena. Anoint your eyes daily yourself, and unite with the prayers which are said here every day between the hours of eleven and two. I will pray for you each day.' We parted; he permitted me to embrace him. I left Tours that same evening, and at four o'clock in the morning I was in Paris.

"On arriving, I went immediately to bed and slept all morning. I arose quite late. My first thought was to make the unctions and say the prayers indicated by Mr. Dupont. They were ineffectual. It was about half-past ten.

"About noon, as I was on my way to attend to some business affairs, I suddenly felt all the heaviness removed from my eyes, and the sensation of a healthy condition seemed to penetrate the eyelids and brow, which had been habitually so much oppressed. The favor of Heaven had suddenly descended in a full stream, like those rains so long desired, which, when they are the least expected, fall like a blessed dew upon the parched earth. I remembered that prayers were being offered at Mr. Dupont's at that very hour.

"From that day, my sight was restored. A year has passed, and I have had no return of the malady. Three or four times I have been conscious of a slight weakness in my eyes, so very slight as not to interrupt my work, or even inconvenience me, to which I would not refer, were it not that I desire to make a perfectly true statement. To relieve these trifles, I have always employed effectually the oil of the Holy Face."

We have purposely preserved the description and the expressions of the celebrated author. His account is an exact picture of what hundreds of others have seen and felt at Mr. Dupont's, what others have either told or written to us, with the same conviction and the same faith in the power of God and the merits of his servant.

XXVII

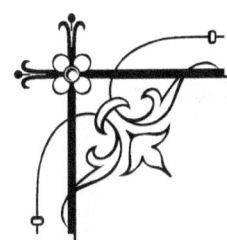

Chapter XIX

His Love of the Church.

THE EVENTS which were occurring before the Holy Face and at Lourdes, the current of Catholic piety so rapidly directed towards these two points from different parts of France, influenced Mr. Dupont in his views with regard to the situation of the Church. The precarious and alarming situation of Catholicity, subsequent to the war in Italy, constantly engaged his attention, and, by turns, excited his fears and hopes. It was the continual object of his prayers at the Nocturnal Adoration and before the Holy Face. But the dominant sentiment with him, was confidence in the future. The world appeared to him to be inundated with supernatural graces; and the trials, through which it pleased God that the Sovereign Pontiff, the Clergy and good Catholics should paas, seemed to him the forerunners of an unexpected and favorable conclusion. His whole correspondence abounds with these ideas. We shall transcribe a few passages which manifest his love of the Church, and the hopes he entertained of her triumph. He does not deceive himself as to the bitter hatred of Satan and his unhappy dupes; but he derives from its manifestation a motive for encouragement.

"Do not the multiplied efforts of Satan prove," he says, "with a force amounting to certainty, that the monster is roaring, because he comprehends that the Church is approaching one of her noblest triumphs?" "One thing comforts me under present circumstances. Evil is, without doubt, in the ascendency, and continues its upward course; but, at the same time, the source of divine mercy is not dried up, and of this we have proofs by the thousands. In my opinion, it is injurious to the power of God to doubt that He is able to overcome our obduracy, and render Himself the Master of our hearts. We are in His hands, and, whilst respecting our free will, He can grant a triumph to His Church, and bring to nought the efforts of hell." "We may know there is consolation in store for our faith, when we calculate the vehemence of the demon's attacks. Animals become infuriated only after having been provoked. Satan, on beholding the wonders of grace at the present day, may now say, as he did on the day of the Incarnation: *Cur venisti ante tempus torquere me?* "Why hast thou come before the time to torment me?"

The Sacred Heart of Jesus, and the Immaculate Conception of Mary, were as the two poles of his hope. Already in 1854, the promulgation of the dogma of the Immaculate Conception had gladdened his faith. In many passages in his letters, he expresses himself on this consoling event with pious enthusiasm. A few days before the definition he wrote: "Behold the approach of the great event which is to confound the enemy of God and man, the old serpent, who will be overwhelmed with confusion, when the Church proclaims that the snares he laid under the feet of Mary have been of no avail. We must, therefore, hope that the triumph of Mary will result in the discouragement of Satan, and, among the children of the Church, in an increase of filial confidence, by the means of which we shall see prodigies of grace renew the face of the earth."

On first hearing of the definition, he cannot restrain the expression of his joy, and pours out his feelings to a friend: "I wished to write to you in order to rejoice with you over the great event which marks an era in the history of the Church. How good God has been to inspire Pius IX with the thought of pronouncing the definitive judgment, by his own authority alone! What an argument in favor of unity, in presence of the pell-mell of errors which form the camp opposed to light! Let us now refer to the beautiful idea of Dom Guéranger when speaking of the prediction of St. Leonard of Port-Maurice: 'On the day of the promulgation of the dogma of the Immaculate Conception, the waves of God's anger will flow back upon themselves.' Mercy, then, will accomplish for us, miserable creatures, what justice formerly did to efface the crimes of the earth at the time of the deluge. Let us hope."

The beatification of the venerable Margaret Mary Alacoque, and the extension of devotion to the Sacred Heart, were to his eyes important events which he regarded as pledges of salvation.

"The triumph of the Sacred Heart," he writes, "introduces us into an era which, according to present appearances, will be very glorious for the Church and very profitable to souls. This last blow will sweep from the earth the defilements of Jansenism. All hail to the Sacred Heart! Hell is unchained, it is true; but is not that, of itself, a sign of future defeat? The marvels occurring in England are more than sufficient to exasperate a monster, who believed himself secure as in an impregnable fortress." In speaking of the triumph of the Church, he frequently alludes to England. The conversions made in that country, with which he had relations, attracted his attention and excited the most sanguine hopes. "What is passing in England," he says, "is magnificent: we are, it seems, on the eve of extraordinary events, which, humanly speaking, will sustain the Church and prepare for her a signal triumph over beastly modern heresy, which rejects faith and demands to behold with carnal eyes."

He dwells with delight upon the grand figure of Pius IX. The promulgation of the dogma of the Immaculate Conception, the beatification of Margaret Mary Alacoque, the Vatican Council, and other memorable acts of this illustrious pontiff, seemed to him like so many rays of light successively added to the antique crown of glory encircling the papacy, and reflected in streams upon Christian society at large.

In speaking of the head of the Church, he always said: "Our Holy Father, our beloved Pius IX." He added once: "Beloved by God and Christians, but hated by Satan and his miserable victims."

In the tempests which toss the bark of the Church, he admires the tranquillity and wisdom of this great pontiff: "It is certainly true," he says, "that the pilot, Pius IX, is tranquil at the helm; he seems to sleep in the bark as the Divine Master: *Novit Dominus pios de tentatione eripere.*" Words of St. Peter, which he applies by a graceful and delicate allusion to the name of Pius IX, that cannot be translated into our language. The encyclical upon the Syllabus, (December 8, 1864,) made a great impression upon this fervent Christian, whose mind was so just and so enlightened in the things of God. He understood at once how wise and opportune in our modern times was this Pontifical act, and he discovered the germ of salvation it contained for civil society. He admired it the more sincerely, because the errors it designated had long been the objects of his abhorrence.

He never separated Rome in his thoughts from the Church and Pius IX. He cherished a devotion to the city of the popes; he had correspondents there; he accompanied in spirit those of his friends who went to pray at the tomb of the holy Apostles, a pilgrimage much less frequent and more difficult in those days than at the present time, and reserved for a favored few. "This journey," he says, (March 24, 1862,) when speaking of a nobleman of his acquaintance, "will be of service to him; great consolations are granted to great sorrows. Now Rome, the home of faith, contains all that binds us closely to Him Who has said: 'Blessed are they who mourn,' and Who can alone pour balm into the wounded heart." To an officer who returned from Rome in 1869, on the eve of the opening of the Council, he writes: "I have just read with intense interest the details you had the kindness to send me of your journey to Rome. Rome, whence light is about to flow in streams upon the world. *Fiat!* How happy one is to be a child of the Church!" The invasion of the holy city in 1871, caused him deep affliction, and really tried his confidence; he writes in a sad strain, (December 24, 1871): "O Rome! alas! the object of our fears and sorrows! And yet we must either hope or faint in the way. There are so many souls walking in the path of the counsels; they can obtain grace both for themselves and others."

France, as well as Rome, is the object of the fears and hopes which, by turns, possess his heart. The shining virtues and the good works which illustrate France, encourage him to hope that his country will pass safely through the ordeal. "Consider," he said, (November 16, 1845,) "all the religious institutions which are spread over France like so many nurseries, whence the plant will be disseminated to the rest of the world. Every wound of society is provided for, from the crib to the pallet of the decrepit poor. At Paris, the *crib*; at Sens, the Sisters of the Holy Childhood, who are increasing in numbers throughout France; at Saint-Servan, a work which will soon be propagated under the attractive name of Holy Old Age. Every Christian comprehends that he is an apostle. Rapid means of transportation are furnished him that he may make a stand against impiety, and whilst Satan forwards his boxes of books and his married missionaries, true Christians vie with each other in bearing the cross of Jesus Christ to the extremities of the earth." The noble enthusiasm of the French youth, who enrolled themselves among the Pontifical Zouaves transported him with joy and admiration. He writes, (November 5, 1867): "The same breath which inspired St. Louis and his gallant cavaliers is, today, animating our Christian youth who fly to the aid of the Holy See." And on the 25th of February, 1868: "The ardent, generous zeal which animates Christian souls at the sight of the dangers which menace the Pope, carries us back to the days of the Crusades."

The disasters which overwhelmed France during the Prussian invasion deeply afflicted him, but did not destroy his confidence in the destiny of the eldest daughter of the Church. "Catholic France seems to arise from the tomb," he writes in 1872. "We have just grounds for hope, since her first act after resuscitating, is to enter into prayer. What a grand sight is the concourse of people at Lourdes, and at other shrines! Let us then redouble our confidence. Satan resists because he knows well where the blow will wound him. The victory will be to the children of God."

Without absenting himself from the Holy Face, he was acquainted with everything connected with the Church. He learned all through his extensive correspondence. There was not a sorrow, a joy, a fear, or a hope in any part of the Catholic world, which did not find its echo in his heart. He received letters from all quarters, requesting his advice, his prayers, light in doubt, or encouragement under trial; in one sense, he might say with the Apostle: Who is weak and I am not weak? Who is scandalized and I am not on fire? This grand Christian was thus identified with the soul of the Church and he lived of her life.

Thence also arose his lively interest in Catholic publishers and authors, who were expending their energies in the good cause. He sympathized in their feelings, kept himself informed as to the works of religious controversy which, from time to time, issued from the press; sometimes be read them, and either directly by letter or through his friends, he offered his congratulations to their authors.

At one time Captain Marceau and himself made the resolution not to read a newspaper, partly through a spirit of mortification and sacrifice, and partly to avoid a loss of time. But he considered himself justifiable in not adhering to this determination, during the celebrated struggle of the French episcopacy to obtain the liberty of Christian education. His relations at the Conferences of St. Vincent de Paul with Mr. Léon Aubineau, one of the principal writers for the Univers, made him acquainted with that paper; he subscribed to it and was in entire sympathy with it. As this sheet solely advocated and upheld the interests of the Church as of paramount importance, and publicly professed the intention of defending only the truth, and of subordinating all human to religious questions, it answered in every respect his dearest desires. For the same reasons, he equally esteemed the Monde, and subscribed to it also. He likewise received some local papers and pious reviews. Mr. Dupont read from these only such articles as related to religion, or had reference to questions of doctrine, or to works which were interesting to his faith and piety, and which might, in some manner, be useful to the Church and to souls..

He was aware of the immense injury inflicted by impious journals upon contemporary society, particularly upon youth; he was bitterly afflicted. "What a frightful abyss," he exclaims, "is opened under the feet of youth by a wicked press!" He relies upon the Catholic press to neutralize its effect, and attributes to its persevering efforts the absence of human respect among men of every rank, and the increase of the number of communicants at Easter in 1862. "Happily," he says, "we learn that in the large cities throughout France, the number of men who have made their Easter Communion, far exceeds that of preceding years." He ascribed the increase to the courage and talent of Catholic editors. He was never indifferent to the Pastorals of the Bishops. Immediately after reading them, he communicated his impressions in his correspondence to his friends. "What a magnificent page," he says, "has been written by Monseigneur of Paris, to confound the enemies of our Lord!" He refers to a Pastoral in which Monseigneur Darboy, speaking eloquently of the divinity of Jesus Christ, answers the impious volume of Renan which had just appeared. "I would like to have a copy of it," he says, "to lend to benighted souls who may need it."

He heartily applauded the publication and distribution of such new works, as were in accordance with his habitual train of thought, or which seemed to him suited to the necessities of the times. Many authors presented him with the first copies of their books, and awaited his opinion and observations. When a book pleased him, he was accustomed to read it carefully, note the *errata*, and send them to the writer, manifesting in his manner as much delicacy and humility as zeal. A historian once requested him to criticize one of his works. "He made but few corrections," says the author; "I had abridged the most sacred names of our religion, and I found beside the initials J. C., N. S., the names *Jesus Christ, our Lord*, written in full by this good Christian. I was impressed and edified, and I said to myself: 'Behold a man of faith!' His just and delicate suggestion has since been of service to me."

Without being a theologian or a man of learning, Mr. Dupont had the gift of discerning in contemporary productions even a shadow of error. Whatever book of piety or religion fell into his hands, on merely glancing through it, he appreciated its beauties, or discovered its defects. He was guided by a kind of Catholic instinct which enabled him to detect the vulnerable point. "I am unfortunate," he said one day to Monseigneur d'Outremont, "when I take up a book, if there is any portion of it objectionable, I am certain to open it at that page."

When reading, he was accustomed to note down the thoughts which particularly impressed him: he used for this purpose a large sheet of paper left lying on his desk. As this sheet became filled with the passages thus selected, he attached another sheet to it, until at last he had made quite a collection. If a book was good and could benefit the reader, he did not wish it to be read carelessly. When sending a book of this kind to a man of the world, he once wrote: "Do not answer me until you have read the book, and do not devour it, as you would an ordinary book containing only wind. There is no question here of an omelette, but of a solid dish."

He is without mercy for bad books which come in his way. Regarding those who had written them as instruments of Satan, he experienced a triumphant delight in destroying their impious works. One day, a number of volumes of Voltaire, Jean-Jaques Rousseau, and others of the same kind, were sent him. Instead of throwing them into the fire, the idea struck him to dig a hole in his garden, and, placing them within, to cover the whole with manure; above this he sowed potatoes. When they were sufficiently large, he ordered them to be dug up. They were remarkably fine; his garden had never yielded better. What should be done with them? His servants, the members of his household, were called upon to give their views. It was proposed to sell them in the market, to cook them, to send them to the Little Sisters of the Poor. Standing with his arms folded, Mr. Dupont listened in silence and with tranquillity, to the different suggestions; suddenly he said: "Throw them to the hogs, they are fit for nothing else." Then, laughing heartily, he turned to a friend, who was present at the scene and who related it to us, and added, in reference to their origin, "they come from Voltaire, from Jean-Jaques; of what good are such productions but to feed swine?"

On the contrary, when he met with a book of piety which he considered a useful work, he would order many copies, and distribute them. He extracted, as we have said, certain striking passages, either for his own benefit, or to communicate them to others. It was thus he composed a charming little volume under the title of *Pensées sur l'Amour de Dieu*, (*Thoughts on the Love of God*), and later, the one entitled *Petit Jardin Céleste, Recueil de Pensées Spirituelles*, (*The Celestial Garden, Collection of Spiritual Thoughts*). These "thoughts" he tells us were inspired by the Little Sisters of the Poor, and were intended for their use. They are simple and touching, and bear the impress of the spirit of God. They are evidently the fruit of prayer and meditation on the Scriptures. We extract a few: "O my God, when shall I be able to read the precept of loving Thee written on my heart by Thy hand? When will it be granted me, O my God, to love Thee without distraction, in the midst of the weariness and crosses of this life?—O my God, since Thou art pleased to call Thyself our Father, how sweet it would be to me to love Thee with filial tenderness and childlike simplicity!—To die in the habit of love, to die in an act of pure love,—what a happy death; but to die from love, would be the accomplishment of all my desires, if it be permitted to a miserable sinner to aspire so high.—The faithful soul is 'the lily amid thorns.' The lily thus situated leans neither to one side, nor the other; it remains upright, and unfolds its leaves, and opens its heart only towards heaven, to receive its dew and warmth, lest it should lose a portion of them by bending towards the earth.— The heart the most abandoned to God is the best guarded.—The heart which meditates upon the goodness of God, should either love Him, or cease to be a heart.—My God, Thou art all love; for Thy works breathe love; Thy commandments are love; our vocation is nothing but love. But how few comprehend the language of love! Sacred altar, when I consider thee, when I turn my eyes upon the spot where the tabernacle reposes, I am unable to resist the transports of joy which fill my soul. In contemplating thee, O throne of the Divine Lamb, my heart opens, dilates, liquifies in the fire of love. When wilt thou arrive, O happy moment, in which my adorable

Saviour will come to repose within it?— Knock at the Heart of Jesus by confidence and love; it will be opened to you, and abundant graces will, thence, flow upon you."

Such was the devouring zeal which animated this pious layman in the presence of the adorable Face of our Lord. His writings breathe only love, and like his conversations and his prayers, had but one aim, pursued but one object: the glory of God by serving the Church, and saving souls.

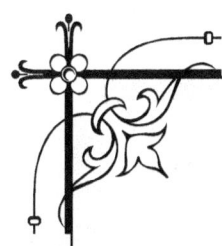

Chapter XX

His Faith, His Humility.

THE INCIDENTS thus far related have brought us nearly to the year 1870. France is on the verge of great trials; the trials which God reserves for the servant of the Holy Face are also about to commence. His virtue, already so exalted, must be purified and perfected by passing through the fire of tribulation. He is to suffer in soul and body. He will see France invaded, the city of St. Martin bombarded and occupied by the enemy, and, consequently, disorder introduced into those works of zeal and piety which he had most at heart, and which formed the happiness of his life. He himself, afflicted more and more in every member of his body, will live in a state of isolation, condemned to inactivity, and suffering all the infirmities of old age.

But, before rehearsing those painful incidents which will bring us to the end of our career, it will not be amiss to dwell awhile upon some of the interior and fundamental virtues which were the soul of his life, and which inspired his heroic acts and noble sentiments. It will furnish us the opportunity, whilst casting a retrospective glance upon his actions, to refer to various characteristics which either escaped us, or which could not be suitably introduced in the previous pages.

Mr. Dupont's predominant virtue was faith. It was, in truth, the motive of all his actions, the soul of his life. One of his friends, a priest, speaking of him, said: "He was truly the man of faith, a strong, simple, and constant faith, which was manifested rather in the uniform and habitual actions of daily life, than by the exceptional practices of an interior and mystical life. I mean, that what was most observable in Mr. Dupont, and what I believe to have been a portion of the mission assigned him here below by Divine Providence, was the *visible* work of faith, the *sensible* presence, as it were, of that virtue which rendered him a docile instrument, *ever ready to do good*. It was this simplicity of divine faith, which constituted the unity of his life, from the course of which he never swerved, either in public or in private; always the same, to such a degree, that it seemed to have almost become his nature. With this simplicity was sometimes united a striking and unaffected dignity, arising, no doubt, from the solidity of his character, but which, in his case, bore the impress of the noble spirit with which his beautiful soul animated every action of his life. Mr. Dupont's faith possessed, also, a distinctive mark; namely, a peculiar instinct in discerning between the good and evil spirit. I remember a certain imposter, Michel Ventras, for whom he felt, from the first, a most decided repugnance. On the other hand, where there was question of events of a really supernatural order, particularly such as the apparitions of the Blessed Virgin, he was strongly inclined to believe, and, although awaiting with respect the decision of the ecclesiastical Superiors, he could not restrain the exterior manifestation of his joy, upon receiving the first authentic accounts of these touching evidences of the divine goodness."

The same priest, a good judge and an intelligent observer, adds: "Precisely because it was simple and upright, the faith of Mr. Dupont possessed a purity and stability which could brook no alloy of human wisdom, nor worldly prudence, still less, of that which Pius IX has so justly branded with the name of 'liberal Catholicity.' The least deviation from what is just and true in a matter of doctrine or principles, called into play an energy which was aroused at the first enunciation of anything fallacious. This same energy of soul maintained his whole conduct in the most perfect serenity and equanimity; he was always the same, always ready for what he called his *daily work*, that was, his constant assiduity before the Holy Face, in union with all who went there to offer their prayers."

In addition to this testimony from a priest of an interior and austere life, we present evidence of another kind, in which we shall find the echo of the best society in Tours at that time: it is that furnished by the Abbé Boullay. Fr. Boullay, dean of the Chapter at his death, and a man of superior intellect, enjoyed among the Clergy and in the world a well-merited reputation for eloquence; warm-hearted, gifted with amiable and brilliant qualities, which were not marred by a degree of oddness and agreeable eccentricity of character, he visited familiarly the most noble families in the country, and he was everywhere welcomed and handsomely entertained. He was about the same age as Mr. Dupont. They lived in the same part of the city, and often met in the street, in the sacristy, and at the assemblies of the cathedral officers; there existed between them a mutual esteem and affection. The witty dean, whose humorous sallies were sometimes tinged with Gallican and materialistic expressions, which came only from the lips and not from the heart, amused himself sometimes with the "holy exaggerations of his neighbor." "I never meet him," he said, "that he has not his pocket full of miracles to relate to me." He professed, however, no less a sincere admiration for the faith and virtues of the "grand Christian." We will give an example. One day, when he was in the sacristy of the cathedral conversing with some canons and other ecclesiastics, Mr. Dupont entered. A circle was formed around him, and they remained listening attentively to a long account of supernatural events. When he had gone away, Mr. Boullay said jestingly: "The holy man really believes that God works miracles as a man would hammer nails. He doubts nothing. The only thing I can reproach him with, is an excess of faith..." But checking himself suddenly, and as if to repair the blunder which had escaped him, he exclaimed with enthusiasm: "That is a noble fault to have an excess of faith! He is right; we cannot have too much." Then, turning to leave the sacristy, he said seriously: "Gentlemen, Mr. Dupont is a saint; let us imitate him."

Faith, as viewed by Mr. Dupont, was that "mountain of God," that fertile mountain of which the Scriptures speak. "How advantageous it is," he said one day, "to place ourselves upon that mountain that we may learn to comprehend the littleness of human plans! Let us live, my dear friend, more and more, the life of faith, in order to appreciate the nothingness of earth and to rise above the instability of the things of this world." He had established himself in this superior sphere, and thence he drew the contrast between the things of God and those of time. "When shall we be able," he exclaimed, "to entertain ourselves solely with things so ineffable? It is necessary that faith should revive, faith, the love of the things of God in opposition to the miserable affairs of time. The Gospel placed above the journal! Heaven preferred to earth! God to man! We shall see that day, I hope."

He entertained so high an idea of faith that, for a long time, he thought of requesting Mr. Auguste Nicolas to add at the end of his *Art de Croire*, a last chapter under this title: *Honneur de Croire*. "And in reality," said he "what greater honor can elevate man?"

"The spirit of faith," said the Curé d'Ars, "consists in speaking to God as we would speak in a familiar manner to a man." Mr. Dupont practiced this to the letter. When kneeling before the Sacred Face in prayer for those who asked his aid, he seemed less absorbed than confident. He spoke to God as to a Being intimately present, and then turning to the invalid, he would inquire if he were cured. He spoke to God as to the proprietor, the occupant of his room. "Miracles!" he would say, "what is easier? It is simplicity, particularly, which obtains them... The class of men who obtain the most abundantly, is the class of the peasantry. I have seen many persons present themselves before the Holy Face, saying: 'Oh! I am not worthy to be heard.' I do not like that. It is not in this manner we should speak. The question is not of what you are worthy. You are worthy of compassion alone and of nothing else. You must express your wants and believe." In order to excite faith, and prove the facility of obtaining a miracle, he would recall to the infirm the title of God: "Creator of all things: *Creator omnium.*" His conviction of omnipotence was a sentiment so lively and so simple, that the most prodigious results would not have surprised those who witnessed it. The very tone of his voice in prayer revealed, in a striking manner, the plenitude and simplicity of his faith. In a layman, it was particularly remarkable. After having been in his company, the most pious priests, the most fervent Religious, felt that their faith was warmed and strengthened.

His unalterable serenity was not less remarkable: he soared, as it were, in a region above the reach of events apparently the most disastrous, ever tranquil, even where the interests of religion were involved, because, in all circumstances, he beheld the action of Divine Providence and the accomplishment of the Divine will. During the ceremonies on a feast of the Immaculate Conception, in a church at Valparaiso, the edifice caught fire, and a large number of people perished in the flames. The papers teemed with accounts of the disaster. A lady of Tours, moved by the recital of the sad news, was tempted—she herself relates the incident—to murmur against God. "Why, O my God," she said interiorly, "didst Thou not save from death, so many pious faithful, employed in honoring Thy Holy Mother, and in celebrating the triumph of her Immaculate Conception?" Whilst occupied by these thoughts, she met Mr. Dupont in the street. Entering at once upon the recent disaster, she gave expression to her sorrow in bitter terms. The servant of God, preserving a perfect tranquillity, interrupted her. "Madame," he said, "your emotion misleads you. You have cause to rejoice, rather than to weep. Behold how God chose the moment, when His children on earth were occupied in honoring their Mother in Heaven, to call them to Himself and transport them, by one bound, to His Paradise. In an instant, they are saved, they are happy; this is not an accident, but a grace, a very great grace." "I dared not answer," added the lady. "He was in quite another sphere: I was looking at earth, he regarded Heaven." Living by faith, Mr. Dupont supposed that all who had faith were like himself. This illusion deprived him perhaps of a correct discernment of others. Losing sight of the evil passions of mankind, he concluded that sanctity accompanied the faith he so much loved. Apparently, he did not take into account the obstacles which may impede the progress of the soul, even when the intellect is convinced, and which may retard the believer in the path of perfection. As for himself, he did not seem absorbed, but firmly established, in God; and his unity of occupation, unity of conversation, and unity of purpose under every circumstance, in every respect, in his room, in his work, in his repose, in his words, gave to all his surroundings the air of a sanctuary; it was God, God always, God alone.

Conversation not relating to God, was insupportable to him; in fact, he would not endure it. Several persons were once dining with him. The conversation, without being worldly in the ordinary sense of the word, turned upon human and profane subjects. Mr. Dupont, after keeping silence for a few moments, suddenly interrupted his guests in an earnest manner saying: "I perceive that you eat like dogs and cats without thinking of God. Do you not know that life is too short to allow us to speak of any thing but God? I know nothing shorter in the world than life." This abrupt remark, if made to his guests by an ordinary man, would have been considered an insult; coming from Mr. Dupont, and in his tone of voice, it charmed every one. In a guard-house one of the men gaped. "You are wearied," said Mr. Dupont to him; "I can readily understand it; it is very natural; one is always weary when not occupied with God, or speaking of God."

He had an extreme respect for priests. When on a pilgrimage or travelling, he treated those whom he met with politeness, preventing kindness, and exquisite charity, taking charge of their baggage, assisting them in the difficulties that arose, saving them from any inconvenience, making himself their obliging servant, and all this with a cordiality and ease that savored, not the least, of affectation, nor proved an annoyance.

He was always happy to serve a Mass. Whenever the opportunity of fulfilling that pious function preseated itself, whether in a private chapel or in a parochial church, in the city or in the country, he eagerly took advantage of it, being careful, however, to avoid interfering with others, or of disturbing the usual routine of the individual or of the place. He would replace the choir-boy with the calm dignity and angelic fervor which always characterized him before the altar. He particularly loved to serve the first Mass which was offered in a new chapel or church. He valued it as a priest does his first Mass, or a Christian, his first Communion.

He had no less respect and deference for his confessors. He took pleasure in rendering them friendly services, and performed these with a delicacy, a kindness, and devotion which never gave them cause to suspect the sacrifices which, in consequence, he was sometimes obliged to impose upon himself. When M. l'Abbé Pasquier, in his old age, was able to walk only a short distance, his pious penitent hired a vehicle for his use, and he would himself drive him from house to house, wherever he wished to go, remaining in the carriage and watching the horse as an ordinary driver. When later, M. l'Abbé Verdier was in the same condition, the result of a long and dangerous illness, Mr. Dupont procured a carriage every day during his convalescence, and drove him in the country, in order to recreate and strengthen him. M. l'Abbé Allouard was invited to dine with him every Sunday. The conversations of these two men of God, the one a profound theologian, the other possessing, as we know, an ardent piety and candor of soul, were as seraphic and elevated as they were simple and joyous. They spoke only of God, of

Jesus Christ, of the Saints, of the Church, and of miraculous events, all passing in a bright and joyous manner, and interspersed with witty jibes and contemptuous attacks upon Satan, "the old man, the animal, the beast," as Mr. Dupont called him, and upon his agents and modern partisans, whom he named the "swine of his band."

He was never troublesome to the priests to whose ministry he had recourse. Simple, upright, and precise in his questions and his accusations, he proceeded frankly, requiring but a few words for the direction of his conscience. If his confessors were indisposed for any length of time, he asked the permission to continue his Communions as usual, sometimes sending the message without constraint through a third person. From the time that he fixed his residence at Tours, he always selected his confessors from the clergy of the cathedral, as he lived in that parish. Notwithstanding his well known veneration for many holy priests of different Religious orders, we do not know that he ever departed from his usual method, or that he had recourse to clergymen not belonging to the parish.

In matters not connected with Confession, he asked advice, consulted different priests at length and frequently; as for example, concerning the interpretation of a text of scripture, the translation of a passage, the form proper for a prayer, an association for pious purposes or practices of virtue, a supernatural or a miraculous event. With regard to this kind of facts, which always excited his liveliest interest, he devoted more attention to their examination, and was more reserved in accepting them than we might be inclined to suppose. His first impulse was to believe simply; but before asserting or making known the incident to his correspondents, he was very careful to be certain of its truth, and awaited the investigations and decision of the proper authority before finally accepting it. We often see him in his confidential communications to his friends discard his first impression, and say simply and frankly: "The investigation did not result favorably; we must be on our guard and wait; Satan can transform himself into an angel of light."

Whilst faith taught Mr. Dupont the greatness of God, it made him feel at the same time the depth of his own nothingness, and implanted in his soul another fundamental virtue which he comprehended and practiced no less faithfully, viz: humility.

This pious layman placed a high value on humility. A gentleman was once relating in his presence a striking action, and seemed to await an expression of his administration and praise. "Ah!" he said quietly, "one good act of humility is worth more than that." Being convinced that one of the most serious spiritual defects of our day is a spirit of independence and pride, he took pleasure in distributing the "Litany of Humility." "The enthusiasm manifested in regard to this Litany," he said one day, "is sufficient evidence that Christians comprehend how thoroughly the world is infected with pride, a malady which can be combated only by humility."

To make oneself little and to seek little things, was one of the principles of his spirituality. "If it is permitted me," he wrote to one who consulted him, "to offer an advice,

I would say to you, that after exposing the wound of your heart to our Lord by elevating your thoughts to Heaven, you should embrace, as your armor on earth, small things, and, of small things, those which are the least. To save the world, Jesus made himself little. And thus, to save ourselves and others we should likewise make ourselves little. I know a person who conducted a great work to a successful issue, by devoting herself to the practice of the smallest works one can imagine. For instance, she would kiss the steps as she ascended the staircase, when she could do so without attracting attention. Absorbed by the thought of obtaining the conversion of her sister, she strove to secure it by performing little and lowly actions, working rather as a vile insect than as a noble animal. This idea suggests the thought that the nearer we approach our nothingness, the nearer in reality we approach to God, by abasing ourselves to our original condition, a sublime condition, because the Divine will meets no obstacle to be overcome."

He frequently reverts in his letters to the "spirit of annihilation," to the "idea of our own nothingness." "Oh! how difficult," he said, "is this return to nothingness, since He, Who created the world from nothing, was forced Himself to mingle with the things of nothing, in order to give us the example! Therefore, being under the obligation of conforming ourselves to Jesus, in order to attain Heaven, we cannot do otherwise than walk in the path of an extreme humility."

A pious young lady from Lyons, who had been introduced to him by Monseigneur Dufêtre, was once complaining to him of not being sufficiently detached and dead to herself. Mr. Dupont replied to her: "An excellent means to obtain this self-annihilation is to consider yourself as one who is being carried to the grave. Of the dead, we can say what we will,— good or evil, it matters not to them; they are insensible to all that passes around them, they hear nothing, they answer nothing. Let us be as insensible as the dead when anything wounds us, when nature revolts within us; let us say: 'It matters not to me what is said, what is thought of me, *I am dead.*' Then the soul recovers its peace, we accept all, we are silent, and we can repeat with truth: '*I am dead.*' Therefore, it is granted that we three are dead. (The young lady was accompanied by a friend.) We will kneel down and say three times the *De profundis*." "From that time," says the lady, "whenever he met us, he would ask: 'Are you really dead?' Yes, or no, we were always obliged to say our *De profundis*, 'as a means,' he would say, 'of attaining the insensibility, the indifference of a corpse.' Experience taught us that the practice was good and efficacious; for, as long as we continued it, we felt our souls become detached from the things of earth."

What he taught others, he practiced himself. He was deeply penetrated with the sentiment of his baseness, and hence arose the terms of sincere contempt which he was accustomed to apply to himself. A friend having addressed him in a letter in a manner expressive of great respect, he replied: "Remark, if you please, that I have added no epithet of any kind to your name; I do so, to force you, when you next write to me, to proportion your style to my miseries. You know what the 'pilgrim' is, and you can well understand how heartily, and with just cause, those who also know him thoroughly, will laugh at the honor you do him." He jests about the "pilgrim sunk in the mire," "the pilgrim in penance." "I hope," he writes to a friend who had made him a visit, "that God will grant me the pleasure of seeing you again; in the meantime, I shall frequently recall with delight the short time you passed with me; I shall be the '*ruminating* pilgrim,' a poor little creature, whom naturalists have not yet classed, because they have no microscope sufficiently powerful to discover his habits." He was requested to join a pilgrimage; he offers in excuse the work of the Holy Face. "I am necessarily deprived of my name of 'pilgrim,' and I assume another I prefer to bear, that of 'servant.' Pray for me that I may be truly an humble servant, ready to do a service for those who may require my assistance." In regard to a project for which his interest was asked, he declares himself to be "only a broom handle, incapable of performing any work... *Ascende superius!* Men and animals need air to support life. I require, in addition, my nothingness."

All his actions bore the impress of great delicacy of feeling, not that purely natural and human delicacy manifested by well-bred persons in the world, but a true Christian delicacy, inspired by faith and an humble charity. He abhorred all worldly parade, pomp, or aiming at effect.

But his humility never appeared more worthy of admiration than in presence of the venerated picture of the Holy Face, or under any circumstances connected with the marvels of grace effected in his room.. His dissatisfaction was decidedly expressed, when letters were handed him bearing in the address some epithet of praise or commendation, as for example: "Mr. Dupont, in his chapel of the Holy Face, Tours;" or, "Mr. Dupont, Miracle-Worker, Tours;" or again, "Mr. Dupont, Physician who cures by prayer, Tours." He destroyed such envelopes at once; ' but the members of his household, by stratagem, obtained possession of some of them in order to amuse his friends.

One was given us, mailed in London, addressed thus: "*Mr. Dupont, Tours, France;*" then in a corner, as indicating the individual, were the words: "*The one who cures people.*" A letter was one day received at the post office simply directed: "*To the Thaumaturgus of Tours.*" Great embarrassment at the office! The postman of Saint-Etienne Street concluded that it was for Mr. Dupont, who made it a subject of merriment, repeating the word in an ironical manner, and imitating the speech of a little child or an idiot: *Thau... ma... tur... gus!* Persons, who were ignorant of his name, frequently wrote: "*To the great physician.*" We have often heard him jest upon this subject. "Humanly speaking," he said in a serious and sincere tone of voice, "our Lord could not have done worse than to select me as an instrument; the wise of this world would have taken good care to make a different choice." When petitions fervently presented to God were not granted, he was afflicted. "But," he added, "since we should derive profit from every event, I do my best to purify *the old man.* I mean, that my duty is to submit with entire resignation in this, as under other circumstances, when my heart was the most earnest in prayer. This proves to me, in a conclusive manner, that I am as nothing in what takes place here. My part is only to register petitions."

He concealed his own action as much as possible, ever seeking obscurity: thence arose his aversion to anything which might tend to bring his work into notice, and attract to himself consideration in the world. A few days after the death of Monseigneur de Montblanc, there was a report at Tours that the Bishop of Versailles had been appointed to the vacant see. Mr. Dupont appeared pained by the news. "His Lordship of Versailles," he said, "is my intimate friend; should he become Archbishop of Tours, I could not avoid seeing him frequently, and that would cause difficulties for a miserable being like myself, who am not fitted to frequent palaces." Another appointment having been made, he spoke of it as a grace from Divine Providence, Who thus had had pity on him, and left him in his obscurity.

He rarely appeared at the archiepiscopal palace, and only on business, never for mere visits of ceremony. Neither Cardinal Morlot nor Cardinal Guibert could induce him to accept an invitation to dine. At first, Monseigneur Morlot insisted, and often renewed his efforts, hoping to succeed after a time. Mr. Dupont always found excellent reasons for declining the honor. At last, he one day accepted an invitation through deference to his mother, who urged him to do so, telling him that he could not politely refuse. He entered the dining-room with the guests. But, as they were about to take their seats at table, it was found that one place was wanting. A gentleman of the company, it appears, not wishing to be crowded, had adroitly removed a chair, a circumstance which did not escape the observation of Mr. Dupont. He immediately passed behind the Archbishop, and whispered to him: "You see, Monseigneur, that I ought not to dine with persons of high rank, since there is no place for me." By the time the disappointed Archbishop had glanced down the table and given orders to supply the omission, Mr. Dupont was already at the bottom of the staircase; and when a messenger was sent to recall him, he had made his escape. The entreaties of Cardinal Guibert met with no better success; Mr. Dupont never appeared at the table of that venerable prelate, even on the festival of St. Martin, on which occasion, the members of the Clothing Society, of which he was president, were usually invited.

He would cordially express his opinion to those who visited him, and who were suffering any anxiety of mind; but, if anyone was apparently seeking in him a counsellor or director, he would exclaim quickly: "Advice? Alas! my dear friend, I ought to hide myself in some unknown spot, and remain concealed there, instead of holding communication with pious souls."

He showed extreme displeasure when some persons, through gratitude or veneration, wished to kiss his hand. To the very close of his life, he refused to permit this mark of respect. A few months before his death, a pious lady of Tours, who was quite infirm, went to see him on the part of a friend. The holy man, noticing that she walked with difficulty, offered her his cane. "Oh! no," said the infirm lady, refusing it, "it is too handsome for me." "Take it," said Mr. Dupont, "it is on that account I give it to you." The lady, touched and grateful, kissed the charitable hand which presented the cane. Mr. Dupont, assuming a stern manner, said: "What are you doing? Were it not for my infirmities, I would kiss your feet."

During his whole life, he never yielded to the urgent solicitations made him by different persons to give his blessing. But, on the other hand, what value he attached to that of the priest! He received one day a pair of scapulars blessed by a Religious of his acquaintance, who was of very low stature. Making a delicate allusion to that circumstance, he said with a charming grace: "This is, in truth, a beautiful present, enriched with many favors by the good little Father who, as soon as he raises his hand to bless the poor, far exceeds them in height. We are the poor, and the hand of the priest is so rich! Moreover, the alms is proportioned to our misery."

He did not restrain the expression of his feelings when strangers, either through flattery or other motives, lavished upon him epithets which wounded his humility. He sometimes replied quickly, and energetically disclaimed the honor done him; at other times, he exhibited his discontent by a serious manner and an expressive silence. When he found these means of no avail, he turned the whole affair into jest, and laughed as though he considered their observations as made sarcastically, in order to amuse themselves at his expense.

An English lady, Madame Viot-Otter, who went to his house frequently and at any hour of the day, and who, whilst venerating him as a saint, spoke to him with perfect freedom and loved to tease him, relates that on one occasion she found him taciturn, gloomy, and, to use her expression, "in a bad humor." To "rouse his spirits," she suddenly said to him very seriously: "'Mr. Dupont, you are not amiable today. That will not do. Take care; it might, at some future time, be an obstacle to your *canonization*.' This observation of mine struck him as so ridiculous and comical, that he laughed heartily. My object was attained; I had succeeded in raising his spirits."

When in familiar conversations he noticed that particular attention was paid to his remarks, or that his answers to questions regarding himself personally, were listened to with avidity, he was troubled, became confused and vexed, assumed an expressive reserve, or observed an absolute silence. He never referred, even when speaking with his relatives or intimate friends, to any event of his life which reflected credit upon him.

The following incident comes to us from a Religious, venerable for his age, austerities, and virtues: "We were, one evening, walking together in his garden, and we were conversing on various subjects. 'What is left of my fortune,' he said to me, 'is invested in the Colonies and in government stocks. In the present unsettled state of the country, I may possibly lose all. My mother is dependent upon me, and I have thought of the occupation I should pursue.' 'What would you do?' 'I should be a bootblack.' 'Why a bootblack?' 'You ask why? Do you not understand? God alone is great,' he said, pointing to Heaven; 'and we!...' I perfectly comprehended his idea. He was speaking simply and sincerely, and the expressions of humility were in entire conformity with his sentiments, and came from his heart."

Another fact indicative of his humility, was told us by a lady who knew him intimately. "When Mr. Dupont's request to vacate the seat assigned him in the cathedral, was at last acceded to, he disappeared, and no one knew where to find him in the church. After some days, I discovered him behind a pillar near the door, with the Brothers of the Christian Schools. As I had noticed that, in every chapel where retreats or other public exercises were being conducted, he always selected a place near a door, I remarked it to him, expressing at the same time my astonishment. He answered me: 'Do you think I read the Gospel to no purpose? I do not wish the Master to make me take a lower place, because I go too high. As it is, I am sure to attain my object, because the last shall be first.' He was also the last to present himself at the holy table at the moment of

Communion, and it grieved him to see persons, on festival days, crowding to the railing, without making way for others, or awaiting their turn with patience."

The same person added: "I never observed but one fault in Mr. Dupont: he, who gave away so much, and knew how to give in so charming a manner, did not know how to ask for anything. The courage to do so was wanting to him." But why did he not have it? Because he represented all his wants to God, Who alone can give all. His disinterestedness equalled his spirit of humility. "One morning," says the same lady, "when I arrived at Mr. Dupont's, I found him surrounded by a party of persons, one of whom had just been the object of a remarkable miracle. They evidently belonged to the class of those who are largely endowed with the goods of this world. In the transports of their joy and gratitude, they offered him any amount which might be necessary for his alms, his poor, his good works. They urged, they importuned him to accept the offering of their gratitude. He refused and remained inflexible. 'But,' I said to him after the departure of the strangers, 'why do you deprive yourself of such aid? See what good you could do with it. What a help it would be to you for the good works in which you are interested, or for the poor!' 'And the Great Poor, Who is in Heaven! His glory!' he replied, pointing upward with a gesture, an expression of countenance I shall never forget. 'Money here!' he continued, 'Never! There are poor-boxes in all the churches of Tours; let them bestow their charity there.'"

Although possessed of an ample fortune, he knew how to preserve poverty in spirit, and to practice the virtue. His losses in the Colonies, which were at times considerable, made but little impression upon him, and he adopted for his own guidance the advice he gave others. "Your zeal in the performance of good works," he said to a wealthy person who had met with heavy losses, "if you did not view all things with the eyes of faith, would naturally cause you to grieve for your present misfortunes. But you do well not to permit yourself to be influenced by this thought. If God wills us to be poor, blessed be His holy name! If He wills us to be rich, blessed be His holy name! But I say to you: How dangerous is wealth! Oh! what a heavy weight is an income of eighty or a hundred thousand francs! Oh! what a load it will be upon the conscience, when God will demand an account of it, and will investigate the use we have made of it! 'I fear nothing so much as a large fortune,' said a lady to me recently, a holy woman, the mother of five children. What a subject for meditation in these few words!"

To return to his humility, we will say with a contemporary writer of great talents who knew intimately and studied Mr. Dupont: "Humility was the source and guiding principle of his whole character; with him the 'I' had ceased to be a motive. There are various kinds of humility. There is the humility of the man who considers himself, in order to excite self-contempt, who is struggling to resist the repeated attacks of a self-love not wholly subdued; there is also the humility of the man who never thinks of himself at all; the latter kind of humility was that of Mr. Dupont. Many persons say with their lips that they are nothing, but their hearts and actions do not accord with their words; it is evident they are something in their own eyes, and, in the secret of their hearts, they esteem themselves a great deal; humility is often a mere formula; as for Mr. Dupont, humility was his life; he was humble as he breathed, always, everywhere; his humility was also perfectly simple… There is an affected humility: a strange thing, worthy of compassion! With Mr. Dupont, humility did not regard self: it was absolutely simple.

"I heard a lady, in speaking to him, call him a saint. It would be difficult to describe the manner in which the unlucky word was received. It was not the false modesty of a man who disclaims a compliment. It was a displeasure so intense, that no one would willingly have been, a second time, the object of it. 'In the works which are performed here,' he said, 'I am the obstacle.' And he believed what he said. He added in the presence of the lady above mentioned: 'If all now in this room were put under the press, nothing but mud would issue from it.' Again: 'Nothing prevents the sun from rising and setting, because it has no self-will. Whilst man! man prevents all things. God acts only on nothingness. When man resists, God withdraws.'

"Mr. Dupont repeated every day the following short and simple prayer: 'From the desire of being consulted, O Lord, deliver me.' His prayer was heard. The room was always more or less filled with pilgrims. They might come from the extremities of the earth; they might offer him the most flattering homage from persons of the highest rank. He was invulnerable. They might remain away; they might neglect him; they might forget him; they might do what they pleased; pay him attention, or pay no attention to him at all; it was impossible to wound his self-love. It was as though he had placed his self-love under the receiver of an air-pump. It had no air to breathe, and no sound was conveyed of the things addressed to it.

"He made those who were speaking to him feel the necessity of not giving him a thought personally. Worldly politeness annoyed him. I beg pardon for the trifling incident I am about to relate; it will interest, because it so perfectly characterizes the man. I was dining with him one day, and his mother was at the table. Having just arrived from the cars, I commenced to make a slight apology for the dusty condition of my coat. Mr. Dupont interrupted me at the first word, in a tone of voice I should like to render, and said: 'Life is too short to permit us to pay attention to such things.' To appreciate the remark, it should be given in his tone and manner.

"In conversation with Mr. Dupont, prayer must necessarily be the sole object of thought. He abhorred the social '*I, myself*, and after having destroyed it in himself, he pursued it to the death in others. Everybody was admitted to his room; but one might remain there any length of time without receiving the least notice from him, unless his prayers were directly asked. He never lifted his eyes to those who did not require his services. You entered and you left: he neither received you, nor bade you adieu. In one word, he was not in his own home. The simple fact was, that the room in which he remained was the room of prayer.

"He repeated the following sentence even to satiety: 'Paganism says: *Me, me, adsum qui feci*. I, I did that. Christianity says: *Vivo ego, jam non ego, vivit vero in me Christus*. It is not I who live, but Christ liveth in me.'

"He had neither exterior nor interior troubles, and the reasons he gave for his tranquillity are worth pointing out. He insisted on the necessity of cheerfulness. 'The devil,' he would say, 'is the prince of weariness. We must be joyous.' As to his exterior tranquillity, he gives the following explanation: 'I sometimes see persons who are tormented and disturbed, because their manner of living is not like that of others. These people are something, it would seem; no one thinks of troubling or annoying me; I am nothing. How could they disturb nothingness? Try to take nothing between your fingers and do it an injury.' And then with a peculiar gesture, he seemed to make the effort to crush something between his fingers and did not succeed, as he held nothing between them."

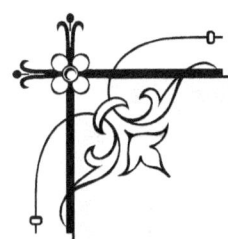

Chapter XXI

His Hope — His Love of God — His Mortification.

From Mr. Dupont's faith and humility, arose that simplicity of heart, that unalterable serenity, which his friends admired, and which strangers never failed to remark at the first glance. It was the radiance of hope. This second theological virtue had its roots so deep in his heart that nothing whatever had power to discourage him. We have seen how he prayed, both at the Nocturnal Adoration and before the Holy Face. He prayed with unshaken confidence and perseveringly, until the grace demanded had been obtained. "It is certain," he said, "that we cannot go against the will of God. But as we rarely know it until the moment of its execution, nothing prevents us from persisting with confidence in our demands. Our Lord has commanded us to be persistent. Moreover, our confidence acquires a degree of merit in proportion to the difficulties which present themselves." Such was his confidence in the providential action of God over the world, that he rejected with disdain all the reasoning of human foresight. "What do we know of the future?" he would ask. "It will, in all probability, be just the reverse of what we expect. All these reflections are time lost. It is a distrust of the mercy, an outrage to the infinite merits of the Divine Victim."

He encouraged his friends to foster such sentiments. To one of them, a layman like himself, and of similar tastes, he wrote: "Let us pray for France. In your solitude, you have a great deal in your power. It needs but one soul united to our Lord, and treating with Him of the interests of eternal life, to draw down from Heaven innumerable graces. Sacred history teaches us this." "Let us pray with confidence," were words forever on his lips. "Let us blush to be wanting in that confidence which obtains whatever it asks."

As to himself, he possessed it to a degree of deliberate conviction, whose truth and solidity theologians themselves were forced to admire. A venerable curate of the diocess of Verdun furnishes us an example of this: "Twenty years ago," he writes, "Mr. Baudier, Superior of the Seminary of Tours, went to visit Mr. Dupont, taking with him his brother, a professor of theology, and myself. After the ordinary salutations were exchanged, we were admitted into the room where the picture of the Holy Face was venerated. With Christian courtesy Mr. Dupont invited us to prolong our visit, during which a very interesting discussion occurred between him and the professor of theology. The subject was confidence in prayer. The professor maintained that when we ask of God benefits of the purely natural order, we should beg them, if not with indifference, at least without an urgency which might be contrary to the Divine will. Mr. Dupont replied with a vivacity of faith, and an appropriateness which gave him the decided advantage. "Not at all, Professor, we should employ a kind of importunity; our Lord Himself invites us to this when presenting us the charming example,—in which no distinction is drawn,—the example of a friend arriving in the middle of the night, and knocking repeatedly at the door of his friend, until the latter, overcome by his importunity rather than inspired by friendship, rises and opens to him.' These words appeared conclusive, and made upon me an impression which the lapse of twenty years has not effaced.

I consider it a duty to recall them now, to the honor of the venerated thaumaturgus, for I am the sole survivor of the four who were present on that occasion."

Regarded as a Catholic dogma, this confidence was in reality unassailable, because it was founded upon the promise of our Lord in the Gospel: "Whatsoever you shall ask in prayer, believing, you shall receive." Mr. Dupont had this sacred text forever upon his lips. He also quoted frequently the beautiful thought of St. Hilary: "God, Who inspires us to pray to Him, cannot refuse to hear our prayer."

A fervent layman of Paris, the director of an important work of zeal and charity, was complaining in Mr. Dupont's presence of a weakness of sight, which threatened to terminate in blindness. The servant of the Holy Face pointed to the venerated picture, and proposed to recite the prayers for his cure. The patient objected, saying humbly: "Would God attend to so small a want of a miserable creature like myself? Have I not other more necessary favors to ask of Him?" Mr. Dupont considered his answer as an evidence of want of faith and confidence, and reproved him severely: "Do you not see that you are placing obstacles to the gift of God? Ask Him decidedly to cure you, only adding: 'My God, for Thy glory.'"

As a true and enlightened Catholic, Mr. Dupont did not fail to rest his confidence upon the intercession and protection of the Blessed Virgin and the Saints. We have already seen the confidence he placed in the medal of St. Benedict, the water of La Salette, and the oil of the Holy Face. He made no less use of the medal of Mary Immaculate, called the "miraculous medal." He was among the first who were informed of the apparition vouchsafed to a pious Sister of St. Vincent de Paul, for the purpose of honoring Mary's privilege of being "conceived without sin." During his whole life, he had recourse to the medal struck on that occasion, and, through it, he obtained from the august Virgin many graces, cures, and conversions. As he considered

Satan, the spirit of evil and the enemy of man, to be the original cause of all our miseries, he constantly made use of prayer and supernatural means, not only to obtain spiritual favors of every kind, but also to combat corporal infirmities, either in connection with medicine which he did not reject, or after a positive decision that remedies were of no avail. He never doubted the efficacy of these means; if employed unsuccessfully, he attributed the failure to want of confidence.

But the chief foundation of his confidence was what he called the "merciful goodness of our Lord." Thoroughly imbued with this sentiment, he was never disturbed by any adverse event. His hope in the future was not diminished by revolutions, and the calamitous disorders which accompany or result from them; they seemed rather to strengthen and augment it, because he viewed such events in their supernatural bearing, and he thought, moreover, that the hand of God was evident in the miraculous incidents so frequent in our day. "Everything concurs to prove," he writes, "that our Lord, in His merciful goodness, wishes to pardon the present generation, and that He no longer holds captive the fire of love with which His Divine Heart desires to inflame the world." He adds: "Do not present this idea to men who are accustomed to regard only the difficulties in the way. He who says: I cannot, never succeeds. St. Paul was more prudent and better informed when he exclaimed: *I can do all things in Him Who strengthens me.*"

He often said: "Many signs convince persons of faith, that the time of combat is near at hand." But what he calls "the time of combat" neither troubles nor terrifies him. When in the midst of the disorders by which society is agitated, he sees Catholics contending with revolutionary men for an election, defending a right, or casting votes for a law, he encourages his friends by quoting the words of Scripture: "Fear not the multitude of your enemies; for the battle is not yours, but God's: *Non est enim pugna vestra, sed*

Dei." He loved to recall the passage in the Second Book of Paralipomenon whence the above text is taken, in which it is related that the holy king Josaphat, in the midst of the perils surrounding him, and uncertain of the issue of the battle about to be fought between the children of Israel and their enemies, cried out to God: "As we know not what to do, we can only turn our eyes to Thee." And this confidence of the pious king and of his people was recompensed by a brilliant victory. "It is good, therefore," he added, "to abandon ourselves to God, and to remember that the result of every combat depends, not upon us, but upon God alone."

The secret of this unalterable serenity and unvarying confidence, was his intimate union with our Lord, and the love which burned in his heart for his Divine Master. "What would we not do to please Him," he said, "if we knew Him, if we had the intelligence of His love deeply implanted in our hearts? Thy enemies, O Jesus, penetrated to the very depths of Thy heart, and we, who desire to be Thy friends, abandon our hearts, alas! too often, to thoughts so frivolous that Thou canst not enter them. Reign over them, nevertheless, O Jesus! and make us free, notwithstanding our cowardice, by subjecting us to Thy holy sovereignty."

Speaking of a man of God who was full of fervor and zeal he said: "He is a soul inflamed with love, burning with the desire of procuring Veronicas for Jesus. It is impossible to reflect upon the Passion, without ardently desiring to offer some consolation to our Lord. It is a certain means of washing away our sins in the ocean of mercy."

From his love of Jesus, came the love of his neighbor and zeal for the salvation of souls. The conquest of souls was ever the leading thought in his works of prayer and charity; for, superior to every other consideration, was the spiritual good of his neighbor. He was frequently recompensed by striking conversions, or sincere homage rendered to the faith. But when the contrary happened, how extreme was his sorrow! We give as an example a circumstance he relates in a letter to a missionary of America, whom he had formerly accompanied to the port whence he was to embark: "I have just been to Nantes, to place, as pilot on board of a vessel, a young man who was recommended to me by an intimate friend. But how far different was the journey we made together to the same port! My young protegé has not faith. I appointed for our rendezvous the church of Sainte-Croix at half-past seven in the morning. I arrived there in time to assist at Holy Mass three times. The hour appointed having passed, I was about to leave the church to discover what had detained the young man. We met at the entrance. 'I am here,' he said to me. 'Very well, we will make a short prayer.' 'No.' 'Why not? You are going on a voyage of three thousand leagues.' *'I would not do so willingly.'* Thereupon, with my heart full of sorrow, we proceeded on our way. Will you not pray for him? I am quite certain you never hear such words from the lips of your savages. It is the rottenness of Europe which engenders such miseries. Pray fervently."

After having travelled in company with Mr. Dupont, Sister Francis Xavier, a fervent Religious, whose life and letters form the subject of an interesting volume recently published, wrote: "God, in His goodness, gave me as a travelling companion a pious man of the world, named Mr. Dupont, a resident of Tours. The night was passed as if we were at the gate of Paradise. We talked the whole time of Jesus and Mary. He is far more devout than I am. After completing the rosary, he made me say a large number of Aves for the conversion or perseverance of persons, who needed the one or the other; from eleven to twelve we made the Stations of the Cross on an indulged crucifix. We meditated aloud by turns. When he proposed the latter, I feared I should either laugh, or be vain if I should have good thoughts. Oh! if you knew the depth of faith, simplicity, and love in the heart of that man! Instead of laughing, I wept. We could not tear ourselves away from the cross of

Jesus, at the foot of which we found Mary. Every journey made by this apostolic man is a pilgrimage. He is a saint, an angel, sent to me by God to support and humble me; for I am a worm in presence of his profound faith and sublime humility. Whenever he perceived a steeple, he recited in Latin a prayer of St. Francis of Assisi: 'There, and in all churches of the world, Thou art present, O Jesus!' And then his soul became absorbed in the thought of the love of our Lord. I slept, but he continued his prayers until morning. When I awoke, he said to me: 'We must speak of God or be silent.' We spoke of our good God, and, to profit by his counsel and example, in my turn, I speak of Him to you."

His love of our Lord and his charity for man so absorbed his whole being, that he wished never to speak on another subject. "It is so consoling," he said, "to converse heart to heart of Jesus, Who suffers so strangely at man's silence in his regard! Before the Incarnation, the Holy Ghost declared that there was an obligation to talk of God: *Omnis enarratio tua in præceptis Altissimi*: 'Let all thy discourse be on the commandments of the Most High.' Then, when Jesus comes in person to explain the old law, and promulgate the law of love, He assures us that where we are collected, even in small numbers, in His name, He is in the midst of us, to make us comprehend the difference between pious colloquies and worldly conversation. Therefore, I think we should often say to the giddy ones of the world: *Si scires donum Dei!* 'If you knew the gift of God.' And of what else ought we to speak? But, in order to speak, we must love; 'for the mouth speaketh from the abundance of the heart.' Let us then be united to our Lord, that not only His blood may become ours, but that His thoughts, His words, His actions, may also become ours! When the great Apostle said: 'We are the good odor of Jesus Christ,' he, undoubtedly, no longer lived, but Jesus Christ in him. How much we might say without going beyond the circle in which a Christian should remain enclosed!"

Even when at table, when making a visit, in his room, on a journey, God was the habitual subject of his conversations. If any other was commenced, he either remained silent or slept. An old sea-captain relates the following incident: "Marceau was one day ascending the Loire on a steamboat, in company with Mr. Dupont. The latter, resting his head on a table, fell asleep. Some engineers were conversing on ships and machines. Mr. Dupont awoke only when they were to land at Nantes.

Marceau inquired why he slept so soundly. 'It appears,' he answered, 'that those gentlemen could talk, during an entire day, of every thing but God. I borrowed several hours from the night, and I shall, at that time, have the leisure to meditate.' Marceau assured me," continued the narrator, "that when he was with him, and long conversations turned upon profane sciences or similar subjects, his friend would sit apart, and recommence the sleep of the steamboat."

But if it happened that the reputation of his neighbor was attacked, or charity was wounded, he did not keep silence; sometimes he even permitted himself a frankness in his remarks which was only authorized by his reputation for sanctity, and softened by the gentleness of his character.

As for himself, an uncharitable expression never escaped him. He was ever ready to excuse the faults of others, or to beg pardon for them of God. One day, a young man who was a fervent Catholic, being inflamed with divine love by his conversation on the Eucharist, went, on leaving him, to the cathedral and knelt in prayer before the altar. Soon after, an officer in full uniform, holding by a leash an enormous dog, crossed the church, and passed before the altar without the least recognition of the presence of our Lord. The pious young man was pained at the irreverence he witnessed, and, on his return to Mr. Dupont's, he gave vent to the indignation and bitterness of his soul. The servant of God interrupted him: "My young friend," he said gently, "be calm, and imagine it was a poor blind man who passed by you. How could you expect him to view things in the same manner as you do? Let us do something better than express our indignation; let us pray God to open his eyes and grant him the gift of faith." Both knelt before the Holy Face, to offer a prayer for the poor unbeliever. The same love of God and his neighbor, which inspired Mr. Dupont with exalted views and delicate sentiments, led him to acts of Christian mortification and evangelical penance. This spirit of mortification was observable in him on his first arrival in France. A Superioress writes us: "We noticed in Mr. Dupont, during his earliest visits to Saint-Servan, an austere virtue; he possessed a rare spirit of recollection and prayer. He made every night the holy hour, and he endeavored to propagate this pious practice." In Lent and upon fast-days, he took no food until noon, and then his meal consisted of one dish; at collation, he took only uncooked salad. On Ash Wednesday, he ate bread which had been cooked under the ashes; on Good Friday and Holy Saturday, he did not break his fast until six o'clock in the afternoon.

The least suffering or corporal inconvenience which God sent him, was food to his spirit of mortification, and he was very careful to derive profit from it. He once had a boil, "which," he says, "is so placed on my right wrist as to prevent my writing, particularly since the incisions and application of caustic. It would have given me pleasure to converse with you. *Fiat*! If God shows me mercy, I shall have a long life, because I have great need to do penance."

In the same spirit, the recluse of Saint-Etienne Street imposed on himself in 1869 a kind of sacrifice, trifling in appearance, but the merit of which will be appreciated by those who, from circumstances, may have been called upon to make a similar one. As it was the common custom among the residents of warm climates, particularly of the Colonies, Mr. Dupont had, from his youth, contracted the habit of taking snuff. He undertook to deprive himself of it. "Can you believe it?" he writes to his friend and compatriot Mr. d'Avrainville, who had the same habit, "after using tobacco for forty-nine years, I have discarded the snuff-box. Next Saturday will be the twenty-eighth day, and I feel not the slightest inclination to resume it."

His elegant and polished manners, partaking of the grace of the nobleman and the dignity of the magistrate, the irreproachable neatness of his dress, his beard shaved daily, the fine white linen he always used, betrayed neither to his friends nor to his servants the austerities he practised. Those who were in the same house with him never suspected his frequent use of the discipline. Only one person knew it during his life, Mother Mary of the Incarnation, the aged Prioress of the Carmelites, to whom, on account of her age, her virtue, and the confidence he had in her, he spoke freely of his interior; and even she drew from him by stratagem the secret she suspected. We have learned through her, that at a certain period of his life, after what he styled his conversion, he practised this kind of penance regularly every evening before going to bed, or when he rose at midnight for the holy hour. The Reverend Mother, having once asked him how he managed not to be heard by the persons of his household, he informed her, that adjoining the room which then served him as a sleeping apartment, there was a private cabinet where he retired, either during the day, or at night, to "practise his devotions." "It is there," said the Reverend Mother, giving these details to her spiritual daughters, "that the holy man disciplines himself to his heart's content." In truth, the holy man did not spare himself. He even requested a hair-shirt of the Mother Prioress, and from her testimony we can say, that no instrument of penance used by austere orders was unknown to him. We have still his iron discipline which was found after his death.* But, like many other saints of the same character, he was extremely careful to remove all proofs of his austerity. If we may accept the statement of another grave authority, when he occupied a car alone in travelling, he disciplined himself in a spirit of reparation, to "expiate," he said, "the sins committed on the railroad."

He belonged, in this respect, to the school of Father Lacordaire. We know from the account of his private life, how constantly the illustrious Dominican practised this mortification, so opposed to the pride and sensuality of our age, and how often he counselled young persons to adopt it as a sovereign remedy against temptation. The servant of the Holy Face also gives the same advice in words which betray his secret. An individual, painfully tempted to sadness and discouragement, opens his heart to him and seeks his advice. "You have," he answers, "in your own hands the means of benefiting yourself. There is a remedy, which is repugnant only to such as have never made a trial of it seriously. I mean corporal mortification. *I chastise my body and keep it in subjection*, said the great Apostle, and justly, since our Lord did not consent to deliver him from temptation. Reasoning on the subject does no good; the body is the animal part, and against it, words are of no avail. It needs blows; the discipline, taken with humility and the intention of inflicting punishment, repairs promptly the forces of the soul, and restores it to its dignity, if I may thus express myself. The body bends to the yoke, and acknowledges the baseness of its extraction. You will soon be restored to peace with yourself, and you will have your eyes fixed, in future, on Heaven." As the person was unwilling to employ this hard and strange means, Mr. Dupont insists: "I am pained to see that you continue to ask advice, and

---

* It hangs in the sacristy of the oratory, in that part called the Chamber of Miracles, bearing the following inscription: "Here the servant of God macerated his flesh by long and bloody flagellations." *Castigo corpus meum et in servitutem redigo.* "I chastise my body and reduce it to servitude."

to reason upon your spiritual condition. You are wrong to reject the means I suggested in my former letter. *Penance! Penance!* that will fill your heart with joy, and establish you in the friendship of our Lord." Again he writes: "You plead in vain, that you have already suffered greatly. Oh! if you knew the value of a voluntary suffering! I pray God to bestow upon you abundant lights on this subject… St. Paul chastised his body; all the saints have followed his example, and our Lord desires to impart new vigor to the spirit of penance, in order that many souls may labor with him for the moral resurrection of the people sunk in philosophism. The evil is greater than we imagine. The number of those who love their bodies is very great, and they are strongly inclined to believe that the sufferings of Calvary suffice. Reason persuades them that it is useless to imitate the saints in their treatment of the flesh. But what is now passing under our eyes, makes it evident that our Lord wishes to lead us back to the only way of salvation, to penance, which He first embraced Himself that he might give us the example."

The above incidents and quotations prove how thoroughly this great servant of God understood, and how perfectly he practised, the fundamental virtues of the Christian life. It might, in strict truth, be said of him that he "was the man of the three theological virtues." We have dwelt upon the "simplicity of his faith," "the fervor of his hope," "the ardent zeal of his charity." Faith, however, was dominant; it vivified every action of the day, was active every moment of his life. He frequently arose at two or three o'clock in the morning, in winter as well as in summer, he prayed, meditated, went to the earliest Mass in his part of the city, and Communicated. Having returned to his room, kneeling or seated between the Holy Face and the Holy Scriptures, he devoted himself to the spiritual occupations we have described; and this was the daily routine for at least the last twenty-eight years of his life. He is depicted by St. Paul: "The just man lives by faith;" *Justus ex fide vivit*.

We should not, however, conclude that this eminent perfection was natural to Mr. Dupont, that he attained it without effort, without a struggle with self, and that it was the result of a highly gifted character and disposition. On the contrary, in his youth, a love of pleasure had a powerful sway over him. One of his relatives describes him when a child, as the life and soul of the sports of his age. As a young man, he was passionately fond of hunting, dancing, driving fine horses, and possessing handsome equipages. By disposition, he was quick, impetuous, gay, self-willed even to obstinacy; he carried written on his hand evidence of the latter quality in the scar, which was never effaced, of the wound received on the gate of the castle of Chissay, the effect of his thoughtlessness and tenacity of purpose. He did not willingly yield to others; he wished to be first, under all circumstances. This natural asperity and violence of temperament were manifest, at the commencement of his life of piety, even in matters of controversy. We must, then, conclude that the virtues of Mr. Dupont, like the virtues of all the saints, were the triumphs of grace. His merit was in his correspondence to the graces bestowed upon him, and in resolutely profiting by them, to advance in the path of perfection.

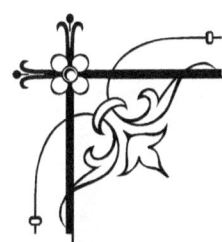

Chapter XXII

His Devotion to the Sacred Heart, the Blessed Virgin, the Saints, the Angels, and the Souls in Purgatory.

The spirit of prayer was the life of the virtues with which Mr. Dupont's soul was so richly endowed. He possessed that gift in an eminent degree, and he found delight in every form of devotion authorized by the Church. He was, in truth, a man of prayer and meditation. We may say of him that "he prayed always." "How often we have contemplated with admiration," writes the Superioress of a community, "his humble attitude in prayer, so expressive of his realization of God's presence, and the sense of his own abjection, his nothingness, before the Divine Majesty." When alone, he sometimes expressed his sentiments by exterior acts not unusual in the lives of the Saints. The following practice was peculiar to himself; he communicated it to a person in his confidence. "I was making the Stations in the chapel of the Petit-Hôpital, and, being alone, I extended my arms in the form of a cross. On reaching the Station where Jesus is fastened to the cross, I considered that my hands were not open as should be those of a mendicant, with the palms turned towards Heaven in order to receive its gifts. I quickly opened them, and presented them in a supplicating manner to our Lord. Thereupon, many thoughts presented themselves to my mind, too long to transcribe; nevertheless, it seemed to me a duty to mention the above practice, and many have derived benefit from thus extending the hands to God. In doing this many words are not necessary. The poor are less troublesome to the rich when they do not enumerate their wants. Now, if that be true in the case of a poor brother supplicating a rich brother, might not the same be said of our petitions to our good God, Who knows so perfectly all our miseries?"

Above all others, he particularly relished liturgical prayers. He noticed the feasts the Church celebrates each day, and united with her in his intentions. On leaving the church at the conclusion of the Office, if he met a priest of his acquaintance, or a pious, well-informed layman, his salutation, his first remark, was to repeat a sentence from the Introit of the Mass, the Collect, the Post-Communion, or an incident of the life of the Saint honored on that day.

Everything connected with the Passion of our Lord and His Divine Heart, excited his deepest emotion. He was a member of the Confraternity of the Sacred Heart, and he was particular in observing its rules and celebrating the special festivals. He speaks of this beautiful devotion, as a pledge of salvation and a motive of confidence: "It is evident that the graces which inundate the earth come from the adorable Heart of Jesus, and are obtained by Mary through the Sacred Heart. As it is a kind of extension of the mystery of the Incarnation, it belongs to Mary to interpose by her Immaculate Heart, since there is question of the last effort of love to restore a dead faith, as was announced by our Lord to Margaret Mary Alacoque. It is certain that St. John alone heard the pulsations of the Heart of Jesus, that Margaret Mary saw this Heart burning with the flames of love, and that Jesus wished us to offer particular homage to His Heart of flesh. When St. Gertrude, who died in 1260, predicted the future worship of the Sacred

Heart, she noticed to St. John that he had not spoken of it in his Gospel. To which he replied: 'This revelation is reserved for later times, that by hearing the pulsations of this Divine Heart, the world might be renewed in the love of God which would be growing cold.' The striking connection which exists between the revelations of St. Gertrude and those of Margaret Mary, explains what is now passing before us, and inspires an unbounded confidence as to the result of the present conflict. For three centuries, humanity wallowed in her reason, and at last found herself in the midst of a disgusting sewer. At this moment, she hears the words: *Hora est jam nos de somno surgere.*"

On the subject of the Sacred Heart, Mr. Dupont was inexhaustible. He wrote a beautiful and ingenious comparison, by which he explains the harmony which should exist between our hearts and the Heart of Jesus; it was suggested by the invention of a spring-pendulum. "*Vivat Cor Jesu sacratissimum!*" he exclaims. "Since it has been granted to human genius to produce the wonderful combination of two clocks, which, when brought into connection, (one serving as a regulator), communicate the time to each other by harmonizing their movements,… might it not be granted to us, in the spiritual order, to place our hearts against the Heart of Jesus, and thus bring all our thoughts in harmony with its divine pulsations? The spring-pendulum clock was sold for its weight in gold (fifty thousand francs) to the Emperor Alexander. What sacrifices should not be made by a Christian to place himself in contact with the Heart of Jesus, which St. Gertrude saw issuing from His sacred side, as if placed outside, to be the regulator of our hearts?"

It would be useless to dwell in this place upon Mr. Dupont's filial devotion to the Blessed Virgin; we have seen him give proofs of it during the whole course of his life. We shall simply recall one or two particular instances, which should not be left unnoticed. Suspended above his chimney-piece was a card, upon which he had inscribed the names of the sanctuaries that he had visited in honor of the Mother of God. This long series, following in succession according to the order of his visits, was marked in different styles of writing, with different dates, and formed a peculiar kind of Litany, which it delighted the heart of the old pilgrim of Mary to recite. Opposite the door of his room, he placed in a small niche, where it still remains, a statue of the Blessed Virgin under the title of our Lady of Good Hope. He visited it frequently, and was careful to surround it in every season with verdure and flowers. It was a souvenir of his pilgrimage to La Salette.

Mr. Dupont held in high veneration our Lady of Miracles honored at the Refuge in Tours. It was with the oil that burned before this ancient statue that he first obtained the cure of the infirm, and he was desirous that this Madonna should be known by persons at a distance. He writes to a friend: "I cannot resist the impulse to send you a little picture which photography has reproduced with great perfection. It is a miraculous Madonna in oak which antedates the age of St. Louis; it is called our Lady of Miracles, and it is justly so styled. This statue is in the chapel of the Sisters of the Good Shepherd, and the Religious conceived the happy thought of having it photographed, and medals struck off, which being distributed, will bear to distant places the name of the divine Mother."

With the Sacred Heart of Jesus and the immaculate heart of Mary, he associated the heart of St. Joseph. He loved to recommend and circulate some Latin and French prayers in honor of this glorious patriarch. His confidence in St. Joseph was once recompensed in a charming manner. Mr. Dupont was accustomed on certain festivals, for example, at the Carnival and New Year's day, to give a supper to the good old people of the Little Sisters of the Poor. One of these occasions, so eagerly anticipated by them, was approaching. The generous benefactor was forced to tell them that he had not the funds necessary to procure the extra provisions he always provided on those days. He advised them to apply to St. Joseph, and to make to the good Saint, the protector of the Little Sisters, a novena, in order to obtain turkeys and chickens for their accustomed feast. "Let us ask for a wild boar," exclaimed several among them. A wild boar! The request appeared strange to Mr. Dupont, but as the old people seemed to give it a decided preference, he consented. Every day they said for this intention the prayers appointed for the novena. The man of God prayed with his habitual fervor and confidence; but he laughed and jested with his friends about the strange idea the good old men had of asking a wild boar of St. Joseph. The day before the conclusion of the novena, a porter from the railroad hastily entered his room, requesting him to direct the large gate at the entrance to be opened, because a wagon was there containing a wild boar for him; at the same time, he handed him a letter. One of his friends wrote: "I am a poor marksman, and I know not by what good fortune I killed a boar in my woods. As I am alone in the country, and cannot eat the boar myself, I send it to you, thinking it may be of some use for your poor." We may readily imagine that it was heartily welcomed; the old men congratulated themselves upon the happy thought, and thanked a thousand times the holy Patriarch who had heard their prayer.

To devotion to St. Joseph, he united devotion to St. Teresa, who was, herself, so devoted to the foster-father of our Lord. The great reformer of Carmel was, for many reasons, very dear to Mr. Dupont. He delighted in reading her works; he learned in her school the secrets of prayer; he inhaled the perfume of her most sublime virtues when visiting her daughters at the monastery of Tours; he always carried about him the sheet called "the little letter of St. Teresa," and kept a picture of the Saint, on the reverse of which, he had noted the different phases of what he called his conversion, but which we, more justly, may style his flight in the path of evangelical perfection and the supernatural life.

His devotion to St. Gertrude originated in his love for the Sacred Heart. He read and enjoyed the writings of the illustrious Benedictine, her *"Revelations"* and her *"Insinuations of Divine Piety;"* he was particularly attracted by the practices she taught. He especially loved to repeat the beautiful salutations she addresses to the wounds of our Lord, and he recommended them to pious souls. By his direction, a picture of the Saint was lithographed; in it she is represented as showing her heart, upon which Jesus appears seated as upon a throne, and beneath are the words: "You will find me in the heart of Gertrude." The very name of Gertrude transported him with joy. On the return of her festival, he cannot restrain the ardent expressions of his love. To one who sympathized in his devotion he writes: "I must say a few words to you this evening before the termination of the day dedicated to St. Gertrude. But a letter does not afford us the means of entertaining ourselves, as we would wish, upon this great Saint, our special patroness. How many graces are attached to the loving devotion we can render to her, who was the living tabernacle of Jesus!" In his pious transports for reparation, he exclaimed: "Let us salute with love the prophetess of the Sacred Heart, the loving confidant of Jesus, who has told us all His secrets! O Gertrude, help us to pronounce with our hearts and lips the invocation which arose from your soul, all on fire at the recital of the blasphemies of the prætorium: 'I salute Thee, my Jesus, vivifying pearl of the excellence of God; I salute Thee, incorruptible flower of human nature!' Our Lord deigned to make known to thee, that all who would thus salute Him with thee when they heard blasphemies, should be recompensed for their zeal in defending the glory of God. We implore thee, then, O amiable virgin, our dear patroness, to help us to abhor, as thou didst, the injuries offered to God and to combat them with thy cry of love: *I salute thee, my Jesus, vivifying pearl!*"

He also held in peculiar veneration his patron, St. Leo the Great. To a friend, an associate of the Nocturnal Adoration, who, on the occasion of his Saint's day, promised to pray for him, he answers with charming modesty: "Either my good angel or my patron saint, must have inspired you to pray for me. The great Doctor of the Church is, in truth, the patron of your poor brother of the Adoration. I have only one patron; but as *God tempers the wind to the shorn lamb*, I have occasion several times during the year to offer my homage to St. Leo, and I confide to him the care of my salvation." On another year, the feast of the great Pope coincided with the joys of the resurrection of our Lord. To a friend, who kindly congratulated him, he replies: "How kind you were to remind me so seasonably that the festival of my holy patron corresponded this year with the *alleluia* of the Resurrection. But, in order to complete your act of courtesy, it remains for you to obtain also for me the grace of resuscitating, by disengaging myself entirely from the old man, and I rely upon your prayers *ad hoc*."

With St. Leo, the terror of the barbarians and the protector of Rome, he associated St. Michael, the defender of the Church. He designed a picture of this archangel crushing the dragon, which was to be represented chained. "It seems to me," he said, "that one head to the dragon is better than many, and expresses more clearly the powerful action of the chain, which the angel is about to place around his neck. The chain could not bind the seven heads; there would seem an uncertainty as to the result of the effort. Let Hercules destroy successively the heads of the hydra. St. Michael said but one word: *Quis ut Deus?* Who is like to God?"

The devotion he professed for St. Anthony of Padua had for its object the recovery of lost or mislaid articles. He applied for even trivial things to this Saint whose name is so popular, and his confidence was always rewarded. We mention one instance out of a thousand. It occurred in 1847. The servant of God was going from Tours to Mans, and met in the public conveyance a Religious of Providence, Sister Francis Xavier, of whom we have already spoken. She was on her way to Havre, whence she was to embark for America. Being the only passengers, our travellers took advantage of the circumstance to pray, and entertain themselves about God during the journey. On their arrival at Mans, Mr. Dupont accompanied the Religious to the house of her community; the Superioress immediately inquired of the Sister if she had a trunk; she replied in the affirmative. "Where is it?" That was a difficult question to answer. The pious layman inquired at the office of the diligence; it was not there. He returned to say to the Sister, who was to leave early the following day for Havre, not to be disturbed, as St. Anthony of Padua would cause the trunk to be restored; he was going, he said, to pray to the Saint, and she must pray also. The large gate of the establishment was then closed, and the Sisters retired for the night. The next morning at five o'clock, when the portress went to unlock the gate, what was her astonishment to find a trunk within the enclosure on the pavement near the gate, which, nevertheless, was still locked! No one had rung the bell, no one had opened the gate, no one had entered; the trunk was not there when they went to bed; it was, however, the very trunk which they thought was lost. When informed of the circumstance, Mr. Dupont seemed to find it quite natural: "St. Anthony had taken care of the baggage whilst they were occupied with our Lord."

In invoking St. Anthony of Padua, the fervent Christian had a special motive not generally known, that of recovering lost graces. In the year 1846, he agreed with several persons, among others Madame des Hayes, a Religious of the Sacred Heart, to make a novena for that intention. He strongly urged this practice upon pious souls in order to obtain the conversion of sinners. He wrote to one of them: "I advise you to have the novena to St. Anthony of Padua reprinted;" and added: "Those who make this novena, after having prayed for themselves, will, no doubt, be impelled to supplicate our good God in favor of some sinner." He adds: "We cannot know how much a true sentiment of faith can accomplish in the search for lost graces." He himself had this novena printed, and he distributed it. He wrote to one of his goddaughters, for whom he dreaded a dangerous intimacy: "I write to make you a suggestion, which is to commence a novena in honor of St. Anthony of Padua, that you may find a good, pious soul with whom you may contract a holy friendship." On all occasions, he manifested an unlimited confidence in this illustrious son of St. Francis, asserting that he had never invoked him in vain, even for the most trivial objects. He, therefore, wrote to a lady who was lamenting the loss of her spectacles: "Pray to St. Anthony of Padua, and you will find your spectacles." For more important things, he advised to pledge oneself, by promise or vow, to make some return.

He particularly honored St. Francis of Assissi, being attracted to the love of the seraphic patriarch by his stigmata, which recalled the pierced Heart and the dolorous wounds of the Divine Crucified, and also by the prayer taken from the Scriptures, in which mention is twice made of the Holy Face, and which is called the "Benediction of St. Francis." He recited this prayer very frequently, and he had it printed on a small sheet by itself, which he distributed and which he carried about him, venerating it with great devotion, pressing it to his lips, and pronouncing with intense delight and an angelic enthusiasm, each of the three parts composing it. He never wearied of commenting upon these three parts, particularly the second, which refers to the Son, and in which is contained the whole economy of the devotion to the Holy Face: "*Ostendat Faciem suam tibi et misereatur tui:* Let him show his Face to thee and have pity on thee."

He made use of it in his attacks of gout or paralysis as a remedy, and as a motive of patience. "This benediction," he says, "can be effectually used in every combat against the old enemy, who afflicts today as in the time of Job with paralysis, as well as leprosy and other miseries, which make us sigh after our heavenly country when we are attacked by them." The precious indulgence of the Portiuncula was one of those which he was most eager to obtain. He never failed to go to Notre-Dame-la-Riche, (the only church in which it could, at that time, be gained), to make the visit prescribed for that intention. His zeal and persevering fidelity may be gathered from a remark in a letter written in 1860: "For the last twenty-five years, I have annually followed the devotion of the Portiuncula; my poor mother never failed to attend."

We must not omit to mention among his devotions, the homage he paid to St. Monica. "The world is filled," he would say, "with afflicted mothers and wives; I recommend you to say the Litany of St. Monica." For a long time, he zealously disseminated those pious invocations, which are addressed, and not without fruit, to the mother of the great St. Augustine. When the association of Christian Mothers, which is under the protection of this Saint, was instituted and at once introduced into Tours, he approbated it with his whole soul; he rejoiced that France, to her honor, had taken the initiative in so admirable a work, and he anticipated from it great advantages to families. "The foundation of the confraternity of Christian Mothers," he writes to a friend in 1856, "will make a new breach in the citadel of Satan. I have been, for some time, in communication with one of the first mothers of the work."

The patrons of the city were not neglected in his devotions. Conjointly with St. Martin, he honored St. Gatian, the first apostle of Tours. He loved the ancient and beautiful cathedral which is dedicated to him; he admired the two magnificent towers which ornament it, and he loved to contemplate them, when, tormented by gout, he remained seated in his garden on a bench whence they could be seen. As he gazed upon them his heart was elevated to God, and his mind reverted to the generation which had erected them to the glory of our father in the faith. He had the church photographed and he sent to all his friends copies of it, with an inscription in the form of a prayer which he had composed. Near Notre-Dame-la-Riche in the primitive cemetery of the Christians, is shown the place where the first bishop of the diocess was buried; Mr. Dupont frequently visited it. When a petition was sent to obtain the benediction of Pius IX on the work of St. Martin, he wished the letter to be dated on the feast of St. Gatian.

His devotion to St. Francis of Paula, the other great protector of the city of Tours, was not less striking. It originated in the prolonged residence of the Canon Pasquier, his confessor and friend, in the ancient monastery of Plessis-lez-Tours. He went frequently at that time to pray at the tomb of the founder of the Minims, in company with the pious Canon and two or three other priests who entertained similar sentiments, and they secretly venerated the blessed, but deserted spot, for which they hoped a brighter future. Whilst he was able to walk, he never omitted to go there on the 2d of April, the festival day of the Saint. For a long time this tomb, formerly so celebrated and so frequented, had been designated only by a wooden cross. Mr. Dupont was among the first who cherished the desire of restoring the ancient church, and reëstablishing the pilgrimages of former days. In the mean time, he solicited the favor of elevating at his own expense a more suitable cross. It was made of iron ornamented and arranged according to his directions. The memorable spot received no other mark of honor, until the first stone was laid of the monument which it is now proposed to construct. The pious layman made his offering so discreetly that few knew from whom it came.

His intelligent piety professed an especial devotion to the patriarchs and saints of the Old Law, whom he had learned to know and love from his assiduous study of the Scriptures: Job, Moses, David, Elias, Eliseus, Daniel, Tobias. He invoked them on certain days and under certain circumstances, recalling their words, their actions and virtues. He did not neglect Saints Anne and Joachim, who were so intimately connected with Mary and the Word Incarnate. "How profitable it is to place oneself under the protection of the august ancestors of our Lord! Grandparents are so proud of the success of their children!!! And thus we may believe that they have benedictions in reserve for all men who felicitate them upon Mary and Jesus."

Besides the honor he paid the great Saints glorified in Scripture and in the Church, the servant of God rendered homage to the holy angels. His confidence in his guardian angel had been greatly increased by an incident that occurred to himself, one apparently trifling, but which made a strong impression upon his mind. We give it as it was related to us by one of his friends: "I was walking one day in company with Mr. Dupont through the street of the Ursulines, and, when we arrived opposite the street which runs from the cloister along the garden of the archiepiscopal palace, I noticed that he respectfully raised his hat as though he were saluting some one. Seeing no one near us, I inquired for whom the salutation was intended. He answered that it was a mark of respect to his good angel; and, on being questioned by me, he related the following incident: Once when passing through that street, he was turning over the leaves of a small book on devotion to the guardian angels. He had just read the passage: 'Beware of disregarding an inspiration to do good, because you thus dishonor your good angel,' when he noticed a stranger, a countryman with a cheerful countenance, in good attire, and apparently in easy circumstances, walking down the street, carrying a cane in his hand. Upon perceiving him,

CHAPTER XXII

the idea immediately came to his mind to offer an alms to the worthy man; seeing the stranger so well clothed, his first impulse was to reject the thought, but, being interiorly urged to act upon the inspiration, and making the application of what he had just read, he drew from his purse a small piece of money and approached the unknown man: 'But,' he said, 'I was so unprepared for a polite acknowledgment of my strange offer that, fearing to feel the weight of his cane, I was ready on the instant to make my escape. Imagine my astonishment when the stranger stopping in surprise, informed me that he lived at the other extremity of the department, that he had lost his purse, and being unacquainted with any one at Tours, he was quite embarrassed how to obtain the means to satisfy his hunger and to return to his home.' 'But,' he asked, 'how could you possibly know of my difficulty?' The servant of God pointed out to him the passage in the little book he held in his hand, replaced the small piece of money by a coin of greater value, and, as the good man refused to accept it, unless as a loan, he requested him to settle the debt by giving an equal amount to the poor. 'From that time,' said Mr. Dupont, 'I never fail to salute my good angel when I pass this spot.'"

So great was his confidence in the protection of the holy angels, that even a remark from him in reference to them, sometimes made an irresistible and indelible impression, as in the following incident related to us by a lady: "I was quite a young woman; I desired to join my husband, an officer in Africa, and it would be necessary for me to undertake the journey alone. I met Mr. Dupont in the street, and I stopped to speak to him of my project. I expressed to him the terror I experienced at the mere thought of going alone, and I asked his opinion as to its propriety. With a tone of confidence and an air of dignity, which I shall never forget, he said: 'But, Madam, you will not be alone. You forget your guardian angel. Go, go without fear...' I went, inspired with confidence by his words, and I arrived in safety at my destination. The incident may appear trifling, but there was left upon my mind so deep an impression of the presence of my guardian angel that it has never been effaced."

A pious lady living in the world relates a circumstance that occurred in her youth, which proves how entirely this fervent Christian relied on the intervention of the good angels: "One Christmas eve, my father, who feared I would enter religion, and who, on that account, never entrusted me to the care of any one else, permitting me to go to Confession only twice a year, and then to the confessor of his choice, had accompanied me to the cathedral, where I was to make my Confession to M. l'Abbé Manceau. After being there a short time he felt the cold, and said to me he was going for his cloak, but he would return immediately. Scarcely had he left, when an irresistible desire impelled me to go to the Carmelite convent which was at that time only a short distance from the Church; I followed the impulse, notwithstanding my fear of being discovered by my father, and the consequent outbreak of his anger. I was not long absent, and yet, on returning to the church, I saw my father standing before the confessional of Fr. Manceau, evidently looking around for me. What could I do? I must necessarily pass before him to resume my place; he would, undoubtedly, see me and suspect where I had been; I knew how violent would be the explosion of his wrath. I dared not advance; I stood undecided, when perceiving Mr. Dupont, I approached him and, in a few words, explained my embarrassment: 'Do not fear,' he said to me gently, 'ask his angel to close his eyes, and he will not see you.' Trembling like a leaf, I went to my father and said to him: 'Have a little patience, my turn will soon come, and I shall not be long.' The holy man had spoken the truth; his good angel, in concert with my father's angel, had closed his eyes; he did not see the direction from which I approached him."

Mr. Dupont's letters to his friends and various persons, often commenced with an act of homage rendered to the presence of the good angels: "I salute your good angel!" or: "Salutations to our good angels!" It was a pious practice for which he would, at times, give his reasons. "I commence my letter in this manner, because it expresses a very natural thought. When we meet a friend, do we remove our hats in salutation to him alone, if he is in company with one or several persons? More than that, if the companion of our friend should be a person of high rank, he would receive the first salutation, and we should enter into conversation with our friend, only with the permission of the noble personage." To another he writes: "I salute your dear angel, my dear friend, and I beg him to unite with mine, in obtaining for both of us the grace to accomplish God's holy will in all things."

In the intimate communications between souls, he perceived the intervention of good angels. He begged them to make known his gratitude to persons who had obliged him. "I desire with my whole heart," he says, "that my good angel, in return for all the services you so kindly render me, would bestow upon you graces for the good of your soul. To ask, is to obtain. Therefore, you will have them. And you will say: 'The angel of the poor pilgrim has manifested gratitude to me.'"

Another of his practices was to pray the good angels to conduct him to the holy table. In the latter part of his life, when he could Communicate but rarely, he had composed under the title of: *Sighs of a soul deprived of daily Communion*, this prayer: "Good angel, dear object of my affections, do not refuse me the aid of thy powerful intercession; help me to transport myself in spirit to every altar throughout the world, at the moment when the Holy Sacrifice is consummated, that I may collect upon my tongue the particles of the hosts which fall at the moment of holy Communion."

The Scriptures suggested to him pious considerations upon the holy angels. "How many graces descend upon us from Heaven at the same time! We may well, therefore, apply to ourselves the words of the prophet Eliseus to his servant, at the moment when the latter tremblingly announced to him that the city was surrounded by enemies: 'Fear not, for there are more with us than with them.' And at the same moment, Eliseus begs God to open the eyes of Giezi, and Giezi sees millions of horses and chariots of fire, and the enemy abandon the siege. I think we should continually fortify ourselves by the thought that the good angels are able to do us more good than the bad angels can inflict evils upon us."

In regard to the "petitions for prayers," which he did not always inscribe upon the register with the detail of particulars which persons desired, he makes this remark: "I am convinced that the good angels comprehend wonderfully well my abbreviations necessitated by want of time." He did not wish those angels who were commissioned to receive a soul at its departure from life, to be retarded by prayer. "Do not make useless efforts," he says, "to detain Sister X—— from her Heavenly Country. When the angels come for such souls, we are very weak to reject them. We say in our poor way, like the inhabitants of Joppa around the body of Dorcas: 'Behold her good works; we have need of her.' But the Saints in Heaven are more powerful. In regard to the service they render us, all the Saints, on leaving the earth, may say with our Lord: 'It is expedient for you that I go.'"

Another devotion dear to Mr. Dupont was that which he practised for the souls in purgatory. He manifested it especially by the Communions he offered for them. He had particular ideas on this subject which he often expressed with an extraordinary enthusiasm. He thus explains himself: "When I have the honor of communicating for a departed soul, at the moment of receiving the holy host, I employ a little formula which I adopted many years ago; it is to say: *Portio mea in terra viventium*: 'Thou art my portion in the land of the living.'

"I adopted it under the following circumstances. On the death of Monseigneur de Montblanc, Archbishop of Tours, during the Mass which I intended offering for the repose of his soul, I lost sight of him completely, and I did not even think of him at holy Communion, when the priest, in giving me Communion, pressed somewhat heavily with his finger, and broke upon my tongue the sacred host in two distinct parts. I feared that one of the particles had fallen; but at the same moment, I felt it in my mouth, and I exclaimed interiorly: *Portia mea in terra viventium!* Immediately, the thought of Monseigneur Montblanc came to my mind, and I said: 'Monseigneur, you say that with more reason than I, who am still in the land of the dying!' From that time, I have always had recourse to my little formula when I approach holy Communion."

He made use of this practice on an occasion which is worth relating. A lady of Tours, with whom he was intimately acquainted, died. The following day as he was leaving the church, he met her daughter, and said to her confidentially and in an extatic manner: "I offered my Communion for your mother, but you do not know my embarrassment At the moment the priest placed the sacred host upon my tongue, it separated into two parts. Several ideas presented themselves to my mind, and, whilst I was thinking of offering to God for the dear deceased the part I intended for her, it seemed to me that she appeared before me with her hands full of gold, as if to say to me: 'I am richer than you.' As I strove to examine this impression, I seemed to hear her pronounce these words: 'My portion is in the land of the living.' Oh! how pleased I was! yes, the dead who die in the Lord go to the land of the living, and it is we, alas! who are in the land of the dying, in that land where, at every moment we are exposed to the danger of losing God, and of dying eternally."

The thought of death was ever present to his mind; the consideration of a future life and a blessed eternity, was a powerful aid to infuse a supernatural motive into his actions. All of them were directed to God. A person, who frequented his house, and sometimes attended to business affairs during his absence, told us that wishing one day to seal a letter, he found only black wafers upon the desk. Mr. Dupont said: "It is the emblem of mourning, and I wear mourning as all sinners should do." This incident recalls another related by one of his friends. "Mr. Dupont always wore black. 'One day,' he said, 'some one asked me for whom I was in mourning. The one who put the question was not a Christian: he asked me for whom I wore mourning! "For you," I replied, "For it is written: 'Seven days you shall wear mourning for the dead, but for the fool and impious all the days of your life."' Mr. Dupont had in his tranquil manner, applied these words to the one who questioned him, and who, in his eyes, was a fool and an impious man. This excessive frankness appeared to him as quite a simple and natural method, and he would relate such instances without ascribing to himself either merit or reproach." His black dress did not, therefore, indicate, as the world might suppose, the loss of a friend. Death, as he viewed it, was life, and instead of weeping over the departure of those he loved, he rejoiced at their eternal happiness whilst awaiting the reunion with them in Heaven.

He had a special practice in favor of the friends of whose death he was informed, and he suggested it to others that they might apply it to him at his death. He explains it to one of his goddaughters in the following terms: "Everything leads me to believe that I shall be called to a severe judgment. Alas! I understand that it is an all-important affair, and that, in such a moment, we invoke, like Job, the aid of our friends. I will tell you one of my devotions taken from St. Teresa, and I beg you to adopt it, in order to make use of it when the occasion may require. St. Teresa, on hearing of the death of an old friend, exclaimed: 'If during my life, O Lord, I have done any good, apply it to that soul.' At the same moment, she understood that the soul was admitted into Heaven."

Whenever he met a funeral procession, he would immediately join it,—it mattered not to what class of society the deceased belonged,—and saying the rosary, follow bare-headed as far as the cemetery. He preferred to attend the funerals of those in the humbler walks of life, and of the poor: he made it a duty to pray for the repose of their souls, an office of charity which is too often neglected.

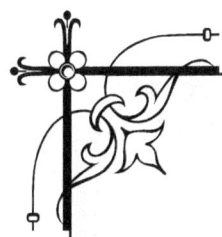

Chapter XXIII

Fourth Period of the Holy Face.

Mr. Dupont lived in a supernatural element. He was ever united to God, and in spirit and heart, in the society of the angels and Saints. The practice of the interior virtues, his unwearied application to prayer, his various exercises of piety, adopted according to circumstances and the necessities of the moment, all these spread around him a sort of heavenly atmosphere, the influence of which was felt by all who approached him. His reputation was great and extended to a distance. Persons from every direction visited him impelled by various motives: the infirm, to be cured; the afflicted, to be consoled; the curious, to study and know him; grave men, to be edified and instructed; others, simply to beg his prayers, and at the same time to receive from him a word of encouragement, or of light in their difficulties and their doubts. We may assert, without fear of passing the bounds of truth, that there was not a work of zeal, of piety, or of charity, founded in France during thirty years, for which his influence was not exerted, either directly or indirectly; not a man of God, of any consideration whatever, who did not make a point of recommending himself to his prayers, or of soliciting his advice as to an enterprise already commenced, or for a project in contemplation.

The visits made to him did not always result in a corporal cure, or in a miracle apparent to the senses; they most frequently proved to be remedies for the soul, leading to a sincere conversion, an amendment of life, or imparting an increase of faith, a supernatural light which poured the balm of consolation into the suffering heart. The room of the servant of God had become a source of graces, a centre of benedictions appropriate to every want of the soul. In illustration of this general remark, we will give in detail a few facts which occurred in the years immediately preceding 1870.

A very aged lady was living in an entire disregard of any religious practice. A dangerous illness having prostrated her, she was recommended to the prayers of the servant of God. He was deeply interested in the salvation of her poor soul, and he made daily inquiries as to her dispositions. Her attendant, seeing her mistress reduced to the last extremity, ventured to propose the ministry of a priest, but her suggestion was indignantly rejected. Informed of the discouraging refusal, Mr. Dupont did not, on that account, lose hope, but continued to intercede for the return of this unfortunate soul to God. His prayer was heard; she became more composed, unexpectedly asked for a priest, and made her Confession. God restored her to health, and prolonged her life four years. She persevered in fidelity to her religious duties, and died in an edifying manner, fortified by the sacraments of the Church.

An old man, without religion, was hopelessly ill. Mr. Dupont was informed of his condition, and exhibited great solicitude for his salvation. His prayers proved efficacious; the hardened sinner himself requested the attendance of the curate of St. François-de-Paul, who found him in excellent dispositions. He was unable to administer the Holy Viaticum; but, at the moment of death, the man received Extreme Unction in the most consoling sentiments of faith.

In 1853, Mr. Dupont was requested to pray for an infant two months old, in a dangerous condition from whooping-cough, which caused violent convulsions. The man of God answered only by the following mysterious words: "*There must be victims in families.*" A few days later, the child died, although the parents had made a pilgrimage to obtain its cure. After the lapse of five years, the grandfather, who did not practice his religious duties, was hopelessly ill. He was recommended to the prayers of Mr. Dupont. For ten years, his friends had vainly solicited his conversion; it was obtained only two months before his death. But the man, who was naturally upright, returned to God with all the simplicity and docility of a child recently enlightened from above. He received, in perfectly Christian dispositions, the Sacraments of Penance, Eucharist, and Confirmation. The friends who were present were edified by the calmness and resignation of the poor man, so long an alien from his God. A fortnight afterwards, he died surrounded by his family, justifying, by his holy death, the prophetic words uttered by Mr. Dupont five years previously.

Mr. D———, a good man in the worldly acceptation of the term, lived, as well as his wife, without religion of any kind. The slightest thing which might recall to mind the Catholic faith, offended them. So strong was this feeling, that upon the division of some family property, when an image of the Saviour fell to their share, Madame D——— gave it away, saying she did not wish to have in the house an emblem which always brought misfortune. God, Who willed the salvation of these two souls, sent the cross of suffering, to force them to turn to Him; but the grace was to be granted them through the intercession of the servant of the Holy Face. Mr. D——— was struck with paralysis, which deprived him of the use of his lower limbs, and kept him a prisoner in an arm-chair, or on a bed of pain. His condition embittered still more his natural disposition, and made him very difficult to manage. Notwithstanding the devoted attentions of his wife, who never left him, and the care of an excellent servant, he was extremely irascible. To complete his misfortunes, the faithful servant was suddenly unable to continue her attendance on him. A blow, which she had accidentally received, was so serious in its consequences, that the physicians considered a dangerous operation indispensable for her cure. The girl, having heard of Mr. Dupont, went to Tours for the express purpose of recommending herself to his prayers: she united with him in prayer before the venerated image, anointed with the oil, as he directed, and she was immediately relieved. Mr. D—— was singularly impressed by the cure of the servant; he thought within himself that the saint who had obtained the restoration of his nurse, could as readily obtain his; but he asked himself what claim he had to such a favor. He, a sinner! he was unworthy of it. He determined, however, to write to the servant of God a very humble letter, in which he begged the aid of his prayers, acknowledged that he had never made his first Communion, that he did not deserve to be cured, but still he hoped. Mr. Dupont prayed for him particularly, and succeeded in winning his soul to God. He received Holy Communion, became patient and resigned, and terminated his life with a Christian death. Instead of health of body, God had granted him the more precious gift of health of soul. Madame D——, touched by her husband's example, was also converted.

A young lady of Tours believed herself called to the Religious life, but she was decidedly and persistently opposed in her designs by her father and mother. Suddenly, her eyes became affected so seriously, as to inspire her parents with the fear of a total loss of sight. The proposition was made to her to visit Mr. Dupont, to anoint with the oil of the Holy Face, and make a novena. She gladly consented, not with the intention of soliciting relief from the affection of the eyes which caused her no anxiety, because she was confident that her vocation was from God, but to beg that her father and mother might consent to her entrance into religion. She performed the pilgrimage, was faithful in reciting the prayers and making the unctions; at the end of the nine days she was no better, but the spiritual blindness of her parents had been removed, and she obtained their entire approbation of her pious design. The affection of the eyes proved less serious than was supposed. The young lady gradually improved; she is, at the present moment, Superioress in a house of her Congregation, and gladly relates this incident, in order to honor Mr. Dupont, to whom she feels indebted for the favor.

It sometimes happened that a simple drop of oil given by the servant of God produced, even at a distance, miraculous effects, not only on an infirm body, but also on a rebellious will. A lady relates a pious stratagem and attests its truth. "A man about forty years of age had not approached the sacraments since his first Communion. His wife, a devout woman, prayed fervently, and offered large alms with the intention of obtaining his conversion; all was in vain; from neglecting the practices of his religion, he proceeded to a denial of the doctrines of the Church, and lost his faith. His wife confided to us her trouble, and asked advice of my daughter who replied: 'Since your remonstrances are fruitless, do not talk to him upon the subject of religion; such conversations tend to embitter his feelings still more, and remove him farther from God. Bring me a shirt belonging to this heart of stone, and we shall melt it.' Upon the shirt, on the side of the heart, they put a drop of the holy oil sent by Mr. Dupont. A few days later, the man suddenly asked for a prayer book. The following Sunday, the same stratagem was employed, and the unbeliever asked for a priest. He was sincerely converted, and his wife blesses from her heart the servant of the Holy Face; but the man was never told of the means employed to bring him to God."

The Reverend Father Bouix, the learned translator of the works of St. Teresa, never passed through Tours without visiting the servant of God. "When I called one day," he says, "I found several persons in his room, who, like myself, had gone to be edified by his conversation. A woman presented herself. 'Do you remember me?' she asked Mr. Dupont; 'you cured me, and I now bring you my son.' He was a boy about fourteen years of age, who suffered so intensely with an affection of the stomach, that in consequence of the violent pain she had spent two hours in dressing him that morning. They commenced the prayers. Mr. Dupont anointed the boy on the forehead, and directed the mother to pass into the adjoining room, and apply the oil to his stomach. The child returned to the room restored to health; Mr. Dupont said to him: 'Take that armchair, my little friend, and carry it around the room.' The boy obeyed immediately, to the great joy of the happy mother. Overcome with gratitude and rejoicing in his recovered health, the boy opened his arms, stood on tiptoe, and warmly embraced the man of God, who, smiling at his simplicity, raised his eyes to Heaven, and, in union with those who were present at the interesting scene, chanted the *Magnificat* in thanksgiving."

Two very pious young ladies, relatives of Horace Vernet, lived in Tours. One of them was so crippled in all her limbs, that for several years she had been unable to go to the church, unless carried in a chair. She requested one day to be taken to Mr. Dupont, and she was perfectly cured. The congregation were astonished to see her afterwards walking daily to church without assistance. The fact was one of public notoriety, and we have often heard it related by the curate of her parish.

The citizens of Tours have not forgotten Sister Angela, one of those worthy daughters of St. Vincent de Paul, whose apostolic zeal equals their ingenious charity. One day, in ascending a narrow and dark staircase to visit a patient, she fell, and, although not injuring herself dangerously, she suffered afterwards from a tumor on her leg, so large as to inconvenience her in walking, and to cause her to limp. Mr. Dupont noticed it, and pointed expressively to the picture of the Holy Face, as if inviting her to seek there her cure. The Sister hesitated and smiled. The servant of God then spoke seriously, and asked in tone of reproof: "What! a Religious deficient in faith! Come, Sister, kneel down and pray." Ashamed of her first feeling of distrust, she fell upon her knees and united in the prayers; after the unctions were made with the oil, the tumor disappeared. The Sister left his house, no longer lame, but free from pain, and delivered from an infirmity which never returned. She is now in America continuing her works of charity.

The cures effected were at times so far above the laws of nature, that the spectators experienced a kind of religious terror, if we may so express ourselves. A venerable and pious lady, who was visiting a friend in Tours, desired to see Mr. Dupont and pray before the Holy Face. A remarkable miracle was operated in her presence. A man entered who had an enormous swelling on his hand; as the servant of God applied the oil, the swelling disappeared under his fingers. Terrified by the wonder she witnessed, the lady ran from the room, went in all haste to the house of her friend, and related what she had seen, exclaiming that she could not believe the evidence of her senses, the thing was impossible, and yet she admitted that the circumstance really occurred as she represented it; her mind was in confusion; the divine, the supernatural had, as it were, transported her into another world. When she became more calm, she recognized a miracle in the event which had transpired before her, knowing that what is impossible to man, is possible to God, Who can do all things.

A lady, living in the vicinity of Tours, was passing some time in that city. One day when walking with her husband and daughter, she requested them to wait a few minutes, as she desired to procure a phial of oil from Mr. Dupont. She entered his room and knelt for a short prayer, not wishing to detain her husband for any length of time. The holy man occupied his usual place at his desk; as she arose to leave the room, he looked at her, and in a tone of authority said to her: "Sit down. You torture yourself, Madame, and are uselessly disturbed; *the woman who fears God will laugh in her last hour*. You would make greater progress in the spiritual life, and you would be far happier, if you abandoned yourself more entirely to Divine Providence." Then referring to the text quoted above, he related the history of his mother who, having feared death during her whole life, died peacefully and with a smile upon her lips; he continued to speak for some time upon confidence, abandonment, and peace of soul. This conversation was so unexpected to the lady, and apparently so uncalled for from one who, was a perfect stranger to her, that she hastened to take her leave, ascribing his remarks to a weakening of his mental faculties, as he was then an old man. However, she begged the aid of his prayers that she might obtain a particular grace which she ardently desired. He answered: "I promise to pray, but your petition will not be granted." In reality, she did not attain the object of her desires. That very evening she dined with a friend in Tours, and among the guests was a bishop, who had been, for a long time, her confessor, and who still continued to be her director. She related the singular interview of the morning. The Bishop took her aside and said: "I have no other advice to give you; Mr. Dupont's words contain all you require; they sum up my opinion in regard to your spiritual condition, and the wants of your soul." The lady then comprehended that the servant of God had been enlightened from above in her regard. She still lives, and the above statement is given upon her own testimony.

A pious young lady of Versailles, who had visited the Holy Face, repeated to us another fact which was personal, and almost of the same kind. "As I had already," she says, "been once cured, I returned to see Mr. Dupont, with the intention of obtaining through his intercession a favor I specified. He listened to my petition, smiled gently, and, taking his pen, wrote upon the register, not the request I had made, but another entirely different. I called his attention to it, but he left unaltered what he had written, and the grace he asked was granted me. I shall never forget the calmness and depth of expression on the face of the holy man; it seemed to say: 'Poor child! you know not what you ask; there is something better for you; God will grant it.'"

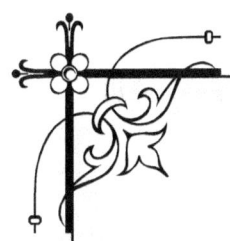

Chapter XXIV

Prussian Occupation — the Commune — Pontmain.

THE DISASTERS of 1870, caused Mr. Dupont a deep sorrow. He loved his country as he loved God and the Church. In common with other Catholics, he had always relied upon the valiant sword of France to defend the Spouse of Christ, whom, as eldest daughter, her mission is to protect against schism and heresy. The faith and charity which animated his private actions, also made him a virtuous citizen, an exact observer of the laws, a sincere lover of his country. Although he always held himself apart from politics, and took no part in the civil administration, he never did so through hostility or a spirit of opposition. He subjected himself to fulfil, even in the smallest point, his social duties, and these he performed as an enlightened Christian, uprightly and conscientiously. We will give only one instance of this. When the National Guard was organized in 1848, Mr. Dupont presented himself with others. He stood guard in his turn, wearing the required uniform, remained faithfully at his post, observed the watchword, and awaited patiently until he was relieved by the corporal, meditating during the time, as he himself informs us, on the words of the Psalmist: *Nisi Dominus custodierit civitatum, frustra vigilat qui custodit eam.* "If the Lord keeps not the city, he watches in vain that keeps it." He would repair from his post if it was night, to rejoin his associates collected at the Nocturnal Adoration, and continue with them, before the God of the Eucharist, his prayers for his country and his fellow-citizens.

When the news of the first defeats arrived, Mr. Dupont was alarmed for the future of France, and he wrote on September 7, 1870: "We can say nothing, we can do nothing but humble ourselves with our heads to the dust, whilst the justice of God passes by." But in dealing a heavy blow upon France, "divine justice" was about to permit the stroke to fall at the same time upon the servant of the Holy Face, and to inflict upon him a succession of bitter trials, which, in the designs of Providence, were to purify his beautiful soul, and associate him to the dolors of Calvary. His first sorrow was the suppression of his cherished work of the Nocturnal Adoration, necessarily interrupted in consequence of the general conscription of able-bodied men, and the public charges imposed on others. He made no complaint, but in his heart it caused him great suffering. In the condition of health to which he was then reduced, he was forced to live solitary and isolated, and content himself with remaining in prayer before the Holy Face.

His house was open during the night, as well as the day, not only to the pilgrims who continued to go there, although in less numbers, but also to the young soldiers who were hastening to the defense of the invaded territory. His hospitality was well known; it was freely called upon, and many, merely passing through the city, carried letters to him from their friends. He writes to some one on October 13, 1870: "The two young men, to whom you gave letters, asked admittance last night at one o'clock. They had but a short time at their disposal, and wisely came to render homage to the Holy Face, and to ask for a medal of St. Benedict..." But already stirring events were crowding upon them, and he adds: "The Prussians are at Orleans. It is not known if they will come to Tours. In any case, nothing will occur without the permission of the Divine Master. *Blessed be His holy Name!*"

The sudden invasion of Paris gave rise to a remarkable event closely connected with the last years of our holy friend. The Religious of the Visitation of Paray-le-Monial, with whom he held frequent communication, had, in concert with him, conceived the idea of embroidering a flag of the Sacred Heart, to be sent to the brave soldiers who were chosen to defend the capital against the contemplated attack of a foreign foe. This flag, of which a *fac simile* may be seen in the present oratory of the Sacred Face, represented the Sacred Heart of Jesus with the aspiration: "Heart of Jesus, save France!" From Paray-le-Monial, it was forwarded to Mr. Dupont, with the request to present it before the Holy Face, and thence send it, either to General Trochu, charged with the defense of Paris, to be planted on the walls of the capitol, or to the volunteers of the West. Mr. Dupont called upon Mr. Ratel, engineer of the railroad, and inquired if there was any means by which the banner could be introduced into Paris. He was informed that Paris was completely invested, and the trains no longer had access to the city. The idea occurred to both of them to present the banner to Charette, who had just arrived at Tours, and whose Zouaves received later the name of the Western Volunteers. They repaired to the hotel where the General lodged; they were met at first by one of his brothers; Charette entered afterwards. He accepted the gift, and a meeting was appointed for the following morning at Mr. Dupont's. There, in presence of the Holy Face, they opened the box containing the banner. Together, they prayed for the salvation of France, and they agreed that the precious standard should be deposited in the tomb of St. Martin until the following day, and that on the reverse side should be embroidered the words: *St. Martin protect France*. The design for the embroidery was immediately drawn by some ladies who were present, and the work was executed by the Carmelite Religious. The history of this memorable flag of the Sacred Heart is well known; how, under its auspices, the Zouaves of Charette were covered with glory, to the admiration of all France, and even of their enemies.*

During the siege of Paris, we trace in Mr. Dupont's correspondence his anxiety and alarm as to the fate of his friends. But he does not interrupt his mission before the Holy Face; he receives those who present themselves from whatever quarter, or for whatever motive they may come; he is even ready "to show the Prussians several remarkable certificates written partly in German and partly in French." "And," he adds, "we could talk about God." He is always the man of prayer, the man of faith and confidence in God, never despairing of the future. "We may be certain that many hearts will now turn to God; this is the plank to save us from shipwreck." Then quoting the words of Josophat, when he was surrounded by a multitude of enemies, he adds: "If we lifted our eyes to Heaven with the faith of Josophat, the enemy would depart."

It was not long before the Prussians entered Tours. They occupied the city during the armistice. To a trial so severe to the heart of a Frenchman, Mr. Dupont submitted humbly, repeating with the holy patriarch Job his habitual aspiration: *Blessed be the name of the Lord!* He wrote this act of praise on the 1st of February, 1871, in the midst of the Prussian invasion, at the commencement of a letter addressed to one of his goddaughters, who had taken refuge in Brittany; but an expression which escaped him, betrays the bitterness of the trial, and the heroism of his resignation: "You have, my dear child, imitated the dove of the ark.

---

* The banner in the church of the Sacred Heart at Paris bears, on one side, the Sacred Heart, and, on the other, St. Martin. It expresses the same idea: that of invoking the Sacred Heart and the Thaumaturgus of Gaul for the salvation of France, and we see that it originated before the Holy Face of Tours, from a happy inspiration of Mr. Dupont.

You are the first to give me evidence that communication has been restored. Your letter brought to my old eyes the tears, which, for so many years, seemed dried up."

As he had predetermined, he did not neglect the opportunity to speak of God and to glorify the Holy Face. "For several weeks," he writes on March 5, 1871, "I have had quartered upon me fifteen or sixteen Prussians; with the exception of two or three Protestants, all are Catholics. Their conduct is irreproachable." On another occasion, he wrote: "Among the Prussians I lodged, the Catholics were in the majority, and they prayed much before the Holy Face; one of them even obtained a remarkable favor. I tell you this for your consolation; but we must pray fervently that revolution may not make progress in Paris. Alas!" He foresaw what was to happen. The revolution is a greater source of alarm to him than the foreign enemy. "The Prussian occupation," he says, (March 20th,) "was not very ruinous to our country, and, in general, the men conducted themselves with propriety; in contrast to this behold at Paris, wretched criminals rising in their ignominious audacity in opposition to the order-loving and healthy portion of the nation. May God in His mercy avert the scourge which seems ready to fall upon us!" "Let us pray," he writes to another friend, "that revolutionary ideas may not gain the ascendency. Alas!" "According to the reports which are in circulation," he writes, (March 5, 1871,) "a fearful crisis is upon us. May the Lord extend to us a helping hand! I hope that the revolutionary hydra has too soon unmasked his batteries." "How often," he writes to a relative in America, (April 14, 1871,) "my thoughts turn to you in the midst of the terrible events which, for nearly a year, have crushed our poor France, abased below all other nations! You know the catastrophe; but you must pray that the abyss may not close over us; I mean, that the revolution, which is Satan unchained, may not swallow us up as it did eighty years ago."

During the terrible days of the Commune, "the incredible recital of La Roquette," touching the massacre of the hostages, wrings from him a cry of agony, (Aug. 15, 1871.) "When will people begin to love each other in Paris, which has become a city of hatred!!" But, immediately, the man of prayer rises above all natural feeling; the following beautiful letter places him before us invoking all the holy patrons of the capital, and uniting their names in the form of a litany, which he proposes to recite every day: "We have had the idea of making a novena of prayers in honor of all the saints who, in any manner, are invoked in Paris, the patrons of the parishes, as well as those whose names have been given to streets and squares. Unite with us, saying for example: Our Lady of Victory, pray for us; Saint Genevieve, etc."... This idea, as eminently Catholic as French, was realized. We have before us the series of these invocations to the number of eighty, under the title of "Litany of the Saints of Paris." Mr. Dupont added a short notice of each Saint. We may be permitted to believe that these secret supplications made by a large number of fervent souls at the suggestion of the servant of God, contributed, in no small degree, to deliver Paris from the horrors of the Commune.

Paris being liberated from it, he expresses a desire of reparation, the justice of which will not escape any of those who are aware of the religious ignorance so common among men. "Shall we," he writes, (June 1, 1871), "put to profit the victory gained over crime? They are going to rebuild, as soon as possible, the ruined walls. It would be a hundred times better to instruct the mind, and force all to learn the Catechism."

But, above all, he ardently desires to see men turn to God in prayer. "Let us place ourselves in the hands of God. He alone can protect us from the shipwreck which menaces Christian civilization." "Happily, God is all-powerful! Otherwise, there would be every reason to fear that evil would prevail. Let us then hope, notwithstanding appearances." The sad condition to which France is reduced, afflicts him, but does not diminish his confidence. "You are bowed down under the pressure of the great affliction which weighs upon every Catholic heart. But as the sentiment of prayer seems to be awakening in a large number of souls, we should, I think, be wrong to yield to discouragement. Abraham's confidence increased in proportion as the number of elect demanded by God decreased. Our efforts, then, should be directed to augment the number of souls destined to incline the balance on the side of mercy."

The supernatural hopes which he cherished, gathered strength from the miraculous event occurring at Pontmain. Mr. Dupont was almost immediately informed of the circumstances attending the apparition, by a relative who was on the spot. "They were very small children who saw the Blessed Virgin; they spelled the words as they were successively formed before them: 'Pray! My son inclines to mercy. France will soon be liberated.'" This predilection of the Mother of God for childhood charmed him; he exclaims: "The preeminence is decidedly granted to children. What a cause of abasement to pride!" He welcomes with pious avidity the least news on the subject, and he hastens to communicate it to his friends.

The situation of Rome caused him constant anxiety. "And Rome," he writes, "alas! a subject on every side for fear and affliction! And yet, but for hope, we should faint by the way. There are so many souls walking in the way of the counsels; they may obtain grace for themselves and for others." His hopes are founded partly on these motives, and partly on others still more elevated. "The promises made to Peter," he says, "repose in their plenitude upon our beloved Pius IX. What more can we ask? The blood of the first martyrs was the seed of the Church. That of the martyrs of the nineteenth century will restore the Church to its primitive vigor. And notice that, for a large number of Christians, there is great need of a new resurrection. The present, then, is an important moment fraught with great interests." A lady of Paris had sent him a pamphlet of Father de Pontlevoy, relative to the events of the period. "I have read," he writes, "the pamphlet with great interest. It is one of those things which bring out clearly the great souls who have received the glorious mission to save the Church in these disastrous times, when the bark of Peter is, apparently, in danger. The blood of the martyrs gave birth to the first Christians; the martyrs of the nineteenth century will arrest the revival of paganism. Let us, then, remain Christians."

The pilgrimage of Pontmain furnishes him food for reflection and hope. "I know," he says, "that General Charette went with all the officers of his battalion from Fougères to this new pilgrimage, and that he and all his companions were struck by what they heard from the children and the, inhabitants of this *little place*, which will become a *great place*, when the prophetic words, spoken a few days before the armistice, will be accomplished. It will be the complement of Salette and Lourdes." On January 29, 1873, he writes: "The grand inspiration of faith which is impelling multitudes to make distant pilgrimages, excites strong hopes for the future. The favors of Heaven, so lavishly bestowed for some time past, strengthen our confidence. I have passed some pleasant hours lately with the author of a pamphlet entitled: *The Miracles of our Lady of Lourdes; a Public Challenge to Free Thinkers*. Ten thousand francs were deposited with a notary. That such a production should reach its seventeenth edition, proves that Satan must have fallen back a great distance. Away then, Satan!!!" Nevertheless, as he knows that France has been chastised, because of her foolish pretensions and her pride, he is persuaded that her salvation must come through the intercession of the humble and the lowly. Some one in Paris proposed to make a novena of prayers. "Think of me," he writes, "during this week, when you will be at the tomb of St. Genevieve. It is the lowly who will save France. Benedict Labre will unite with St. Genevieve, with Joan of Arc, Germaine Cousin, and other little ones who are unknown to men."

Two extensive manifestations of Catholic faith at Tours rejoiced his soul, and convinced him more and more that the work of St. Martin was destined to play an important part in the providential mission of France. The tomb of the Blessed Jeanne-Marie de Maillé, one of the glories of the province of Tours had been exposed, and devotion to her had, through the exertions of Cardinal Guibert, just been solemnly recognized and approved by the Holy See. Under Monseigneur Fruchaud, successor of Monseigneur Guibert, it became the occasion of a triduum of religious festivals, during which the ancient faith of Tours gave evidence of its vitality, and awoke to its early splendor. The new glory of this illustrious servant of St. Martin imparted additional brilliancy to the annual celebration of the feast of the Thaumaturgus. The solemnity of the 11th of November, 1872, and the exercises preceding and following it, were the occasion of an outbreak of piety and of transports of fervor, which had not before been seen at Tours. Mr. Dupont takes pleasure in referring to this in his correspondence: "The novena of St. Martin," he says, "is performed here in a most consoling manner through the marvellous eloquence of Father Felix. The metropolitan church is too small to contain the crowds of men who attend." The joy of these festivals was to the servant of God, as are the last rays of the setting sun to the belated traveller. The days of entire isolation and acute suffering were approaching.

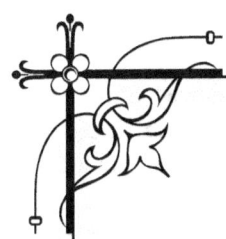

Chapter XXV

Isolation and Suffering — Last Period of Devotion to the Holy Face.

God, designing to purify his servant more and more, was about to afflict him in all that he held dear. The Nocturnal Adoration, which had been interrupted for a long time, was resumed with great difficulty; the associates were unable to assemble oftener than once a month; the meetings were continued, thanks to a few fervent men whom Mr. Dupont had inspired with his own sentiments; but he was no longer there to keep alive the flame by his words and example. This was a painful privation to him as well as to them. On the other hand, it is well known that our public disasters during the war of the Prussian invasion, by dispersing or removing members of families by death, were necessarily attended with changes and interruptions of social relations. The pilgrimage to the Holy Face, as a consequence, became very different from what it had previously been. Visitors, without ceasing entirely, diminished sensibly in numbers. We may truly say that the devotion was the same, as is proved by the correspondence of that time; many, who could not undertake the journey, requested by letter to have phials of the holy oil forwarded to them, and begged the prayers of the servant of God. But crowds no longer thronged his room; isolated pilgrims presented themselves, one at a time. Already he was, himself, scarcely able to receive them: he began to feel the weight of his infirmities. "I regain with difficulty," he said, (February 2, 1871,) "the strength I lost two or three years ago. I am at an age when this should not surprise me. I am now in my seventy-fifth year. It behooves us all to endeavor to walk perseveringly in the ways of God."

There is a void around him occasioned by the death of his dearest friends, his relatives, his neighbors. He speaks with deep emotion in one of his letters, which constantly become shorter, of the death of the "Rev. Abbé de Solesme," of the loss of his "dear cousin Adrien de Beauchamps," and also of the death of "a good neighbor, with whom he had been intimately associated for more than forty years...."

To his other infirmities, was added a partial loss of sight. "I have discovered," he says, (December 10, 1874,) "that my sight is very defective. I was forced to guess at all that portion of your letter written in red ink. You cannot imagine the effort I was obliged to make in the attempt to read it, and unfortunately, it was trouble lost! Another misfortune is, that as only a few come, at rare intervals, to visit the prisoner of Saint-Etienne street, I have not the chance of aiding my old eyes by young ones. Add to this, the gout in my hands forces me to write so slowly that I forget half the words."

He makes no complaint of a state in which he views the divine will. "Yesterday evening, I suffered from vertigo," he writes to a friend. "The physician assures me it is of no consequence. Still, I realize that it does not require a cannon ball to destroy this earthly envelope. I have evidently entered into a state beset by infirmities, the true way of penance, in which, willingly or unwillingly, we must do the will of God. Ask for me the grace to receive this penance lovingly." He is ready to accept all the incommodities of old age, particularly the loss of his memory which had always been good. "If my limbs render me very slight service," he says, "my memory scarcely serves me at all. Such is my condition; humanly speaking, it is sad; but God wills it, *amen!* it is right, and just as it should be."

He aspires more than ever to "silence," desires "to be forgotten," and requests a friend to help him to maintain himself in these dispositions. An excellent person was endeavoring, through kindness, to divert him. "I shall write him," he said, "that the greatest need of my soul is to remain in perfect silence. You know what good reasons I have to keep myself at anchor in the port of abjection." Another lady proposed to him to interest himself in a good work; he answers: "You ask me what is simply impossible. In my present state of decrepitude, I am entirely unfit for service. I *am able* for nothing, I *do* nothing, I *am worth* nothing."

He had not, however, lost his serenity, nor his amiability in receiving his friends and in entertaining his guests. The following incident is a proof of this, and it is also an evidence that the decay of his faculties was not such as, in his humility, he supposed. We quote from the letter of a gentleman living at present in the North, who had formerly frequent communication with him. "One became an admirer, a disciple, a friend, after having seen or heard him, or even after having received one of his letters. To see him was a powerful attraction to me to visit Tours. My last visit was in November, 1874. I had received several invitations to dine, but I preferred accepting one from Mr. Dupont. His health appeared to me much weakened by age and infirmities; but his kind reception was the more gratifying, and his memory had not failed. On entering, I met a countryman walking at an ordinary pace, his countenance wearing a contented expression. It was only after he left that I learned the following fact.

"An inscription, which Mr. Dupont was attaching to a crutch placed in his hands by the countryman, certified that the man was lame when he entered, being unable to walk without the support of a crutch. After having prayed before the Holy Face, he arose perfectly well, and deposited his crutch as evidence of his cure. The servant of God informed me, with the simplicity which characterized him, that when the countryman came he was a cripple, and that after having prayed he returned home with the full use of his limbs. I dined with him alone. I cannot express to you the happiness I experienced in being near this holy man. His whole conversation consisted of quotations and admirable comments upon the Old and New Testament. My memory, imagination and heart were fed, enlightened, and charmed by the fervor of this beautiful soul. He gave me, at my departure, a small parcel of earth brought to him by a pilgrim from the garden of Olives. He sealed the envelope, inscribed on it: *Ex pulvere Gethsemani*, and kindly signed his name."

The above represents in what manner Mr. Dupont at that time received his friends when they visited him. This was undoubtedly one of his last receptions. For the future, he was to live in silence and solitude. When the pilgrims, who went to pray before the Holy Face, did not inquire for him, or when he was unable to receive them, he sent his servant, whom he had trained to that pious employment, to supply their wants.

He made use of the sacrifices imposed upon him by this isolation, as a means of advancing in virtue. His patience was unalterable; his humility was beyond expression. One of his intimate friends had the idea to test it, and she gives us the following account: "In order to amuse myself, and enjoy his humility, I said to him one day: 'Would you believe that I was really impatient this morning with a good man who was going away, because you were not in your room! I told him he had no faith, that he was an unbeliever,... that *you were nothing but the distributor of the oil*, and that it was the Holy Face which performed all the cures.' 'Oh! how truthfully you spoke,' he said, as he extended his hand to me; 'I will put on your forehead some of that excellent oil, which is miraculous in its effects upon the mind as well as upon the body.'"

He kept himself aloof, as far as he could, even from his ecclesiastical superiors, avoiding with great care everything which might attract to himself any mark of esteem or interest. In the latter years of his life, he was visited by the Archbishops of Tours; far from being elated by this honor, he seemed embarrassed and confused rather than gratified. His only desire was to be unnoticed and forgotten. It was from this motive, that he constantly refused to allow either his portrait or photograph to be taken. One of his goddaughters was very urgent in her request for his photograph: "I am not in a position," he replied, "to have my photograph taken. I am called upon to see so many persons that I could not enter into so puerile a distribution." To a friend presenting the same petition, he answers: "I have an excellent reason for not sending you my photograph: it has never been taken."

He no longer engaged in any active work of zeal or charity, except in that of the Clothing Society, of which he was president. The meetings were always held in his room, such being the wish of the members; and they never left him without being filled with the odor of his sanctity. He could not assist actively, and often he spoke very little. "But it was enough for us," says one of them, "to know that he was there in continual prayer. Wherever we might be employed in the work of the Society, we were encouraged and hopeful, considering his prayers to be efficacious to secure our success. It seemed to us that he, individually, had a power of prayer as mighty as that of a Religious community, whence the divine praises and the perfume of prayer ascend unceasingly to Heaven.

It was about 1874, that he remarked when reading a life of St. Edmund, Archbishop of Canterbury, a prayer which that illustrious pontiff daily addressed to the Apostle St. John, whence he derived at the hour of death a sweet consolation. The prayer was as follows: "O beloved disciple of Jesus! O virgin Apostle! obtain for me from our Lord the happy death which was granted to thee and the Saints. May I end my life in sentiments of true faith, firm hope and perfect charity! May I, preserving consciousness to the last, be able to confess my sins sincerely, and be fortified with the viaticum of salvation, and the unction of the dying! May I expire, ardently desiring to see the Face of our Lord Jesus Christ!" The concluding words, particularly, delighted Mr. Dupont. This fervent invocation corresponded so entirely to the secret aspirations of his soul, that, like the holy Bishop, he repeated it continually. He spoke of it to those who visited him, pronouncing the words slowly, as though he found in them an infinite delight; with his own poor hand, swollen and painful as it was, from gout and paralysis, he made a large number of copies of this prayer which he presented to his friends, or enclosed in letters.

For a long time he deprived himself of the pleasure of visiting Religious communities and attending to the works of charity in which he was interested. The only exception he made was in favor of the Little Sisters of the Poor, whom he occasionally visited; his habit was to arrive during their recreation, and pass it with the Sisters. He would then see the old people, and speak a few kind words to each. They collected around him, they called him Father Dupont, they were perfectly at home with him. The mere sight of him was a joy to them and did them good; his words animated by an ardent faith, and his example, encouraged the most suffering to bear their cross with patience. These charming visits, which, by degrees, became very rare, were festival days for the whole community.

When the paralysis and gout gave him a little respite, he took advantage of it to assist at the Holy Sacrifice, a happiness he could no longer enjoy frequently. He would go to the chapel of the Carmelites. It was the sanctuary of his choice, and, for some time, he had selected it as the one in which to hear Mass and receive holy Communion. He edified all present by arriving, every morning in summer at half-past five, and at six in winter, braving the inclemency of the seasons, and all the inconveniences arising from the early hour. When the morning was dark, he made use of a pocket lantern. Knowing that the body of Sister Saint-Pierre lay in the chapter-hall directly beneath the holy-water font, he would stop when near it, and, with his simple faith, entertain himself an instant with the dear deceased, concerning the interests of the Sacred Face and reparation.

As his sufferings increased, he was forced gradually to resign himself not to leave the house, and at last was confined to his room. That small apartment on the first story, was about to become the scene of the last trials of this true Christian, and then of his death. We should first mention how it happened that he was occupying it. For a long time his bedroom was the one which he called his drawing-room, and which in reality had become the oratory of the Sacred Face; it was a pleasant apartment, situated upon the ground-floor, and opening into the garden. He had in it a small iron bedstead concealed by a curtain; he was thus enabled, both night and day, to satisfy his devotion. He was so happy to sleep in the presence of the adorable Face of our Lord. And how often, when alone, he prayed kneeling before the cherished and venerated picture!

On the occasion of his last visit to the baths of Bourbon, he anticipated a long absence. Before his departure, his servant, Adele, requested his permission to order some repairs in that part of the house which was daily thronged with strangers. She had the different rooms on the lower floor, connecting with the oratory, properly cleaned and painted; she was, above all, particular in arranging in the best manner, that spot sanctified by so many prayers and miracles. At last, she was so daring as to remove the iron bedstead, on account, she said, of the inconveniences resulting from its remaining in a room frequented at all hours by strangers. She purchased a new bedstead, and placed it in a room above, which had formerly been used by Madame d'Arnaud as a sitting-room. On his return, astonished to find that he was no longer to pass the night near the Holy Face, Mr. Dupont, calmly folding his hands, said gently: "Can it be possible! Why was this done, Adele?" She explained to him, in her manner, how inconvenient it was to him to pass the night in a room where he was subject to receive so many visitors. Without shewing the least dissatisfaction, the good servant of the Holy Face conformed his will to the Divine will, and resumed his occupations as though the sacrifice had cost him nothing. This happened after 1860. From that time, he always slept in the room in which he died, and it was there, that he remained continually during the last few years of his life, a prisoner from paralysis and gout.

But before following him to this new Calvary, let us stop a moment with him in this first room, his drawing-room and oratory, to which he no longer goes, unless occasionally to receive visitors and write his letters, but where, by the power of his prayers, miracles continue to be effected.

We have said above that the people no longer went in crowds as formerly; but petitions by letter for prayers became far more numerous. The quantity of notes of this kind received during the last years of his life is incredible. We have looked through a portion of those found among his papers.

We see in them marks of the wonderful confidence placed in him by persons of every condition, and from every country. His reputation for sanctity was so great and universal, that petitions were presented him for prayers, as though the address was being made to a saint in Heaven. He is not only requested to recommend their necessities to what they call his "confraternity of the Holy Face," and to his work of the Nocturnal Adoration, but they apply to him personally; his individual prayers they particularly desire; these they esteem as peculiarly efficacious, and the simple thought, that he remembers them, consoles and encourages. Every kind of necessity is referred to him. An infirm person writes to be cured. A mother recommends her daughter; a wife, her husband. What is most urgently solicited, is the conversion of a sinner, the return of a prodigal son. His prayers and "blessing" are asked for children preparing for their first Communion. Strangers open their hearts to him with simplicity and candor, confide to him their troubles, as they would do to an intimate friend, to a confessor, or we might rather say, as they would do to an angel of Paradise, to God Himself. Urgent telegrams are forwarded begging his prayers for a relative dangerously ill, for one in his agony who has not made his peace with God, for a departed friend, for relief from temporal misfortunes. Again the petition comes from a deacon about to be ordained a priest, or a mother recommends the examination of her son; a father, the first Communion of his daughter; a curate, the sick of his parish; a wife, her husband threatened with blindness. A poor widow begs him to aid her to pay her rent due since All Saints. The Trinitarians, recently established, ask him to send them novices. A Christian mother relies upon him for the cure of her son, and his vocation to the ecclesiastical state. Thanks are returned for phials of oil, or additional ones requested. He is desired to unite in novenas for particular favors which are specified. His house was a centre, a sanctuary, as it were, towards which thousands of hearts turned with confidence.

Those who know the state of his health are afflicted, and promise him to pray for his restoration; but the greater part supposing him to be still at his desk before the Holy Face, are astonished at his silence, and beg for a few words in answer. Many such letters to his address were received long after his death; they come even to the present day. For his part, notwithstanding his gout and other infirmities, he was particularly desirous not to interrupt his correspondence;

he continued it until the last month of his life. But it caused him much pain, as we may judge by the account he himself gives of his condition. He jests about his hand-writing with a friend in America: "My dear friend," he says, "what a difference between our writing! yours becomes that of a giant; and mine, as age advances, diminishes to nothing. But, after all, that is of no consequence: our business is to advance in the path which conducts to Heaven. The one who arrives there first, will not forget the friend he has left on earth." In the meantime, he is perfectly resigned: "The gout, without leaving the left hand, seems disposed to settle in the right hand; should this be the case, my insignificant letters must cease entirely; in advance, I say: *Fiat!*"

From that time he wrote only when circumstances rendered a few lines absolutely necessary. Each of these letters short, simple, and containing a pious sentiment, carried to those who received them a precious emanation of the "good odor of Jesus Christ," which perfumed his conversations.

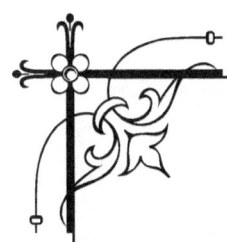

Chapter XXVI

His Last Illness — His Death.

For three years Mr. Dupont, having suffered intensely from gout, was unable to leave his room. The attention required by his helpless condition, brought his servants more immediately in communication with him, and they were edified both by his example and conversation. They admired in him the man of faith and confidence. They were astonished by his simplicity in prayer. "What are we but poor little creatures?" he would say to them. "What can a little creature do, but extend his hand and offer a prayer to his heavenly Father? Can it be possible? God does the will of his creature! Let the creature, then, do the will of God!" "Never," he said on another occasion, "never ascend the mountains; but always take the level road which runs at their base." He strongly recommended to those who served him, "fidelity to the good angels." "Listen attentively to the good thoughts with which they inspire you," he said; "to disregard them would be an infidelity to God." He urged them never to disgrace their name of Christian by giving ear to the suggestions of Satan. "Depart," he said, addressing Satan in a contemptuous manner, "depart! *Vade retro!*" Then raising his cap, he would salute him ironically: "Good evening!" His animation and gayety never flagged when he was speaking of Satan to his servants. "How can one," he said, "be a child of God, and hold communication with the reprobate! The wretch! leave him his cunning; it is all that remains to him; he has no heart." "As for you, you can obtain everything. You have only to extend your hand like a pauper to God; that suffices for prayer, and after you have received from the hand of God, lift that hand in imagination to your lips, kiss it with gratitude; a sincere kiss, and a simple 'I thank Thee.'"

Returning to the poor, to those poor whom he loved so dearly, he said: "Let us be very exact in serving the poor; never delay, for they are kings; they will be kings in eternity!" And he would relate incidents which occurred to himself personally, to prove how important it was not to delay doing the good act which it was in our power to perform. Thus he mentioned that he was once preparing to visit a poor person who was ill, when the rain commenced to pour down in torrents. Madame d'Arnaud opposed his exposing himself in so terrible a storm. Whilst waiting for the cessation of the rain, he took up a book: it was "St. Gertrude." As he opened it his eyes fell upon the following words: "The poor are the princes of the heavenly court; they should never be kept waiting." This ray of light shone upon his mind at an appropriate time, and nothing could detain him longer at home. He went immediately to the house of the poor invalid. On arriving, he found the man in his agony. He had only time to call in the priest to administer the last sacraments. He determined, from that moment, to profit by the lesson thus taught him, and never to delay rendering aid to the poor, when inspired to offer it.

There was a proverb he loved very much, and which he repeated frequently: "Da et accipe: Give and receive." He made use of these words, to induce others to bestow alms promptly and generously, saying that we "receive" from God in proportion as we "give" to the poor. He very particularly recommended that the linen given to the poor should be clean, well mended, and that it should retain no bad odor.

On another subject, Mr. Dupont was equally inexhaustible; it was the necessity and happiness of holy Communion. "A Christian, without holy Communion," he said, "is a fish out of water." In support of this, he quoted the Sacred Scriptures, saying that the Bible, from beginning to end, from the first page wherein it is written: *If you eat of this fruit you shall die*, to the last page of the Apocalypse, in which mention is made of the "tree of life," and the "river of the water of life," is a continuous invitation to nourish ourselves with the Eucharistic bread. He applies to Communion the verse of the Psalm: "*Qui dat jumentis escam et pullis corvorum:* Who giveth to beasts their food and to the young ravens that call upon him." He used these words as illustrating, in the mystery of the Eucharist, on the one hand, the greatness and goodness of God, and on the other, our nothingness.

Such were the subjects of his familiar conversations with his domestics; and the pious persons of the neighborhood who went to render him any service. They all delighted to recall his ideas, which we have endeavored to reproduce as nearly as possible in his own words. But it is impossible to convey in writing the attractive joyousness, the flashes of wit, the expressive gestures, the winning manner, which threw a charm around his every word.

Mr. Dupont always gave a cordial welcome to children. He made himself a child with them, questioned them in a familiar manner, made them talk, sing, recite the catechism or their prayers. When he was visited by the young who were about entering boarding school, he encouraged them to study diligently, and never omitted to impart to them a method by which they could succeed in obtaining prizes at the conclusion of the scholastic year, and, as an example of its efficacy, he would relate an incident which happened to himself. One of his friends had placed his son at the Lyceum in Tours, and, as he anticipated being absent several years, he begged Mr. Dupont to see him occasionally, and give him the benefit of his advice. The child, who entered at Easter, was the last of his class in composition. As this was the case several times in succession, he became thoroughly discouraged. His kind protector finding he could animate him, neither by his visits nor his advice, was pained, particularly as the father had entrusted the boy to his care as to a friend who would be interested in his progress. On visiting the child one day, and finding him more dejected than usual, he said to him: "I know a secret, a means by which you can obtain the first place in the class of composition, and secure a prize at the end of the year." The pupil regarded him in astonishment. "If you promise me to employ it I will tell you what it is." The child promised. "You will obtain success by repeating frequently this little prayer: 'My God, when shall I love Thee?'" During several weeks, Mr. Dupont daily visited the boy, to inquire if he had been faithful to his promise, and had repeated the prayer. At the close of the scholastic year, the boy was at the head of the class of composition, and received in recompense one of the first prizes. The professor, astonished to find that a new pupil, who had entered only at Easter, should have made such progress and gained so honorable a rank, expressed his surprise to the servant of God, and inquired what mysterious means he had used to effect so desirable a result. "It is my secret," said Mr. Dupont seriously, "which I will communicate to you, upon condition... that you tell it to all your pupils. It is to have recourse to God with faith, and to place confidence in prayer, repeating frequently: 'My God, when shall I love Thee?'" We may add that the same means was employed by other children to whom he recommended it, and their parents have assured us that it always proved efficacious.

He loved children; their simplicity charmed him. A little boy, six years of age, had received a picture representing St.

John the Baptist with the Lamb of God. In childish glee, he exclaimed to his mother: "Oh! look, Mamma, I have a little lamb." Mr. Dupont entered at the moment, and, bending over the child as he stood behind him, he placed his hands on his shoulders and said laughing: "My little friend, you have received a lamb, because you have been a good boy; if you had not been good, you would have had a wolf." "A wolf!" replied the child, half turning towards him, "I wish you would hush. A wolf! wolves eat people." The mother chided the boy for what she called his impoliteness, and offered excuses to Mr. Dupont. "Let him say what he pleases," answered the man of God, charmed with the words of the child; "he has spoken well; truth is found in the mouths of little ones: the Lamb saved men; the wolf eats them."

During his last illness, he accepted with infantile candor and touching simplicity the least object of piety which was offered him. A pious young lady living in Saint-Etienne Street, had just returned from a pilgrimage to Paray-le-Monial. When visiting the celebrated grove of nut trees in the garden of the monastery, the scene of the ecstasies of blessed Margaret Mary, she had gathered a nut which she took home with her. She planted it in a flower-pot. After a time this fruit, so precious to the eyes of her faith, germinated, and a little sprig appeared above the earth, on which a leaf-bud was opening. She showed it to Mr. Dupont, who was at that time incapable of moving from his chair. At the sight of this leaf, the holy friend of the Sacred Heart and the Visitation, devoutly bowed his head, and pressed his lips to the little plant, testifying his respect and faith, even with regard to so trifling an object, because it came from a spot illustrated by so many miracles and virtues. The lady, thinking to please him, left the shrub with him. He placed it in his window, and took care of it until his death. The plant grew, and it is now in the possession of the Carmelites, for whom it has a two-fold value.

Suffering and privations were to be, to the very last, the portion of this generous lover of the cross. In detaching him from every earthly affection, our Lord wished to associate him still more to the mystery of His dolorous Face. For example, it was noticed that the pious recluse was not as insensible, as he appeared, to the solitude formed around him, and particularly to the isolation in which, against their will, he was left by some friends, among whom were those he had loved the most dearly. He was grieved, but he bore his sorrow in silence.

A still greater privation to him was to forego assisting at Mass, and communicating daily, as had been his habit for a long time. A sacrifice of this kind, prolonged for more than two years, must have been a great pain to him; he never made a complaint. Once a week, the parish priest carried him holy Communion. The day on which the God of the Eucharist thus visited him, was, for the fervent solitary, one of ineffable delight and holy joy. But he asked nothing more. One of the vicars proposed to obtain permission of the Archbishop to celebrate Mass occasionally in his house. He refused, not desiring for himself personally anything extraordinary or singular. And, with a delicate humility so characteristic of him, he even refused to have the divine Eucharist brought to him too frequently, thinking it a want of respect to Jesus Christ and His ministers to oblige them to come so often to so miserable a creature. On such occasions, the curate was forced to use a gentle constraint.

He had, moreover, a method of his own to indemnify himself. He told a friend: "To indemnify myself for my inability to Communicate as I formerly did, I go in spirit every morning from church to church in all parts of the world; I beg our Lord to give me in Communion the small particles which fall from the sacred host, and I occupy myself in collecting them." Charming words which depict the ingenuous candor and humble love of this zealous adorer of the Eucharist, comparing himself to the Cananean woman, and, like her, finding his happiness in receiving the crumbs which fall from the table of the Divine Master.

Deprived of the power of either reading or writing, unable to leave his chair, condemned to a complete immobility, and, at times, to acute suffering and sleepless nights, he prayed without intermission. Early in March, he was still more prostrated by paralysis, and he suffered more acutely from the gout. From that time he was confined almost entirely to his bed. In this situation, more and more alone with God, wholly absorbed in Him, he seemed, by contemplation and the exercise of mental prayer, to have already attained the repose of the beatific vision.

One of the last words he spoke was to ask for the God of the Eucharist, Whom he loved to adore and receive, but of Whom, in his humility, he always considered himself unworthy. Thus, to an offer made him a few days before, to administer the holy Communion as Viaticum, he had replied: "Oh! no, I am too miserable a creature to have our Lord come to me as viaticum." But when Mr. Léon de Marolles, his relative and executor arrived the following morning at six o'clock, he said to him: "Léon, I have a commission to entrust to you, I desire to receive my God." Mr. de Marolles did not understand, because, in order to catch the meaning of his words, it was necessary to be accustomed to hear him speak. Adele entered at that moment, and approaching, asked what he wished. "My God," he replied earnestly. She objected that "it was late;" that "the morning was too far advanced for one in his weak condition to remain fasting," and she suggested that he should delay receiving. "No, no," he said, "because it will be pleasing to our Lord." "Certainly, sir," answered Adele; "I will send for the priest, and then I will prepare the little nuptials as we did for Madame d'Arnaud." She alluded to the flowers and lights which, in Martinique, it is the custom to use on such occasion; and which he himself had carefully arranged for the last Communion of his mother. He bowed his head in acquiescence. One of the vicars of the cathedral notified him that he would administer the holy Communion to him at a quarter before twelve. In the interval, Mr. Dupont frequently inquired when he would come. His pious servant was greatly disturbed by the fear, that in his exhausted condition, the patient might be unable to receive the sacred host. But at five minutes before twelve, the servant of God received, with more facility than was anticipated, the adorable body of his well beloved, with a clear mind and perfect consciousness. He spoke with difficulty; but he murmured prayers without ceasing, sometimes closing his eyes, and, again, lifting them to heaven.

He soon entered his agony, which was prolonged for eight days. He was fully conscious when the sacrament of Extreme Unction was administered; he followed the ceremonies attentively and piously, uniting in the liturgical prayers, answering calmly and with presence of mind, even reminding the priest of a slight omission, which his emotion prevented him from noticing. The following days were to the dear invalid, days of merit and patience. He lay extended upon his bed as upon a cross, being unable to move either to the right or to the left; his hands were crossed upon his breast. As the left hand had been for some time rendered useless by the paralysis, it would sometimes slip from its place, but with his right hand he would immediately restore it to its position, so that both should be clasped. He suffered acutely; not a murmur, however, escaped his lips.

That nothing might be wanting to his perfection, God permitted him to be tried, as were St. Martin and many other great Saints in their last moments. Satan, whom this valiant Christian, armed with the medal of St. Benedict, had combatted with so much energy, and so contemned during his whole life, seemed eager to avenge himself in his last hour. One day his attendants perceived, with anxiety, that the servant of God, habitually so calm, appeared excessively agitated, and as if troubled by the sight of a painful and odious object. This occurred several times, and Mr. Dupont acknowledged that the demon was tormenting him. On Monday evening at seven o'clock, he said suddenly: "Adele, to think of such a thing! Satan has just dared to make promises to me...; the miserable wretch!" "Sir," said the old servant, accustomed to the language of her holy master, "do not fear; say to him: *Depart from me, Satan!*" and then she added: "you have a medal of St. Benedict." Recalling the example of St. Teresa, to whom a little holy water sufficed to put to flight the evil spirit, he asked to be sprinkled with some. "I took the asperges," says Adele, "and after doing as be desired, I put a little on his hand, and said to him: 'Make the sign of the cross,' which he did several times." The next day about six o'clock in the evening, she lighted a blessed candle, knowing that this religious custom would be in conformity with his wishes. Each time the demon was, apparently, renewing his temptations, the aspersions with holy water were repeated, after which the patient recovered his habitual peace, and thus victorious over his enemy, the latter was put to flight and desisted from his infernal attempts.

At last, he could not make himself understood, but he evidently comprehended all that was said to him. Those who were around him were impressed by his beautiful countenance, calm and peaceful as usual. He made known by signs that he was uniting in the prayers offered near him, for they prayed continually. He had often requested this of Adele before he was in imminent danger. "Pray, Adele," he would say to her, and he would answer her in a low tone. During his agony, the faithful servant, seeing the importance of the continual prayer which her venerable master begged so earnestly, persevered to the very last in fulfilling his desire. She made the aspirations suggested by her piety and her heart, as for example: "Jesus, Mary, Joseph! My Jesus mercy! Heart of Mary, be my salvation!" "It was not I who prayed," said the pious servant, "it was my good angel." Sometimes she said to him: "I pray so badly, do you understand me?" Once he answered: "Continue to pray in the same manner." Fearing to annoy him, she took his hand and said: "If you understand me, press my hand;" and he at once pressed it.

He remained motionless lying upon his back, suffering a crucifixion, his eyes nearly always closed, a sweet serenity upon his countenance, his respiration somewhat oppressed and gasping, but without rattling in the throat, expressing in his whole appearance the idea of his cherished invocation to the Holy Face, which in his heart, he no doubt, frequently repeated, although his lips were unable to pronounce the words. This agony lasted eight days; the body was crucified, but the mind was clear and conscious.

On Friday evening, Adele saw that the end was approaching; controlling her emotion and raising her voice, she bade him adieu in her own name, and in the names of the two other servants, Zepherin and Adelaide, who had been in his service, the one, fifteen, and the other, twenty-eight years. They had formed his little adopted family. The three, kneeling by his bedside, begged him not to forget them in Heaven, promising him to persevere in the path of virtue he had taught them by his example, with the hope that God would grant them the grace of being reunited with him.

His confessor reiterated the absolution daily. On Saturday morning they commenced again the prayers for the agonizing, which had already been said several times. As they pronounced the words: *Beati immaculati in via*, the commencement of Psalm cxviii, which he had loved to repeat and meditate upon, the attendants noticed that this good servant of God smiled sweetly, a peaceful, heavenly smile which he had himself noticed upon the lips of his dying mother. One of the last words of his confessor was to recommend to his prayers himself and the citizens of Tours. "We have just prayed for you, Mr. Dupont," he said, "to St. Martin, in whom you have all your life had so much confidence. Pray for us in eternity."

About four o'clock on Saturday morning, March 18th, feast of the Archangel Gabriel, with his eyes still closed, and without the least rattling in the throat, he three times drew a heavy breath at long intervals. At the third, Mr. Léon de Marolles, his cousin, who had never left him, said with emotion: "He is no more!" It was indeed the last breath of his holy relative which he had the consolation of receiving. He died without a struggle; nothing extraordinary had occurred in his last moments to the eyes of those who surrounded him. He preserved in death the angelic calm of his beautiful face, which had long indicated that his soul no longer dwelt on earth. His eyes remained closed. He was seventy-nine years of age.

His body was laid in his oratory before the venerated picture of the Holy Face, in the very spot where pilgrims from all countries daily thronged, where his lively faith and his fervent prayers had obtained so many miraculous cures and conversions. His color was but slightly changed; the sight of him inspired neither sorrow nor sadness, but rather excited a sweet emotion of joy and confidence.

"It would be impossible to describe the edifying scene which is passing before my eyes;" writes a witness of it, "crowds, succeeding each other in a continuous stream, come to kneel in prayer by the mortal remains of him whom they already regard as a protector and a saint. It is equally impossible to number the pictures, the rosaries, the medals, which have touched the face or hands of the dear deceased. All feel and realize that they are near one who was a friend of God, and they pray with fervor."

Such was the scene presented by his oratory during Saturday, Sunday, and on Monday, until ten o'clock in the morning, the hour appointed for the funeral. His obsequies were a kind of religious triumph, one of those public manifestations, such as the influence of true virtue has alone the power to produce. The prefect of Indre-et-Loire, the municipal officers, the vicars general, and the metropolitan chapter were present. The cathedral was filled as on days of extraordinary ceremonies. In this immense crowd were seen the faithful of every condition and rank, priests, Religious men and women of different communities, representatives from all the associations of charity, the heads of different trades, workingmen, the poor in large numbers, the children of the Orphan Asylum, the old people of the Little Sisters. This interesting cortege went to the house of the deceased in Saint-Etienne Street, and accompanied his remains to the church, whence they followed it to the cemetery.

"The Lord, Who delights to exalt the humble," permitted, in order to add to the pomp of this religious ceremony, that they should be obliged, in consequence of the rising of the waters of the Loire, to make a long detour, and conduct the funeral procession over the stone bridge connecting with Royale Street. The venerable deceased had requested a simple funeral. His idea was understood and carried into effect. The front streamers of the funeral car were held by an old man and an old woman from the pensioners of the Little Sisters, and the other two, by little children from the Asylum. Whilst, the corpse was being lowered into the grave at the cemetery, some among the crowd were heard to say: "Is that the place for so holy a man? He should be laid in a church." Others added: "The day will come when his body will be removed, and he will receive the honor he deserves." Whatever may be in this respect the judgment of the Church, which it does not belong to us to anticipate, his mortal remains, whilst awaiting the resurrection, repose, as he requested, under the same marble slab which covers the bodies of his mother and daughter. On the cross which surmounts it, has been engraven simply his name and the date of his death. The only distinguishing mark of this tomb, is the white marble *prie-Dieu*, originally erected in memory of Henrietta. Pilgrims and the friends of the venerated deceased, when kneeling there, offer their prayers in the very spot where he so often prayed for others.

We have no correct portrait of Mr. Dupont. There was a small one painted on wood, which was quite a good likeness of him as he was in his youth; attaching no value to it, he gave it to Adele. Foreseeing towards the end of his life, that after his death it might be used in a manner not agreeable to him, he took advantage of the absence of his servant, entered her room, removed the picture which she had hung on the wall, and threw it in the fire. It was in winter, and he quietly took his seat near the fireplace. When Adele returned, she noticed at once that the precious portrait had disappeared. She ran to her master, lamenting the loss, and found him rubbing his hands with delight; laughing heartily, he pointed to the frame which was nearly consumed. He would never allow his photograph to be taken. His portrait which hangs at present in the room in which he died, was drawn by a friend, from memory, and from an imperfect photograph taken after death. The picture in the hall at the entrance of the oratory is from the pencil of Mr. Lafou. The head of the venerable deceased reposes upon his couch, and he appears to sleep. A breath of the resurrection, a ray of heavenly joy plays over the closed eyes and the lips: it is the reflection of the image of the Sacred Face, which the artist, by a master-stroke of genius, has represented as soaring above in the dim distance. A more striking or charming illustration could not have been given to the oft-repeated aspiration of this grand Christian: "May I expire, ardently desiring to see the Face of our Lord Jesus Christ."

Those who knew Mr. Dupont in the prime of life, love to recall his fine form, tall, straight, and well-proportioned, deriving additional advantage from his dignified carriage and magisterial gravity. His bright, clear eye, his broad brow, his noble and regular features, gave an air of distinction to his physiognomy; habitually calm and serene, his countenance mirrored the various emotions of his soul, and, in this respect, strikingly reminded us of the sweet and tranquil, and, at the same time, sympathetic and expressive face of the holy Pope Pius IX. When kneeling in adoration before the Blessed Sacrament, when presenting himself for holy Communion, or making his thanksgiving after Communion, his countenance was sometimes seen to glow with a kind of "phosphorescent light,"— these are the words of the ecclesiastic who had often witnessed it—an emanation, as it were, of the interior fire of his soul, which added to the beauty of his features. An author who visited him towards the end of his life said of him: "The abiding sentiment of the presence of God gave a certain majesty to his bearing. His countenance shone at times with a soft light which commanded respect."

In conversation, his gestures were natural, often expressive and picturesque, lending a particular interest, an additional charm to his descriptions and narratives. He had a habit of expressing his admiration or surprise by extending his arms and lifting his eyes to heaven. A shrug of the shoulders testified indifference or contempt. He threw himself back in his chair, laughing or rubbing his hands, when relating the discomfiture of Satan, of the "old man" as he called him. He exhibited an exquisite politeness and urbanity in his intercourse with every one; he had the elegance, culture, and refinement of good society, and yet, without any art or affectation.

His dress and habits of life were simple and without luxury, but, in every respect, conformable to his rank and of irreproachable neatness. He was accustomed to walk with a recollected air, at a rapid pace, enveloped in a long overcoat with deep pockets and wide sleeves; he politely saluted his acquaintances and his friends, accosted them readily, detaining them at the corner of a street, or on the side walk to communicate to them a pious anecdote, to relate an edifying piece of news, to quote a verse of Scripture, or a sentence from the Office of the day, if the individual was an ecclesiastic or a Religious. To him could be applied with perfect truth the following description taken from the prophet Isaiah: *Honorabilem vultu et prudentem eloquii mystici:* "The honorable in countenance, and the skilful in eloquent speech."

Modesty and propriety accompanied him as an atmosphere; nothing in any manner connected with him was either neglected or affected. He was the same in his drawing-room; he was cordial and polite to all who visited him, treating each as became his condition and office. His conversation was lively, playful, rendered interesting by its originality, and always interspersed with edifying incidents. Courteous and amiable with all, he expressed frankly and simply his sentiments to those who were irreligious and unbelievers, unless discretion or charity obliged him to keep silence. On such occasions he controlled himself in his speech, and took refuge in a chilling reserve, or an absolute silence.

In order the better to appreciate the culminating point of virtue to which we have seen him attain, we will cast a retrospective glance upon his whole life, and briefly recapitulate its principal phases.

Mr. Dupont, during the course of his seventy-nine years, endured trials evidently sent by Divine Providence, as so many steps to conduct him by degrees to that summit of perfection which He designed him to attain. Death deprived him, suddenly, of an amiable wife whom he tenderly loved; this was the first blow. Again death visited his home, and robbed him, successively, of his daughter and his mother, thus breaking the two dearest and sweetest ties of nature. He resigned himself, not without keen sorrow, but with the generosity of faith and the heroism of holy love.

Forced to leave his native isle, he is guided by the hand of God to the city of St. Martin, where he fixes his residence, and where graces are lavished upon him. The career of piety and good works invites him, unfolds itself before him, appearing easy and attractive; he enters upon it with all the vivacity of his southern temperament, and the ardor of his firm faith; he finds in it his occupation, his delight, the charm of his life. By a special illumination from above, he is detached, by the example of St. Teresa, from many worldly pleasures which he still loves, and he determines to embrace, although remaining in the world, a more fervent life of prayer, penance, and union with God. He passes a portion of his nights in Adoration before the Blessed Sacrament. His communications with Sister Saint-Pierre, and devotion to the Holy Face, complete the work and make of him a man of prayer and reparation. The afflictions of the Church, the humiliations of France, and later, his own infirmities, conduct him, towards the end of life, to the road to Calvary, and finally, "nail him to the cross with Christ," according to the expression of St. Paul. The sufferings endured during his last illness, furnish him with occasions of frequent and minute sacrifices, which render him more and more conformable to the Divine Crucified, and elevate him to a degree of perfection which is found only in the Saints of God.

A letter was one day received at the post-office, simply directed: "To the Holy Man of Tours." This epithet was so universally applied to Mr. Dupont, that it caused the clerks no embarrassment. The letter was forwarded to its destination, the pilgrim of Saint-Etienne Street. Men the most eminent in science and virtue, entertained the same opinions of him, and used the same language as the people. Not long since, the venerable Coadjutor of Bordeaux, Monseigneur de la Bouillerie, wrote to us: "Mr. Dupont enjoyed the highest reputation, and in Paris, where I then lived, his name was familiar to all. I will mention a circumstance which occurs to me as I write. When I was nominated Bishop, and was about to leave for my diocess, a good girl, who had been for some time under my direction, was lying dangerously ill in a hospital at Paris. She asked me if she could not write to Mr. Dupont, of whom she had heard so many wonderful things. I answered there was no objection whatever to her applying to him, and gave her his address. Then the good girl said, in all simplicity: 'Father, should not the letter be directed to *Mr. Dupont, Thaumaturgus, Tours?*' I mention this circumstance as an evidence of the popular belief in his sanctity."

The pious prelate adds: "I knew him, principally, by general report, having only once had the gratification of conversing with him. His ardent love of the Holy Eucharist, and the Christian affection existing between himself and the Reverend Father Hermann, made me acquainted with him. I prayed in his little oratory of the Sacred Face, and even from one short interview, I became convinced that his soul was intimately united to God."

The same impression was made upon all who approached him. During his life he was accused of being "an enthusiast," "exaggerated in his sentiments." Let us consider if this imputation was merited. It is certain that this supposed "exaggeration," or "exaltation," whatever name they may choose to use, led to no reprehensible consequences, because it never induced him to step beyond the bounds of the charity due to his neighbor, nor beyond the limits of the obedience he owed legitimate pastors. This fervent layman was ever a docile child of the Church, strictly governed by the regulations she imposes in relation to the acceptance of revelations and events, which are considered miraculous. We find in many of his letters expressions of his sentiments in reference to such circumstances; in them, he asserts that he awaits with respect and deference the decision of ecclesiastical authority. Until that was made, he advised his friends to observe a prudent reserve. In writing of an instance of the kind he says: "I am told that the pretended miracle is a notorious fraud. Silence, therefore. Let us wait awhile."

Mr. Dupont was "an enthusiast" in his confidence in the power of God and the Saints, in his implicit reliance upon the efficacy of prayer, in his hatred of the demon and of the instruments of Satan, in his ardent devotion to whatever concerned the exterior adoration of the Eucharist. Granted! But can we be too enthusiastic on such subjects? Does not the enlightened Christian regard as a supernatural and extraordinary degree of zeal and fervor in the practice of virtue and fidelity to duty, that which is qualified by the careless and the unbeliever as enthusiasm? Was not this same divine folly the characteristic of the Saints, for which their contemporaries reproached them? Were not the solitaries of Palestine and the Thebiade "enthusiasts," when, issuing from their deserts in their penitential garb, they suddenly appeared in the streets of Antioch or Alexandria, in order to defend the faith attacked by the Arians, and to fortify, by their example and discourses, the wavering faithful? Were not the martyrs of the first centuries "enthusiasts," who not only suffered death with fortitude, but who boldly presented themselves before the pagan judges, defied them in their tribunals, and proceeded to torture with a triumphant joy? And at an era nearer our own day, did not men stigmatize as "enthusiasts" those heroes of the Middle Ages, a St. Bernard, a St. Francis of Assissi, and many others, whose love of poverty and mortification led them to practise those virtues with a rigor considered impossible to the strength of man? Mr. Dupont was an "enthusiast" after the manner of these illustrious Saints. Gifted, as they were, with a sensitive and sympathetic soul, like them also he abandoned himself, with transports of joy and unreservedly, to the things of God. His feelings were easily roused by any manifestation of the action of the Holy Spirit. But his was not a thoughtless enthusiasm; it originated in the most solid and correct supernatural motives. The two following incidents will illustrate our idea on this point.

CHAPTER XXVI

A Jew, the son of a zealous and learned rabbi, who had hitherto lived as a man of the world, careless and unbelieving, was converted, and, having been prepared by Mr. Dupont, was baptized and made his first Communion. After this holy action, the darkness was removed, as it were, from his eyes; he quoted from memory long passages of the Holy Scriptures with facility and correctness, adding admirable explanations. Every thing he had formerly learned from his father concerning religion recurred to his mind; he comprehended and interpreted all in a Catholic sense; he had become at once a fervent and well-informed Christian. Mr. Dupont, charmed with the wonderful operations of grace in this soul, never wearied conversing with him, and, in his admiration, he would exclaim: "Behold him! yesterday he was ignorant; today, he knows far more than ourselves."

One day when there was a number of persons in his room, and they were about to commence the prayers, two workmen presented themselves to be cured. On their entrance, Mr. Dupont was struck by their peculiar manner; he interrogated them and discovered at once that they had no idea who he was, but supposed they were dealing with a bone-setter. The servant of the Holy Face explained to them that cures were obtained there only by prayer. They did not comprehend him. The unfortunate men had lost even the first ideas of religion. Immediately, on the spot, the charitable apostle began to instruct them, and running through the principal truths and the commandments, he touched upon Confession. Until then they had listened with interest; but when he explained the Sacrament of Penance, they commenced to shake their heads and mutter to themselves. Mr. Dupont repeats the instruction, and insists upon the necessity of this dogma, which is so salutary and consoling to mankind: they are not convinced. At last, the zealous catechist exclaims: "It is not hard to throw yourself at the feet of the minister of God, and say: 'Bless me, Father; for I have sinned.'" "Oh! certainly not, it is not hard," cried out an old peasant who was seated at the other end of the room. "You may well believe it was not men who invented that. Men! they would have told us to say: 'Punish me, Father; for I have sinned!' and our good God makes us say: 'Bless me, Father; for I have sinned!'" Mr. Dupont arose, and walking to the peasant with his peculiar air of dignity, laid his hand on his head, saying: "Let me kiss the head which, through the Holy Spirit, has conceived so beautiful a thought!" Thus did this great servant of God know how to admire and feel!

Perhaps also, some may be surprised that he was inclined to consider as providential the coincidence of certain dates and facts, or to attribute directly, either to a Divine action, or a satanic influence, the least good or evil event which came under his observation, or of which he was informed. But, in reality, was this disposition of mind which did not exclude the exercise of free-will, opposed to the doctrine of the Gospel? Does not Jesus Christ emphatically call Satan "the prince of this world?" Is Providence an empty name? Does it not designate the paternal solicitude of the Creator, watching over His creatures even in minute affairs? Does not our Lord represent to us the hand of our heavenly Father extended towards His children, numbering even the hairs of their heads, feeding the birds of the air, adorning the flowers of the field, not letting even a sparrow fall to the ground without His permission? Was then, this constant reader of the Holy Book so very wrong, when he reduced to practice, in his conversation and sentiments, those divine and touching lessons contained in the instructions of the Gospel? If his conduct and language were at variance with the views of his contemporaries, of those who saw him only from a distance, or who were scarcely acquainted with him, and who formed their judgment of him without knowing his supernatural motives and his mystic explanations, was it not that the result of the pernicious influence of an age sunk in materialism, or the effect of the ignorance of a multitude of Christians, who, at the present time, are accustomed to speak, judge, feel, and act in direct opposition to the Gospel? Here again, it was evidently the simplicity of faith which elevated the servant of God to those sublime heights, and inspired him with his clear ideas.

Another general observation on Mr. Dupont's life should not be omitted. This grand Christian of the nineteenth century, like the greater part of the holy personages whom the Church honors with a public veneration, did not attain at once the summit of perfection. It was successively developed, had its phases, its degrees. And, as in the ascetic and moral order, there was progress, so in the intelligence of his faith, and consequently, in his expression of it, there was a marked difference, a sensible advance, which presents him to us ascending, as it were, higher and higher, under the impulse of the breathing of the Spirit of God.

If his natural temperament, the vivacity of his disposition, the ardor of his zeal, and the poetical turn of his imagination, rendered him in his youth inexact, extreme, and too human in the manifestation of his faith, by degrees he gained the mastery over these defects, and he acquired a correctness and clearness of sentiment, an exactitude of expression in accordance with the most vigorous theology. On his part, there was the same enthusiasm for the beauties of the supernatural, the same jubilation of heart at every manifestation of the Divine action; but there was also more distrust and reserve in the acceptance of human testimony. His peace of soul and purity of heart, increasing as holy love augmented, were more and more reflected in his words and his exterior acts.

Such was Mr. Dupont during the last fifteen or twenty years of his life. Such we have ourselves known him, and we give personal testimony to the truth of the description of the holy man as presented above. We have known eminent priests, men of experience in the things of God, who never conversed with him without being struck by the correctness of his ideas on different texts of Scripture, or on various matters of doctrine and piety.

We may add that the aureole of sanctity which environed him, brought Mr. Dupont, by letters or visits, in communication with laymen, priests, or Religious, of an impetuous and eccentric zeal, inclined to introduce new works or devotions, who went either to consult him or to engage him to adopt their views. He was likewise in correspondence with Religious women, or ladies of the world, of ardent temperament and keen intellect, with imaginations easily inflamed, who fed upon chimerical projects, or who were the victims of a bitter deception, and who applied to him for light, consolation, and encouragement. We have in our possession a large number of letters written by the servant of God to persons of this kind. What particularly attracted our attention in these confidential communications, which are frequently only short notes, and what characterizes them, is the sobriety of language, the calmness of judgment, the prudence of the counsels, joined to the utmost delicacy of charity; but above all else, there is a firmness of opposition, decided and candid, to whatever appears extreme and far-fetched, and on that account regarded by him as false or impracticable. Every line reveals the impress of a sound mind, of a mind humble, upright, and always aiming at what is practical. It was not in vain that this fervent layman so often repeated the invocation to our Lord: *Faciem tuam illumina super servum tuum, et doce me justificationes tuas*: "Make Thy face to shine upon Thy servant, and teach me Thy justifications." The spirit of wisdom with which he was filled, proves that his prayer was heard.

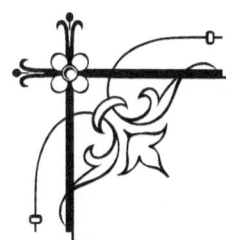

Chapter XXVII

The Oratory of the Holy Face — Conclusion.

After Mr. Dupont's death, there was a natural desire to know what would become of the venerated picture of the Holy Face, which, for so many years, had been the one object of his life, and which had been honored in his home by so many miracles. The servant of God was unwilling himself to leave any direction in regard to its disposition. When making arrangements concerning his property, his confidence in God and his humble discretion had dictated to him the following words: "That I do not speak of the Holy Face in my will, is not the result of forgetfulness. I do not wish to interfere in the question which may arise, when I shall no longer be there to maintain the lamps in my oratory. God will provide according to His holy will."

The confidence of "the good servant" was not frustrated. The "will of God" was about to manifest itself in a striking manner, and assign to this dear object an exalted destiny far beyond all human foresight. In consequence of family arrangements, the house was to be sold. This was publicly known, and great anxiety was felt lest the holy spot should fall into careless and profane hands: it was, however, soon announced that it had become the property of a Religious community. The purchase had been accomplished secretly, and the Carmelites were the happy proprietors.

Notwithstanding their poverty, by a concurrence of providential circumstances, these humble virgins, worthy inheritors of the grand idea of reparation which had taken its rise in their midst, had succeeded from the seclusion of their cloister in making the important acquisition. The combined influence of Sister Saint-Pierre and Mr. Dupont was manifest, and, for the future, Carmel and the Holy Face were to be inseparably united.

Great was the joy of the Carmelites, as was also that of the pious faithful of Tours, and all the friends of Mr. Dupont. The Archbishop, Monseigneur Colet, not only authorized the Reverend Mother Teresa of St. Joseph, Prioress of the Carmelites, to take this generous and bold step, but he was desirous of giving a proof of his sincere devotion to the Holy Face, and his profound veneration for the memory of the grand Christian, who had died in his archiepiscopal city, "in the odor of sanctity." Such were the terms used by the pious prelate in the decree, by which he "converts into a chapel the oratory where the servant of God has, for so many years, kept a lamp burning night and day before the picture of the Holy Face of our Lord, and where so many marvellous events, attested by public report, occurred after unctions made with the oil from this lamp." This posthumous eulogy of Mr. Dupont, and the indirect acknowledgment of the miraculous events of his life, were very remarkable from the pen of the successor of St. Martin. His Lordship announced that he would himself bless the new sanctuary. We will give a glance at the arrangement of the holy place.

The oratory of the Holy Face is composed of the two apartments, which were formerly the small dining-room and the drawing-room of Mr. Dupont. It is a chapel of expiation, and it has been arranged in conformity with this idea, but in such a manner as, at the same time, to express to the eye of the public what it had formerly been, namely, the apartment in which the servant of the Holy Face habitually remained and prayed. The partition-wall, separating the dining-room from the drawing-room, has been removed, and in its place are now isolated pilasters connected by a balustrade; the idea was taken from the Sixtine Chapel at Rome. The altar covers the marble mantel-piece, and the flagstone upon which Mr. Dupont was accustomed to kneel in the midst of the pilgrims. A statue of the Ecce Homo is placed in a niche above the tabernacle. The picture of the Holy Face, in a handsome frame, the gift of the Christian Mothers of Tours, surrounded as with a crown by numerous *ex voto* offerings, hangs on the right, viz., the Gospel side, in the same place as formerly, with the same lamp always burning before it. On the left, or Epistle side, is displayed the flag of the Sacred Heart, a fac simile of the glorious standard which was unfurled by the Zouaves of Charette, and which preceded them at the battle of Patay. Quite near and on the same side, open on his desk and honored, as heretofore, by a lamp ever burning, appears the Holy Bible, the very one which Mr. Dupont used. On the interior wall, in imitation of the rooms of St. Ignatius and St. Philip Neri at Rome, are painted pious sentences and touching inscriptions, recounting the virtues of the servant of God, and the principal incidents of his life.

The 29th of June, feast of St. Peter, was appointed by Monseigneur Colet for the benediction of the oratory. The prelate wished to bless it himself, and offer the first holy Mass at the new altar. The ceremony was performed with great solemnity in presence of several members of the metropolitan chapter, the curates of the city, the superiors of communities, a large number of priests and of the faithful, all rejoicing in this episcopal act, which converted into a public oratory consecrated to works of reparation, what had hitherto been, in the house of a fervent layman, only a sanctuary of private devotion. At the same time, Monseigneur Colet canonically erected there the confraternity in reparation of blasphemy and profanation of the

Sunday, which, according to the rules, was affiliated to the archconfraternity of the same name at Saint-Dizier, for the establishment of which Mr. Dupont, seconding the desires of Sister Saint-Pierre, had formerly exerted himself so zealously. The Archbishop of Tours, however, using his right, and wishing to render the spirit and regulations of the said association more intimately conformable to the character and title assigned to the new oratory, introduced in the rule notable modifications relative to the particular devotions of Adoration, prayer, and love with which it was intended to honor the Face of our Lord, outraged and disfigured in His Passion. He thus made it a special confraternity "in honor of the Holy Face." He inscribed his own name the first upon the list, and appointed a priest to serve the chapel, with full power as director, to aggregate to the confraternity the faithful of both sexes.

By these different acts the devotion of reparation to the Holy Face—that cherished devotion of Mr. Dupont—assumed only three months after his death a new form, was proposed by legitimate authority to the faithful at large, and, in future, permitted to be the object of a regular and liturgical pilgrimage. Very soon one priest did not suffice for the duty. Already, the oratory was too small; the faithful, priests, Religious, succeeded each other almost without intermission; some, to celebrate Mass; others, to receive Communion; all, to offer prayers and petition for graces. The pilgrimages to the Holy Face, which, during the latter years of the life of the servant of God, had diminished in numbers, or had even been interrupted, were resumed with such activity and fervor that a more complete organization became necessary.

The Archbishop, under these circumstances, decided to establish in the house of Mr. Dupont, under the auspices of this apostle of the Holy Face so devoted to St. Martin, a society of priests especially charged to attend the oratory, and to serve the faithful who might visit it as pilgrims.

He regularly appointed and named them "Priests of the Holy Face," a title sufficiently indicating the particular mission which is confided to them,—that of promoting and extending by every means in their power, the devotion of reparation to the dolorous Face of our Lord, such as Mr. Dupont understood and practiced it for twenty-five years.

As soon as they were installed, the priests of the Holy Face had sensible evidence that the hand of God directed the current of events occurring in this holy place. Even more than during the life time of Mr. Dupont, his little oratory became the centre of adoration, supplication, thanksgiving, and works of reparation. It continues to be visited without interruption by persons from all parts of France, and also from different countries. From England, Poland, America, Cochin China, applications are received for tickets of admission to the Confraternity, and petitions to participate in the prayers and merits of the work. Twice a day the pious invocations improperly called the *Litany* of the Holy Face* are recited there, and sometimes amid a considerable concourse of the faithful. Innumerable petitions, and often touching letters of thanksgiving are presented. "*Ex voto*" offerings are from time to time sent as expressions of gratitude, and they are added to those which already surround the venerable picture. Pilgrimages, solemnly organized, are made to the oratory at certain times of the year.

For instance, during the last weeks of Lent, which are more particularly set apart for the commemoration of the Passion, the different parishes of the city, and the greater part of pious associations and boarding schools, are accustomed to make thither a pilgrimage of public penance and expiation. That of the men, on the evening of Good

---

* This "Litany" composed by Sister Saint-Pierre is not liturgical, and can be recited publicly like any other approved prayer. It has been authorized by several bishops. Without giving to it a formal application, Pius IX blessed it, and enriched it with an indulgence.

Friday, is every year attended by large numbers whose zeal and fervor give great edification: on that day, and on several extraordinary occasions, many of these men of the world, assembling by hundreds when the appeal is made to them, seem eager to prove that they have not lost the remembrance of the heroic virtues of Mr. Dupont, their fellow-citizen and their friend. The associates of the Nocturnal Adoration, inspired by the same sentiment, requested permission to establish their work in the oratory of the Holy Face: once a week on Tuesdays, there is now as there was formerly during Mr. Dupont's time at the chapel of the Lazarists, a holy vigil from half past nine in the evening until five o'clock in the morning, before the Blessed Sacrament publicly exposed. On Wednesdays, Adoration during the whole day prolongs this prayer of reparation, and thus completes a day and a night of uninterrupted Adoration.

Not less striking is the irresistible attraction, an attraction full of sweetness and unction, which is felt by all souls for this holy spot. It is experienced, not only by the simple faithful of all ages and of every condition who go there to pray, but priests, and Religious the most accustomed to pious emotions, assert that this little sanctuary possesses for them a charm, and imparts a peace not found elsewhere, and this they attribute to the memory of the pious layman who so long had made it his abode. There is scarcely a strange prelate, an eminent ecclesiastic, who, after visiting in our city the tomb of St. Martin, does not desire to offer a prayer in the oratory of the Holy Face. It seems as though a heavenly influence hovers over the spot, that a celestial perfume embalms and attracts souls, and that there they inhale the good odor of the virtues of Jesus Christ. All retire deeply and delightfully impressed. They echo the words of a pious prelate, Monseigneur Richard, who exclaimed on leaving it: "Oh! how devout is your little sanctuary!"

The extensive correspondence of Mr. Dupont continues, although under a different form. The priests of the Holy Face daily receive letters, in which petitions are made for divers kinds of graces. Nearly always, the name of the venerated deceased is mentioned in terms of eulogium, and his memory recalled with gratitude; the writers refer to visits made to him, cures, and other favors obtained by his prayers and the unctions with the holy oil; they evince deep emotion when narrating his kind attentions, his goodness to the sick and poor; they never weary of rehearsing the wisdom of his counsels, the charm of his virtues. In some of these letters, with a beautiful simplicity, they speak to him as though he were still alive; they beg his intercession; they ask his aid, as they would that of a saint in Heaven. They do not hesitate to call him "the saint," "the holy man," "the thaumaturgus," "St. Dupont."

Those who visited him in his last illness, retain a vivid remembrance of it. "I shall never forget," writes one of them, Mr. Joseph Lemann, "the pressure of my hand by the dear deceased, and the look of love he raised to Heaven, when, speaking of his death, I said to him: 'During your whole life you have adored the Holy Face; now, you have a right to the Heart? From the Holy Face he must, in truth, have passed to the Heart of his God. He might well be called a man of the two Testaments: of the one, through the Holy Scripture, with which he was perfectly familiar; and of the other, through the Holy Face. He had, moreover, the venerable majesty of the patriarchs, and the inexhaustible charity of the apostles. I knew he was near his end; one of his hands was entirely paralyzed; with that which he could still use, he selected two prayers, handed them to me, and expressed the wish that I should make them known, if I thought them suited to do good to souls. If I thought them worthy! They are burning darts of love. One is the sigh of his soul *deprived of daily Communion*. The other is the sigh of his soul, which he imagined already in the other world, but *deprived*, for a time, of *Paradise*. I do not think that our good God allowed him to recite the second prayer."

It has been necessary several times, in order not to infringe the laws of the Church, to repress the popular enthusiasm, and to put a stop to the demonstrations of veneration and honor to his memory and tomb. At least, all which the Church does not forbid is practiced; they invoke his name and pray in private at his tomb. And this spontaneous confidence in the efficacy of the prayers of the venerable deceased, and in the power of his intercession with God, is rewarded at the present moment, as it was formerly, by cures, conversions, and other favors. We have no intention of now relating these facts, which form a series to themselves; perhaps the occasion may present itself at some future time. We will, however, mention some.

A paralytic of Orleans having been taken to Mr. Dupont's grave, and having made interiorly in union with him a novena of prayers, at the same time anointing with the oil, was perfectly cured, was able to go herself to the oratory and deposit her crutches as an *ex voto* offering before the picture of the Holy Face. A young person, a lunatic, having been without result under treatment at Paris, at the house of a physician who made insanity a specialty, was suddenly restored to reason during a novena of Masses, prayers, and unctions offered through the intercession of Mr. Dupont. An inhabitant of Alsace was afflicted with an immense internal tumor, for which a painful and dangerous operation was judged necessary; he was anointed with the oil, invoked Mr. Dupont, and promised to make a pilgrimage to his tomb. The tumor and all pain disappeared in a few days. In the month of August, 1880, he undertook the long journey, accomplished his vow at the tomb of the servant of God, and requested a Mass to be offered in thanksgiving at the altar of the Holy Face. A short time previous, a venerable lady of Rennes fulfilled a similar promise: after using the oil of the Holy Face, and invoking the name of

Mr. Dupont, she recovered her sight, of which she had been nearly deprived. We could mention other instances of the same kind, which manifest the power of the servant of the Holy Face in favor of those who continue to visit his oratory with faith. The large number of placques of marble, which already cover the walls of the lateral chapels, are unexceptionable witnesses of the truth of the statement.

Another point which we can, likewise, affirm with certainty, is the wonderful increase of the devotion to the Holy Face. Mr. Dupont's drawing room, when converted into a chapel, became very soon too small even for the ordinary exercises of piety. It was necessary to enlarge it. This was accomplished without depriving it of the character proper to it. Two lateral chapels were added, one of which was dedicated to St. Peter penitent, and the other to our Lady of Dolors. These two little apartments, lighted from above by a dome in the oriental manner, constructed in a pure and austere style after the model of the most ancient Latin Churches of Rome, are as two precious jewels on either side of the simple sanctuary; they enable the faithful on days of large pilgrimages to make their stations more conveniently. From all directions we receive petitions for the picture of the Holy Face, which is the true representation of the veil of Veronica, and identical with that venerated by Mr. Dupont. The priests of the Holy Face obtain them from Rome, and distribute them. It would be impossible to count the number of these pictures exposed in different places, and almost always with a lamp burning before them. They are to be found in private houses and oratories, in hospitals and convents, in public chapels, in parochial churches and in cathedrals. They were venerated, even in Mr. Dupont's time, at the hospital of Vincennes, the Visitation of Paray-le-Monial, and the Benedictines of Arras. Now they adorn Notre Dame at Paris, the Cathedral of Perpignan, the Basilica of Lourdes, and the chapel of the Sacred Heart at Montmartre.

This rapid increase, this moral progress, this unexpected expansion of a purely private devotion, which is becoming a Catholic and universal work, may well be interpreted as manifest signs of the intervention of Divine Providence. The servant of the Holy Face was unwilling to make on this point any arrangement looking to the future. He had said: "God will provide." And we see how God has provided and He ceases not to provide.

Has this adorable Providence ulterior designs on the name of the great Christian, whose history we have just related? Shall we one day have the privilege and joy to see decreed to him the honors of canonization? It would be rashness on our part to engage in such inquiries, or anticipate in any manner the decisions of ecclesiastical authority. We must pray and hope. We can do no more: let us glorify, love, invoke, what our holy friend glorified, loved, and invoked during his life. Let us do so with the generous faith and unshaken confidence which he himself possessed. Following his example, let us be, above all, men of prayer and reparation. God raised him up, a simple layman, to manifest, in a striking manner, what can be done in our day by a Christian who is worthy of this name.

The world is apparently verging towards its decline; the Church is attacked with surpassing rage by the powers of hell; princes, governments, nations, those whose mission it is to aid and defend her, turn against her or abandon her; there is no earthly arm upon which she can lean. But the Spouse of Christ, apart from the privileges of infallibility and immortality with which she is endowed, has within herself for the service of her children, a divine force which no human force can overcome, that which a great doctor characterizes when he says: *Nihil potentius homine orante.* "Nothing is more powerful than a man in prayer," (St. John Chrysostom,) that which the servant of the Holy Face knew so well how to use: a good prayer, a prayer animated by faith, supported by hope, directed and inflamed by a charity of reparation. Such a prayer, arising from the soul of Catholics united and associated for a common expiation, is an efficacious, as well as invincible power. Prayer made Mr. Dupont what he was; it gave him as a crown of glory to the city of St. Martin: it will give, we hope, to contemporary society, what it needs for its salvation; to France, what is wanting for its regeneration, namely, enlightened minds, charitable hearts, noble characters, in a word, true Christians.

FINIS

BRINGING YOU SPIRITUAL RICHES
OF THE HOLY ROMAN CATHOLIC TRADITION
AT THE MOST AFFORDABLE PRICES POSSIBLE.
CARITASPUBLISHING.COM

www.ingramcontent.com/pod-product-compliance
Lightning Source LLC
Chambersburg PA
CBHW070043080526
44586CB00013B/890